SAVING APARTHEID

GLOBAL AMERICA

Edited by Jay Sexton and Sarah B. Snyder

Columbia University Press's Global America series pushes the history of US foreign relations in new directions, sharpening and diversifying our understanding of the global dimensions of American history from the colonial era to the twenty-first century. Books in the series explore America's global encounters, including how external forces have shaped the development of the United States and vice versa; why American encounters with the wider world have produced volatility, ruptures, and crises; the shifting contours of US power over time; and the impact of hierarchical attitudes regarding identity in shaping US foreign relations. Taken together, the series analyzes the global history of the United States; its authors employ a diverse range of methodological, chronological, disciplinary, geographical, and ideological perspectives.

Augusta Dell'Omo, *Saving Apartheid: White Internationalism at the End of the Cold War*

Samantha Iyer, *Agrarian Superpower: Food, Development, and the Global Ascendancy of the United States*

Robert S. G. Fletcher and Alec Zuercher Reichardt, eds., *Inlands: Imperial Formations, Contested Interiors, and the Connection of the World*

Rumi Yasutake, *The Feminist Pacific: International Women's Networks in Hawai'i, 1820–1940*

Robert B. Rakove, *Days of Opportunity: The United States and Afghanistan Before the Soviet Invasion*

M. Todd Bennett, *Neither Confirm Nor Deny: How the Glomar Mission Shielded the CIA from Transparency*

Dario Fazzi, *Smoke on the Water: Incineration at Sea and the Birth of a Transatlantic Environmental Movement*

SAVING APARTHEID

WHITE INTERNATIONALISM
at the
END OF THE COLD WAR

AUGUSTA DELL'OMO

Columbia University Press
New York

Columbia University Press
Publishers Since 1893
New York   Chichester, West Sussex
cup.columbia.edu

Library of Congress Cataloging-in-Publication Data
Names: Dell'Omo, Augusta Lynn author
Title: Saving apartheid : white internationalism at the end of the Cold War / Augusta Lynn Dell'Omo.
Other titles: White internationalism at the end of the Cold War
Description: New York : Columbia University Press, [2026] | Series: Global America | Includes bibliographical references and index.
Identifiers: LCCN 2025030450 | ISBN 9780231215886 hardback | ISBN 9780231215893 trade paperback | ISBN 9780231561020 EPUB | 9780231565592 PDF
Subjects: LCSH: Apartheid—South Africa | White supremacy movements—South Africa | Apartheid—Public opinion | South Africa—Foreign public opinion | South Africa—History—1961–1994 | United States—Relations—South Africa | South Africa—Relations—United States
Classification: LCC DT1757 .D44 2026
LC record available at https://lccn.loc.gov/2025030450

Cover images: Shutterstock

GPSR Authorized Representative: Easy Access System Europe, Mustamäe tee 50, 10621 Tallinn, Estonia, gpsr.requests@easproject.com

FOR JOHN, HEATHER, AND CANYON

CONTENTS

III. WHITE POWER WITHOUT APARTHEID

SAVING APARTHEID

INTRODUCTION

On March 24, 1977, Donald deKieffer, a paid lobbyist of South Africa's apartheid government, approached the American Legion, the single largest US veterans group, with over two million members, about a potential arrangement. After a meeting with the Legion's executive committee, the Legion committed to partnering with the South African government. They would run twelve feature articles on South Africa in its magazine, which had more than 2.5 million subscribers; offer speaking engagements for deKieffer and South African military officials; and arrange a Legion visit to South Africa. DeKieffer reported to his South African bosses that the partnership would drive "very good impact at the grassroots level" through the Legion's political influence and conservative—but "not extremely right-wing"—credentials.[1] After these forays, deKieffer attended the Legion's 1977 convention and lobbied for the passage of resolutions that supported the forced removal of black South Africans into ethnically homogenous states and continued American military and economic investment.

Perhaps most interesting was the agreement between deKieffer and the Legion to distribute a twenty-minute presentation crafted by the South African Department of Information to all 16,000 Legion posts and other civic engagement groups at no cost.[2] In deKieffer's assessment, the Legion "urged a tremendous nationwide educational campaign on behalf of South Africa" and would be "strong dependable friends."[3] He expected an average of fifty presentations per month, reaching a sympathetic audience of 500,000 to 1 million people in the first year.[4] The data seemed to pan out. In a Legion report from October 1978, one speaker reported giving over a dozen speeches to audiences numbering over 1,500 attendees. Hundreds of discussions with business, labor, and clergy leaders took place across Texas, Iowa, Illinois, Colorado, Kansas, and Missouri, and the reaction proved "strongly supportive of the American Legion's positions on South Africa."[5] One presenter testified that "the blacks were impressed and shared my views that the United States would be better off if we would lift the embargos and sanctions and stay out of the internal affairs of the nations of South Africa."[6] DeKieffer was thrilled with the Legion's efforts, crediting them with creating "incredible opportunities I haven't seen in four years," driving the formation of new pro–South Africa groups and the support of dozens of national organizations like the Conservative Caucus. DeKieffer gushed that they were reaching "literally millions [they'd] never managed to reach before."[7]

When deKieffer met Minister of Information Connie Mulder of South Africa in January 1974, Pretoria was on the precipice of escalating its propaganda efforts across the West.[8] The relationship between deKieffer—representing the firm Collier, Shannon, Rill and Edwards—and Mulder signified something new for South Africa. Under Prime Minister B. J. Vorster, the Department of Information massively expanded its operations from 1974 to 1977, spending millions of rand and calling upon a web of supporters throughout the United States and Europe.[9] DeKieffer and his associates operated seen and unseen at the levers of American power, building political and social support for South Africa in response to rising antiapartheid sentiment across the West. They had a new strategy for winning support in the United States that eroded anti–South Africa attitudes, provided cover for conservative friends, and built a bridge to liberals.[10] This new strategy would be a campaign of influence at the elite and grassroots levels. They had specific targets: the congressional Foreign Relations, Armed Services, and Finance Committees; the ranking minority and majority members; legislative aides; and the Republican and Democrat Policy, Steering, and Research Committees. The liberal friends pulled in by deKieffer and his associates were ideologically heterogeneous: segregationists, big government skeptics, Watergate babies, and Cold War Warriors.[11] They funded Black legislators as counters to ardent critics of

South Africa and slandered antiapartheid organizations as Soviet driven.[12] According to deKieffer, Republicans remained their "natural support[ers]": "If one organization could be singled out in its willingness and ableness to assist us, it is the Republican Steering Committee." DeKieffer also forged partnerships with groups like the Young Americans for Freedom and Young Republicans.[13] These efforts proved fruitful—deKieffer secured favorable congressional winds, staving off further sanctions and limiting criticism of apartheid policies.

The South African lobbying effort was not without its challenges. DeKieffer and his team worried about appearing "too far-right," warring internally about how to involve white citizen groups and John Birchers and ensure their surrogates were not "right-wing nut[s]."[14] DeKieffer worried that if their advocacy was not moderate, they would only empower South Africa's critics.[15] But conservatives did not get off easy: some of deKieffer's associates expressed "disgust at the cowardice of our so-called conservative colleagues," who "lack the spine" to work against South Africa's dark prognosis.[16] This frustration only increased as deKieffer's firm struggled to change the grassroots view of apartheid in the United States, even as they identified emerging pro–South Africa groups that deKieffer struggled to coordinate thanks to personality, geographic, and legal differences.[17]

DeKieffer's efforts came to an abrupt halt in 1978. The South African newspaper *Rand Daily Mail* implicated Vorster; Mulder; General Henrik van den Bergh, the head of the Bureau of State Security; and Secretary of Information Eschel Rhoodie in a massive conspiracy to use South African government funds to wage a global propaganda war. Mulder and Rhoodie, under Vorster's directive, set up a secret slush fund of 64 million rand to buy off Western politicians, bribe international news agencies, and distribute propaganda within South Africa. This became known as the Information Scandal. The scandal, in all its tawdry details, led to Vorster's resignation, Mulder's political exile, and deKieffer's own legal troubles in the United States.[18] Minister of Defense P. W. Botha pounced on Vorster's woes to seize power, promising to end the apartheid state's propaganda war, which he instead continued upon his rise to South Africa's highest office.[19] However, damage had been done. Revelations about the Information Scandal and global outrage at Pretoria's spiderweb of influence spooked more moderate partners in Congress and at the grassroots. Botha's response to the Information Scandal—public distancing and a sham investigation into Vorster's financial malpractice—bred a consensus among apartheid's defenders that an undeniable change in Pretoria's willingness to defend apartheid had occurred. South Africa stood alone, refusing to make her case, and white South Africans would pay a deadly price. How real Pretoria's retreat was remains up for debate. Critically, for apartheid's supporters, that shift felt very real, demanding a new kind of activism in the wake of the Information Scandal—a more decentralized, grassroots, and reactionary movement to save white rule.

DeKieffer's lobbying was both an ending and a beginning. What happened in 1980 catalyzed over a decade's worth of far-right organizing and activism supporting the apartheid state. As global antiapartheid sentiment grew throughout the 1980s, a powerful countermovement emerged, consisting of political, religious, and paramilitary actors invested in preserving white rule in South Africa. *Saving Apartheid* offers an examination of this "pro-apartheid" movement and its organizing in the United States and South Africa, from the election of Ronald Reagan in 1980 to apartheid's end in 1994. A global ecosystem of white supremacist actors took up the mantle of white rule amid South Africa's isolation on the international stage. Those invested in preserving apartheid included more than just white South Africans. The effort to save white rule took on personal meaning for white supremacist actors globally and included all kinds—journalists, historians, veterans, and state representatives mobilized by a landscape of political operatives, evangelicals, and think tanks. These men and women attended conferences, went on cross-country tours, organized fact-finding missions, and conducted refugee rescues. Cross-racial relationships supporting apartheid included black South Africans who formed political and social alliances with the pro-apartheid movement. Apartheid's defenders had a volatile relationship with global conservatism, sharing fundamental political beliefs about anticommunism and free markets while also seeking to dramatically push conservative political parties down an explicitly authoritarian and racist path. The pro-apartheid movement positioned itself as the torchbearer of real conservatism in the West, advocating for an antidemocratic and anti-multicultural path inconceivable to weak conservative leaders. Ordinary people, animated by the claims of white supremacist internationalism, undertook a global effort to preserve white rule as the apartheid state crumbled and the post–Cold War world emerged.

The political gains of the conservative movement in the United States and Europe catalyzed those who wanted to save South Africa from its international pariah status. Long positioned as the anticommunist bulwark in Africa, the apartheid state increasingly found its currency as a premier Cold War partner devalued in the face of global antiapartheid lobbying against white rule. An international ecosystem of white supremacist actors mobilized in response to this threat, lobbying friendly governments against economically sanctioning South Africa. Yet they failed. Centrist right-wing opposition to the violent atrocities of the apartheid state overpowered the sympathetic aims of President Ronald Reagan and Prime Minister Margaret Thatcher, and Western legislative bodies began to pass sanctions on South Africa in 1985. This betrayal by centrist conservatism enraged the pro-apartheid movement, creating a critical shift in its activism. Right-wing governments in both the United States and South Africa became the enemies of white rule, not its defenders, which in turn demanded new tactics that were more grassroots, more antistate, and more violent. As the apartheid government and the Cold War came to a close, white internationalists faced a changing geopolitical landscape that demanded a reimagining of the future of white power. To create this future, apartheid's defenders put forth a new version of their ideology that could survive—and maybe even thrive—in a colorblind, human-rights-centric, and neoliberal world.

This story is a middle piece in the puzzle of global white supremacy that leads into the antistatism of the 1990s. The somewhat lost decade of the 1980s, as US far-right activists transitioned from anti–civil rights activism to the violent, antigovernment tactics of the 1990s, was a critical point of exploration for the far right. The effort to save apartheid brought together a global coalition of actors who sought to influence the conservative Western governments they believed to be allies. Their successes and failures influenced the trajectory of far-right organizing in the 1990s and beyond, revealing a far more dynamic coalition than first appeared. The landscape of apartheid's defenders, their victories and defeats, and their vision for the future offer critical explanatory power to the trajectory of the contemporary far-right and conservative movements. In 2025, as President Donald Trump and his former advisor Elon Musk's defenses of white Afrikaners drive media to ask about "what's really driving Trump's fury with South Africa," *Saving Apartheid* offers a prehistory of the present.[20]

THE APARTHEID GEOPOLITICAL LANDSCAPE

In 1948, the National Party rose to power in South Africa, campaigning on the promise of implementing apartheid. The victory of the National Party, led by radical Afrikaner nationalists, proved a shock, edging out the sitting United Party by a handful of votes to seize control of the Senate and form a government. The National Party arose as a result of tensions between Afrikaner and English whites in South Africa, with the United Party maligned during the campaign as being tied to the interests of English capitalists. In contrast, the National Party promised to address the issues of working-class Afrikaners: urban poverty, poor services, and rising unemployment. The "Africanization" of urban centers, exemplified by Johannesburg's African population outnumbering whites for the first time in 1946, fueled white fears of the swart gevaar, or black peril.[21] The National Party's victory cast black and white South Africans as being fundamentally different and was seen as a "triumph" of Afrikanerdom and the protection of Afrikaner upward mobility against English capitalist interests.[22]

Although the National Party "did not have a complete blueprint" for apartheid upon its assumption of power, their system had seven components: "starker definition of races; exclusive white participation and control in central political institutions (and repression of those who challenged this); separate institutions or territories for blacks; spatial segregation in town and countryside; control of African movement to cities; tighter division in the labor market; and segregation of amenities and facilities of all kinds from universities to park benches."[23] The National Party committed to its core of Afrikaners, creating job reservations for working-class Afrikaners, pushing out English-speaking whites from civil service roles, and limiting voting to only whites. Throughout the 1950s, the National Party implemented the Group Areas Act (1950), which initially divided South Africans into three racial groups, white, colored, and native, later evolving to white, Colored, Black or African, and Indian.[24] The "slow pace" of apartheid implementation angered the National Party's ardent supporters, even as the Group Areas Act removed 600,000 Colored and Indian people from Cape Town and Durban, along with thousands of Africans.[25] The National Party built a vast apparatus of influx control that limited black South Africans' ability to live in urban centers

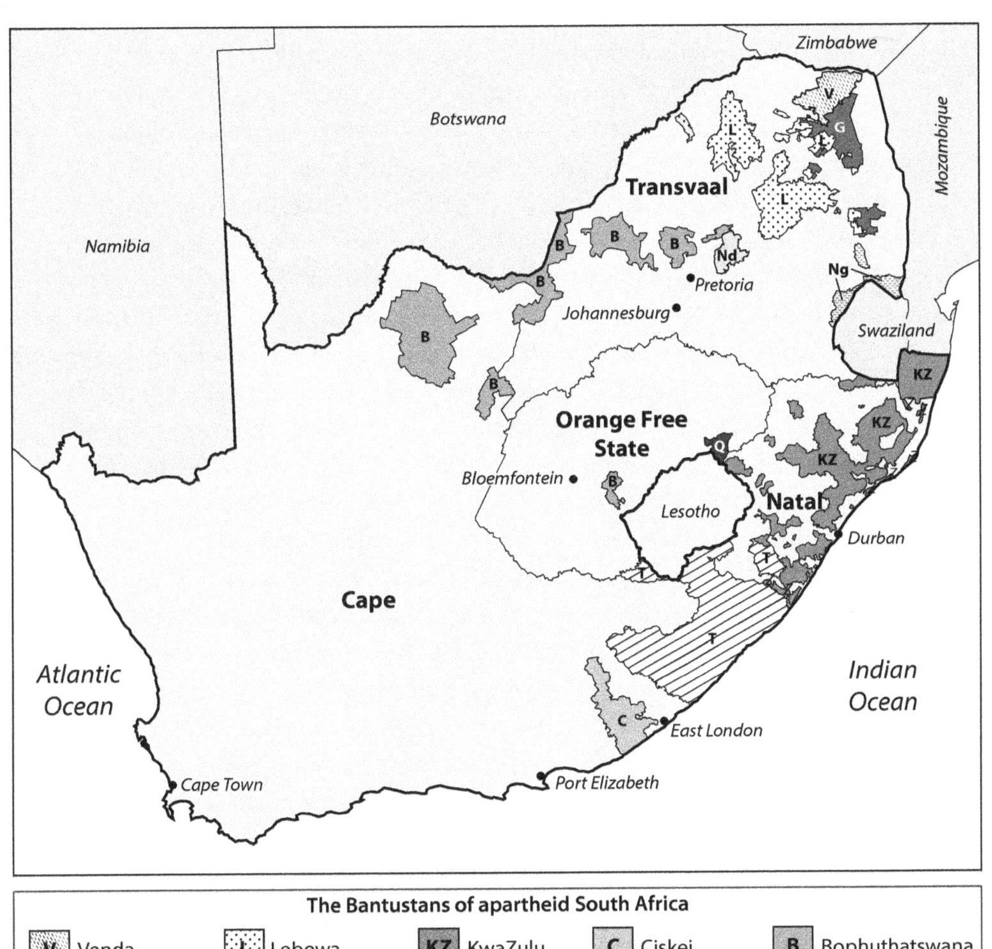

FIGURE 0.1 Map of the bantustans and provinces in South Africa during the apartheid era (1948–1994). Source: Htonl, Bantustans in South Africa, produced with Bantustan boundary data from the Directorate: Public State Land Support via Africa Open Data, May 8, 2013. Used via the CC Attribution-Share Alike 3.0 Unported license, https://commons.wikimedia.org/wiki/File:Bantustans_in_South_Africa.svg. Changes to the source are the inclusion of major cities in South Africa.

while meeting the demand of manufacturers for a settled labor force.[26] The apartheid policies solidified the National Party's hold on power.

The 1960s brought dramatic changes as the apartheid state navigated the dual challenges of decolonization and growing internal rebellion to white rule. In 1960, seventeen African countries became independent. Prime Minister Harold Macmillan of the United Kingdom declared 1960 the "Year of Africa" as Africa sat at the crossroads of decolonization, the global Black freedom struggle, the Cold War, and economic development.[27] As independence transformed the continent, racial oppression intensified in South Africa upon the election of Prime Minister H. F. Verwoerd, the "father of apartheid," in 1958. "Verwoerdian apartheid" expanded the social engineering of white rule. Verwoerd put into place a vision of separate development within the "homelands," or "bantustans"—homogenous ethno-states created by the forced deportation of nearly 3.5 million people—under the control of African tribal elites.[28] According to Chief Albert Luthuli, president general of the African National Congress (ANC), 1960 was also the "Year of the Pass" as the protest movement planned a series of mass actions against the grotesque pass laws. The pass laws, used to control the movement of black South Africans, drove widespread national disobedience by the ANC and the Pan Africanist Congress (PAC). This culminated at Sharpeville on March 21, 1960, when a group of 300 police officers opened fire on over 5,000 protestors, leaving 69 dead and 180 seriously wounded.[29] After the massacre, a new era of state violence began in South Africa. Verwoerd's administration suspended habeas corpus, tortured detainees under the Sabotage Act, massively expanded military spending, and mass arrested and banned the ANC and PAC. In response, the ANC and PAC became underground liberation movements, moving toward armed struggle.[30]

International outcry after Sharpeville changed the posture of the apartheid state. In response to criticism from the Commonwealth and other African states, South Africa voted to leave the Commonwealth in 1961 and form an independent republic. Verwoerd's administration began appropriating a decolonial rhetoric centered around capitalism, inviolable state sovereignty, and anticommunism to justify white rule.[31] The bantustans, in Verwoerd's rendition, became independent states within the southern African confederation, an authentic, African federal system against radical African decolonization.[32] Simultaneously, the bantustans became counterinsurgency labs for the security state to drive Cold War anticommunist repression; local authorities partnered with Pretoria to gain access to housing, education, employment, security, and weapons.[33] Sharpeville brought real repercussions for whites, who previously remained largely isolated from the demands of maintaining apartheid. Political confidence "eroded" among whites as private capital fled the apartheid economy.[34] In 1967, the Defense Amendment Bill came into effect, making service in either the South African Defense Force (SADF) or the South African Police compulsory for all white men between age seventeen and sixty-five because of "new threats" on South Africa's borders.[35]

These threats took on new life with the collapse of Portugal's right-wing dictatorship in a bloodless coup in 1974. Two forces struggled to control Portugal's former colony Angola—the communist People's Movement for the Liberation of Angola (MPLA) and the anticommunist National Union for the Total Independence of Angola.[36] Cuban combat troops and Soviet materiel pushed the MPLA to the brink of victory in November 1975, triggering military intervention by SADF and its covert American backers.[37] The Angolan Civil War amplified the Border War within the territory then known as South West Africa, considered by some scholars as the "most comprehensive, costly, and traumatic" of all the apartheid wars.[38] After the MPLA gained power, it supported the South West African People's Organization in its struggle for independence, and the SADF responded with cross-border raids.[39] Aiming to curtail South Africa's military activity, the UN Security Council put forward Resolution 435 in 1978, proposing a ceasefire and UN-supervised elections in South West Africa, which Pretoria opposed. Meanwhile, Mozambique's communist forces consolidated power in 1974 and faced Rhodesian- and South African–backed counterinsurgency campaigns.[40] After the 1965 Unilateral Declaration of Independence, in 1978, Prime Minister Ian Smith of Rhodesia conceded to majority rule, sending shockwaves through white South Africa.[41] Black political power, backed by communism, was the existential threat to white rule, and it now surrounded South Africa.

Challenges to white rule existed in the international organizations in which South Africa sought membership, principally the United Nations, who tied apartheid's end to the global struggle for self-determination.[42] Throughout the 1950s, the UN passed eight different resolutions challenging the apartheid regime as being in violation of "commitments made by all Member States to uphold fundamental freedoms." After the ANC and PAC were banned, the General Assembly established the UN Special Committee on Apartheid and, in 1969, called on all member states to assist the liberation movements in South Africa.[43] The UN's antiapartheid activism came to a head in the 1970s, when the General Assembly declared 1971 the International Year for Action to Combat Racism and Racial Discrimination. This high-water mark of antiapartheid activity in the UN included declaring apartheid a crime against humanity (1973), working with the Organization of African Unity to "take all necessary steps" to support those in the fight against apartheid (1970), supporting sporting boycotts (1970), denouncing the "intolerable conditions" in Southern Africa and the denial of self-determination (1974), and instituting the UN Security Council's mandatory arms embargo (1977).[44] The struggle against apartheid provided recently decolonized African and Asian countries a means to challenge continued Western support for the apartheid state and raise larger critiques of the liberal project.[45]

The struggle also catalyzed a growing antiapartheid movement across the Americas and Europe, spurred on by the liberation movement in exile and rebellion inside South Africa. After the imprisonment of high-level ANC members, including Nelson Mandela, Walter Sisulu, and Govan Mbeki after the Rivonia Trial in 1964, the ANC established its operations in exile in London.[46] Deputy President Oliver Tambo, after fleeing South Africa, set up the ANC's armed wing, Umkhonto we Sizwe (MK), forging relationships in East Germany, China, and the Soviet Union and establishing bases in Tanzania, Zambia, and Angola—among others.[47] As the historian Rob Skinner argued, the turbulence of the 1960s worked to create "organized anti-apartheid movements and coordinated sanctions campaigns" across Europe, Africa, Asia, and the Americas.[48] The United Kingdom's Anti-Apartheid Movement proved particularly successful in the 1960s, pressuring the UK government to impose an arms embargo in 1964.[49] The global antiapartheid movement responded to conditions within South Africa. From the 1950s to the 1970s, "Black Consciousness" animated a younger generation of students, clerics, and artist-activists who engaged in a robust diasporic exchange with West Africa, the Caribbean, and African American activists.[50] Steve Biko's South African Students' Organization sat at the vanguard of Black Consciousness, charging black South Africans to act "*in themselves* and *for themselves*" to participate in the struggle.[51] Antiapartheid organizing by Black Americans dovetailed with evolving pan-Africanist and anticolonial politics within the global Black freedom struggle.[52] In the aftermath of the civil rights movement, apartheid's existence—and the US government's complicity in it—activated Black Americans in groups like TransAfrica, the Free South Africa Movement, and the Third World Women's Alliance.[53] This activism took on new urgency in the aftermath of the June 1976 Soweto Uprising, when police fired tear gas and live ammunition into a crowd of several thousand students protesting the imposition of mandatory Afrikaans-language instruction.[54] The Soweto Uprising sparked internal rebellion that "rocked apartheid to its foundations [as] townships became epicenters of protest."[55] Pretoria's crackdown inspired a new, multiracial coalition for South Africa composed of students, religious organizations, political committees, and labor groups across the United States and Europe, who pressured Western governments to divest from the apartheid state.[56] Antiapartheid activists in capitalist and social-democratic countries disagreed on how to bring about apartheid's end as political organizations and business and labor leaders debated divestment as a tactic of ending white rule.[57]

This pressure challenged the existing Western powers' posture toward South Africa—one that acknowledged apartheid's immorality while refusing to sacrifice strategic and economic Cold War interests.[58] This posture gave the Nixon and Ford administrations cover during their escalating interventions in southern Africa after Soviet and Cuban involvement in the Angolan Civil War, tying the United State even closer to the "anticommunist" apartheid state.[59] The election of Jimmy Carter in 1976 seemed to promise a new direction for US foreign policy in Africa because of his concerns about the global struggle for racial equality and the particular dynamics of the region.[60] Carter's willingness to engage with Mozambique's Samora Machel and Zimbabwe's Robert Mugabe and deepen ties with Zambia's Kenneth Kaunda and Tanzania's Julius Nyerere signaled a radical change in posture for the United States. Although the Carter White House refrained from levying economic sanctions against the apartheid government, the administration's negotiations with the Frontline States horrified the white regime. The South African government accused the Frontline States, a loose coalition of African countries committed to ending white rule in South Africa and Rhodesia, of harboring communist terrorists and plotting white genocide. Carter engaged in frequent condemnations of the apartheid state, pushed white South Africans to encourage racial reform, and joined the UN Security Council in establishing a mandatory arms embargo in 1977.[61]

As apartheid came under assault domestically and internationally, white South Africans evaluated what it meant to preserve white rule—and what it meant to be white. At its inception, the National Party positioned itself as the champion of Afrikaners, not English whites, casting its victory in 1948 as one of Afrikaner upward mobility against the tyranny of English capital.[62] This dynamic changed under Verwoerd in the aftermath of Sharpeville in 1960. Verwoerd called for white unity to preserve the apartheid state, crafting an "inclusive white nationalism" that would "retain white dominance over the bulk of South Africa as it also countered claims for majority rule."[63] As Roger Southall argued, "as racial tension mounted, and as black political consciousness increased, the Afrikaner-English conflict had begun to recede in the background," and the National Party "correctly claim[ed] they had fostered white unity."[64] By "binding disparate strands of nationalism together," the National Party allied with English capital to preserve physical and economic security for whites as apartheid came under the twin threats of Afrikaner nationalism and communism.[65] These twin threats slighted both white Afrikaners and English, as South Africa became subject to cultural and sporting boycotts: it was barred from the Olympics in 1964, and rugby had "abandoned" South Africa by the mid-1980s.[66]

The Botha administration, led by Minister of Defense General Magnus Malan and SADF head General Andre Viljoen, utilized this new inclusive white nationalism to further weld all South African whites to maintaining the apartheid project. An "overarching narrative of crisis" dominated Pretorian military planners, who by the 1970s imagined the "Total Onslaught" of global communism against South Africa.[67] The Total Onslaught was one part of Botha's "Total Strategy," which paired "reform" with violent security repression inside South Africa. In one of his first speeches as prime minister, Botha declared that white South Africans must "adapt or die." He presented himself as a verligte, or enlightened, liberal white, in contrast to verkrampte, or hard-right whites.[68] Botha proposed political changes to apartheid, including the repeal of "petty apartheid" restrictions around mixed marriages and segregation in public places and the recognition of black trade unions.[69] However, as the historian James

Barbar stated, "reform under Botha was always double-edged, designed to divide as well as rule and always more than matched by repression."[70] A key fixture of Botha's Total Onslaught Plan was the low-intensity conflict waged by South African security forces domestically, applying counter-insurgency lessons learned from its operations in the Border Wars.[71] In April 1979, Botha and Magnus Malan rectified what they saw as Information Scandal weaknesses in the State Security Council by creating the National Security Management System (NSMS). The NSMS consolidated power within the executive state president's office, "drove security expenditures deeper into the recesses of the state," and expanded financing for the police and the SADF to operate domestically.[72] In 1979, Pretoria established the Vlakplass unit, the "special forces" of state security, which used ANC and PAC defectors as soldiers in their death squads.[73] According to Christi van der Westhuizen, Botha's expansion of the security state revealed the "underlying problem" of these "half-hearted" reforms: "the real intent was to sustain white domination."[74]

Black South Africans responded to Botha's "reforms" with widespread insurrectionary violence. Outraged at the limited reforms from the South African government and the security crackdown, resistance to white rule spread across the country. This resistance ranged across a spectrum of antiapartheid politics—communist, socialist, capitalist, and white liberal. Labor unions, specifically the Congress of South African Trade Unions, unleashed waves of mass strikes and stayaways, building on the 1973 Durban Strike.[75] The South African Communist Party and the Azanian People's Organization mobilized underground.[76] "Above ground" resistance occurred as well—through civic organizations, religious groups, lawyers, parliamentary opposition, universities, and the media—putting forth a liberal democratic vision of a new South Africa.[77] Organizations like the Black Sash, predominantly composed of middle-class white women, used legal and nonviolent tactics.[78] Other whites fled South Africa, joining the ANC or PAC in exile or even joining the MK.[79] Some chose parliamentary politics—through Alan Paton's Liberal Party (1953–1968), Helen Suzman and Colin Eglin's Progressive Party (1959–1975), and eventually the Progressive Federal Party led by Frederik van zyl Slabbert and Zach de Beer (1977–1989).[80] Tambo declared 1980 the "Year of the Charter," referencing the ANC Charter calling for mass action against the Botha regime and the bantustans as the ANC infiltrated South Africa.[81]

The question of the bantustans in this antiapartheid paradigm remained constant. By the time Botha assumed power, the apartheid state had created ten ethnic bantustans, with four receiving independence—Transkei (1976), Bophuthatswana (1977), Venda (1979), and Ciskei (1981)—and the other six designated "self-governing." Independence went unrecognized by the international community. As the historian Laura Evans argued, the apartheid state used the Department of Bantu Administration and Development to purge the ANC and PAC from the bantustans via influx control and rural planning.[82] The bantustans could not function without the apartheid state, especially their security forces, which the SADF and police supported as part of a larger colonial project of quashing rebellion.[83] Those who governed the bantustans walked a challenging line in their governance of these illegitimate states, what the historian Shula Marks calls "mastering the politics of the tightrope" between white state power and antiapartheid organizing.[84] Within South Africa, black collaboration with apartheid was nothing new as whites made up less than 20 percent of the population. According to historian Jacob Dlamini, for "most black South Africans, the face of apartheid was black," with "the lines of complicity running like veins and arteries inside the human body."[85] In this project of control in the bantustans, apartheid officials and their African intermediaries crafted "new forms of regional ethnic sovereignty" that moved away from the "flexibility and ambiguity" that had categorized ethnicity within South Africa for centuries.[86] Corruption fueled the power of local authorities within the bantustans, who relied on patronage to prop up sham states. The bantustan leaders, principally KwaZulu's Mangosuthu Buthelezi, Bophuthatswana's Lucas Mangope, and Ciskei's Lennox Sebe, all sought various means of legitimacy—ethnic nationalism, security, international tourism, tribal authority, and even their antiapartheid credentials—to retain power.[87] Ethnicity was a powerful organizing principle within the bantustans that evolved throughout the 1980s and 1990s as its leadership sought to justify its existence and forge a new South Africa.

The bantustan leaders were more than pawns of the apartheid state: they also signified an evolving form of black conservative politics within South Africa. The bantustans were "incubators of a black middle class and bureaucratic elite," as the apartheid state "pumped" in money that fomented a "capitalist class" of entrepreneurs and business development.[88] Opportunities for a "burgeoning African bourgeoise" of educators, government bureaucrats, traders, and lawyers existed within the bantustans to create a generation of literate, comparatively socially mobile, and business-savvy black South Africans.[89] Undergirding this capitalist development of the black middle class was a conservative social politics, encapsulated by KwaZulu's leader Mangosuthu Buthelezi, that was patriarchal, hierarchical, traditional, and explicitly Christian.[90] Christianity, especially Pentecostalism, surged within South Africa in the 1990s building on a bedrock of American Christian networks and white megachurches that promised a vision of economic prosperity to black South Africans.[91] These entangled movements of black conservatives, bantustan officials, and black Christian leaders looked abroad to forge relationships with a global conservative movement. Black conservatives who questioned the necessity of economic sanctions, lambasted the communist ANC, and propped up the reformist credentials of the National Party found new allies in Western states. They tapped into a global network of conservatives, especially from the United States, who were eager to coopt black South Africans into the power structures of white supremacy as justification for delaying apartheid's end.

The US far right understood the apartheid issue through the lens of its own transformations in the 1970s and early 1980s. In the 1970s, white power activism was ignited by the Vietnam War, economic turmoil, and civil rights successes. Formally unified in 1979, the white power movement in this period possessed revolutionary commitments and new organizing strategies against a perceived rejection of whiteness by 1960s civil rights' successes.[92] White power organizations waged war as part of what historian Kyle Burke called the "anticommunist international." Often dovetailing with anti-Soviet global organizing on the right, the white power movement fashioned an imagined community of actors in the Global South committed to curbing civil rights. The World Anti-Communist League's 1974 conference proved to be the high-water mark for international anticommunism, as global right-wing forces became convinced of Western governments' weak commitment to the cause.[93] The white power movement in the United States looked to white southern Africa for inspiration as it planned for the coming "race war," detailed in books like *The Turner Diaries* and *The Camp of the Saints*.[94]

These white power activists, who came together across classes, geographies, and educational levels, were a fringe piece of a mainstream right wing that wanted to pull together its primary coalitions—free marketers and social conservatives—into a winning combination for the Republican Party. As Carter's policy agenda struggled to bring together the economic politics of the 1930s with the social politics of the 1960s, disenchantment with the state by the white working class only grew.[95] The emerging new right offered a cultural refuge for white, blue-collar workers in the 1980s, bringing a new, more populist right to the forefront of the US conservative movement. This new appeal to the white working class by the elite business leaders of the new right relied on the rise of "colorblind conservatism" in response to the explicit focus on race in the 1960s. Emphasizing market forces and individual meritocracy rather than discriminatory, structural realities provided the basis for opposition to affirmative action and other race-based public policies throughout the 1970s.[96] In addition, the distinct evangelism of 1970s social conservatives wove together right-wing ideas about the free market, family politics, and racial colorblindness.[97] These new conservative positions in the 1970s and 1980s reflected the challenges within the Reagan coalition. Anticommunist hardliners stood shoulder to shoulder alongside evangelicals fixated on social issues like abortion. Throughout the 1970s, establishment conservatives and the grassroots right diverged over a spectrum of issues—from support of anticommunist activists to immigration, civil rights, and voting.[98] The question of race in the Republican Party took on central importance in the post–civil rights United States, and apartheid South Africa sat at the heart of the issue.

Therefore, as the Reagan administration prepared to take power in 1981, officials sought a new strategy for dealing with South African intransigence in the interlocking Angolan, Namibian, and Mozambican crises in southern Africa. In what the writer William Finnegan called "an academic essay cum job application," Chester Crocker, the incoming assistant secretary of state, laid out his vision of southern Africa policy in a 1980 article in *Foreign Affairs*.[99] In his essay, Crocker coined the term "constructive engagement," which denoted a new strategy for ending apartheid based on an emerging "window of opportunity" to engage with the "reformist" South African government under Botha. Under the policy of constructive engagement, the Reagan administration would avoid punitive economic measures, provide diplomatic support to South Africa, and implement educational and training programs for black South Africans.

Crocker's policy reflected the US government's view that it should extend empathy not only to black South Africans "but also for the awesome political dilemma in which Afrikaners and other whites [found] themselves."[100] According to the historian Piero Gleijeses, Crocker's statements reflected the Reagan administration's empathy for South African whites and Reagan's endorsement of policies like separate development.[101] The policy was, at its core, an "antiapartheid" strategy to diffuse the calls for sanctions.[102] Crocker outlined this regional dimension of constructive engagement in February 1981, linking together Namibia and Angola—South Africa should only implement Resolution 435 if Cuban troops left Angola.[103] According to Crocker, the SADF used its Namibia presence to guard against possible invasion by the Cuban troops via Angola, and linkage offered a "major visible, strategic quid pro quo" for a United States with little leverage to pressure South Africa.[104] By pitching constructive engagement as a regional strategy that benefited all of southern Africa, Reagan officials tried to avoid the accusations of an American "tilt" toward the apartheid state.

Linking Namibia to Angola allowed administration officials to focus attention on the Cuban and Soviet roles in southern Africa, which reflected the anticommunist priorities of Reagan himself. Reagan entered the White House on a groundswell of American support for "peace through strength" against the unique threat posed by the Soviet Union.[105] Assembling a team of like-minded anticommunists, Reagan positioned the early foreign policy of his administration in opposition to the Soviet Union goal of creating a one-party international state.[106] With anticommunist hardliners in the White House, the administration refocused on rolling back Marxist gains throughout the Global South.[107] Although not explicitly declared until 1985, the Reagan Doctrine of support for anticommunist resistance fighters around the globe emerged in Reagan's early days on the campaign trail and delighted right-wing Americans.[108] Conservative media like *Human Events* magazine, intellectuals like Allan Brownfeld, and paramilitary figures like John Singlaub pushed the administration to go further in its support for anticommunist allies in the Global South.[109] Southern Africa took on unique importance to hardline right-wingers. The anticommunist guerrilla leader of Angola, Jonas Savimbi, became a favored patron of the Western right, with Crocker describing him as "one of the most talented and charismatic leaders in modern African history."[110]

The Reagan administration's southern Africa strategy appeared promising to hardline conservatives.

Furthermore, the administration's rejection of economic sanctions against South Africa reflected the conservative internationalist vision of Reagan and other right-wingers. Throughout the 1980s, the Reagan administration focused on expanding economic liberty and used capitalist policies to solve a variety of foreign policy problems.[111] Reagan's capitalist individualism tapped into a long history of right-wing advocacy for deregulated markets and free trade. Constructive engagement not only eschewed economic sanctions but also offered the possibility of infusing American capital into a budding South African black middle class.[112] In this effort, the Reagan administration found allies in American multinational corporations that believed apartheid could be reformed through enlightened business practices and that feared calls for disinvestment. The 1977 Sullivan Principles drafted by Leon Sullivan, a Black American and member of the General Motors board of directors, offered a set of voluntary conduct rules for corporate social responsibility that incentivized racial reform through corporate success.[113] The Sullivan Principles drew the attention of Reagan State Department officials and right-wing business leaders, who viewed these capitalist reform programs as complimentary to constructive engagement. Constructive engagement seemed a broad church for Reagan's right-wing base, bringing anticommunist hardliners and capitalist interests into southern Africa policy, but a more militant far right had a vision of its own—preserving apartheid.

TOWARD A NEW HISTORY OF US–SOUTH AFRICAN RELATIONS

The relationship between the United States and South Africa has been well-documented by historians, and the histories, especially from scholars of US foreign relations, tell a familiar story.[114] Scholarly consensus indicates that although US policymakers acknowledged apartheid's immorality, they refused to sacrifice strategic and economic Cold War interests, which came to a head in the 1980s as Reagan's constructive engagement strategy ran afoul of his political allies and adversaries.[115]

Reagan's positioning of South Africa as part of the West drew on a much longer history. For much of the nineteenth and early twentieth centuries, the United States and South Africa existed as part of a network of "white men's countries" that circulated strategies of racial knowledge to oppress nonwhite peoples.[116] This relationship was political, social, cultural, and, crucially, economic and relied on state power.[117]

However, as Brenda Gayle Plummer argued, scholars of US foreign relations must pursue "hybrid histories" that move away from a nation-state framework to consider "how power operates in multiple registers."[118] Jamie Miller echoed this point, arguing that the next frontier for scholars is to consider the intersection of the global Cold War and local political agendas.[119] This shift away from focusing only on state policies reflected work by historians of US foreign relations—particularly those studying African American organizing—who did not put policymakers at the center of their narratives.[120] In doing so, a broader vision of US foreign policy emerges by considering how women, people of color, and LGBTQ activists sought to make domestic and global equality national security issues.[121] This shift is especially essential considering the burgeoning literature on US antiapartheid efforts and grassroots organizing across the Atlantic.[122] The antiapartheid movement transformed the global Black freedom struggle and American politics because all organs of US state power—local city councils, Congress, and the American presidency—faced pressure to divest from the engines of the apartheid regime. The story that emerges through these two interlocked literatures is of the pressure from antiapartheid activists to push often unwilling American lawmakers to actually punish the apartheid state.

The end of apartheid in South Africa and the global divestment movement's role in apartheid's demise reflect one of the great triumphs of movement politics across the West. But just how complete was this victory? What forces, beyond the intransigent Reagan and Thatcher administrations, sought to protect apartheid in the West? Focusing on activism for equality and human rights misses the parallel organizing for inequality and racial hierarchy by the right wing, which scholars often dismiss as having an exclusively domestic agenda. The preponderance of analysis on the US right-wing's domestic activism masks the movement's equally ambitious international vision and its connections to a broader, global conservative organizing. That conservative organizing specifically fixated on the apartheid state as a location of its activism. Transatlantic white supremacist actors were aware of Black organizing efforts to push the US government toward an openly confrontational geopolitical posture with the apartheid state and actively combated that effort. In the late twentieth century, in response to the civil rights movement's successes and global decolonization after World War II, official and unofficial efforts to protect white rule persisted. The pro-apartheid movement reveals how efforts to lobby the United States and South African states clashed with imaginative discussions in American white power spaces about the very meaning of preserving white rule. Far-right churches, community organizers, and newspapers remained hyperfocused on local, domestic realities as they examined apartheid. South Africa's pariah status was never complete—a broad landscape of Americans connected their struggles with transatlantic discussions about the role of race and racial hierarchy in international affairs.

The triumphalist story of apartheid's end has also come under increasing scrutiny by historians, especially in light of the struggles of the modern-day ANC. The apartheid state's construction, maintenance, and persistence into the 1990s continue to draw attention, as scholars combat the realities of official state secrecy and record destruction, especially from 1990 to 1994.[123] As scholars like Jamie Miller note, we know little about how the leaders of white South Africa sought to keep their regime viable at home and abroad and how the government operated in practice.[124] Thus, analyzing the South African apartheid state brings a unique set of challenges to scholars, who wrestle with the regime's repressive realities while attempting to avoid essentialist accounts of the power it wielded.[125] Nevertheless, these studies focus almost exclusively on the apartheid state itself and miss the profoundly personal and grassroots nature of right-wing activism in this period, which was both in alliance and in conflict with the South African state.

The ANC and its associated allies were not the only movement in the 1990s envisioning a "new South Africa." In the late 1990s, the far-right alliance between white power groups and black nationalist leaders who refused to participate in the negotiations to end apartheid requires particular consideration within the framework of the pro-apartheid movement. The relationship between black Bantustan leaders—specifically Bophuthatswana's Mangope, Ciskei's Oupa Gqozo, and KwaZulu's Buthelezi—and the state reflects the changing nature of resistance and collaboration at the heart of apartheid and the need to move beyond this binary paradigm.[126] The decision by Buthelezi, Mangope, and Gqozo to align with the paramilitary white right in the 1990s provoked a violent rebuke from the ANC and other antiapartheid parties, which lambasted the "partnership of convenience" as a continued defense of white rule. The far-right alliance that emerged in the 1990s originated in the pro-apartheid activism of the 1980s, as South Africa's bantustan leaders walked another political tightrope in their relationship with US and South African white power activists.

Scholars have neglected the study of nonwhite, right-wing politics, especially in the United States, which leaves critical gaps in understanding the rise of a global, cross-racial far right. Political, religious, and economic conservatism remains a potent strand of Black American intellectual thought underexamined by scholars, with the "very notion of a black conservative [being] oxymoronic" for many.[127] As right-wing movements become more global and increasingly multiracial, exclusively focusing on the white right offers only part of the story. The prominent global activism of the antiapartheid movement and the popularity of figures like Desmond Tutu and Nelson Mandela masked a bedrock of black conservative religiosity and politics. Focusing on the "low-intensity conflict" between antiapartheid and conservative Christians offers a unique examination of black right-wing religiosity that existed before the apartheid state that emerged more fully in the postapartheid world.[128] As the South African government–ANC negotiations began, pro-apartheid groups reframed defenses of white rule, moving away from preserving the apartheid system and toward crafting Christianity-based defenses of financial, social, and cultural stability. These relationships struggled to come to fruition in an apartheid world. However, as Siphiwe Dube argues, this New Right appeals to an "undeclared coalition" that includes the black middle class and aspiring middle class in "neo-apartheid."[129] These paradoxical positions around apartheid and "colorblindness" reveal the tensions at the heart of a budding new conservative movement oriented around free markets, Christianity, and right-wing politics emboldened by a neoliberal resolution to the apartheid era.

The trajectory of apartheid's end and the evolution of the pro-apartheid movement reveal how the global far right became disenchanted with the center-right at the peak of its political power and sought to create a new vision of conservative power in a postapartheid world. Scholarly analysis of the white power movement languished throughout most of the post–Cold War era, with studies focusing disproportionately on the Ku Klux Klan or the 1990s white power movement.[130] The cognitive tissue that connected the various eras of the Klan to the white power separatism of the 1990s eluded scholars before Kathleen Belew's *Bring the War Home: The White Power Movement and Paramilitary America*, which places the white power movement's antistate turn as a response to the Vietnam War.[131] However, other factions of the white power movement in the United States and South Africa underwent a similar transformation in their pursuit of defending apartheid. This renewed scholarly focus on right-wing extremism globalizes our understanding of white power movements, moving away from the view of these networks as strained, convoluted, and backward looking.[132] White supremacist organizing and efforts to preserve racial hierarchy have always been global projects.[133] As Daniel Geary, Camilla Schofield, and Jennifer Sutton argue, international links "both real and imagined . . . undergirded the pursuit of white racial nationalism long before the internet."[134] Although often nationalist in their goals, white power projects persist transnationally in their inspiration and identification, with the case of apartheid South Africa as a prime example of this paradox. The global defense of apartheid by a vast array of political, religious, and paramilitary actors reveals how the white power movement evolved at a critical point of expansion in the 1980s and 1990s. Despite apartheid's prominent place in the white imaginary, scholars remain focused on US and European white power influence in and responses to South Africa. Constructing an international history of the pro-apartheid movement demands focusing not only on US white power actors but also on how South African ideas of whiteness found purchase in the United States. Everyday South Africans proved flexible and sophisticated in their efforts to influence white Americans' views on apartheid—and they were not just tools of Pretoria. US and South African pro-apartheid factions clashed over their competing visions of how to preserve white rule even as they organized globally.

The story of the pro-apartheid movement then is not one of radicalization, as is the common story of white supremacist groups. Rather, it is one of recalibration, as the far right considered how to defend white power in a changing world that in two decades saw the Cold War end, apartheid fall, and neoliberalism rise. Telling the story of the pro-apartheid movement showcases the landscape of white supremacist activism at the international, national, and local levels, revealing the deeply personal nature of the apartheid issue to Americans and South Africans. As Elizabeth Gillespie McRae argues, white supremacist politics historically created platforms that translated political support for racial hierarchy into broader geopolitical debates.[135] These geopolitical connections and conversations—about global communism, failing US power, the United Nations, and anti-Christian violence—provided the basis for local racial oppression. Apartheid—as the last white-ruled state—took on particular urgency for white supremacists at both the global and community levels. US pro-apartheid organizers not only supported Afrikaans-language papers but also wrote man-seeking-woman advertisements looking for partners who were friends of white South Africa. This tension between geopolitical and personal choices does not fit neatly into international relations theories but rather encompasses white supremacist actors making choices about what "security" looked like to them.[136] As apartheid crumbled, pro-apartheid actors consciously turned away from the state as a provider of white security and created their own forms of protection, reevaluating the meaning of white power.

The pro-apartheid movement existed as a transnational, loosely connected and affiliated network of political, religious, and economic actors focused on undercutting attempts to end white rule in South Africa.[137] These actors included not only paramilitary white power militias but also religious organizations, community organizers, conservative media outlets, and politicians.[138] Those who worked to defend the apartheid state are part of what I call the "white supremacist international ecosystem" of the 1980s and 1990s. The word "ecosystem" highlights the pro-apartheid movement's existence within global white supremacy, where apartheid was only one issue. In this international ecosystem, intellectual, religious, political, paramilitary, and terrorist actors fixated on apartheid sat within a swath of global right-wing activists, from paramilitary US fighters in Rhodesia and mercenaries in South Africa to the antigovernment militias of the 1990s.[139] The pro-apartheid movement's activism was—and its legacies remain—part of a larger war within the right over its ideology. The pro-apartheid movement's worldview fits with Seymour Martin Lipset and Earl Raab's definition of the right as an ideology of preservation.[140] Nevertheless, Noam Gidron and Daniel Ziblatt caution against constructing a single type of the right.[141] This call is essential in understanding how support for white supremacy evolved in tandem with and beyond the apartheid state. In that effort, I use "center-right" to describe the parties that brought together Christian, free market, and conservative politics with a commitment to internationalism and "far right," as defined by scholar Eviane Leidig, as constituting nativism, extreme nationalism, and authoritarianism.[142] The interplay between the far right and electoral right creates a "dialectic of extremism and respectability" between the two factions, well present in the US and South African right wings of the 1980s and 1990s.[143] Although the pro-apartheid movement was global, lobbying conservative governments across the West, the decision to focus on the United States reflects three factors: the unique white supremacist relationship between the United States and South Africa, the United States as the last sanctions holdout, and the nexus of conservative thinkers and activists operating through and within the United States.[144]

The pro-apartheid movement shared a worldview sympathetic to white rule; connected like-minded individuals; exchanged propaganda material, money, and techniques for legitimizing the apartheid state; and worked to build a new cross-racial right wing in and outside the state. In this vision, "whiteness" and "white supremacy" were a "configuration of power, privilege, and identity consisting of white racialized ideology and practices, with material and social ramifications."[145] Although they all supported white power, each actor did so from various political, religious, and social contexts that dictated the particular choices and partnerships within the pro-apartheid movement. Critically, this vision of "saving white rule" changed over time. Many of these organizations eagerly described themselves as white nationalists, committed to creating separate white states and reinstituting explicit racial hierarchies. Others tried to remove race in their support for white rule and create colorblind defenses for protecting the apartheid state for strategic, economic, and religious reasons. However, a series of core beliefs animated all factions of the pro-apartheid movement—it was devoutly Christian—often Pentecostal—militantly anticommunist, overtly capitalist, and explicitly antidemocratic. The question of race—the heart of the apartheid project itself—perhaps vexed the pro-apartheid movement's individual members the most, as white rule's defenders imagined a world with and without the enshrined protections of apartheid.

Saving Apartheid intentionally takes a far broader definition of white power than most US histories of right-wing extremism, which focus narrowly on explicit hate groups like the Ku Klux Klan and the separatists of the 1990s, preferencing the activities of paramilitarists in these analyses. Focusing only on the most explicit, violent, and vile aspects of white power misses the landscape of support for apartheid in the 1980s and 1990s. Support for the apartheid state was an uncomfortably broad church. Even more worrisome, taking such a narrow definition of "white power" risks diluting it to just physical violence, which is ahistorical in the United States and South Africa and disregards the political, religious, social, and economic apparatus of apartheid that kept whites in power. Conversely, taking a broader view of those who supported the most explicit form of white power allows us to ask more complicated questions about the conservative coalition, about race, about how white supremacist politics evolved, and about who was and remains invested in this project.

Writing this history presents a particular set of archival challenges. At best, the documentary record of white power organizations remains fractured because these groups intentionally learned to hide their membership records, obscuring the movement's objectives. Paradoxically, white power groups often attempt to overinflate their numbers, reach, and power, making it difficult to determine their influence. Far-right organizations form, metastasize, and collapse within a matter of years or months, challenging a researcher to track the reach of these networks successfully. Many religious and political organizations that advocated for white rule remain active but have attempted to destroy the historical record of that support. Record destruction by the apartheid state compounds this difficulty. At times, people and organizations appear only once across the archives I visited. Sometimes, a single pamphlet circulated, zombie-like, across the United States and South Africa, with its origin nearly impossible to uncover and biographical information about these actors even sparser.

To reconstruct the pro-apartheid movement, I tracked its activity across over a dozen archives in the United States and South Africa. These archives included official state records and the records of religious organizations, grassroots groups, and watchdog entities, among others. Their materials ended up in collections in a variety of ways. Some were traditional, being deposited by family members or sold to archives by independent investigators of the far left or the far right. I spent two weeks at the Ronald Reagan Presidential Library just sorting through mail sent to his office to identify which people and organizations were invested in protecting South Africa. Sometimes I got lucky. At the Alan Paton Centre in Pietermaritzburg, while wandering around a conference room, I found every issue of the *Aida Parker Newsletter*, one of the most prolific South African pro-apartheid newsletters circulated in the United States. The Archive of Contemporary Affairs in Bloemfontein proved more fruitful than I could have possibly hoped on the inner workings of the black-white conservative alliance to prevent democratic elections. Tracking other individuals required more unconventional techniques—in a moment of desperation, I ordered from Amazon bound copies of the Trinity Broadcasting Network's newsletters from 1970 to 2000. The gamble paid off. Over several years, I constructed what I began to call the "pro-apartheid movement," tracing its arc from the 1980s to apartheid's end.[146] By weaving together a fragmented and disjointed movement, the bottom-up mobilization and grassroots learning in local white power movements came into focus, as they navigated an evolving geopolitical world, showcasing a kind of far-right organizing too often derided as only possible with the advent of the internet.

Saving Apartheid intentionally tells the story of the grassroot support for white rule and its intersections with religious, intellectual, nongovernmental, and state actors. The question of South African state involvement in financing and directing these actors within the pro-apartheid movement is impossible to ignore. These actors, especially those that found success in lobbying conservatives in the United States, undoubtedly were useful to the regime. Some of them were even caught up in the Information Scandal and tried to rebrand as independent of the South African government. These men and women, however, had their own motivations and agendas outside and beyond the South African government's vision of white rule. That duality is important for considering the agency and intellectual imagination of not only white South Africans but especially black South Africans who navigated their stances vis-à-vis the regime throughout apartheid's existence. The tension between the "prostate" and "antistate" activity of the pro-apartheid movement allows us to see how white power organizing evolved, its relationship to power, and its vision of white supremacy beyond the state.

Saving Apartheid proceeds in three parts. Part I begins by constructing the pro-apartheid movement in the United States and South Africa. Two chapters on stories, bonds, and evolutions map the religious, social, and economic international exchange that formed the basis of the political relationships within the pro-apartheid movement. Part II examines the effort by the pro-apartheid campaign to prevent the passage of economic sanctions against South Africa throughout the 1980s across the West through white women's activism and within the Reagan White House. The three chapters in part II consider how the global failure to prevent the passage of economic sanctions by conservative-led governments in the United States and Europe pushed pro-apartheid organizations to partner directly with the South African state and bantustan governments. Part III focuses on the move to enforce white rule on the ground in South Africa, even as apartheid itself crumbled. In this final section, the violent antistate direction of these white supremacist actors emerges globally, as the movement no longer viewed Western states as sufficiently committed to white rule. Apartheid South Africa is one of the few geopolitical issues that spans almost the entirety of the Cold War and into the post–Cold War era. As a free South Africa rose, *Saving Apartheid* showcases the evolving relationship between white power and conservative politics throughout the Cold War and as South Africa navigated a new neoliberal world.

I

BUILDING THE PRO-APARTHEID MOVEMENT

1

TELLING THE STORY OF WHITE POWER

At first glance, David Otto's 1993 advertisement for a man seeking a woman appears rather conventional. A thirty-one-year-old from Burlington, Iowa, Otto's interests included dining out, good music and movies, long walks, and animals. However, Otto added one nonnegotiable caveat for his prospective bride—she needed to be "a friend of white South Africa."[1] Otto's advertisement appeared in *Citizens Informer*, the semiregular newsletter of the Council of Conservative Citizens (CofCC). A 1980s iteration of the segregationist Citizens Councils of the 1960s, CofCC's slogan, "the voice of the no longer silent majority," reflected the organization's virulence. The CofCC was and remains a hate group, self-described as a white-rights group that actively opposes nonwhite immigration.[2] Founded in 1985 by Gordon Baum, a personal injury attorney turned white power activist, and thirty compatriots, the CofCC grew to more 15,000 members in twenty-eight states by 1999. It reached into the annals of American power with Congressman Bob Barr (R-GA) and Senate Majority Leader Trent Lott (R-MS) speaking to the organization multiple times.[3] The organization allegedly inspired the mass killing of nine people at a historically Black church in Charleston, South Carolina, by Dylann Roof in 2015.[4] But in the 1980s, the CofCC and its members focused on South African apartheid and the ill omens its end would spell for whites globally. "Are you a conservative young lady, nationalist, and invested in the struggle for Afrikaner freedom and independence," the advert wrote. If on the "same wavelength"—and no older than thirty-three—"please don't be shy" and write today, the ad said.[5]

Otto's advertisement appeared in a tense issue of *Citizens Informer*; the main story of the issue was titled "Where Do We Go from Here?" The story focused on the failed presidential bid of George H. W. Bush in 1992, which CofCC members agreed hardly counted as a defeat for the right wing because of Bush's poor conservative credentials. Nevertheless, CofCC leadership remained concerned about many issues, particularly the "deteriorating situation" in South Africa.[6] In one column, Lieutenant Colonel Robert Slimp elaborated on the fall of white South Africa. Slimp, a minister in the conservative Presbyterian Church in America, a retired army chaplain, and a director on the CofCC board, was the CofCC's primary columnist on the state of South Africa.[7] He reported visiting southern Africa twelve times since 1976, four times as a tour guide. Almost every article about South Africa in *Citizens Informer* in the 1980s or 1990s included Slimp's perspective. Slimp gave lectures at CofCC meetings across the United States, presenting secret footage of African National Congress (ANC) attacks on black South Africans.[8] If the ANC came to power, Slimp wrote, "the future of nearly 6 million whites [would] be sacrificed," resulting in the "complete destruction of the most stable and friendly government in all of Africa."[9]

For white supremacist organizations like the CofCC, preserving South African apartheid remained the crucial foreign policy issue throughout the 1980s and 1990s. The urgency of protecting South Africa dramatically increased in the 1980s as international protests against apartheid raged and activists across the Global South, the Soviet Bloc, and increasingly the West targeted US and European governmental complicity in supporting white rule. The global antiapartheid movement brought Black activists, business leaders, university students, religious organizations, conservatives, and liberals together to rally against the South African government's horrific racial oppression. As global antiapartheid sentiment grew throughout the decade, a powerful countermovement emerged, consisting of religious, political, and economic actors protecting white rule in South Africa. The rising power of the religious and political right in the United States and Europe catalyzed pro-apartheid actors like Slimp and Otto, who lobbied conservative Western governments to support the apartheid state. However, the US–South African relationship was not just a geopolitical issue. Slimp and Otto saw themselves as part of an international white supremacist ecosystem that viewed apartheid as profoundly personal.

As the international profile of the antiapartheid movement and black South African activists grew, transatlantic white supremacists countered them. To defend white rule in South Africa, a transatlantic network of activists—called here the "pro-apartheid movement"—emerged as a coherent force in the 1980s, catalyzed by the election of Western conservative leaders and the desire to fill the void left by the Information Scandal. The pro-apartheid movement existed as a powerful adversary to the antiapartheid movement and created specific discourses around apartheid that permeated right-wing thought in both the United States and South Africa. South Africans created a particular portrait of white preservation to be exported abroad and co-opted by other white power actors in the United States and Europe. These networks grafted onto existing conservative discourses on communism, colorblind capitalism, and Christian persecution to justify apartheid. Through these interlocking narratives, white supremacist actors on both sides of the Atlantic built an expansive and inclusive case for preserving apartheid that accomplished two tasks simultaneously. It mobilized embattled far-right actors to protect the last bastion of white rule by whatever means necessary and created a palatable discourse defending white rule that could accommodate, attract, and mobilize conservatives of all stripes. These discourses were the bedrock of the pro-apartheid movement, the guiding rhetoric that sustained white supremacist organizing as it built a transatlantic partnership across factions of Western conservatives.

CATALYZING WHITE POWER

The election of Ronald Reagan in 1980 came right on time for the South African government. Riding a wave of global conservatism that brought Prime Minister Margaret Thatcher to power in the United Kingdom in 1979 and Chancellor Helmut Kohl to power in West Germany in 1982, the former Hollywood actor and Republican governor of California crushed incumbent Jimmy Carter. From the 1980 campaign trail to the first days of the Reagan administration, the White House distanced itself from the "failed" Carter years.[10] Reagan officials eagerly charted a new path on southern Africa, specifically to reverse Carter's criticism of the South African bantustan system. In a November 1976 editorial in the "arch-conservative rabble-rousing" *Manchester (N.H.) Union Leader*, Reagan offered his positive comments about the "independence" of the Transkei bantustan.[11] Ritualistic denunciation of the bantustans ignored the state's positive promise of self-rule and autonomy for black Africans, Reagan wrote, insisting that the United States "stop acting foolish" and recognize the bantustans as independent states.[12] Reagan's comments, which came after his narrow defeat for the 1976 Republican presidential nominee, seemed out of touch given the Soweto Uprising in June of that same year. Nevertheless, the editorial reinforced Reagan's commitment to a "party that prioritized rightwing ideology, rather than shied away from it."[13] The Reagan Revolution in 1980 thus promised a new US–South African relationship.

A potentially less critical United States suited the P. W. Botha regime as it stared down the twentieth anniversary of the apartheid republic. The beginning of the 1980s saw the "remotivation of the white electorate," as Christi van der Westhuizen put it, via "the borrowed ideological innovation of 'total onslaught.'" Upon its assumption of power, the Botha regime needed to fend off internal rebellion by black workers and urbanites, a brutal recession, a bloated apartheid bureaucracy, an increasingly rightwing electorate, and regional and international pressure against the state. Botha united the administration, business elites, and the security state in service of the Total Onslaught Plan, which became the ideological undercurrent defending apartheid.[14] As Pretoria waged overt war in Namibia and Angola and covertly backed anticommunist forces in Mozambique, it relied on a powerful military apparatus revamped under Botha. The National Security Management System (NSMS) centralized the security state after the Information Scandal, creating a "parallel, militarized bureaucracy" that identified and eliminated security threats.[15] The State Security Council (SSC), with Botha at the helm, oversaw the NSMS and launched attacks in violation of international law on the ANC-in-exile headquartered in Maputo. Domestically, the Botha administration consolidated existing security measures into the Internal Security Law, which codified draconian death penalties and decades-long prison sentences for those convicted of terrorism, subversion, or sabotage.[16] A friendly American president was a needed boon.

White South Africans largely rejoiced at Reagan's triumph over Carter—an election that South African readers followed closely. Reagan appealed to reformist, centrist, and far-right factions across the Atlantic. With Reagan, white South Africans could count on a more approachable, friendly, and helpful United States. This improved relationship proved especially important considering the divisions among white South Africans about the trajectory of the apartheid state and the international response to the perpetuation of white rule. The Afrikaner nationalist newspaper *Die Transvaler* wrote that Reagan's runaway victory would usher in years of favorable policies for South Africa.[17] One editorial lamented the possibility of the Americans deciding "to saddle themselves and the Free World with the peanut farmer for another four years."[18] Upon Reagan's victory, writers in the Afrikaans-language press said that a refreshing new strategy would emerge from the Reagan White House. The United States was now willing to support its allies for the survival of civilization.[19] One leader of the Namibia faction of South Africa's National Party wrote that Reagan's new South Africa attitude would give whites "valuable breathing space."[20]

Although there was still skepticism of Reagan, his foreign policy strategy for southern Africa won praise. Constructive engagement, publicized during Reagan's campaign as part of the wider strategy of the Africa Working Group, was seen as a boon to US–South African relations and proof that Reagan did not accept the inevitability of white downfall. Conceived by Assistant Secretary of African Affairs Chester Crocker, constructive engagement promised a new direction for US–South African relations, one of behind-the-scenes negotiation with the apartheid state. In Crocker's vision, the Reagan White House would link together the regional conflicts in Angola, Namibia, and Mozambique, pushing the implementation of UN Resolution 435 while Cuban troops left Angola. For apartheid's defenders, constructive engagement reflected the realities of life in southern Africa, in which white South Africa stood alone against the onslaught of communism in Africa. That Total Onslaught vision, propagated from the Botha administration, permeated all facets of South African life, especially in how the apartheid state dealt with rebellion at home and conflict abroad. To South Africa's defenders, the Reagan administration's backing away from engagement with the Frontline States and resisting calls for sanctions seemed to reify a new, realistic assessment of the communist threat in southern Africa. Ringing endorsements for Reagan's foreign policy appeared in a September 1981 issue of *Die Beeld*, a pro–National Party but marginally more independently minded newspaper. One unnamed writer wrote that Reagan's foreign policy team did not see southern Africa as a black-and-white issue but rather as an issue about the threat of communism that would cause destabilization and conflict.[21] Whites' place in South Africa should be assured in this view, not pushed aside, as it had been under the Carter administration. *Die Beeld* previewed a dynamic new alliance between Secretary of State Alexander Haig and Foreign Affairs Minister Pik Botha of South Africa.[22] This new reality likely occurred because the Reagan administration "came to power without the support of the black public . . . and owes nothing to the black American," *Die Beeld* wrote.[23] White writers largely reacted with delight to Reagan's election, which promised to change South African policy. Americans were now in the fight against the Total Onslaught.

Right-wing thinkers in the United States expressed similar views to South Africa's writers, immediately imploring Reagan in the months before his inauguration to right the wrongs of the disastrous Carter years. One letter writer from West Virginia sent his concerns directly to the Reagan-Bush transition office in December 1980, requesting that Reagan task his new secretaries of state and defense to review US foreign policy toward South Africa. The writer insisted that armed with the "cold facts," Reagan would come to South Africa's aid.[24] As the president of United Continental Land Corporation relayed from his conversations with National Party ministers, "If Carter had been re-elected, the Russians would have been at the Cape within one year."[25] This sentiment reflected the view that South Africa was the last anticommunist bulwark on the continent and revealed that this belief was held not just in the elite circles of foreign policy. It trickled down to everyday Americans who saw white South Africa as a Cold War ally. They saw Reagan as understanding that relationship to a different degree than Carter. Others put an even finer point on the importance of Reagan's election. Writing on behalf of nineteen other Rotarians and Rotary Anns, one Rotary leader wrote to Reagan in November 1981 after a trip he and his wife led in South Africa.[26] He noted a feeling of optimism about the country that he said came from Reagan's election.[27] Reagan's election activated conservatives to support South Africa throughout the United States, empowered by the belief that the man who led the highest office in the country was a friend to white South Africa.

For apartheid's defenders, Reagan's victory came at a critical inflection point in the global assault on South Africa. The apartheid state's militant transformations responded to a massive ramp-up of protests, demonstrations, and subversion by the ANC, which by 1981 "had built a solid base among the popular masses," and made inroads with Colored, Indian, and even white South Africans.[28] Escalating black resistance to the apartheid regime posed an existential threat to white life under apartheid. Botha became prime minister in 1978 with a mandate to contain black rebellion after the Soweto Uprising in 1976 and increasing rebellion in the townships. His attempts to push the economic development of a black middle class to siphon off support for the ANC and limit political representation for Colored and Indian South Africans failed to appeal.[29] In response to hollow political and economic offers, organizing bodies like the United Democratic Front (UDF) and the Congress of South African Trade Unions emerged in the mid-1980s, operating as expansive, multiracial coalitions. They brought together labor, political, and student organizers in reinvigorated antiapartheid activism.[30] Simultaneously, the ANC-in-exile was "reviving its primacy in the liberation struggle" and continued its pursuit of armed resistance and its international advocacy, inspiring activists across the West.[31] As in South Africa, diverse, multiracial coalitions emerged in the United States, including congressmembers, political committees, labor groups, students, and religious entities, and demanded divestment from South Africa, building off decades of African American activism against apartheid before the 1980s.[32] It was this reality—Black Americans and Africans working together, mobilizing a cross-racial, cross-political, international movement against apartheid in the former safe zone of the West—that horrified white supremacists.

Thus, the antiapartheid movement was an existential threat to white supremacist actors. Internal and global rebellion against the apartheid state, in the view of pro-apartheid supporters, fundamentally weakened South Africa's ability to wage war against radical Black communism in Africa. Pro-apartheid authors railed against the antiapartheid movement as a "death lobby" and enlisted the services of Soviet defectors to attack the antiapartheid movement as nothing more than Kremlin subterfuge.[33] Targets of the pro-apartheid movement's venom included a who's who of ANC leaders, such as the imprisoned Nelson Mandela, the internally exiled Winnie Madikizela-Mandela, then-president of the ANC Oliver Tambo, and Bishop Desmond Tutu, as well as African American activists such as Randall Robinson, founder of TransAfrica. As Tambo and Tutu crisscrossed the Western world, rage against these agitators filled pages of white supremacist publications. As John F. McManus, future president of the John Birch Society, put it, organizations like TransAfrica publicly backed terrorism, working side by side with communists at home and abroad.[34] White supremacists were concerned about black activists' mobility and visibility and their potential to attract allies in the white world. The antiapartheid movement's success necessitated a challenge.

To protect white rule in the 1980s, apartheid's defenders developed three overlapping narratives of why the United States needed to protect white rule that grafted onto existing conservative rhetoric. First, the pro-apartheid movement wielded an anticommunist defense, arguing that South Africa alone could stem the tide of radical Black communism in Africa. Second, by leveraging existing colorblind discourses, pro-apartheid activists contended that South Africa no longer suffered from issues of race and thrived under a race-neutral capitalism. Finally, narratives of Christian betrayal dominated, as pro-apartheid activists insisted that Christians remained under assault from communist Black liberationist groups at home and abroad. These arguments mutually reinforced one another, providing a wide tent of overlapping and sustaining talking points in defense of white rule. In the early 1980s, the pro-apartheid movement deployed these arguments simultaneously, but as the West passed sanctions against South Africa and the Cold War ended in 1989, the threat of communism receded. As the 1990s began, pro-apartheid actors increasingly shifted to a rhetoric of colorblindness that further reinforced their Christian and free-market arguments. It is impossible to disentangle these arguments, which were not just simultaneous but mutually reinforcing and ever evolving, woven into the very fabric of global conservative thinking.

Throughout the 1980s, many pro-apartheid activists insisted that they were not actually operating in defense of apartheid, that they wanted South Africa to evolve, and that they were not racist. They used many rationales: They touted their heritage as part of the English liberal tradition, their work in multiracial organizations, and their black partners.

They showcased research produced by the South African government as proof that apartheid was on its way out and just needed to be left alone by the West. These claims are disingenuous in many obvious ways—their dilution of the horrors of apartheid, their dismissal of black suffering, and their deep and abiding hatred for those that fought against white rule. However, their insistence that they did not support apartheid does reveal an existential question at the heart of the pro-apartheid movement: What did it mean to protect white power at apartheid's end? Was it the apartheid system they were protecting? Or was it something else? Within these defenses of apartheid is a true wrestling over what South Africa looked like beyond legalized white rule that was, at its core, anticommunist, Christian, and capitalist.

EXPORTING THE TOTAL ONSLAUGHT TO THE WEST

The pro-apartheid movement drummed up fears of a communist attack against the anticommunist partner of South Africa as the first line of defense against critics of the apartheid state. The South African government had long used anticommunism as a "diffuse ideology of social control."[35] The capitalist-communist binary of the Cold War offered the South African government status as a geopolitical ally to the United States, especially important with the rise of communist liberation movements in Mozambique and Angola and what became Zimbabwe and Namibia. Throughout the Cold War, White Africa—South Africa and Rhodesia—proved adept at positioning itself to the West as the only force holding back the tides of communism's political control, thereby demanding toleration and acceptance of their abhorrent racial practices.[36] Both state and nonstate bastions of white power leveraged South Africa's geopolitical importance—economic interests, military-grade uranium, and the Cape of Good Hope's strategic value—to position Pretoria as a vital anticommunist ally to the West.[37] As the apartheid state's pariah status grew, complicating the US–South African relationship, right-wing activists sought to remind Westerners of the price of complacency and apathy toward revolution in South Africa. As they put it, only South Africa stood between a total communist takeover of the continent.[38]

It is here that grassroots pro-apartheid actors overlapped most heavily with the arguments from the South African government. Botha's Total Onslaught and his wider Total Strategy created a vision of a South Africa under assault at home and abroad, fighting desperately to reform in the face of communist extremists who sought to destroy white life in the country. Grassroots pro-apartheid actors deeply believed this vision and aligned with the National Party's explicit hatred of the ANC, deep fear of the Frontline States, and support for the militarization of the nation. However, a strong undercurrent of frustration with the Botha regime existed in tandem, particularly after the 1983 reforms and the rise of insurrectionary violence. To some of the militarized white right and their wider conservative allies, the Botha regime was failing in its duty to fight communists. Their rhetoric in the mid-1980s sought to export the Total Onslaught Plan to the United States and to push the National Party to stay the course.

Although a nebulous, evolving set of actors without a clear hierarchy or leadership, the pro-apartheid movement had several prominent organizational drivers in the 1980s and 1990s, specifically the umbrella group United Christian Action. United Christian Action, an influential right-wing religious group in South Africa, coordinated over a dozen pro-apartheid groups, launched new organizations, and established an information service that was sent to over 800 partners worldwide. Edward Cain led United Christian Action and considered it his mission to "provide valuable information to top American opinion informers."[39] Born in Johannesburg in 1935, Cain served as a missionary in Mozambique with WEC International from 1964 to 1975, where he married a US missionary. Cain and his family left Mozambique after the assumption of power by Samora Machel in 1975 and the transition to a one-party state under the Liberation Front of Mozambique (FRELIMO). FRELIMO's power terrified anticommunist activists across the transatlantic, who monitored Mozambique closely and agitated for the United States to join South Africa and Rhodesia in supporting the anticommunist Mozambican National Resistance (Renamo).[40] After Machel's rise, Cain established the bimonthly publication *Signposts* targeting American Christians with his propaganda.[41] He published *Signposts* for over twenty years and also wrote the *Roca Report*, a monthly review of current affairs and political and social analysis for his subscribers.[42] United Christian Action, based out of Cape Town, coordinated fourteen of the most influential transatlantic pro-apartheid organizations, such as the *Aida Parker Newsletter*, Frontline Fellowship, the Gospel Defense League, and the Reformed Independent Churches Association. Disciples of Cain described him as an advisor to political elites, a counselor to church leaders, and a government lobbyist. His United Christian Action was an umbrella body to mobilize opposition to the plot to turn South Africa into what Cain called a political, social, and economic nightmare. Many of these individuals possessed deep ties to the South African security state and used their influence to distribute government propaganda across the West. Cain himself had ties to the Christian League of Southern Africa, implicated in the Information Scandal as a beneficiary of the secret slush fund.

One of the member organizations of the United Christian Action, Frontline Fellowship, was run by Peter Hammond, a lynchpin in the pro-apartheid movement's effort to expose the realities of communism and the necessity of the Total Onslaught Plan. No one mobilized the interlocking logics of anticommunist and Christian defenses of apartheid better than Hammond. As chairman of the right-wing religious group Frontline Fellowship, Hammond built his case for supporting South Africa on tales of violent Black communism. Born in Cape Town in 1960 and raised in Rhodesia, Hammond formed Frontline Fellowship after his 1977 conversion to Christianity and service in the South African Defense Force (SADF). Hammond described his operation as a prayer fellowship of soldiers to Africa's communist terrorists and claimed to command members of the Rhodesian Army, the South African Infantry, and the US Marines.[43] According to his biography, Hammond "has been ambushed, come under aerial and artillery bombardments, been stabbed, shot at, beaten by mobs, arrested and imprisoned."[44] Hammond undoubtedly cut a charismatic figure. In one theatrical tale, Hammond showed up at a Zimbabwe military camp. The soldiers claimed that the prime minister of Zimbabwe, Robert Mugabe, was their God and arrested and interrogated Hammond.[45] However, the strength of Hammond's Christian testimony overwhelmed the interrogators. Upon hearing Hammond's testimony, the troops asked for New Testaments, cured of their communism by God's message.[46] Hammond takes center stage in the pages of Frontline Fellowship's reports. Although he mentions dozens of fellow missionaries, his story dominates as he ministers with the sounds of mortars, machine guns, and helicopter gunships overhead, reminding him of his gratitude for South Africa's freedoms.

Hammond embodied an overt, muscular Christianity popular among American and South African men and an important contrast to the defections taking place from the SADF by white South Africans. As the Botha regime expanded conscription in the 1980s and white men began serving longer terms in South Africa and the Border Wars, the regime cracked down on those that fled, refused service, or joined the End Conscription Campaign that began around 1984.[47] Hammond, in his service to the SADF and his heroic actions across the border of South Africa, stood in stark contrast to a weak white South African man who resisted conscription. Hammond exemplified the hegemonic Afrikaner masculinity of the apartheid state, even though he himself was an English-speaking white: "simple, honest, steadfast, religious, and hardworking."[48] Hammond described Frontline Fellowship as a group of evangelical Christians from military backgrounds dedicated to missionary outreach in neighboring communist countries. The self-proclaimed pioneer of evangelical-military-missionary outreach, Hammond regaled his subscribers with tales of verbal and physical sparring with hardened communists in Mozambique, Zimbabwe, and Angola. He conducted mass literature distributions with South Africa; hosted a weekly radio program *Salt and Light*; sponsored Bible colleges and Christian schools in Zambia, Sudan, and Zimbabwe; and wrote Christian textbooks.[49] But Hammond's largest activity was Bible smuggling. In 2020, he wrote that after his conversion to Christ in 1977, he conducted over 140 missions behind enemy lines smuggling Bibles.[50] In his work, Hammond reported receiving visits from Military Intelligence, Security Police, and the National Intelligence Service as he fought off Black communism.[51]

Hammond's militant and muscular Christianity aligned with the expectations of not only his American readers but also those in South Africa anxiously following the decolonization around them.[52] White soldiers fought and died in Angola and Namibia as the war in Angola turned unfavorably against the anticommunist National Union for the Total Independence of Angola (UNITA) and Cuban troops and Soviet material entered the fight. The 1960 Year of Africa had slowed, with only four nations becoming independent between 1967 and 1974.[53] Many of these new African states fell "victim to the authoritarian trend . . . governed by a single party that was intolerant of divergent views" as they struggled to cast off the undemocratic colonial structures.[54] These authoritarian trends became useful tools of organizations like Frontline Fellowship to deny legitimate black aspiration for majority rule as only leading to violent excesses, repression, and death. Hammond and Frontline Fellowship exemplified the fight between white supremacy and decolonization, balking at the trend toward majority rule. In contrast, the apartheid state and its hierarchies were "essential" to fight the Cold War and decolonization. Hammond's travels provided critical evidence for the pro-apartheid movement as it made its case that soulless, violent communism menaced the borders of civilization. Only Pretoria kept it at bay. Hammond wrote a monthly newsletter to subscribers, informing them of his discoveries. According to Frontline Fellowship, South Africa sat at the doorstep of a "bleeding continent of poverty, bloodshed, famines, corruption, dictatorships . . . communist interference, and civil wars."[55] Hammond warned that one-party dictatorships of communist slavery and exploitation spread godless, atheistic propaganda into schools and newspapers just kilometers from Johannesburg.[56] Worried Westerners needed to act to prevent a Marxist takeover of South Africa, specifically by supporting the United Christian Action and its partner organizations, which fought on the frontlines of this invasion. The colonial invocations used by Hammond reimagined whites as the oppressed, positioning them simultaneously as civilizers and victims of an imminent threat from communism. The decolonialization of Africa framed the pro-apartheid movement's vision of the world and the case presented to the United States.

According to Frontline's supporters, African communists focused on South Africa to transform the state politically, socially, and economically into a Marxist nightmare that would terrorize not only white South Africans but also its black citizens.[57] South Africa's communist enemies collaborated with the systematically orchestrated international campaign of boycotts, demonstrations, sanctions, and disinvestment to harm South Africa's majority-black population. Black South Africans—apartheid's defenders argued—did not want to be pushed into a Marxist system. According to United Christian Action, black South Africans feared their "beloved land [would] be plunged into the poverty, misery, and enslavement which exists in all Marxist countries."[58] It was not enough for pro-apartheid actors to invoke the fear of a Marxist South Africa. These groups needed to show that the communist onslaught directly threatened black South Africans.

In doing so, the pro-apartheid movement insisted that communism—not white rule—posed the greatest threat to black South Africans. As a chairman of the Manatee County branch of the CofCC put it, "There is nothing wrong with apartheid . . . and it is time someone said it."[59] According to the CofCC, the most significant impediment to the United States forming an intelligent policy toward South Africa was ignorance. American "do-gooders" were unaware of the benefits of the apartheid system for black South Africans. Pro-apartheid publications like the *Aida Parker Newsletter* touted wildly misleading statistics on high literacy rates, rising wages, and returned citizenship for black South Africans in its editions, often taken directly from Pretoria's propaganda machine.[60] In contrast to the benevolent, reforming National Party that ruled South Africa, black Africans, especially those in the Frontline States, suffered under violent communist regimes. The pro-apartheid movement's racist worldview reimagined Africa's black revolutionaries as colonizers and enslavers. In their view, African communists were uniformly Black and violent, on the precipice of tipping white and innocent black South Africans into poverty, instability, and godless depravity.

COLORBLINDNESS, CAPITALISM, AND RADICAL BLACK ACTIVISM

The anticommunist arguments of the pro-apartheid movement dovetailed with colorblind discourses that portrayed South Africa as under attack from race-obsessed Black Americans. The pro-apartheid network tapped into evolving racial narratives in the United States, particularly the colorblind rhetoric of the post–civil rights era. As the historian Matthew Lassiter argued, suburban white Americans found comfort in colorblind politics, which allowed them to view racial progress through free-market ideas of a growing middle class and the power of rugged individualism.[61] Pro-apartheid groups used colorblind messaging to drive support for white rule.[62] These activists argued that white Americans and black South Africans shared similar politics: free market, family values, racial colorblindness, and local autonomy in churches, neighborhoods, and schools.[63] This colorblind conservatism signified an evolving form of white supremacist rhetoric and policies in the United States that justified the preservation of hierarchy under the guise of conservative values. It was actually Black Americans, in this telling, who were obsessed over race and fomented hatred of the apartheid state, rather than black South Africans. Black South Africans, in the pro-apartheid movement's view, were focused on stability, economic security, and family values. Radical Black activists in the United States and the ANC had led well-meaning Americans astray.

The weaponization of colorblind capitalism and the cooptation of Black activism in both the United States and South Africa were essential. As the American studies scholar Justin Gomer put it, "colorblindness entered the oval office with the election of Ronald Reagan": Reagan used colorblindness as "an effective ideology through which to roll back the victories of the civil rights movement." As Reagan refused to enforce civil rights legislation and attacked civil rights via the judiciary, his civil rights officials accused Black leaders of "practicing a 'new racism' in their defense of affirmative action."[64] Capitalism underpinned these colorblind arguments in both the United States and South Africa. Reagan and his conservative Western compatriots came to power promising to unleash the free market. The belief in capitalism as a "panacea" also existed in South Africa. Botha, building on the 1970s marriage between the National Party and English capital, pushed the development of a black middle class to solve the demand for a consistent urban labor force from businesses and to defuse rebellion from black South Africans. In their effort to convince black South Africans that "'capitalism' could deliver benefits," big business-backed foundations spent millions in the townships on education, and the Botha administration rolled back restrictions on trade unions, job reservations, property rights, and housing and relaxed influx control.[65] These reforms became the bedrock of the National Party's presentation abroad—a reforming, increasingly colorblind South Africa, more focused on capitalist development than racial oppression—and a key tenet of pro-apartheid grassroots organizing as they prepared to fight against sanctions. By 1980, the UN Security Council voted to make its arms embargo mandatory and the OPEC oil embargo was firmly in place. The Botha administration faced a new sanctions challenge—multinational, multilateral, and specifically targeting trade—and needed a strategy to defuse calls for more economic punishment.[66]

Pro-apartheid organizations created an image of a threatened South Africa assaulted on all sides by radicals who fixated on the racial politics of the apartheid state. United Christian Action, for instance, argued that the ANC relied on the inculcation of class and race hatred, identifying any white South African as the enemy.[67] United Christian Action also leveraged its member organizations to portray itself as a mouthpiece for black South Africans. According to Cain, United Christian Action was mostly composed of black Christians, including the Reformed Independent Churches Association, a four-million-member-strong church led by a black bishop.[68] Even a cursory examination of United Christian Action and the Reformed Independent Churches Association revealed their claims of black participation to be demonstrably false.[69] Nevertheless, Cain insisted that contrary to the image portrayed internationally, the difference in South Africans was not between the races but between those who advocated revolutionary overthrow and those who did not. Do not be fooled, Cain implored, "South African Blacks do not applaud the activities" of revolutionaries.[70] Citing remarks from "black civic leaders," United Christian Action reported that any injustice of the white government would be insignificant in comparison to the violence of radical black leaders.

According to apartheid's defenders like the *African Intelligence Digest*, the ANC caused the South African government to step in to prevent radical blacks from terrorizing and murdering black South Africans who rejected radical-liberal racial politics.[71] This publication was written by Donald McAlvany and the executive director of Conservative Caucus, a US grassroots right-wing organization, Howard Phillips, who was also a founder of the New Right and a one-time presidential candidate. The Conservative Caucus's juxtaposition between "moderate" and "radical" black South Africans—based on their stance on sanctions—was crucial in the pro-apartheid movement's strategy. For instance, Hammond cited his travels throughout Mozambique and Zimbabwe to claim that black Africans rejected the radical racial politics of the antiapartheid movement. Hammond insisted that black Africans did not want an explicit focus on race; rather, they preferred "(what the world calls) 'oppression' in South Africa to . . . 'freedom' under a Black dictatorship." Hammond's Frontline

Fellowship ran dozens of "testimonials" from black Africans insisting South Africa was "Number One" and that laborers hoped to work in the apartheid state to become "fat with lots of money."[72] Pro-apartheid actors alleged that black South Africans possessed no commitment to the radical, leftist, race-based politics of antiapartheid organizations like the ANC and, in actuality, viewed the apartheid state as a bastion of peace and financial security.

The positioning of apartheid as a backer of financial security for black South Africans was essential in tying the colorblind and capitalist pillars of the pro-apartheid movement's rhetoric together. Positioning black South Africans as the beneficiaries of white rule, especially in the bantustans, would be a critical part of the strategy against the calls for sanctions. In the mid-1980s, antiapartheid activists in the West put into motion calls from the ANC, Pan Africanist Congress, labor unions, and the UDF to boycott businesses working in South Africa and to force their governments to divest. The pro-apartheid movement, in contrast, presented a different vision. False claims about black South Africans' high quality of life animated pro-apartheid publications throughout the 1980s. According to these groups, antiapartheid organizations' narrow focus on black South Africans' lack of political representation missed the favorable financial and personal security afforded them under white rule. As Hammond said, antiapartheid organizations were "trying to kill the goose that lays the golden egg" for black South Africans.[73] The pro-apartheid movement upheld South Africa's black bantustan leaders as paragons of capitalist, colorblind development compared to other parts of "backward" black Africa. In the *Washington Times*, the right-wing newspaper read regularly by Reagan and Thatcher, the conservative columnist William Murchison lauded the bantustans of Transkei, Bophuthatswana, Venda, and Ciskei as transformed by economic freedom.[74] According to Murchison, the bantustans became free-market havens by abolishing corporate and local taxes, deregulating small businesses, and selling public housing to the private sector. Ciskei's "rugged independence," Murchison said, showed "the capacity of African blacks to enjoy and profit from freedom, precisely as white Westerners."[75] *Reason*—a libertarian magazine—praised the bantustans as freely working for the South African government and a potential hotbed of Western investment. Would it not "be a delicious irony," *Reason* reported, if the bantustan would offer a new development model for the continent, after no state or international body demurred to recognize the bantustan as an independent country.[76] Pro-apartheid actors praised the separate development system as providing economic security for South Africans, contrasting the violent, abusive bantustan states favorably to the race-obsessed, communist ANC.

This focus on race-based politics emerged not from black Africans, the pro-apartheid movement insisted, but from Western white liberals obsessed with South Africa. As the American African Affairs Association put it, the ostracism of white-dominated governments in Rhodesia and South Africa undercut the economic and strategic interests of the free world. William Rusher, founder of the US conservative movement and publisher of the magazine *National Review*, and Max Yergan, an African American activist turned anticommunist agitator, ran the American African Affairs Association and pressured the Ford and Carter administrations to recognize Rhodesia. The organization fell apart after Yergan's death in 1975. However, its arguments in support of white Africa showcase how the defenders of white rule wove together Cold War, colorblind, and capitalist politics. Rusher, Yergan, and their allies attacked the antiapartheid movement's vision of South Africa as a fixation on race alone rather than on the larger threat of communism. Hammond took a similar tack, saying that the United States, United Nations, international media, and nongovernmental organizations became "inordinately obsessed" with the internal affairs of South Africa.[77] Amazed at the preoccupation with alleged "oppression" in South Africa, Hammond chalked up the Western condemnation of apartheid to ignorance about the positive realities of black South African freedoms. The pro-apartheid movement concluded that a global conspiracy possessed designs on South Africa, wielding the boogeyman of racial oppression to justify destroying a stable nation.

Despite their claims to the contrary, throughout their private letters and memorandum and their public newsletters and communication, a deep and abiding disdain for black South Africans permeates the pro-apartheid movement. Individual black leaders—like Mangosuthu Buthelezi of KwaZulu—are essentialized as "different" than other black South Africans, who were described as violent, unintelligent, and in need of governance. The creation of a black middle class and the possibility of educational and financial security in the bantustans were in white's interest as long as they proved the benevolence of white rule and, most importantly, did not challenge the existing apartheid hierarchy that put whites atop it. Throughout the 1980s, white defenders of the apartheid state in both the United States and South Africa constantly searched for black South Africans and Americans willing to echo their positions. But the shallowness of their support and the narrow vision for black "freedom" reveal an ultimately hollow position.

For black South Africans, their ability to achieve financial security and safety in South Africa was not a game. The 1980s unleashed open, violent rebellion across South Africa's townships and bantustans, as people demanded freedom beyond what the apartheid state had to offer and debated if they would participate in the Botha reforms. As the National Party sought to cultivate black urban elites and created parallel governance structures of ethnic parliaments and black local councils, opposition mounted. Pressure mounted from the UDF, led by religious leaders like Allan Boesak, Frank Chikane, and Tutu and ANC powerhouses like Winnie Mandela and Albertina Sisulu of the ANC Women's League. The very reforms Botha put into place, devolving power from the apartheid state to urban people in limited areas, fueled rebellion. The townships only saw 12 percent voter turnout in 1983 in these local elections. Those black community councilors became the front lines of the apartheid state, controlling businesses, rents, and licenses, and their inadequacy drove millions of Africans to the streets.[78] By 1984, open rebellion against apartheid and its surrogates raged.

CHRISTIANITY AS APARTHEID'S SHIELD

South Africa's right-wing religious groups became particularly adept at merging these anticommunist, colorblind discourses by insisting that South Africa's problems were not political, racial, or economic but a result of the state's spiritual degradation by anti-Christian forces. This Christian organizing became essential as open rebellion began in the townships and bantustans from 1984 onward. Pro-apartheid organizations sought to weaponize violence against the apartheid state and transform it into evidence of the spiritual failings of South Africa. By weaponizing Christianity, apartheid's defenders put forth a status quo version of their theology, one that reified stability and hierarchy and attacked antiapartheid theologians as urging on violence. As Tutu and his compatriots became more popular abroad, efforts to denigrate their work only increased.

Even before the formal creation of the apartheid state, the South African Dutch Reformed Church (DRC) theorized separate development. The DRC claimed a central role in South African white spiritual life; in 1980, the DRC counted almost 1.7 million members, representing two-thirds of Afrikaners and nearly half of all white South Africans.[79] Throughout the 1930s, the DRC established segregated congregations, and in 1935, the DRC's Federal Council stated its unequivocal opposition to integration. As the sociologist T. Dunbar Moodie put it, "There can be no doubt that the DRC played a foundational role in the establishment of racial grounds for the apartheid system."[80] Indeed, the DRC became known as the "National Party in prayer" for its central role in Afrikanerdom and Afrikaner Christian Nationalism.[81] According to the DRC's apartheid theology, God acted as the original divider, giving each volk a separate soul and thereby mandating that the state needed to support each "nation's" separate development.[82] As the historian Ruhan Fourie argued, the DRC not only upheld state apartheid but also formed the "theological bulwark" of Afrikaner anticommunism.[83] In contrast, the multiracial South African Council of Churches and its leaders Frank Chikane, Allan Boesak, and Beyers Naudé used their prophetic voice to oppose the ruling National Party and its version of Christianity.[84] A religious critique of South African racial practices threatened apartheid and the anticommunist narratives that undergirded Afrikaner identity and security. Right-wing religious groups, be they Presbyterian, Catholic, or Pentecostal, focused on South Africa's antiapartheid theologians and organizations, wielding their faith as a tool against black activists and taking their cues from the DRC. Christianity and white power for these activists went hand in hand, animating all other facets of their pro-apartheid argumentation.

The Christian challenge to the DRC arose through the Kairos Document. Published in 1985 by the Kairos theologians, the document's signatories came from many Christian traditions—Catholic, Protestant, Evangelical, Pentecostal, and the African Independent Churches—united in their loathing of apartheid theology. The Kairos Document demanded a more active role for the church in the antiapartheid struggle.[85] Kairos responded to several concerns, including the use of Christianity to justify white rule and the ineffectiveness of the church's response to apartheid.[86] In Kairos, theologians critiqued the apartheid government's state theology, which used Romans 13:1–7 to demand absolute and divine authority. Kairos theologians argued that the state branded anyone who rejects apartheid theology as a communist, opposed to the will of God.[87] Although Kairos theologians were open to reconciliation and nonviolent tactics as a way to resist apartheid, they insisted that such measures were insufficient. They argued instead that apartheid oppressors would need to repent, centralize black South African grievances, and recognize why factions of the antiapartheid movement resorted to violence; otherwise, church theology would continue to be unsatisfactory. Pastors could no longer be neutral and should instead participate in the struggle, engage in civil disobedience, and serve as moral guides for the nation. Over 32,000 Kairos Documents, published in Xhosa, Sotho, English, and Afrikaans, spread across South Africa. Some parts of the international Christian community regarded Kairos "as the most important theological document" of the past decades.[88] The Kairos theologians published a second edition in January 1986 and a revised version in September of that same year.[89]

Kairos's global reach was one part of the rise in popularity and global recognition of antiapartheid Christians within South Africa. Archbishop Desmond Tutu was perhaps the most famous of these Christian antiapartheid activists and the pro-apartheid movement's biggest target. Tutu spoke before the United Nations several times, met with Reagan and Thatcher, and drummed up support for sanctions at rallies and legislatures and in fiery speeches across the West. Although the pro-apartheid movement had long detested Tutu, when Tutu won the Nobel Peace Prize in 1984, white supremacist anger rose to a fever pitch and made him a target of their attacks, describing his victory as "an insult to the black man in South Africa."[90] The US political commentator and conservative darling Pat Buchanan best summed up the feelings of the pro-apartheid movement on Tutu's award. Whatever his "moral splendor," Buchanan wrote in a November 1984 article for the *Washington Inquirer*, Tutu was a "political ignoramus."[91] Apartheid's defenders derided Tutu as out of touch with true black Africans, morally superior, and unaware of the complexities of ending white rule. Right-wing religious groups devoted their energy to destroying Tutu's reputation, accusing him of fundraising for the South

African Council of Churches abroad and alleging that Tutu's 1985 and 1986 appointments elicited walkouts. Those "walkouts" were from white clergy, although the KwaZulu leader Mangosuthu Buthelezi and the white liberal Alan Paton also privately expressed their misgivings about Tutu.[92] The pro-apartheid movement's most prominent attacks involved tying Tutu to radical Marxist theology, specifically the Kairos Document. Pro-apartheid actors preached that black theologians were betraying South Africa from the inside, engaging in naked militant Marxist ideology. This radical ideology preached atheism, false theology, and a malignant concept of social justice designed to destroy South Africa.

The primary agent driving this discourse was the Cape Town–based Gospel Defense League, part of United Christian Action, which insisted that South Africa's suffering was not the product of unjust social structures, as Tutu argued, but of individual sin.[93] Formed in the early 1970s by Charles and Dorothea Scarborough, the Gospel Defense League described itself as experts in the spread of liberation theology, which "reread Christianity from the perspective of the oppressed . . . and [advocated] the construction of . . . political and economic organization that would replace an unjust status quo."[94] Charles Scarborough, born in England, and Dorothea, born in Germany, served as members of the London Missionary Society to South Africa beginning in 1969. The two married a decade earlier in a bomb-damaged Lutheran cathedral in Lübeck, Germany. In 1974, the Scarboroughs joined the Christian League of Southern Africa, which journalists exposed as a front for the apartheid government during the Information Scandal just three years later. After the League's demise, the Scarboroughs formed the Gospel Defense League in 1980.[95] According to Dorothea, at the Gospel Defense League's peak, the readership grew to over 18,000. Some publications reached over 100,000 copies.[96] The Gospel Defense League directed much of its financial and publication resources to attacking Tutu, which continued until Tutu's death in 2021, when the organization published a final "evaluation" of the Bishop, lambasting his "decades-long record of supporting . . . theological liberalism, collectivist economic theories, and Marxist class warfare," drudging up talking points honed in the 1980s.[97] Dorothea and Hammond formed a friendship in their work, with Dorothea serving on the board of Frontline Fellowship and Hammond taking over the Gospel Defense League after Dorothea's death in 2002.

Right-wing religious groups argued that antiapartheid theologians saw everything in South Africa as the devil's work. Pro-apartheid Christians attacked Tutu and other theologians for ignoring the "manifold good that the white government has accomplished."[98] The theology practiced by the South African Council of Churches, they said, had a bias for communist, socialist-terrorist, and guerrilla groups hellbent on the destruction of South African society.[99] Pro-apartheid organizations routinely accused the South African Council of Churches and others of politicizing religion, arguing that South Africans needed a theology of peace, not one of revolution that justified and incited civil disobedience. Jesus rejected revolution, according to Hammond, the Gospel Defense League, and United Christian Action, which also said that the South African Council of Churches offered violent South Africans an open call to engage in rebellion, revolution, and assassination.[100] The theology of these white supremacist churches was a status quo theology, using apolitical salvation as a guise for the continued defense of white rule.

Right-wing religious groups insisted that they—and not antiapartheid theologians—spoke for "real" South African Christians. "The vast majority of township inhabitants are thankful that there is a controlling factor [the South African government], which has saved them from a tyranny and cruelty never before known," insisted one organization.[101] By creating a narrative of anti-Christian violence targeting black South Africans, the pro-apartheid movement tied its work to US evangelical activism in the 1980s focused on global Christian oppression.[102] The anti-Christian violence that targeted South Africans came from the ANC and its radical pastors, who were not Christians at all, but rather violent communists and atheists. In a special issue of the popular *Aida Parker Newsletter* titled "The Enemies Within—Part I: The Priests Take on Pretoria, 'Comrade Jesus' and the SA Revolution," editor Aida Parker decried the "illusion" of Christian liberation promised by Tutu. The South African Council of Churches was not a Christian organization but a revolutionary club that paid out millions to support those charged with treason, murder, and arson against everyday Christians.[103] In her telling, Kairos unleashed a "bloodthirsty clerical band that sanctions violence," as roving gangs of communist radicals destroyed law-abiding black South Africans, specifically those in Pretoria's new community governance structures.[104] The Gospel Defense League accused Kairos theologians and the South African

Council of Churches of refusing to focus on black South African Christians and instead subscribing to imported ideas and strategies to impress foreign donors.[105] According to Dorothea, the South African Council of Churches allegedly raised millions from West Germany, Denmark, and Norway in imported income, whereas only 2 percent of income was raised locally. Pro-apartheid organizations argued that they represented "real" black South Africans while accusing black theologians like Tutu of being part of an international, anti-Christian conspiracy that targeted white and black South African innocents. The melding of white saviorism and paternalistic rhetoric to white supremacy proved a potent piece of pro-apartheid organizing.

Throughout the 1980s, apartheid's defenders developed three overlapping narratives defending white rule that grafted onto existing conservative rhetoric in the United States. First, the pro-apartheid movement argued that South Africa alone could stem the tide of radical black communism, tying into longer anticommunist justifications for the US–South African relationship. Second, pro-apartheid activists contended that South Africa did not have a "race" problem and that black South Africans experienced a high quality of life and economic prosperity, which dovetailed with existing colorblind-capitalist rhetoric. Finally, anticommunist and colorblind discourses united into narratives of Christian betrayal, as pro-apartheid activists insisted that black liberationist groups threatened to destroy South Africa's Christian populace. Although each strand had distinct features, these narratives remained profoundly interwoven and mutually sustaining, braided together to create a rich conspiratorial tapestry of forces working against apartheid rule.

In 1984, the Student Moderate Alliance, the University of Witwatersrand affiliate of the pro–South African government National Student Federation, announced the "relaunch" of its quarterly publication, *The Standard*: patriotic South Africans needed to face facts—it was "time to stand up for South Africa."[106] As the international profile of the antiapartheid movement and black activists grew, transatlantic white supremacist actors reacted with horror—and with an agenda. Catalyzed by the election of Western conservative leaders, the pro-apartheid movement emerged in the 1980s as a coherent network of activists invested in preserving white rule in South Africa. Throughout the 1980s, pro-apartheid organizations honed interlocking defenses of white rule that provided the intellectual kindling fueling its assembly and organization. These ideas became the guiding principles that sustained white supremacist organizing as it built a transatlantic partnership.

2

THE ONLY TRUE FRIENDS SOUTH AFRICA HAS

On March 22, 1982, Senator Jeremiah Denton (R-AL) called to order a series of hearings on "the Role of the Soviet Union, Cuba, and East Germany in Fomenting Terrorism in Southern Africa." Denton, in his capacity as chairman of the Senate Judiciary Subcommittee on Security and Terrorism, set out the investigation's purview. These hearings would determine the USSR's penetration and takeover of two southern African liberationist movements: the African National Council (ANC) and the South West Africa People's Organization (SWAPO). While arguing that not every ANC member shared the leadership's communist sympathies, Denton insisted that the United States refused to acknowledge how black Africans would suffer if communist movements expand or triumph.[1] Over the course of five hearings, Denton argued that although Americans may "sympathize with the original goal" of the ANC, ostensibly making an overture to the ANC's antiapartheid activism, "we cannot, however, delude ourselves that their purpose now is the achievement of those praiseworthy objectives."[2] The ANC, Denton concluded, was a USSR-directed terrorist organization that sought to bring communism to power in South Africa.

Denton's support for South Africa was one part of his anticommunist agenda while in Congress. During the Vietnam War, Denton was a US naval aviator, taken captive by the North Vietnamese in 1965, after which he endured eight years of confinement as a prisoner of war.

The North Vietnamese forced Denton to take part in a 1966 televised interview, during which he blinked "T-O-R-T-U-R-E" in morse code, confirming the treatment of American prisoners of war.[3] While captured, Denton endured the Hanoi March in July 1966, where North Vietnamese soldiers and civilians paraded and beat US soldiers through the streets, and endured years of solitary confinement while in the infamous "Hanoi Hilton" and "Alcatraz" prisons. In 1981, Denton became the first Republican elected to the Senate from Alabama in over a century, riding a New Right wave and campaigning on "uncompromising stands on defense and social issues."[4] Denton was a key part of the congressional Republican blockade against economic sanctions, working with right-wingers like Jesse Helms (R-NC) and Strom Thurmond (R-SC) during his single congressional term to defend Pretoria as the premier anticommunist partner of the United States in Africa.

Denton relied on a series of witnesses—black South African former members of the ANC Nokonono Delphine Kave, Ephraim Mfalapitsa, Jeffrey Motutuzele Bosigo, and Bartholomew Hlapane—to prove the ANC's primary agenda was terrorism of moderate black South Africans. Historian Jacob Dlamini described these hearings as "one of the strangest dramas in Washington D.C.," a "co-production staged by Denton and the South African government." As Denton acknowledged in his opening remarks, the presence of the four former ANC members was not possible without the cooperation of the South African government. Contrary to Denton's hearings and their testimony, these four witnesses were not simply innocent victims of the ANC's radicalism. Bosigo and Mfalapitsa were askaris, former liberationists turned soldiers of the apartheid security apparatus, "denouncing, defaming, and hunting their former compatriots," with Hlapane a "professional state witness for the apartheid state."[5] The testimony of these four witnesses proved essential, crafting an image of the ANC as unbridled with terrorist violence and ill-prepared for rule. Over five days, these witnesses, using materials created by the South African government, regaled the subcommittee with stories about the physical, emotional, and sexual violence committed by the ANC against black South Africans who wanted to end apartheid but did not subscribe to the ANC's communist vision.[6]

Throughout the 1980s, pro-apartheid organizations forged a defense of white rule through interlocking conservative narratives around anticommunism, colorblind capitalism, and Christianity. This organizing was more than a global propaganda campaign. It built upon a tangible network of partners working to save South Africa. The urgency of South Africa's situation required, as one pro-apartheid writer put it, creating "people-to-people organizations to build contact and understanding between Americans and South Africans."[7] They forged intimate connections through fact-finding missions, speaker series, conferences, community meetings, and apartheid tourism. These kinds of activities contributed to solidarity building and knowledge production that translated into collective action.[8] Pro-apartheid organizers leveraged these activities to disseminate support for white rule into cross-racial conservative spaces. The transnational collective action of the pro-apartheid movement highlighted its ability to operate across levels of power, organizing conferences at midwestern churches while also influencing US congressional hearings that targeted the ANC. In the 1980s, the pro-apartheid movement's obsessions over "truth"—the true black South African, the situation under apartheid, and defenders of white rule—dominated. This truth required disciples who stood firm in their knowledge in the face of antiapartheid activists. In the constructed pro-apartheid world, within a far right obsessed over ideological purity, tensions between its disciples proved constant. The coalition fractured and evolved, with some of apartheid's most ardent defenders targeting other right-wingers as insufficiently committed to white rule.

THE TRUE BLACK SOUTH AFRICAN

The pro-apartheid movement's strategy for building support for South Africa relied on interlocking narratives premised on combatting black South African suffering. To bring this position to life, defenders of white rule uplifted conservative black South Africans as the opposition to the ANC. The pro-apartheid movement challenged the idea that the ANC and its antiapartheid allies spoke for black South Africans. Rather, in a silent majority refrain, the pro-apartheid movement characterized Pretoria's supporters as white and black South Africans disinterested in the communist policies of the ANC. Apartheid's defenders referred to these black right-wingers as the "black moderates." This title acted as a foil to the ANC, implying that the ANC was nothing more than a small set of terrorist actors unpopular within South Africa and propped up by the USSR. These projects relied on black South Africans to build a legitimacy impossible to obtain solely on the testimony of whites. Some bantustan leaders possessed independent power and influence to pick and choose cooperation with more unsavory actors. Others did not, elevated almost exclusively by white pro-apartheid actors looking for black South Africans willing to support the limited apartheid reforms of the National Party. The shared support between the pro-apartheid movement and black conservatives regarding Christianity, anticommunism, and colorblind capitalism bred cross-racial collaboration. Throughout the 1980s, apartheid's supporters in the United States, taking their cues from their South African partners, elevated the testimonials of a subset of South Africa's black conservatives, bringing them across the West to share their challenge to the ANC.

In the 1980s, Black conservatives became a critical part of the Republican Party. Black conservatives, mobilized by Reagan's commitment to individual liberty, free markets, law and order, and family values, found a place in the New Right.[9] A post–civil rights rejection of overtly racist language in favor of colorblind equal opportunity capitalism appealed to Black conservatives. Black conservative advocacy revealed a faith in traditional conservatism and the pragmatic political view that joining the Republican Party was the most efficient way to achieve sociopolitical power.[10] When Reagan took office, he appointed several African Americans to positions within his administration such as Alan Keyes as assistant secretary of state for international affairs. Keyes became a leading spokesman of constructive engagement, with members of the Reagan White House lobbying to elevate Keyes as ambassador to South Africa to defuse calls of racism from sanctions agitators. TransAfrica director Randall Robinson, who debated Keyes on television about the apartheid state, called Keyes's advocacy for constructive engagement putting "a black face on an antiblack policy."[11] Right-wingers weaponized the presence of Black conservatives in their ranks as evidence of their increasing acceptance of diversity, but cross-racial conflict stemming from white regressive politics highlights the tenuous nature of that bond.[12] Keyes resigned from the Reagan administration in 1987 after his allegations of being "treated in a racially demeaning manner by Deputy Secretary of State John

Whitehead." Before his resignation, Keyes defended constructive engagement before Congress, arguing that it was Americans' responsibility to not enact measures that could cost two million jobs and wreck the future for black South Africans upon apartheid's end.[13]

The possibility of a black-white coalition in the pro-apartheid movement accelerated with P. W. Botha's reforms in 1983 and the 1984–1986 insurrectionary period. Botha's efforts to create a black middle class faltered in the face of rent increases, corrupt black local authorities, and the inauguration of the first Colored-Indian Tricameral Houses. On September 3, 1984, the Vaal Uprising began. The townships of the Vaal Triangle—the industrial area forty-five miles south of Johannesburg—descended into an open rebellion of mass stayaways, arsons, and the murder of the black deputy mayor of the Lekoa Town Council. By 1986, strikes involved more than 240,000 workers. The apartheid government's oppression proved swift and brutal; 7,000 troops were sent to the Vaal Triangle townships, leading to the death of over 300 people.[14] Hundreds of ANC militants in exile entered South Africa, and Pretoria issued a state of emergency, the first since Sharpeville, in July 1985, increasing the power of state security. By 1986, the South African government detained 8,000 people, charged 22,000 more, and were responsible for a fivefold increase in police-linked deaths from 1984 to 1985.[15] As Franziska Rueedi argued, this period in the mid-1980s was a debate about "what type of life was envisaged as acceptable and desirable" for black South Africans, with Botha's reforms pushing "the issue of rights and representation to the center of public debate."[16] As a contrast to rebelling black South Africans and to buttress the reformist claims of the National Party, pro-apartheid actors relied on black South Africans, who largely fell into three categories: those part of the existing apartheid governance structure, like the leaders of the bantustans and local town councils; religious figures, specifically operating within the network of right-wing religious groups; and anti-ANC activists, who either defected from the organization or rejected its communist sympathies. These black South Africans deeply held the anticommunist, colorblind capitalist, and Christian politics of their partners and united in their opposition to further US economic coercion. Their stories and testimonials against the ANC and in favor of the South African government became the lifeblood of the coalition building and organizing against sanctions in the 1980s.

One of the most prominent figures on the US evangelical circuit was Bishop Isaac Mokoena. Mokoena was the bishop of the Reformed Independent Churches Association (RICA), formed by a group of fundamentalist black churches that included 864 churches and 2.5 million members. RICA partnered with the South African Council of Churches to operate a theological school training black pastors and church leaders. Mokoena partnered with the South African Council of Churches until 1979, when the organization took him to court over misappropriation of funds, with Desmond Tutu testifying against Mokoena. Fifty-two theologians charged Mokoena of financial and sexual "malfeasance," charges that the court ultimately threw out. He then moved the college to the Evaton township with the support of the Christian League, the organization caught up in the Information Scandal.[17] Upon the collapse of the Christian League, RICA operated under the United Christian Action umbrella, allegedly ministering to 4.5 million people by 1981. Based on assessments from the African Spiritual Churches Association, Mokoena was "an opportunist money-lover co-opted by apartheid oppressors," possessing no more than 500,000 followers at the highest estimates.[18] Others put his followers at less than several thousand.[19] Mokoena's speaking engagements brought him across the United States, where he positioned himself as a foil to Tutu, as the "reasonable" black clergyman versus Tutu's radical liberation theology. Famously, Mokoena called Tutu's 1984 Nobel Peace Prize an "insult to the black Christians in South Africa"—there was very little love lost between these two or antiapartheid activists for Mokoena. Mokoena survived an alleged assassination attempt in 1986.[20] Just a year later, Mokoena received the Decoration of Meritorious Service medal from Botha in 1987 as recognition of his service to the government.

United Christian Action reported positively on Mokoena's travels and his dozens of transatlantic speaking engagements including ones that he attended with bantustan leader President Lucas Mangope of Bophuthatswana.[21] Mokoena spent a significant amount of his time on the evangelical circuit in the United States, honored at the National Religious Broadcasters forty-third and forty-fourth annual conventions in 1986 and 1987 and appearing at the booths on South Africa escorted by Afrikaner-Pentecostal ministers. In his speeches at the conventions, Mokoena spoke against sanctions and demanded that Americans invest more in South Africa, particularly in the bantustans. Mokoena's efforts reached the ears of the Reagan White House. In a press conference in August 1986, Reagan, while mispronouncing Mokoena's name as either "Moreno or Monorem," said that Mokoena was the leader of 4.5 million Christians and that "all of them are deadly opposed to sanctions." Mokoena described his efforts to set up a new moderate multiracial political party in his travels; in 1986, Mokoena established the United Christian Conciliation Party with Thamsanqa Linda, former mayor of Ibhayi township near Port Elizabeth, elected as part of the 1982 Black Local Authorities Act.[22] The party seemingly never fielded candidates for an election, and antiapartheid activists picketed US appearances by Mokoena and Linda, including a 1991 event sponsored by the John Birch Society.[23]

Conference events put on by think tanks were sites of fervent intellectual exchange, bringing black right-wingers into US conservative spaces. At an antisanctions conference put on by the Jefferson Educational Foundation in conjunction with the National Center for Public Policy Research in 1987, Mokoena joined with fellow antisanctions black South Africans to attack the antiapartheid movement. The chairman of the Jefferson Educational Foundation cut his teeth with the Young Republican National Federation, and the National Center for Public Policy Research boasted close ties to Jack Abramoff and his apartheid-friendly International Freedom Foundation.[24] The conference was a three-part event. First, a panel was held with Republican congressmen. The second panel was on sanctions, led by Clarence Pendleton, chairman of the US Commission on Civil Rights; Herman W. Nickel, US ambassador to the Republic of South Africa; and two businessmen. The third panel, "Voices from South Africa," included Mokoena and Esau Mahlatsi, mayor of the Lekoa City black town council and the successor to the mayor murdered during the Vaal Uprising. During the panel, Mahlatsi supported the Botha government reforms: Mahlatsi famously invited Botha to visit his township and present him with the "Freedom of Lekoa" award, sparking fury from residents.[25] Mokoena's remarks mirrored Mahlatsi's, attacking the sanctions supporters as driving black South Africans into the hands of Marxists.

The Q&A session included a who's who of apartheid partners. Rich Schmidt, of About My Father's Business, asked the first question. Run out of Lexington, Kentucky, About My Father's Business was a video-production company creating films for distribution to foreign and national ministries. After graduating bible school, Schmidt embarked on a four-month mission tour of Johannesburg, Durban, and Port Elizabeth, setting up in South Africa in 1984. Schmidt saw his work as shining a spotlight on the ANC and their Marxist-Leninist activities and produced a documentary in 1984 titled *ANC—a Time for Candor* that promised the "real story about the ANC." According to Schmidt, stations all over the United States asked for airing rights on the documentary, with the documentary also shown in Italy and France. Disciples of Schmidt circulated the documentary in Australia before a visit from Oliver Tambo, and Schmidt commented how refreshing it was to see people "stand on their convictions and oppose this evil man." The US antiapartheid movement also drew Schmidt's attention, calling TransAfrica leadership "racist of the highest degree in [their] hatred of all whites."[26] Schmidt encouraged readers to sponsor demonstrations against any antiapartheid evildoers that came to their area, using materials from About My Father's Business. From 1989 to 1993, the US government registered About My Father's Business as a foreign agent of the GMR Group, a South African company assisting in subverting global sanctions.[27]

Schmidt was likely not the only paid agent at the conference. Bishop Mzilikazi Masiya stepped up to the mic next and defended Botha's progress toward accommodating black people.[28] Masiya served as the head of several organizations, most importantly Jesus Christ for Peace. Jesus Christ for Peace received its backing funds from David Balsiger of Orange County, California, who helmed the Christian media production company Bible News Service.[29] In the 1980s, Balsiger focused on sanctions, and Masiya seemed a perfect fit for his work. Masiya joined the South African Police in 1973 as part of their counterinsurgency work and turned into a "killing machine." In 1977, South African police arrested and charged him with fourteen counts of robbery, murder, and theft, and upon his sentencing, Masiya escaped from prison. He was captured, resentenced, and released in 1981. Following his time in prison and as a fugitive, Masiya turned to Christianity and began his antisanctions activity by launching Jesus Christ for Peace in 1986. The organization seemingly had no congregation but launched the "One Million Anti-Sanctions Signatures Campaign" in 1988. The campaign allegedly collected 500,000 signatures of black South Africans who opposed sanctions. Masiya later admitted the campaign was "started by whites," specifically by "the owner of [a] Johannesburg travel agency," after they struggled to "get anywhere overseas on their own without blacks."[30] Although Masiya denied any involvement of the South African government, he likely referenced Balsiger, who ran a travel agency in Johannesburg, as the backer of his efforts. These conferences became key nodes of intellectual exchange between black South Africans and American conservatives. Black South Africans provided legitimacy, as Masiya himself stated in 1989, to the talking points curated by pro-apartheid actors, who recognized that without black voices they could not work against sanctions. Mokoena's and Masiya's checkered backgrounds and their financial backing from US conservatives and the South African government could lead one to conclude that those who worked against sanctions did so only for personal enrichment. However, for black South Africans, the anticommunist, colorblind capitalist, and Christian worldview proved to be powerful glue, especially for those who worked against the ANC.

The ANC's violence toward its dissenters was real, even if taken disingenuously by apartheid's defenders. From the late 1970s onward, the ANC-in-exile in southern Africa used brutal punishments, torture, and murder to combat dissent. In 1981, the ANC purged the *Umkhonto we Sizwe* (MK) after discovering South African Police infiltrators and informants, which became the justification for expanding the ANC's security apparatus, *Mbokodo*, which rooted out dissent.[31] The ANC leadership sent mutineers to the prison known as Quatro, where Mbokodo agents brutally beat, isolated, tortured, and executed enemy agents from 1981 to 1984.[32] The brutality in Quatro catalyzed mutiny within the rank and file of the ANC's army, especially those sent to fight against UNITA in Angola where they sustained heavy casualties. The Denton hearings encapsulate the use of the ANC-in-exile's violence to delegitimize the organization's opposition to the apartheid state. Denton, himself a survivor of torture, stated that when he read Kave's testimony that he "actually encountered a woman who has undergone more suffering than I or any of my colleagues."[33] The historian Jacob Dlamini characterized Kave, who described horrific sexual abuse after refusing to accept Marxist-Leninism, as an agent related to Ciskei dictator Lennox Sebe "used by apartheid intelligence to infiltrate the activist circles around Steve Biko."[34] Over five days in late March 1983, Kave, Mfalapitsa, Bosigo, and Hlapane described the true face of the ANC—forced indoctrination, torture, and sexual, physical, and mental abuse. Each of the four witnesses testified to how poorly informed

Americans were about the realities of South Africa. Kave, Mfalapitsa, Bosigo, and Hlapane positioned themselves as doing "genuine black politics," in contrast to the ANC, which "carved up" elders, women, and children and engaged in international terrorism and communism. Mfalapitsa testified to the targeting of black right-wingers, stating that he left the ANC because of the "lack of political support for our people."[35] Rounding out the testimony, Hlapane agreed with separate development, which brought self-determination to South Africans.

Hlapane became a martyr of the pro-apartheid movement after his appearance at the Denton hearings and proof positive of the ANC's violent killing of dissenters. Nine months after his appearance in Washington, the ANC killed Hlapane. The ANC confirmed the killing in 1997, citing Hlapane's "propaganda exercise [that] sought to seriously damage the reputation of the ANC in the international arena, and set back the liberation struggle by portraying the movement as a terrorist group under the control of the Soviet Union."[36] Hlapane's assassination became part of the pro-apartheid movement's evidentiary chain of the ANC's violence. It held up Hlapane as proof of what happens to black South Africans who oppose the ANC's vision of apartheid's end. The story of Hlapane's murder appeared next to a full-page spread on necklace killing, a particularly gruesome method of killing used by the ANC against collaborators of the apartheid states. A tire would be placed around the victim's shoulders, filled with petrol, and set alight. Necklacing attracted specific attention from pro-apartheid activists, as the images of these executions were especially horrific, but the ANC remained divided on the tactic.[37] The ANC did not execute Hlapane via necklace killing: an MK unit shot him and his wife outside their home in Soweto.[38] Nevertheless, United Christian Action, Gospel Defense League, and others upheld Hlapane as a true victim of terrorism, positioning his story next to black South Africans murdered at the hands of ANC necklace killings.

Hlapane's assassination allowed for propagandist crafting of a narrative of beyond-the-pale ANC violence, especially as the townships engaged in open rebellion and collaborationists came under assault. After the Vaal Uprising in 1984, the ANC "put in place the command-and-control networks necessary to develop a people's war," and youths targeted state agents and suspected police collaborators with homemade weapons, bombs, and necklace killings.[39] The ANC drew a clear line in the sand between apartheid's enemies and those who held up its structures. That stark division placed the black bantustan leaders outside liberation forces, who demanded an end to the separate development system. KwaZulu's leaders felt this exclusion acutely. KwaZulu, a semi-independent bantustan located on the eastern coast of South Africa, was the homeland of the ethnic Zulus and headed by Mangosuthu Buthelezi, a Zulu chief, chief minister of KwaZulu, and leader of the Inkatha National Cultural Liberation Movement (Inkatha). Buthelezi was a former member of the ANC, but his formation of Inkatha and his use of the KwaZulu bantustan to shore up his own power made him an enemy of the ANC. Inkatha positioned itself, and not the ANC-in-exile, as the "true inheritors of the 'old' ANC," before they turned to violent resistance.[40] Inkatha's politics was a "class-based politics created by the KwaZulu Homeland elite who invoked Zulu culture and tradition to mobilize its constituencies."[41] Buthelezi presented himself as working to change South Africa from within, ending apartheid through free market capitalism and a federalized system.

Inkatha and Buthelezi's decision to operate within and in concert with the apartheid state put it fundamentally at odds with the ANC and the United Democratic Front (UDF), nearly leading to outright civil war in KwaZulu in the 1980s. The bantustan of KwaZulu and its explicit reliance on Zulu ethnicity limited Buthelezi's appeal to Zululand and Natal, and Inkatha fought the UDF and the ANC covertly on behalf of the apartheid state to retain its hold on power.[42] As part of Botha's Total Onslaught strategy, the apartheid state funneled weapons, money, and South African Defense Force (SADF)–led training to Inkatha and other vigilante organizations to try and curb the UDF and ANC and its trade union partners. The Natal Civil War led to an estimated 12,000–18,000 deaths, with 200,000–500,000 refugees displaced from 1984 until apartheid's end in 1994.[43] The violence was brutal and personal as youths turned crude homemade weapons on each other and against Inkatha's militias (impis) and KwaZulu police.[44] The apartheid state and international media labeled the violence as "black on black," covering up how Pretoria fueled the violence through its proxies to blame Africans as incapable of governance.[45] The pro-apartheid movement ate up this rhetoric: Balsiger published statistics that black-on-black attacks accounted for nearly four times the number of deaths as those caused by security forces, with 172 deaths by necklacing accounting for 65–70 percent of all black violent deaths.[46] In reality, necklace deaths peaked in 1986 at 306, a meager number in comparison to the 14,000 "unrest incidents" across South Africa during the same period.[47]

As the pro-apartheid movement grabbed onto the black-on-black violence label, its disciples focused on Buthelezi. Buthelezi was the West's favored antiapartheid activist throughout the 1970s and 1980s. As a self-described moderate, Buthelezi bought favor in US conservative spaces by presenting himself and Inkatha as opposed to the radical direction of the ANC and instead as the true mantle of antiapartheid activism.[48] The charismatic, undisputed leader of Inkatha, Buthelezi meticulously maintained his image; he "sued or threatened to sue for defamation just about every journalist and scholar" who connected him to the apartheid state and violence in KwaZulu-Natal. Born in 1928, Buthelezi tenuously claimed descent from the First Zulu King, working his way through the apartheid bureaucracy to grab as much as power as possible through the KwaZulu bantustan, becoming its leader in 1976.[49] Buthelezi was fully in line with the pro-apartheid movement's triumvirate as an anticommunist, colorblind capitalist, and Christian, and he used that positioning to find supporters in the West. Calling Buthelezi "South Africa's Champion of Nonviolence," congressmembers circulated Inkatha's claims to be the "only mass movement of consequence operating legally among South African blacks," as Inkatha fueled violence in Natal.[50] Buthelezi insisted that his Inkatha was the nonviolent platform for democracy, touting its offers to negotiate with Pretoria on apartheid's transition and its contributions to a discussion of a new South Africa "without violence." The apartheid issue, according to Inkatha, was one of political representation and did not demand drastic redistribution of economic wealth. Inkatha rejected the one-man-one-vote democracy championed by the ANC in favor of the kinship, chieftaincy, and traditional authorities engrained within KwaZulu.[51] Inkatha, which operated in close concert with the administration of KwaZulu, was also procapitalist. The organization supported the introduction of Western capital into South Africa instead of divestment, with US and South African firms pouring millions into KwaZulu education systems.[52] Inkatha leaders traveled the West, lobbying governments, nongovernmental organizations (NGOs), and businesses to put money into projects in KwaZulu, to the fury of the ANC. The Inkatha vision, where capitalism fueled social change, clashed with the socialist, communist vision of the ANC, which demanded a radical redistribution of land, resources, and wealth, in addition to political reform.

An Inkatha-led transformation of multiracial political representation and capitalist development would mirror what conservatives saw as the US civil rights transformation: political equality without challenging free market ideals. This set Inkatha, not the ANC, as the successor to the apartheid state. Buthelezi publicly opposed sanctions. Sanctions, he argued, harmed black South Africans more than whites, and Inkatha's 1.75 million membership overwhelmingly opposed sanctions.[53] The pro-investment position of Inkatha appealed to Republicans in the 1980s, who saw economic investment as a strategy for liberation—an exact phrase used by Inkatha in the 1985 edition of its magazine *Clarion Call*.[54] The 1982 Buthelezi Commission showcased Inkatha's support of a new, federalized South Africa. In its recommendations, the commission indicated that South Africa should pursue an open consociation between Buthelezi and the central government, with the latter retaining authority over defense, foreign affairs, and transportation.[55] Buthelezi would maintain political and economic control of KwaZulu and incorporate neighboring Natal. In his presentation to conservative Western leaders, Buthelezi decried the radical redistribution of land advocated by the ANC. In practice, Buthelezi drove land redistribution within KwaZulu, consolidating land and port access at Richards Bay and even trying to claim parts of eSwatini.[56] Buthelezi's language of rejecting land redistribution and taking on apartheid from within put Inkatha on the side of Western conservatives. The ANC and its partners continually referred to Buthelezi as a stooge, a sellout, and a lackey of Pretoria, whereas Buthelezi insisted these attacks were designed to weaken the antiapartheid credentials of the Inkatha, even as Inkatha became "a full-fledge surrogate of the apartheid regime in an international proxy war" in the 1980s.[57] However, during this period, the extent of Inkatha's ties to the apartheid state were not yet known, but enough evidence of collaboration—weapons, funding, and meetings between the National Party elites and Buthelezi—fueled suspicions. Inkatha's dialogues not only included the National Party but also the Conservative Party's Andries Treurnicht and the neo-Nazi Afrikaner nationalist Eugene Terre'Blanche, an omen of alliances to come.

White pro-apartheid propagandists used Buthelezi and the other black bantustan leaders to argue that South Africans needed changes but not those coming from the ANC. Apartheid's defenders demanded patience with the white regime, stoking fears of a "cure worse than the disease" in an ANC-led, communist government and using Buthelezi as evidence for this worldview. As William R. Kennedy Jr., publisher of *Conservative Digest*, claimed, responsible black South Africans did not want ANC policies. He highlighted Buthelezi's observations that the ANC was a terrorist organization not at all representative of South Africa.[58] According to *Chronicles: A Magazine of American Culture*, a paleoconservative, neo-Confederate magazine that "caters to the more intellectual wing of the white nationalist movement," "Black masses, especially the rural masses, are indifferent [to apartheid]. . . . There is no racial, but only tribal hatred in South Africa." In this claim, the writer cited Buthelezi, who could "not be brought under a common roof" with the "Xhosa-led" ANC and rejected total independence.[59] Pro-apartheid writers traveled to KwaZulu, lauding Buthelezi's territory as economically viable but still tribalized, not yet at cultural attainment and political sophistication.[60] Buthelezi's moderacy was all that stood in the way of white suicide; as Howard Ruff, chairman of the neoconservative group Free the Eagle, argued: backing Buthelezi was the only way to "prevent a Night of the Long Knives" for whites.[61]

US and South African pro-apartheid activists formed connections with black South Africans to bolster panels, conferences, and meetings. These leaders were meant to attest to the antisanctions ideas of true black South Africans and to create cover for centrist right-wingers who abhorred apartheid but remained skeptical of the efficacy of sanctions. This skepticism of sanctions was coupled with suspicion of the communist ANC; in this space, pro-apartheid activists could thrive, creating enough cover for centrist Republicans to be both antisanctions *and* antiapartheid. Black South Africans played an essential role in organizing against sanctions, positioning their suffering under sanctions and ANC terror as the true battle. The pro-apartheid movement regularly used grotesque images of black South Africans killed in the 1984–1986 rebellions with little regard to the dignity of those depicted. Although some black right-wingers, like Buthelezi, tried to carve out a space for their own power as the moderate black leaders of South Africa, others remained trapped in the reactionary racial politics of the pro-apartheid movement as nothing more than victims of terror. Buthelezi possessed more autonomy than most—in 1986, he famously rejected coming to the United States to campaign against sanctions unless invited by Reagan. The archival record of Hlapane, Mokoena, Masiya, and others is limited, filtered through the pro-apartheid activists who endorsed black South Africans' continued degradation and oppression at the hands of white rule. What these men and women truly thought of their pro-apartheid partnerships remains unclear, shrouded by the very far-right forces that professed themselves truthtellers.

FINDING THE "TRUTH" ABOUT THE APARTHEID STATE

In the flashy *Family Protection Scoreboard*'s South Africa issue, editor Balsiger offered an intriguing advertisement—the come see for yourself South Africa tour. For just $1,595 per person (just over $4,000 in 2023), *Scoreboard* organized a twelve-day leisure and learning tour of South Africa, complete with VIP luxury accommodations and fact-finding activities to interface with the Christian community.[62] This luxury tour was not a one-off experience or the only game in town for apartheid tourism. Throughout the 1980s, dozens of editorials appeared in local and national newspapers across the United States, with writers citing their positive experience in South Africa as they learned the truth about apartheid.[63] These writers went on tours like Balsiger's, some paid for by the South African government, their nongovernmental intermediaries, or private entities. Testimonials about the true South Africa, discovered after a fact-finding mission, permeated white supremacist newsletters, conservative university groups, and even the Reagan White House.[64] These tours targeted not only Americans but also conservative politicians across the West.[65] Although these tours began in the 1960s, after the Information Scandal and concerns about Pretoria's influence peddling, the fact-finding missions increasingly became the domain of nonstate and grassroots organizations. They varied in scope. The leisure and luxury learning excursion of *Scoreboard* fell under what scholars call the "racialized landscapes of tourism."[66] South Africa's game reserves and beaches were paired with luxury resorts, including one in the Transkei bantustan, as part of an international mythmaking that separated South Africa's abhorrent racial practices from its stunning geography.[67]

Others looked different. The South Africa Foundation financed many of these trips for high-level American policymakers, positioning itself as a nongovernmental, cross-racial, and cross-political collection of South African business leaders advocating reforms of the apartheid state. Founded in 1959 by a group of South African businessmen and backed by Harry Oppenheimer of the Anglo American Corporation, the South African Foundation focused on preventing the passage of economic sanctions. It included Afrikaners and English alike, drawing in wealthy American and British benefactors. As journalist Ron Nixon argued, the South Africa Foundation sat atop a web of lobbying that sought to quell sanctions, attempting to appeal to liberal and Black U.S. politicians by offering some criticisms of apartheid while still refusing to support true political equality.[68] The foundation's activities included financing congressmembers' South Africa visits, crafting favorable publications on Botha's reforms, testifying before US legislative bodies, financing antisanctions academic studies, and directly lobbying presidential administrations.[69] Although not explicitly an arm of the South African government, it worked in close concert with the Department of Information. It had a $2.3 million annual budget and $350,000 dedicated just to the United States in 1985.[70]

US and South African pro-apartheid actors pitched their travels as going beyond simple tours to instead act as fact-finding missions, pledging to provide their subscribers with firsthand accounts of life under white rule. South Africa's defenders modeled their efforts on the exploratory missions of the United Nations and human rights groups throughout the Cold War.[71] These fact-finding missions became essential tactics of the antiapartheid movement, with NGOs conducting independent investigations to expose the abuses of white rule.[72] The pro-apartheid movement simply coopted the rhetoric from transnational justice groups that used fact-finding missions to uncover atrocities around the globe. The fact-finding missions conducted by apartheid's defenders, these actors charged, would reveal the "truth" about South Africa that mainstream media hid. This was more than an international lobbying push; it also built people-to-people relationships and experiences that would sustain a social movement. These multiweek tours, operated by luxury tour companies and led by the SADF or other apartheid bureaucrats, cost thousands and included stays at resorts in Bophuthatswana or the Kruger

Park and Sabi Sabi game reserves. It also included controlled visits with black South Africans; closed tours of Soweto and Crossroads; and curated meetings with white and black teachers, workers, and industrialists and, almost always, representatives of Inkatha or local black mayors.[73]

A particularly infamous example of these tours occurred in August 1985. The *Fundamentalist Journal* published a special report on the "Untold Story of South Africa," featuring columns from Jerry Falwell, Ronald Godwin, executive vice president of the Moral Majority Foundation, and William Rusher. Along with nine pastors, Falwell traveled to South Africa in August 1985 for a fact-finding mission, returning armed with pro-apartheid propaganda that insisted that the true bringers of violence were Marxist organizations and not the South African government. Featuring testimonials from pastors and South Africans with whom they spoke, *Fundamentalist Journal* insisted that if "communism takes over in South Africa the oppression will be greater than under apartheid." Over five days, Falwell's group met with Botha and other apartheid bureaucrats, Soweto's black local council, white doctors, Colored and Indian members of the Tricameral Parliament, and KwaZulu officials.[74] Falwell committed the Moral Majority to "do everything we can" to work against sanctions, making video recordings of their trip to send "into a million homes."[75] After returning from the visit, Falwell declared Desmond Tutu a "phony" and began to campaign against sanctions. According to Falwell, Tutu's testimonials of the horrors of apartheid were fiction and Falwell's experience revealed a nation actually under the threat of communism, not racial unrest, and he returned more convinced than ever of the need for a robust, white-ruled government. Evoking the "greater fear" of Marxist totalitarianism, Falwell decided that Pretoria had made enough race relations progress.[76] Falwell contended that black South Africans would suffer the most under sanctions. Americans needed to trust in Botha, who assured Falwell "that he is committed to abolishing discrimination."[77] Republicans like Richard Lugar (R-IN), Newt Gingrich (R-GA), and Vin Weber (R-MN) maligned Falwell's comments as an "overtly racist, segregationist discourse [and] . . . a publicly unacceptable position in the post-Civil Rights Republican Party."[78]

Although Falwell stepped out of line according to some Republicans, he was operating in concert with other conservative activist organizations in the 1980s. Conservative titans like Howard Phillips went on their own fact-finding missions. Phillips returned from Southwest Africa (now Namibia) in February 1983, describing a "genuine thirst for the vision of victory and the techniques for achieving them which have been characteristic of the spirit and purpose of the New Right in America."[79] Phillips was dedicated to touring South Africa. In partnership with Duncan Sellars of the pro-apartheid International Freedom Foundation and Donald McAlvany of the *McAlvany Intelligence Advisor*, Phillips led an annual geopolitical/financial tour of South Africa. McAlvany was a born-again Christian who ran a precious-metals firm. He got his start in 1960 at the University of Texas in counterintelligence work, cooperating with the FBI to surveil "communist professors" on campus.[80] He formed the Council on Southern Africa after visiting South Africa following the Soweto Uprising in 1976, which motivated him to educate Americans about the real situation on the continent. McAlvany lectured to thousands of South Africans while giving these tours; in one lecture, he verbally attacked Tutu, urging the South African government to "remove the idiot's passport . . . and somebody might want to even shoot him."[81] Starting in 1975, Phillips and McAlvany led thirteen tours of the "unique, controversial, and strategic country," with thirty hours of lectures given to tour members by cabinet ministers, parliamentarians, business executives, and military leaders, complete with cocktail party dinners—for only $357 a day. McAlvany had traveled to South Africa thirty-one times by 1988.[82] These tours promised unfettered access to a state ignored by liberal media.

A key part of McAlvany's tours and other luxury ventures was the Sun City gambling experience. Hotelier Sol Kerzner established a series of casinos in the bantustans: Wild Coast Sun in Transkei, Fish River Sun in Ciskei, and most notoriously, Sun City in Bophuthatswana. Built in 1979, Kerzner designed Sun City in the Las Vegas style, with gambling, pornography, multiracial shows, musicians, and Gary Player–designed golf courses. Sun City served two important purposes for apartheid South Africa. It provided an outlet for white South Africans who wanted to evade the 1965 gambling prohibition, and it helped sustain the economy of Bophuthatswana and the illusion of its independence under its president Lucas Mangope.[83] Throughout the 1980s, Sun City drew investment from Western firms that parroted the apartheid state's line on Bophuthatswana's independence.[84] Sun City successfully booked many American artists, including Tina Turner, Elton John, the Beach Boys, and Frank Sinatra.[85]

In 1985, Artists Against Apartheid released the protest single "Sun City" to pressure other artists to turn down Sun City contracts and raised more than $1 million for antiapartheid projects.[86] Apartheid's defenders had no such qualms. Sun City became a premier destination point and the crown jewel of Mangope's efforts to preserve the power of independent Bophuthatswana.

These fact-finding missions were not just the domain of the conservative intelligentsia—grassroots organizations also participated. The Council of Conservative Citizens (CofCC) called upon Colonel Robert L. Slimp as a tour guide.[87] In October 1990, Slimp announced his fourth tour to South Africa, where tour participants could personally meet the top political, military, and Christian leaders of South Africa. Activities included welcoming braaivleis (barbeques) with South African military and police officers and their wives and visiting military units that patrol the Zimbabwe border. South Africa "still resembles America's Old South" so "now is the time to go," his advertisement concluded.[88] CofCC members had been going to South Africa for years. In the summer of 1984, the St. Louis chapter elected to take their own fact-finding mission to South Africa, returning convinced that it would avoid the perils of Black takeover that plagued Africa. The St. Louis chapter proved devoted to the white South African cause, taking out a full-page "message to South Africans," assuring them that liberals do not speak for most Americans. Similarly, the Metro chapter insisted that "average Americans in organizations like ours are stepping up efforts to counter anti-South Africa propaganda," placing an ad of support in the Afrikaans-language newspaper *Rapport*.[89] During their trip, CofCC members met with the Foreign Affairs Department and visited the Voortrekker monument—the Afrikaner nationalist commemoration of the 1835 and 1854 Boer exodus from the Cape Colony into the interior, built and paid for by the apartheid government in 1949.[90] In their report, CofCC members highlighted that "blacks [were] not nearly as eager to see the white government deposed as the liberal news media implies." They were "content," with a "relaxed, carefree attitude." These reports came from their "firsthand interactions" with black South Africans and their meetings with South Africa Foundation researchers, who stated the "Blacks [want] to repudiate white liberalism."[91] These trips bolstered the image of the apartheid regime and the claims of those who said they knew the true black South African experience.

South Africa's fact finders brought the "truth" about the apartheid state and also the horrors of the communist onslaught on the South African border. Amid the Mozambican Civil War, pro-apartheid organizations told tales of the harrowing resistance of the anticommunist Renamo and African Christians against the violent excesses of Samora Machel's Frelimo. Renamo, backed by the SADF, expanded far into the north in Zambezia Province, whereas Frelimo was part of the fragile "big five" liberation alliances in southern Africa. The ANC, under Machel's protection, had a network of bases and safe houses in Mozambique used to deploy MK operations in KwaZulu and Natal. The SADF's cross-border raids targeted these underground units in Mozambique, Botswana, and Lesotho.[92] Peter Hammond's Frontline Fellowship was a focal point for truth-telling around the cross-border conflict in Mozambique, conducting "field trips" to research communist activities.[93] Frontline Fellowships' field workers became crucial in obtaining so-called eyewitness testimony of the abuses of black communist radicals menacing the South African border. In his reports, Hammond claimed that he used "the strictest research methods possible," with only firsthand accounts "confirmed by separate eyewitness testimony."[94] Proffering reliance on careful cross-examination, sworn testimony, and joint confirmation by entire villages, Hammond reported harassed Christian leaders, burnt villages, unburied corpses, and destroyed Bibles. During one trip to northern Mozambique, Hammond claimed to receive reports of "42 village burnings, 72 church destructions, 60 Bible burnings, 28 massacres, and children forced into re-education camps."

The International Society for Human Rights (ISHR), a nonprofit with connections to US and European conservative groups, circulated this particular report, drumming up fear of a communist onslaught nearly at the brink of overrunning South Africa. The ISHR's British Section invited Hammond to speak at its March 29, 1986, branch meeting and published the full Mozambique report—sixteen pages with allegedly over 300 interviews—in its September 1986 newsletter.[95] Delegations from the ISHR visited South Africa in January and February 1986 and confirmed that religious freedom for Christians was encouraged under apartheid with any privileges curtailed by communist liberationists, not the government. Sponsored by the ISHR, Hammond and United Christian Action sent a fifteen-member group to West Germany for Kirchentag, an international conference on Christian faith, democracy, human rights, social responsibility, and the fight against discrimination.[96] That particular Kirchentag included a closing service led by Dr. Allan Boesak to over 100,000 people. The Hammond delegation, which also included Dorothea Scarborough of the Gospel Defense League and Cindy Leontsinis of Victims Against Terrorism, picketed the sermon.[97] The fifteen members also held a large event with the ISHR, called the "Partnership Against Violence," that attacked the ANC, drew over 700 attendees, and distributed literature that allegedly Kirchentag subsequently banned. Hammond said all ten black members of the delegation were "threatened with necklacing, petrol bombing, or murder, including a paralyzed 18-year old Black girl."[98] United Christin Action and its partners would go on to protest Kirchentag for the next several years.

International observers disputed Hammond's accounts, accusing him of instigating violence across southern Africa. As the director of the Southern Africa Research and Documentation Centre put it, Hammond took "the list of horrors it is well known the [anti-communists] continuously carry out and turned it around by trying to claim that the [liberation] army are doing them."[99] Watchdog groups struggled to find credible accounts of government workers destroying Bibles or communists "butchering" churchgoers. Hammond's connections to the SADF, his ability to access parts of Mozambique, and his questionable contacts and language skills all opened the possibility of cooperation with state authorities.

Fact-finding missions by US and South African actors were channels worn smooth by the transatlantic travels of hundreds of men and women in the 1980s. United Christian Action held semiregular meetings throughout 1986 in cooperation with the US Christian Anti-Communism Crusade, inviting any friends of South Africa to visit and see the true plight of the nation.[100] In May 1987, Hammond shared his plans to host and organize programs for Americans with Donald McAlvany on the real southern Africa.[101] McAlvany returned the favor, conducting frequent speaking tours throughout South Africa.[102] Slimp and his wife hosted the Rhodesian pastor Arthur Lewis in 1982. Everywhere Lewis went, he reported "a concern to know the truth of the Rhodesia tragedy, and the facts about South Africa"—with media "more sympathetic" than expected.[103] Lewis had plans to use a Bloemfontein farm to create a "little Rhodesia" in South

Africa for Americans to visit, built by the Rhodesia Association of South Africa.[104] Hammond reported positively his relationships with overseas friends, principally Slimp and McAlvany.[105] This transatlantic exchange was more than a simple propaganda campaign: it aimed at building true solidary between Americans and South Africans for the purposes of bolstering white rule.

THE TRUE SUPPORTERS OF WHITE RULE

Reagan's resounding presidential victory in 1984—winning an astonishing 525 electoral votes—seemed to signal the unstoppable power of global conservatism. Although Reagan's first term signaled a watershed conservative revolution in American politics, by the mid-1980s, the political infighting within the Republican Party had paralyzed the White House.[106] The US far right had viewed Reagan as the ideal conservative candidate, but these supporters increasingly questioned his administration's commitment to defeating global communism. The far right became convinced that a fifth column had entered the White House, fixated on undercutting Reagan foreign policy. The British and West German conservative movement also faced charges of insufficient commitment to conservatism as its leaders struck an uneasy bargain with various right factions.[107] These far-righters animated the grassroots of conservative political parties across the globe, rousing the base and driving turnout at the ballot box. However, upon election, right-wing political parties, often helmed by more centrist figures, struggled to hold the coalition together.

A similar tension existed in South Africa, as the *verligte* (enlightened) and *die regses* (far-right) divisions absorbed white political energy in the 1980s.[108] While under its control from 1948 to apartheid's end, the National Party faced consistent opposition from other visions of white rule, specifically the more liberal but still prowhite rule United Party and the Progressive Party. Far-right parties, like the Herstigte Nasionale Party, which splintered off in 1969, failed to win seats in the whites-only House of Assembly, even as it captured 13.1 percent of the national vote in 1981.[109] Its percentage of the national vote revealed a deep undercurrent of white anger toward the National Party. That anger had an outlet in

1982 with the formation of the Conservative Party. Twenty-three members of parliament, led by Andries Treurnicht, broke from the National Party, opposed to Botha's power-sharing proposal for a tricameral parliament that included Colored and Indian South Africans. The Conservative Party accused Botha of abandoning traditional Verwoerdian-style apartheid, but that criticism allowed Botha and his National Party to grab the verligte label. Botha could present himself and his party abroad as the reformers, holding the line against die regses. Within South Africa, Botha weaponized his verligte credentials to expand the security state, positioning his administration as tough against global communism, violently rooting out subversive dissent. For the rest of the 1980s, the center and far-right-wingers in South Africa battled for the white vote, part of a Western trajectory of conservative infighting.

According to some of the most virulent strands of the pro-apartheid movement, any attempt by the West, especially the United States, to pressure reform in South Africa—even as its leaders resisted economic sanctions—revealed an insufficient commitment to white rule. In an open letter to Botha, McAlvany warned that the US government—but not its people—was Botha's deadly enemy. No amount of racial reform, McAlvany continued, would satisfy the apartheid state's enemies in the "US Congress, State Department, media, academia, and liberal eastern establishment."[110] The State Department became the favored target of the pro-apartheid movement, which insisted that the State Department's real goal was the overthrow of the South African government by any means necessary.[111] This distinction between Reagan's true policies and betrayal by the State Department became a standard line of the pro-apartheid movement throughout its 1980s and 1990s activism. Simultaneously, the pro-apartheid movement aimed at the "reformist impulses" of the South African government. As Aida Parker put it, "if ever South Africa falls to the enemy and is totally lost to the West, it will be because of the 'enemy within.' . . . Today's fifth column would have us settle with terrorists. . . . It comprises those who would have us 'negotiate' our country into oblivion."[112] Pro-apartheid writers insisted that the integrationist policies of the National Party betrayed whites, encouraging readers to throw their support behind the Conservative Party and the even further right Herstigte Nasionale Party, which was geared up for a great struggle to defend Grand Apartheid.[113] Whites could no longer trust Botha and the National

Party to protect their interests.[114] One writer for the Holocaust-denying Institute for Historical Review insisted that the Botha regime betrayed Grand Apartheid and that Afrikaners would need their own ethnostate to survive.[115] The National Party had forsaken the Afrikaner.

Although the pro-apartheid movement grew increasingly critical of the Reagan and Botha administrations, it remained committed to people-to-people solidarity. As United Christian Action put it, regardless of the actions of conservative politicians, US right-wingers are "the only true friends South Africa has."[116] Reagan had betrayed the white race, and the white right needed to look for new partners.[117] Other organizations took a similar tone. The National Socialist Vanguard, a US neo-Nazi organization, stated that the white right needed to support black ethnic groups—specifically Buthelezi's Zulus—to create a truly segregated society.[118] Extreme rightists advocated a state's rights solution that would divide South Africa on ethnic, racial, cultural, and tribal lines.[119] Although politicians might have failed them, the people-to-people relationships between white and black right-wingers could save South Africa. These fringe, far-right factions of the pro-apartheid movement remained more muted throughout the 1980s, as defenders of white rule primarily focused their lobbying on saving South Africa from sanctions. However, as the sanctions effort failed, their voices grew, pushing the pro-apartheid movement to schism from centrists toward a more violent path, planting the seeds of the black-white conservative alliance that challenged apartheid's end.

Throughout the 1980s, pro-apartheid organizations weaponized their three-part rhetoric of anticommunism, colorblind capitalism, and Christianity to defend white rule through a vast network of people-to-people organizations. Pro-apartheid actors and organizations forged intimate connections through tourism, lectures, newsletters, lobbying, and fact-finding missions, bringing solidarity, knowledge production, and networking for white rule into cross-racial conservative spaces. This organizing moved across levels of power: it included speaker series at churches, far-right community groups across the United States, and high-powered conferences funded by the intelligentsia of the New Right. Black South Africans were an essential part of this organizing as they navigated their relationship to the apartheid state and its defenders in the West. Tensions between the disciples of apartheid proved constant. White rule's most ardent advocates fought among themselves and the conservative governments they lobbied to defend apartheid.

Looking ahead, the pro-apartheid movement deployed these people-to-people relationships to accomplish a singular goal—preventing the passage of economic sanctions. They would operate throughout the United States and Europe, seeing initial success in the Reagan White House, relying on networks of white women to build their case, and ultimately openly fighting Congress. As the antiapartheid movement stepped up the pressure for sanctions, pro-apartheid actors responded, mobilizing their coalition to find friendly conservative partners who would save the last bastion of white rule.

II

AN INTERNATIONAL ANTISANCTIONS CAMPAIGN

3

MAKING AND BREAKING CONSTRUCTIVE ENGAGEMENT

On July 23, 1986, Ed Cain of the United Christian Action sent a telegram to Ronald Reagan, thanking him for his antisanctions stance. Sanction advocates, Cain contended, were not those suffering under apartheid but those who "enjoy privileges which people in other parts of Africa do not even dream."[1] Perhaps more interesting was Cain's commentary on apartheid itself, which he described as "not defended by people of influence." To Cain, reform was a "reality" in South Africa, as the "legislative pillars" of white rule fell under P. W. Botha. In Cain's telling, apartheid was on the way out in the country and hardly worth focusing on: the true villain, the international sanctions movement, lurked around every corner, ready to destroy reform in South Africa.

By the time Cain sent his telegram to Reagan in 1986, the antiapartheid movement's sanctions advocacy was in full swing across the United States, Europe, Canada, and Australia.[2] In the face of existing cultural and sporting boycotts like the "We Won't Play Sun City" campaign and the "Halt All Racist Rugby" ban, economic sanctions loomed.[3] As internal rebellion against white rule reached a fever pitch, apartheid's defenders worked to convince conservative governments to ignore calls for sanctions, insisting that the West could be both antiapartheid and antisanctions. This positioning argued that the ruling National Party was on a true path to reform and sanctions were not only unnecessary but also a tool of radical communists intent on destroying black and white South Africans.

The antiapartheid, antisanctions position appealed to centrist right-wingers who remained skeptical of the ANC and wanted to use capitalist incentives, not coercion, to induce reform, leveraging existing conservative ideas around capitalism and anticommunism. Reagan's election in 1980 and the announced plan of constructive engagement encapsulated this messaging. In the 1980s, a debate existed among Western conservatives: Could you both be opposed to apartheid and stand against sanctions? Reagan officials firmly believed this was possible and sought to make that position a diplomatic success in southern Africa. The pro-apartheid movement and a sympathetic Reagan administration sought to reset the Western dialogue about South Africa. No longer would sanctions advocates claim sole ownership of the antiapartheid position: the "true" opposition to apartheid came from those who resisted sanctions, were committed to the freedom of black South Africans, and negotiated in southern Africa through the mechanisms created by constructive engagement. After initial success, constructive engagement began to falter by 1984, and congressional right-wingers started to revise their view of sanctions. To hold onto centrist conservatives, who increasingly considered economic coercion, the pro-apartheid movement dialed in their efforts to win the political battle against sanctions. The malleable middle of Western right-wingers, bolstered by conservative governments under Reagan, Margaret Thatcher, and Helmut Kohl, became the pro-apartheid movement's targets, casting the real antiapartheid activists as those who opposed sanctions: the antisanctions international. The strategic failure of constructive engagement paved the way for the sanctions showdown of 1986 and the schism of the Western right over defending apartheid.

FORGING A TRANSATLANTIC RIGHT ALLIANCE UNDER CONSTRUCTIVE ENGAGEMENT

As Reagan took office in 1981, centrist conservatives and their grassroots allies believed that constructive engagement and its antisanctions vision could pay dividends. In the early days of the Reagan administration, Pretoria's senior leadership sought to establish a close working partnership with US officials without committing to end apartheid. In a letter sent

May 12, 1981, Botha wrote that Reagan's public support of South Africa led him to believe this to be an opportune moment for the two governments to promote mutual interests and improve relations. Botha insisted that the two nations shared a history of development, with the same values and democratic tradition in the face of Soviet encroachment. Expressing his skepticism of sanctions and favor toward constructive engagement, Botha refused to commit to a plan of ending apartheid, instead stating that he had a mandate to promote an "acceptable accommodation between the different population groups of our country."[4] Reagan congratulated Botha on his election victory as a clear call for a changed, modern, and strong South Africa.[5] In an initial meeting between Alexander Haig and Foreign Minister Pik Botha a week later on May 20, 1981, Haig reported that he established a new relationship with South Africa based on a realistic appraisal of their mutual interest in southern African. Ending "unproductive ostracism," Haig relayed to Pik Botha that there would be "no Soviet flag in Windhoek" or deadlines on internal reform.[6] This reorientation toward open dialogue with South African officials marked a stark change from the Carter years.

Although American spokesmen denied that the invitation of Pik Botha to the White House signified a tilt toward South Africa, Pretoria sought to capitalize on this visit. In his first meeting with the newly appointed US ambassador to South Africa, Herman Nickel, Botha welcomed the Reagan administration's acceptance that public pressure merely strengthened Afrikaner intransigence.[7] The *South African Digest*, a newspaper produced by Pretoria's Department of Information, expressed unbridled enthusiasm over Reagan's new approach. On March 20, 1981, the *South African Digest* insisted that American foreign policy would be less timid and more realistic, with the South African government never having so much encouragement until Reagan.[8] In an interview with the *Digest*, Pik Botha stressed that he was greatly encouraged by Haig's realism, which would be South Africa's "golden opportunity."[9] Although South Africa was "not exactly about to become the 51st U.S. state," the improvement in relations teased the possibility of budding allies.[10] There was recognition "that South Africa [would] never have a better friend in Washington than Ronald Reagan."[11] This public enthusiasm proved a strategic choice for Pretoria in an effort to convince white South Africans that a renewed US diplomatic relationship would pay dividends for their regional security.

The South African government was right to be optimistic, as the internal policy discussions of the Reagan administration prioritized white South Africans. Haig presented his strategy for southern Africa in a National Security Planning Group (NSPG) meeting on March 24, 1981, that focused on assuring white rights.[12] Haig recommended advocating for the creation of a Namibian constitution protecting white minority rights, along with strengthening public and covert support for the anticommunist UNITA party in Angola. This approach, Haig argued, would restore South Africa's sense of confidence in the United States and show the Frontline States that US influence over South Africa would be more substantial if the Cubans phased out military assistance. The NSPG expressed skepticism of Haig's plan, noting that it seemed unlikely that Western allies or the Frontline States would support a constitution that explicitly protected white rights.[13] In discussing this plan of action at various National Security Council (NSC) meetings, significant concerns emerged from Haig and other presidential advisors that involving Reagan too directly in constructive engagement policy would "jeopardize [Reagan's] prestige."[14] These concerns emerged after a disastrous television interview given by Reagan on March 4, 1981, during which Reagan questioned abandoning a loyal ally like South Africa. International media widely publicized Pretoria's praise of Reagan's statements, with the *New York Times* describing Reagan's policy change as "diplomatic manna for P.W. Botha."[15] Chief of Staff James Baker III, with support from Reagan himself, pushed to not involve Reagan in an upcoming trip to South Africa by Assistant Secretary of State Chester Crocker.[16]

Reagan's absence from constructive engagement and Haig's pro–South Africa vision created a unique window of opportunity for Pretoria, allowing South African officials to insist publicly that a close relationship between Reagan and Botha existed. Although critical of the US government—and increasingly the State Department—the Botha administration emphasized that the relationship with Reagan remained strong. In the correspondence between the two men throughout Reagan's first term, Reagan clearly expressed warmth toward Botha. In a letter from Reagan to Botha on November 23, 1983, Reagan welcomed the "clear willingness by white South Africans" to cooperate with "other elements" of South African society. Invoking his status as leader of the "nation that leads the West and represents the founding principles of our Judeo-Christian tradition," Reagan expressed his appreciation for Botha's courage, strength, and perseverance.[17] "Heartened" by Reagan's commitment to constructive change, Botha, unsurprisingly, responded to Reagan's emphasis on a Judeo-Christian relationship with enthusiasm. "The fact that you, Mr. President, and your Government are prepared to maintain a constructive dialogue with my government in these matters helps to make our task a little easier." Raising the specter of communist influence in southern Africa, Botha flattered Reagan, stating "since you became President, the U.S. has played a more effective role in meeting the communist threat."[18] Reagan's unwillingness to publicly condemn South Africa proved essential for Pretoria in convincing domestic far-right detractors that sticking with regional negotiations would increase the security of white South Africans through constructive engagement.

US officials worked to keep white South African interests top of mind. If the South African far right "put steam behind charges that anything short of maintaining white supremacy is selling out the white man," Pik Botha warned that any possibility of regional settlement would end.[19] But "given the right cards to play," Pretoria's security officials would go to Namibia to lobby the merits of settlements to the rest of the Namibian far-right wing.[20] The "right cards" Pik Botha needed would prove US backing of a constitution that explicitly protected white property and political and physical security. In the weeks that followed, Pik Botha and his counterparts played those cards, lobbying to the internal far right US assurances of constitutionally guaranteed white minority rights, protections to property owners, and military and economic support upon SADF withdrawal from Namibia.[21] In a big win for Reagan officials, the far right seemed willing to accept a SWAPO-governed Namibia "as long as our current South Africa diplomacy stays on course." To the head of the US mission in South Africa, it seemed that the principal worry for the South Africans concerned protecting the National Party's "political flank at home." While Haig's plan to seek an interconnected schedule for Cuban troop withdrawal faltered, South African officials signed off on Phase I of the Namibian proposal on January 29, 1982, privately citing that Haig "nailed" the security concerns of the Namibian white right.[22]

Constructive engagement seemed to be paying dividends in these early years, and the British and West German governments lined up behind Reagan's constructive engagement strategy, citing the possibility of capitalist reform, geopolitical realities, and South Africa's preexisting cooperation.[23] Prime Minister Margaret Thatcher blocked economic measures against South Africa at Commonwealth summits in 1981 and 1983, casting the lone vote against sanctions in 1985.[24] Thatcher's hardline stance against sanctions unsurprisingly put her as the key ally for the Reagan administration, even as it isolated the British from their Commonwealth and Scandinavian allies.[25] Within Britain, free market capitalism, colonial nostalgia, skepticism toward sanctions as a policy tool, apathy, and a persistent, if fringe, far right created a bastion of support for South Africa that bolstered Thatcher's stance.[26] Thatcher's government took these stances despite pressure from the British Anti-Apartheid Movement, which pro-apartheid writers argued had deep ANC roots, infiltrating the Labour Party and prodivestment businesses.[27] In West Germany, Kohl's support for the stance of his American and British allies ran afoul of the Anti-Apartheid-Bewegung, a broad church engaged in strikes, protests, and physical attacks against petrol stations, technology companies, food stores, and automakers like Mercedes-Benz.[28]

In contrast, in Canada and Australia, conservative politicians were skeptical of constructive engagement. In Canada, Prime Minister Brian Mulroney and Secretary of State for External Affairs Joe Clark saw working against apartheid as a moral issue and the driver of regional insecurity.[29] The Mulroney government, in defiance of conservative thinking in the United States, Britain, and West Germany, saw sanctions as a "tool to demonstrate disapproval of apartheid and concordance with norms of global racial equality, not the goal in itself."[30] In response, Canadian defenders of the South African government "shifted from backroom persuasion to a more openly aggressive defense of South African reforms and demonization of the ANC."[31] A similar pattern of defiance occurred in Australia, where the center-right prime minister Malcolm Fraser drew the ire of the pro-apartheid movement for his outspoken critiques of white rule.[32] The succeeding prime minister, left-leaning Bob Hawke, drew even further fury, and apartheid's defenders urged South Africa to be "hawkish with the Aussies."[33]

These differences between these conservative-led states became apparent throughout the activity of the Western Contact Group. Established in 1977 to negotiate the Namibia transition to independence, the Western Contact Group consisted of five member countries: France, the United

Kingdom, the United States, Canada, and West Germany. Although Reagan officials continued to deny the possibility of a "tilt," Haig gloated about the prospects of this US–South African pivot to skeptical members of the Contact Group.[34] In his discussions with the Australian prime minister Malcolm Fraser, Haig said that without South Africa, the United States could not force a settlement, justifying closeness with Pretoria.[35] Simultaneously, the South Africans sought to sow conflict between the United States and the other members of the Contact Group. In cables from the US embassy in Cape Town, officials communicated frustration that South African officials purposely overemphasized US differences with the rest of the Western Contact Group.[36] This dynamic reared its ugly head after Pretoria leaked details of a bilateral meeting between Crocker and Pik Botha in Zurich, outside the channels of the Contact Group.[37] The US deputy chief of mission in Pretoria expressed his frustrations that he had to hide details of this meeting from the West Germans. Pik Botha trashed the Contact Group to US officials, lamenting the "European identification with black Africans' anti-SAG rhetoric," insisting that the Contact Group increased the popularity of the far right by refusing to recognize Botha's racial reforms.[38] Pik Botha continued the pressure to split the United States from the five, Crocker concluded. "In my view," one US official concurred, "Pik would not mind a more difficult relationship among the Contact Group."[39]

CRACKS IN CONSTRUCTIVE ENGAGEMENT

Dramatic changes to the US–South African relationship came in 1982, as the Botha government put its Total Strategy into action. The emergence of a significant challenger—the Conservative Party—to Botha's government in that same year showcased the extent of far-right resistance to the National Party's vision of South Africa. The Conservative Party was launched in response to the Tricameral Parliament scheme, a proposed power-sharing agreement that created legislative representation for Indian and Colored South Africans but explicitly not black South Africans. US officials privately called the Tricameral Parliament a "blueprint for enshrining minority rule" with "little basic difference" in the legislature, full of safeguards against the loss of white control, and with its "most glaring omission [being] the absence of any reference to future accommodation of blacks."[40] Nevertheless, after its announcement, white support for Botha fell sharply from a high of 65 percent in the South African 1977 general election to 47 percent in 1982 after the split in the National Party. Afrikaners fled the National Party and joined the Conservative Party in droves: the National Party lost 31 percent of the Afrikaner vote from 1977 to 1982.[41] The National Student Federation launched cross-university campaigns condemning Botha's foreign policy, arguing that regional negotiations endangered the "security, freedom, and liberty of all South Africans."[42] After 1982, the National Party would defend white rule at home and Western civilization from communist invasion abroad as part of the Total Onslaught Strategy. South African cross-border raids into Mozambique, Angola, and Namibia to hit the ANC-in-exile rapidly increased. Regional negotiations stagnated as the Botha administration proved unwilling to make foreign policy concessions that could make the National Party appear weak to the domestic right wing. Pik Botha attempted to bring US military forces into southern Africa to appeal to the white right, accusing Reagan officials of being "dogged by the Vietnam syndrome" and fearful of using troops to combat the Soviets in the region.[43] South African officials increasingly used American refusal to commit ground troops as justification for expanded military action in Angola. Under pressure from the South African far right, the National Party took a more confrontational posture with the Reagan administration.

This renewed Pretorian intransigence came on the heels of Haig's resignation as secretary of state on June 25, 1982. *Die Transvaler* lamented Haig's departure, hoping that the "measure of understanding that presently exists between us and the Reagan administration will still be maintained."[44] Haig's successor, George Shultz, assumed the post on July 16, 1982, and brought a distinct shift in the State Department's approach to Pretoria. Whereas Haig proved willing to slow the linkage strategy to appease the South Africans, Shultz was not, pushing for regionally connected settlements in Angola and Namibia and extending constructive engagement to Mozambique. Furthermore, Shultz's arrival brought a chilliness to the US–South African partnership, particularly to the relationship between Shultz and Pik and P. W. Botha. Haig's chummy relationship with

Pik Botha evaporated with Shultz, who prioritized rebuilding US relations with the Frontline States. Shultz focused on Angola, optimistic in October 1982 that through dialogue with the ruling communist party, the People's Movement for the Liberation of Angola (MPLA), the United States could gain concessions from the Cubans on withdrawal. In a follow-up letter to Pik Botha sent August 28, 1982, Shultz stressed this as a "make or break moment" for talks after the Americans had exerted enormous effort to pacify the South African right wing.[45]

The US and South African foreign offices struggled to maintain their conservative transatlantic alliance in the following months. Although Washington and Pretoria both recognized Soviet influence in the region, Pik Botha subscribed to the "most pessimistic" readings of SWAPO and MPLA as taking advantage of Pretorian restraint, according to the American consulate.[46] As Shultz and the ambassador to South Africa Herman Nickel expressed their belief that Angola and Mozambique were not just Soviet client states, confrontation with the Foreign Office rose.[47] This frustration only grew as the South Africans downgraded the profile of talks with the Angolans and terminated dialogue with Mozambique, a key initiative from Crocker and Shultz to slow cross-border violence. Pik Botha insisted that the Angolan manipulation of South African military restraint and Mozambique's support for the ANC were diplomatic nonstarters. The Botha administration had concluded that Mozambique was "not master in its own house," and thus Pretoria would not negotiate with its leadership.[48] Reagan officials called on the National Party to respect its efforts to consider the South African government's "problems with the conservatives" and cooperate fully with constructive engagement.[49] "We face a tricky situation with the South Africans," Shultz concluded. Despite their alleged commitment to settling regional conflict, Botha was not eager to take the domestic political risks involved, with the Reagan administration successfully restraining the South Africans from "serious military activity . . . only with the greatest difficulty."[50]

Unsurprisingly, South Africa's renewed intransigence and American wedding to constructive engagement won the Reagan administration few friends on the African continent. Although Africa's statesmen privately supported the Americans serving as a southern Africa intermediary, Reagan did not appear to grasp how nonnegotiable apartheid was for its leadership. For instance, in a meeting with President Kenneth

Kaunda of Zambia on March 30, 1983, Reagan expressed his belief that the South African government was on the road to reforming apartheid. Although Kaunda supported the US–Angolan–South African discussions, he rejected the South African fear of "Soviet encirclement" relayed by Shultz and Crocker.[51] Kaunda insisted that Botha was resisting talks and that South Africa would collapse unless it opened up a dialogue with the ANC. President Mobutu Sese Seko of Zaire expressed similar sentiments: he remained hopeful about the American-led peace process but believed that "unfortunately he could not say that publicly" because of South Africa's continued commitment to apartheid.[52] Other Frontline State leaders questioned the entire premise of constructive engagement. In a meeting between Crocker and Zimbabwe's president Robert Mugabe on September 13, 1983, Mugabe firmly told Crocker that South Africa was the "architect of destabilization in the area" and that the Americans should not give them any encouragement in their continued aggression.[53] The president of Cape Verde, Aristides Pereira, raised a similar point: the Reagan administration's strategy of linkage allowed the South Africans to derail multiple stages of the negotiations process.[54] The message from the African states remained clear: although the United States should pursue regional negotiation, constructive engagement would never win their support.

As the Reagan administration took the temperature of Africa's statesmen, it enraged apartheid's defenders who increasingly questioned US support for white South Africa. Pretoria's propaganda outlets blamed the State Department—specifically Crocker—for the increasingly regional approach to constructive engagement. The press began to attack Crocker's efforts to settle regional conflict, insisting this was not Washington's business. The *South African Digest* relayed that although Afrikaners "welcome the friendly concern" of the Reagan administration, Crocker should bear in mind that "what happens in South West Africa and South Africa is primarily the concern of their peoples." A letter to the editor from *Die Burger* stated, "If America is so concerned about relations between Zimbabwe and South Africa, it should try using its influence to try to bring Mr. Mugabe and his cabinet to their senses."[55] These writers predicted that the Reagan administration would go the way of South Africa's former Western allies and engage in predictable hostility, unable to "see any good in anything that the Government does."[56] However, apartheid's defenders saw Reagan as betrayed by internal enemies. A "fanatical upsurge of anti-South Africa rhetoric" emerged because of Reagan's image as a friend of the Pretoria regime, the *South African Digest* reported, which risked damaging the new transatlantic partnership.[57] The appeals by the *South African Digest* and other South African reporters were both sincere and strategic, attempting to separate Reagan from the "failings" of his State Department and drumming up momentum for a renewed US–South African partnership.

South Africa's US defenders watched developments under Shultz with great concern, accusing the US government of intentionally destabilizing South Africa and forcing the National Party to cave militarily to the UN and the Frontline States.[58] For instance, one writer worried about South Africa's standing internationally if "things go horribly wrong" in the US election of 1984. In light of this possibility, South Africa must remain steadfast and must not cave to US demands.[59] In the summer 1984 edition of *Citizens Informer*, the editors reminded readers that terrorists target South Africa to topple "its white, pro-West government." According to *Citizens Informer* sources, including Johann Stauch of Pretoria's Foreign Affairs Office, Angolan and Namibian terrorist activity increased during constructive engagement. In meetings with members of the St. Louis Council of Conservative Citizens (CofCC), Stauch lauded South Africa's military successes and the National Party's ability to maintain internal stability while calling on Reagan officials to raise military support for the apartheid state. *Citizens Informer* reported efforts by South African officials to lobby the Reagan State Department that robust military efforts were the means to command regional respect.[60] As Carl Nöffke, former head of the South African Information Services and friend to US conservatives, put it in a letter to right-wing titan William Rusher, "it is essential that we muster all support available during the next phase ahead in southern Africa."[61] According to the pro-apartheid movement, Reagan officials needed to move from diplomatic to military support for Pretoria.

Botha echoed these demands from the far right in his conversations with Reagan. In a letter from Botha to Reagan delivered February 14, 1984, Botha expressed his gratitude for the "tentative possibilities of peace" opening up in southern Africa. However, the United States could not expect South Africa to continue to fight Soviet expansionism alone, "deprived of certain weapons." "Can we rely on the U.S. to provide us with the kind of help we will need to resist Soviet expansionism effectively and decisively?" Botha questioned.[62] It was vital for South Africans to know that they had a friend in the United States and an ally who went beyond identifying with the cause to provide military support. Reagan's response seemed to leave open the door to military support. On May 11, 1984, Reagan celebrated the "remarkable degree of understanding" between Pretoria and Washington on the need for "positive, evolutionary change within South African society, and a new constructive spirit in our bilateral relations." Highlighting the successes of the bilateral relationship to minimize Soviet interference in southern Africa, Reagan committed to not leave Pretoria in the face of Soviet ambitions, which "would be inconsistent with all we have done these past three years."[63] Calling Botha's request for military support a "premature" shift, Reagan insisted on international settlement as best suited to achieve results. Constructive engagement, Reagan argued, was the path to success in southern Africa.

ANTIAPARTHEID, ANTISANCTIONS AT THE END OF CONSTRUCTIVE ENGAGEMENT

In a February 1984 letter to Howard Phillips from Representative Jack Kemp (R-NY), Kemp embodied the existing policy of constructive engagement, insisting that Americans had a special obligation of promoting the cause of human rights while rejecting sanctions as the tool in South Africa.[64] Yet between 1984 and 1985, the landscape of what conservative support for South Africa looked like evolved, with Kemp moving to vocally support sanctions as mass resistance to apartheid grew.[65] The year 1984 proved to be the most violent year of resistance yet by black South Africans. Widespread student protests and boycotts over the Tricameral Parliament drove the demonstrations. Botha tried to break the insurgency by arresting forty-three leaders and 150 followers of the United Democratic Front (UDF) and the Natal Indian Congress the night before the 1984 South African general elections and implementing a state of emergency that reached thirty-six districts across the Vaal Triangle and would later include the Eastern and Western Capes. As historian Alex Thomson argued, the sustained nature of the Vaal Uprising "provided a clear message that the majority in South Africa were not prepared to accept the political settlement pressed on them by the National Party."[66] Publicly, Reagan officials called for a greater understanding of black community grievances amid the tentative "but real steps" toward reform in South Africa; privately, analysts possessed no illusions about South African repression. As one Reagan official put it, unrest was a cyclical manifestation of "deep-seated black grievances against apartheid exacerbated by . . . heavy-handed repression of black protestors." Officials recognized that violence would remain until whites actually dismantled the cornerstones of apartheid.[67] The fragility of constructive engagement became even more apparent as black trade unionists—allegedly the major beneficiaries of Western economic investment—engaged in massive labor strikes and demanded sanctions. ANC-aligned unions led major stayaways like the Sarmcol strike in 1985 against British Tyre and Rubber and the National Union of Mineworkers' strike in 1987, which involved over 200,000 black workers and lasted weeks.[68] Cosatu, the umbrella union federation, adopted the ANC's Freedom Charter in 1987, firmly placing it in line with the prosanctions, mass democratic movement for South Africa.

Black political and social advocacy groups and congressional Democrats appeared ill content to wait on the Reagan administration to change its strategy toward South Africa and rallied against the antisanctions posture of the White House. On November 21, 1984, four Black leaders—TransAfrica president Walter Robinson, Congressman Walter Fauntroy, US Civil Rights Commission member Mary Frances Berry, and former chair of the Equal Employment Opportunity Commission Eleanor Holmes Norton—staged a sit-in at the South African consulate in Washington, DC, in protest of National Party crackdowns against black labor unionists. That crackdown included the arrest of the leadership of the Federation of South African Trade Unions and the Council of Unions of South Africa, representing over 300,000 unionists.[69] After their arrest and release, Robinson, Berry, and Fauntroy announced the formation of the Free South Africa Movement, initiating weekly national demonstrations at South African consulates, federal buildings, and US businesses linked to South Africa. The Free South Africa Movement, TransAfrica, and the Congressional Black Caucus began a direct action campaign in favor of economic sanctions.[70] In a letter to Reagan, the Congressional Black Caucus stated that constructive engagement has "contributed to a false sense of confidence on the part of Pretoria that it can give full rein to its most brutal impulses without risking serious censure by the U.S."[71]

By 1984, demands for a more active policy toward ending apartheid did not just come from Democrats. In a November letter from Senator Richard Lugar (R-IN), the incoming Senate Foreign Relations chair, and Senator Nancy Kassebaum (R-KS) to Reagan, Lugar and Kassebaum argued that US policy toward apartheid in South Africa was of "crucial long-term importance to the Republican party." Lugar and Kassebaum questioned the force of Reagan's condemnations of apartheid, with official policy statements "undermined by an insistence on defending the South African government or portraying its intentions as more benign than they are in reality." "The unwillingness of the State Department to attack the evils of apartheid and the violations of human rights in a straightforward, understandable manner," Lugar and Kassebaum concluded, undermined private efforts, especially in the context of the Vaal Uprising and the stalling of constructive engagement.[72] After this letter, Reagan officials began to liaison with Republican leadership—specifically Chair of the House Republican Conference Jack Kemp (R-NY), House Minority Leader Robert Michel (R-IL), and House Minority Whip Trent Lott (R-MS)—to organize briefings on constructive engagement and shore up centrist support. Crocker worried about Lugar pulling Congress apart, arguing it was "paramount" that the administration engage in public bargaining with "individuals or blocks from the Hill" that could unravel the southern Africa strategy.[73] The State Department needed to make sure it could continue to sell centrist Republicans on constructive engagement.

Lugar and Kassebaum's defections from the constructive engagement camp was a warning signal to apartheid's ardent partners. South Africa's defenders needed to retool their approach and pressure centrist right-wing politicians to hold the line, insisting that they—and any "reasonable" person—were against apartheid. The old racial system was on the way out. According to the South African Student Moderate Alliance, the University of Witwatersrand affiliate of the National Student Federation, the foundations for a new South Africa were "being well laid" by the ruling National Party, holding the line against a resurgence of neo-Nazism under the Conservative Party and other far-rightists.[74] The South African government's benevolence, in this telling, led to a massive expansion of workplace safety, land cultivation, infrastructure, and educational facilities for black South Africans.[75] Their sister organization at the University of Cape Town cheered the "peaceful evolutionary societal and political change" under the Tricameral Parliament while urging moderacy against "rapid reforms" like abolishing the Group Areas Act, the premise of separate development.[76] The National Party, and any reasonable conservative in this telling, saw apartheid as on the way out. International right-wing human rights groups validated the "reformist" impulses of the South African government. In 1986, the Peter Hammond–affiliated International Society for Human Rights highlighted the "process of reexamination" of apartheid under Botha and indicated that, in light of these genuine reforms, Western states must immediately terminate the "preposterous isolation" of South Africa.[77]

The "moral imperative"—in contrast to the antiapartheid movement's claims—was for the West to stay economically invested in South Africa.[78] In 1986, the International Freedom Foundation (IFF), which counted among its allies US congressmen Jesse Helms and Dan Burton and received over half of its 10 million rand budget from the South African military, published its take on the global call for sanctions.[79] The IFF decried the "sheer arrogance" of Western politicians in their support for sanctions, highlighting a rally of 90,000 black South Africans attending the launch of the Inkatha-led, antisanctions trade union, the United Workers' Union of South Africa.[80] Those clamoring for sanctions ignored that apartheid "is a dying institution; and that the free market mechanisms of commerce and industry are what is killing it." Two "fallacies" upheld the sanctions activism: that apartheid was a free market system and that economic decline provided the best means of ending apartheid. Instead, the IFF positioned the apartheid state as "racialism plus socialism" and uniquely vulnerable to a colorblind market. Sanctions would undermine reform, bringing massive unemployment at a key moment of accepted power-sharing and slow down economic deregulation that would lead to black entrepreneurship. The IFF concluded that those who were antiapartheid and antisanctions were the true supporters of black South Africans, explicitly evoking bantustan leadership: KwaZulu's Mangosuthu Buthelezi, Ciskei's Lennox Sebe, and Transkei's George Matanzima.[81] The IFF relied on questionable surveys that showed strong black opposition to sanctions, specifically the 1984 Schlemmer Report, which found that 75 percent of black workers opposed divestment.[82] The IFF argued that most South Africans were "in tune" with the reality of apartheid, committed to its eradication, and the best judges of what needed to be done to end it.[83] Only a vocal minority of black South Africans supported sanctions, the IFF concluded, with those in this camp more committed to the destruction of South Africa than apartheid's end.

The antiapartheid, antisanctions position would become the frame to beat back calls for sanctions. In an interview on a radio show in California in July 1985, a Conservative Caucus field director argued that a simplistic and one-dimensional focus on sanctions would not serve as a policy solution.[84] Conservatives needed to reframe the issue: apartheid's ethnic socialism is wrong, and its "most powerful enemy" was free enterprise.[85] The strategy should be to mobilize South Africa's friends at the grassroots, who could bolster antisanctions Republicans and pressure those waffling in their stance. Support for sanctions would be a vote against America and her allies.[86] In July 1985, Senator Malcolm Wallop (R-WY) perfectly articulated this paradigm in his remarks on the Senate floor, slamming economic sanctions as irresponsible and masquerading economic destruction under the guise of human rights.[87]

Perhaps the best example of someone with an establishment antisanctions view who sought to hold out against the calls for economic coercion was Shultz. Shultz was no fan of the apartheid state and had a contentious relationship with the apartheid bureaucrats, specifically Botha, who seemingly loathed Shultz. However, Shultz remained adamantly opposed to sanctions and would remain so throughout his tenure as secretary of state, embodying US conservative, corporate, and Black empowerment debates about the role of capital in apartheid's end. An experienced government operator, Shultz served in the Nixon administration as secretary of labor, director of the Office of Management and Budget, and secretary of the treasury. After leaving the Nixon administration, Shultz became executive vice president for the Bechtel Group, fully implementing his business credentials—a PhD in industrial economics from MIT and service on the Council of Economic Advisers. Shultz was a devoted free market capitalist who believed in the power of economic incentives to drive social change. Shultz shared his belief in economic empowerment as a tool of reform with other Republican congressmembers and American corporate executives. As the historian Jessica Levy argued, in the 1980s, America's multinational corporations rebranded themselves as "allies in the fight against apartheid," working with Black American and black South African businesspeople.[88] In comments before the Senate Foreign Relations Committee, Shultz argued that the South African government needed to reform and the American responsibility was to "ensure that expanded political liberties" were matched with economic opportunity for black South Africans. A rapid downward spiral of the South African economy would hurt "over a dozen states with some 150 million people." Shultz regularly highlighted that, since 1977, American businesses had spent over $200 million on black South African empowerment programs.[89]

These black empowerment programs were part of the US corporate-sponsored Sullivan Principles. More than 150 US companies committed to fighting apartheid on the inside through desegregation of workspaces, equal pay and employment opportunities, black training programs and management roles, and quality-of-life improvements for black South Africans outside of work.[90] Although black trade unionists "gained little from workplace and labor reforms," they utilized their "experience, skills, and political and social capital" to agitate for apartheid reforms beyond the vision proposed by corporate America or the apartheid government.[91] These union actions undertaken from 1984 until apartheid's end and the numbers the unions commanded stood in contrast to the Sullivan Principles, which came under constant criticism from antiapartheid activists.[92]

This emerging Republican critique of constructive engagement policy and potential conservative support for sanctions enraged antisanctions advocates. In *Washington Dateline*, Howard Phillips wrote that anti–South African sanctions would "do more to reduce *your* [American] economic and personal liberties" and release terrorists from prison.[93] South Africa's defenders accused Congress of being "fixed on the race issue as if no other existed," with Pretoria not being the "real enemy."[94] Pro-apartheid publications ran weekly stories highlighting black leaders who refused to endorse sanctions, accusing Republicans of "swallowing the Soviet bait and plumping for sanctions that strike at white Afrikaners."[95] In March 1985, the Conservative Caucus prepared material that attacked members of what it called the "Conservative Opportunity Society," men like Representatives Newt Gingrich (R-GA), Bob Walker (R-PA), and Vin Weber (R-MN). Their failing was that their openness to consider sanctions proved that they were political opportunists "on the verge of surrendering [Americans] civil rights, in an attempt to score public relations points with the media at the expense of the Republic of South Africa."[96] Any deviation from the antiapartheid, antisanctions position was met with strong criticism, with the Conservative Caucus targeting Republican congressmembers who expressed some willingness to put sanctions in place.[97] The policing of the Republican congressional contingent on sanctions reflected the reality that constructive engagement was losing momentum and that apartheid's defenders could not afford to increase Republican skepticism.

Even the Reagan administration could not escape criticism. Throughout 1984, *Human Events* accused the White House of "singling out a free world ally" and joining "the anti-South Africa brigade." *Human Events* editorials accused Reagan officials of abandoning Botha as the government began reform in earnest, which "smack[ed] more of a ploy to try and win the black vote than an attempt to lay down a strategic vision."[98] These critiques emerged as the Reagan administration spent the early months of 1985 trying to play all sides of constructive engagement by pushing the South Africans to reform, centrists to resist sanctions, and far-right-wingers to stick with the Reagan administration. In a report on Pretoria's plan to reform apartheid, officials argued that Botha's assurances broke little new ground. "Nearly all the positive positions are sufficiently caveated and occasionally contradictory that we would be foolish to embrace it simplistically as 'a solution' to the problem of apartheid," wrote one official.[99] In meetings with the Reagan administration, South African officials insisted the administration was "unduly pressuring South Africa to proceed at a faster pace of reform than it wished and trying to take credit for those reforms."[100] State Department intelligence highlighted Pretoria's determination to break the opposition.[101] The Pretorian response to protestors was arrest or detention of opposition leaders and stringent security force action with massive casualties. The under secretary of state for political affairs concluded that this continued crackdown would hurt the Reagan administration's ability to prevent sanctions.[102] Calling the limited reforms made by Botha "a dash of reform in the apartheid stew," NSC officials determined that the timing of these measures suggested "there [was] no coordinated strategy for reform."[103] Yet in a public statement on the apartheid state crackdown in March, the Reagan administration maintained that Pretoria was still pursuing a "genuine process of reform," trying to salvage the value of constructive engagement.[104]

Simultaneously, Reagan officials spent March catering to centrist and right-wing Republicans in Congress to try and hold the line against sanctions. Philip Ringdahl, director of the NSC African Affairs Directorate, arranged for two groups of conservative legislators to receive White House briefings on the status of southern African negotiations.[105] In the first group, Reagan officials invited right-wingers such as Senators Steve Symms (R-ID), Jesse Helms (R-NC), and Strom Thurmond (R-SC) and oriented the briefing around assuaging concerns about selling South Africa and the anticommunist UNITA downriver. In the second group, key fence-sitters like Mitch McConnell (R-KY), Frank Murkowski (R-AK), and Pete Domenici (R-NM) heard White House talking points around regional stability and the benefits of the Reagan-Botha relationship. Ringdahl prepared particular points for each group. In the meeting, National Security Advisor Bud McFarlane reinforced that Pretoria needed to control the pace and nature of the reforms or risk stiffening Afrikaner resistance.[106] Recognizing that the fence-sitting centrists remained more concerned about apartheid than regional relations and that Helms, Symms, and Thurmond's hostility to the State Department likely could not be improved, Reagan officials worried about the tangible gains from these meetings.[107] Swaying both right-wingers and centrists to stick with the Reagan administration's interpretation of constructive engagement proved a challenge.

This domestic criticism of constructive engagement could not have come at a worse time for the Reagan administration as reform efforts within South Africa stagnated and external violence by the apartheid state escalated. Significant white uncertainty over Botha's limited reforms translated into "hardening" at the polls in 1985, as the National Party narrowly avoided losing traditional strongholds in Johannesburg and Orange Free State to the Conservative Party.[108] This hardening at home led to aggressive military action abroad on June 14, 1985, when the SADF raided US-allied Botswana in search of ANC-in-exile base camps. Furious, Shultz stressed with Reagan the State Department's favorable relationship with President Quett Masire and Botswana, "one of Africa's rare democracies."[109] Shultz stated that this attack raised "serious questions" about Pretoria's behavior. In response, the Reagan administration recalled Ambassador Nickel in the hopes of sending a clear signal to the South Africans and cutting off growing congressional momentum against sanctions. South Africa's lobbyists bristled at Nickel's recall, calling it a "severe over-reaction" of antiterrorist action.[110] Privately, Ringdahl, McFarlane, and Nickel agreed that Pretoria seemed determined to project a forceful, aggressive regional policy free of US influence, refusing to acknowledge the Reagan administration's efforts on its behalf.[111]

The international antisanctions movement seriously stepped up its criticisms of the Reagan administration in 1985 in response to the Reagan administration's decision to recall Nickel over the SADF's raid, which the pro-apartheid movement saw as a valid defense against black terrorism. The National Student Federation put on an international "Youth for Freedom" conference during which the members discussed South Africa's military strength and attacked the stance of the Reagan administration. The *American Review*, the South African conservative publication written by Carl Nöffke, a longtime pen pal of William Rusher, titled its summer 1985 newsletter "The Reagan Doctrine: Getting Out Before Really Getting Hurt."[112] On the US side, *Citizens Informer* attacked the "naïve," so-called "conservative" Republican congressmen who took steps to punish the white-led nation of South Africa.[113] The most prominent target of these attacks was undoubtedly the Reagan State Department. At the Conservative Political Action Conference in March 1985, attendees booed Shultz and questioned why Reagan would "tolerate a State Department" that resists military assistance to South Africa.[114] *Human Events* produced a full-page advertisement titled "Why Is Chester Crocker Trying to Sell 20 Million Black Africans Into Communist Slavery," with Crocker depicted as a slave driver. Attacking Crocker's failure to combat "Soviet puppets" and accusing him of deploying a "Carter-style" foreign policy, the ad concluded, "please wake up [Mr. President], before it's too late, to what Shultz and Crocker are perpetrating in your name."[115] One fanatical white supremacist publication based in Britain stated that Reagan's policy of "constructive engagement" was just being used to give him a popular conservative image to mask a campaign against South Africa.[116]

Meanwhile, the Reagan administration hoped that an upcoming speech by Botha on his reform agenda for the apartheid state would silence domestic critics—centrist and right-wing Republicans alike. While the South African government reported ANC and Soviet infiltration into South Africa, the NSC privately reported on July 22, 1985, that it did not have any hard intelligence to show the Soviets' interference.

In the subsequent NSC meeting, CIA officials noted that Botha seemed determined to maintain order in South Africa at all costs. NSC officials argued that the situation was likely to "become even worse in the short-term."[117] In response, State Department and NSC officials undertook their most significant push to move the South Africans toward internal reform to stave off domestic critics, pegged to Botha's upcoming speech on constitutional development on August 15. In a meeting with Pik Botha on August 2, American officials relayed that the nondialogue between government and black leaders was the most pressing issue for the Reagan administration. Pik Botha insisted that Botha's statement "should be powerful enough to cool tempers in the U.S., especially in Congress, and in Europe."[118] McFarlane, Crocker, and Nickel met with Pik Botha in Vienna on August 7, a five-hour meeting that ran the gamut of internal and external reform possibilities. McFarlane reported that although all of the discussion was in very "general terms," Pik Botha offered a fundamental commitment to reverse the bantustan system, restore citizenship, and create a federal system.[119] Reagan officials pegged their hopes to the August 15 speech to show a genuine commitment to reform from the South African government.

The reaction to Botha's "Crossing the Rubicon" speech on August 15 proved nothing short of a disaster. In front of a crowd of 2,000 people, Botha chastised his domestic and international critics, attacked global media, and invoked the specter of Black communist destruction. Under pressure from the South African far right, Botha refused to release Mandela, integrate the bantustans, or credit US regional negotiation efforts. Botha's decision to end his speech stating, "I believe that we are today crossing the Rubicon. There can be no turning back," coined the speech in public memory—even more so given the statement's sharp contrast to a speech that seemingly closed off large avenues of apartheid reform.[120] Privately, Regan officials called Botha's speech "vague and evasive" and believed that black activists would undoubtedly view it as disappointing and without meaningful political implications.[121] American officials on the ground in South Africa concurred that the terms of the address were firmly grounded in continuing separate development: "They have yet to cross the Rubicon until they have done their part to build the confidence necessary to begin a dialogue," with Botha missing a golden opportunity to turn South Africa around.[122] The foreign reaction to the speech was highly critical, in particular by Europe and the Organization of African Unity.[123] Publicly, officials defended the speech as an important statement toward the end of apartheid.[124] However, Botha's ill-received speech could not have come at a worse time for the Reagan administration as it tried to prevent domestic sanctions passage. In the face of overwhelming questions about the efficacy of constructive engagement, the Reagan administration considered how to save the dying policy. Nickel contended that if they continued to recite the evidence of change, they "risk[ed] sounding like South African government propagandists."[125] In particular, Reagan's remarks reinforced the belief that he supported the apartheid state. South Africa's intransigence, McFarlane argued, called into question three key assumptions: South African willingness to reform, engage in regional peace talks, and heed the recommendations of the Reagan White House.[126] The entire premise of Reagan's South Africa policy came into question just as centrists and right-wingers lost faith in constructive engagement.

Ronald Reagan's policy of constructive engagement electrified white power actors in the United States and South Africa, motivating pro-apartheid networks to bolster the US and South African governments to collaborate on regional security. Throughout Reagan's first two years, mainstream conservative's fears of far-right power translated into success in regional negotiations in southern Africa and holding onto support from British and West German governments. However, conservative defections took place as Canada's and Australia's leadership questioned Pretoria's motivations as its intransigence grew. Despite the Reagan administration's best efforts to promote white security in its meetings with the Botha administration, constructive engagement atrophied, and Republicans at home questioned the efficacy of resisting sanctions. In response, the pro-apartheid movement took the constructive engagement case to the grassroots, arguing that one could simultaneously be antiapartheid and stand against sanctions. This antiapartheid, antisanctions position would be put to the test as the congressional battle over sanctions began in earnest in 1985.

4

WHITE WOMEN FOR APARTHEID

In 1990, Accuracy in Media (AIM), a conservative media outlet, released a short film titled *Winnie Mandela's Secret*, as part of their effort to push congressional Republicans to "hold the line" against calls for sanctions. An attractive, blonde South African woman, Cindy Leontsinis, utters the film's first words, stating, "ANC terrorism right now is focused on moderate blacks." She immediately transitions into her credentials for speaking on the issue of ANC terrorism: her work with the black community, "growing up in Zululand," teaching in black schools, and speaking several "black languages." According to Cindy, the ANC directed its terrorist attacks on black town mayors and councilors who would negotiate with the apartheid government. This terrorism—Cindy alleged—led to the ANC targeting the businesses and homes of black moderates and killing their children. In a graphic and false claim, Cindy stated that the ANC issued a decree that every town councilor must "have one child under the age of ten killed."[1] In the AIM film and in her advocacy, Cindy appeared alongside black town councilors and mayors describing intimidation to force resignations; black women who overheard ANC threats to burn homes, women, and children; and survivors of attempted necklace killings.[2] The AIM film concludes with spliced footage from Madikizela-Mandela answering questions about her statement that "we shall liberate with our necklaces." One of the final shots of the short film depicts Madikizela-Mandela laughing at the necklacing question, drawing a sharp contrast to the grave, protective Cindy, who appears alongside "actual victims" of ANC terror.

AIM released the film immediately after Madikizela-Mandela's bodyguards kidnapped four United Democratic Front (UDF) activists and killed one, fourteen-year-old Stompie Sepei, and dumped his body near Madikizela-Mandela's home. Madikizela-Mandela's chief bodyguard and law enforcement accused Madikizela-Mandela of involvement in the violent attack, sentencing her to six years in prison on kidnapping and accessory to assault charges.[3] Madikizela-Mandela proclaimed her innocence throughout her trial, claiming the charges were part of a larger pattern of sustained targeting by the apartheid state, which saw her jailed for 491 days in 1969 in Pretoria Central Prison and internally exiled from 1977 to 1985 in the Free State.[4] At a 1997 Truth and Reconciliation Commission hearing on the activities of the apartheid state, testifiers revealed that security forces had "disseminate[d] a 'veritable mass of disinformation' to local and international media to discredit the ANC and its leaders, in particular, Madikizela-Mandela."[5] These revelations of state targeting of Madikizela-Mandela, suspected at the time but validated only later, and the AIM film demonstrate the important role of white women in their efforts to undermine those who advocated for sanctions. Madikizela-Mandela, known as the "mother of the nation," cultivated a specific feminine but militant motherhood, "arguably more militant than any male ANC leaders."[6] But it was not just Madikizela-Mandela who cultivated this image; the ANC's magazine *Sechaba* published images of the "mother activist" carrying a spear or a gun and claiming her political power through this militant motherhood.[7] Attacking Madikizela-Mandela via her support for violent uprising against the apartheid state required a foil: white women—both South African and American—who testified to the horrors of the ANC and the evils of sanctions.

Throughout the 1980s, Cindy sat within a vast web of pro-apartheid organizations and intellectuals, building a case against sanctions that "reasonable" conservatives in the West could support while still calling themselves "antiapartheid." Cindy was not alone in her efforts to beat back the tide of sanctions. Leading the charge against "sanctions agitators" were American and South African white women, who played a fundamental role in building the antisanctions, antiapartheid case. Apartheid's end threatened white supremacist women in different ways. The pro-apartheid movement's female advocates provided critical fuel for the antisanctions, antiapartheid position by upholding their roles as defenders of womanhood, family, and faith. Women built a robust case for protecting the apartheid state, positioning themselves in the center of the movement. White women advocated in fundamentally different ways from the Peter Hammonds of the movement. They spread the "truth" about white rule, not through swashbuckling tales of heroism but through reporting on apartheid. Some women fulfilled traditional supporting roles within pro-apartheid organizing, arranging tours for high-status white supremacist men. Women used Christianity, age, patriotism, benevolence, and white saviorism to carve out a complex, multilayered case against sanctions. White women were not bit players in the pro-apartheid movement. They provided the logistical, intellectual, and political labor that challenged emerging centrist, conservative opposition to apartheid, fashioning an antisanctions, antiapartheid case that needed women to make it come alive as constructive engagement faltered.

These pro-apartheid women navigated the gendered expectations of women's activism within spaces of white supremacy and broader conservatism. In this, white women carried out conservative feminism by not threatening the white heteropatriarchal order but still carving out their own purview of expertise.[8] Pro-apartheid women acted as "centerwomen"—social network "keystones" providing and sustaining social energy, organization, and knowledge—by recognizing social need, interpersonal connections, and new ties.[9] As centerwomen, they positioned themselves as a hybrid of white women's "wife and mother" and "activist" roles in racist gender images. As wives and mothers, women in hate movements were responsible for education, "transmitting racial hatred and racial activism across generations," finding appropriate socialization for their families, and recruitment, all skills that were leveraged in pro-apartheid organizing.[10] In their activist roles, white women relied on "elusive, indirect, and personal" leadership to initiate direct and indirect action.[11] Through these roles, pro-apartheid women presented themselves as conduits of appropriate knowledge, directing those around them toward proper education about the perils of apartheid ending. In doing so, women "translated" support for white rule into tangible pro-apartheid priorities, such as preventing the passage of economic sanctions.[12] One woman, Aida Parker, built the most sophisticated media apparatus of the pro-apartheid movement, creating a "public square" of antisanctions advocacy for over twenty years. The pro-apartheid movement also relied on in-person, people-to-people connections to sustain its activism. Speaker series, coordinated by women, proved a critical node of pro-apartheid activism, with tours across the United States bringing South African testimonials for white rule into American homes, churches, and community groups. These women were political actors who leveraged gains from the global feminist movements they attacked to derail the anticolonial movements that threatened a social order with them at the helm.[13]

The stories of women supporting white power reveal key differences in the gendered dimensions of pro-apartheid activism, mapping onto larger historiographic insights about the distinct roles of men and women in white power spaces.[14] First, white women's pro-apartheid activism regarding sanctions, while similar to that of their male counterparts, leveraged women's identities as mothers, wives, teachers, and faith keepers in a far more personal way than their male counterparts. This positioned white women, in addition to black South Africans, as the potential victims of an economic boycott, thereby weaponizing white victimhood against the potential loss of white economic security via sanctions. That narrative of victimhood—and white women's weaponization of gender roles—also built a space for American women, who built a claim of harm on their own with the passage of economic sanctions, specifically through faith and motherhood. Second, the international dimension of the pro-apartheid movement provided an opportunity for women to take on "activist" roles internationally, which was especially critical for South African women.[15] These South African women—Aida Parker, Dorothea Scarborough, and Cindy Leontsinis—were not born in South Africa and were not Afrikaners. Their organizing seemed disconnected from Afrikaner women's organizations, despite the central role of women in Afrikaner nationalism throughout the twentieth century.[16] This disconnection shows that the pro-apartheid movement was not an exact fit with the Afrikaner nationalism that upheld apartheid. Rather, these women operated in a different part of the international ecosystem of white supremacy that focused specifically on whiteness in the Global North. White South African women used the freedoms they gained from operating in the Global North to uphold the militarization of South African society at home.

THE PRO-APARTHEID MOVEMENT'S CASSANDRA

Conservative white women became a critical part of pro-apartheid organizing in the 1980s in response to the growth of Black nationalist women's activism before World War II and leftist women's activism during the Cold War.[17] The 1949 Conference of the Women of Asia, the 1958 Asian-African Conference of Women, and the 1961 Afro-Asian Women's Conference marked a new beginning for women's anti-imperialist internationalism that "sought to restructure the economy as well as social relations and cultural and political practices to enfranchise all women."[18] South African women who worked against white rule operated within this landscape. For example, ANC women-in-exile combined anticolonial and feminist analyses to envision democracy and an end to white rule.[19] Multiracial organizations such as the Federation of South African Women, founded in 1954, navigated these global movements by proposing a "militant analysis of their everyday life . . . alongside a theory of motherhood that emphasized vulnerability and danger."[20] These women used an explicit invocation of motherhood to place black women at the center of anti-imperial activity, rejecting the apartheid rhetoric that positioned black mothers as "social problems."[21] Although they used different approaches, a multiracial segment of South African women participated in the international leftist struggle for equality.

Conservative women viewed this landscape of global leftist activism with suspicion, and they organized within it to try and build their case for the preservation of white rule. Their decision to work within the Global North conservative spaces reflected changes in South Africa's domestic political landscape. While the Conservative Party and its far-right allies grew as a major threat to the National Party after Botha came to power, reform of the apartheid state was a growing position among white South Africans. Although it was a piecemeal step toward apartheid's end, the 1983 Tricameral Parliament received 66 percent approval from white voters and the left-leaning, liberal Progressive Party. Even for South African whites who wanted to preserve their power, Botha's "adapt or die" strategy reflected the calculations that some changes to apartheid would be necessary to survive. Both the National Party and the Progressive Party cast themselves as "reformists" in the early 1980s, and the militant, pro-apartheid apologism of right-wing women saw limited appeal within white South Africa. Outside of South Africa, in Western countries led by conservative leaders with strong right-wing movements sympathetic to South Africa, these women could expand their reach and their influence both in concert with and in opposition to the state. In the wake of the Information Scandal, these men and women were useful pawns of the regime—be it through funding, access to information or resources, or sponsorship for trips abroad.

The reality of collaboration within the state does not deny their agency or intellectual thought, even as they marched in lockstep with the regime as it came under threat from sanctions. White women turned their attention out of South Africa and into the Global North specifically because of the real threat of economic divestment and what it meant to white security. Apartheid was never just a system of racial segregation—it was also a system of economic power that put English and Afrikaner whites atop the racial-capital hierarchy. Sanctions threatened white economic power in South Africa as the apartheid economy took a hit in the 1970s and early 1980s. From 1974 to 1987, South Africa's year-over-year growth in GDP dropped to 1.8 percent from 4.9 percent from 1964 to 1974. The drop in growth was especially concerning when foreign capital fled South Africa after the Soweto Uprising in 1976. From 1976 to 1980, foreign capital flowed out at a rate of 2.3 percent of the GDP per year.[22] The outflow of foreign capital upended the South African economy, which relied on external capital to offset internal deficits caused by the bloated apartheid bureaucracy as it struggled to stay afloat amid massive internal resistance.[23] Additionally, in the 1970s, the apartheid government shifted its "social spending from whites to blacks," as part of its broader relaxation of controls on African labor to right the sinking ship of separate development.[24] These changes did not result in desegregation in the labor force but rather reified segregation as whites remained in skilled labor roles and black South Africans remained relegated to semiskilled jobs.[25] For white South African women, these changes to the economics of apartheid were a unique threat.

The threat of sanctions required white women to intervene. In November 1984, the director of the Institute for American Studies at Rand Afrikaans University, Carl Nöffke, lamented to William Rusher that the "disinvestment issue" had assumed dangerous proportions. According to Nöffke, the effort to impose economic sanctions against South Africa was not only a political crisis but also a media one.[26] Nöffke was correct. Global public opinion had turned against South Africa by the mid-1980s in response to horrific media coverage of brutal repression by the apartheid state's forces. AIM reported that the US media, led by the *Washington Post* and the *New York Times*, targeted the South African government for demolition, running over 400 hit pieces against Pretoria. AIM concluded that this propaganda campaign "deliberately took pains not to report the views of the South African blacks who oppose sanctions and who detest and fear the ANC and the communists who run it."[27]

Women of the pro-apartheid movement answered AIM's call to change the narrative around the apartheid state. One publication, the *Aida Parker Newsletter* (*APN*), took on a central role in the pro-apartheid activism of the mid-1980s, with its sole editor, Parker, a prime example of the power of women within the movement. Parker acted as the pro-apartheid movement tastemaker, curating narratives of defense for white South Africa.[28] One of the most regularly produced newsletters among pro-apartheid publications, the *APN* acted as a focal point for rationalizing white rule. She reported on "anti–South Africa" activity across the West and southern Africa, bringing together a who's who of apartheid's defenders in her pages for nearly thirty years. Parker's newsletter was unique among the materials published by women writers of the pro-apartheid movement. Parker acted as spider sitting atop the pro-apartheid media web. She filled a traditional role played by women by creating a space for men's intellectual inquiry, weaving together publications from across the West and pulling in commentary from conservative writers across the Atlantic. But Parker was the dogged reporter—she possessed deep and persistent connections to the US and South African right wing. In the two-hundredth issue of *APN*, Parker's network is clearest: famous conservatives from around the globe sent effusive well-wishes to the *APN* commending its illustrious run. According to Mangosuthu Buthelezi, in the face of ANC atrocities, international condemnation of those who opposed sanctions, and media censorship, the *APN* alone stood for truth and justice.[29] Parker's admirers included grassroots well-wishers from Quebec, Monaco, Australia, Switzerland, Greece, and the United States. Her paper circulated among Reagan officials and congressional Republicans, and her pen pals included Howard Philips and SADF military intelligence head

Tiene Groenewald. She was on the scene for the formation of the black-white right-wing alliance against ANC negotiations with the apartheid state in 1992. Parker published an edition of the *APN* almost every month from 1983 until her death in 2003, offering a rare glimpse at how the pro-apartheid movement's antisanction defenses developed and evolved throughout the 1980s and 1990s.

Throughout the years, her magazine depicts the rise and fall of the pro-apartheid movement, its evolving relationship with various conservative politicians, and how white women worked against sanctions at a critical point—the lead up to the 1985 sanctions debates. Aida Parker was the storyteller of the apartheid state, using her publication to politically, ideologically, and socially unite personal, everyday experiences with "truth-telling" about the political realities of life under apartheid.[30] In the United States, women like Aida Parker engaged with a growing landscape of right-wing media like *Human Events* and the *National Review* to create their own media landscape that had a profound influence on local and national politics.[31] In South Africa, white women were the material and ideological backbone that held up the anticommunist militarization of South African society.[32] Parker's tight links with the SADF and her defense of the Total Onslaught strategy made her a key part of this defense with her activity focusing abroad on fighting back the call for sanctions.[33] Her international reach allowed her to become the "Cassandra" of the pro-apartheid movement, telling the truth of South Africa's doom if the West decided to pass economic sanctions.

According to Parker, the West completely misunderstood the intentions of the divestment campaign, which was really a tool of those engaged in the "total onslaught" against apartheid South Africa. Antiapartheid activists demanded the total isolation of South Africa and full-throated support for the terrorist ANC's destruction of South Africa. Parker used the pages of the *APN* to build a counterstrategy with three prongs to help centrist Republicans hold the antisanctions and antiapartheid line. First, Parker sought to expose the "true intentions" of the disinvestment movement in the United States as committed to the destruction of South Africa and married to radical communist forces across the globe. Second, Parker aimed at the ANC, devoting entire issues to exposés on the terroristic tactics of the organization and its leadership, in contrast to the reforming apartheid state. Finally, Parker worked at her third goal—preventing conservative defections to the sanctions camp—by providing cover for those skeptical of economic coercion. These three interlocking objectives worked to create a bulletproof narrative against sanctions. The stylish and professional *APN* was circulated to right-wing politicians across the West and was the media keystone connecting the US and South African factions of the pro-apartheid movement.

Although she rose to fame with the *APN*, Parker had long embedded herself in the defense of white rule and the skepticism of Western designs for the region. Born on October 24, 1918, in Atherstone, England, Parker got her start with the South African newspaper *The Star* before moving to the progovernment *The Citizen*.[34] Parker's most infamous reporting at *The Citizen* occurred in June 1977, when she published a two-week-long exposé on "The Secret U.S. War Against South Africa." Across ten parts, Parker laid out her case that the United States intended to "finish" South African whites, with Pretoria "No. 1 on the American liberal hit list," linking Black power to Adolf Hitler's *Mein Kampf*. These themes—conspiracy against South Africa's whites, US government complicity, and Black radicals—would dominate the *APN*. Parker's reporting raised her profile among US pro-apartheid actors. Donald McAlvany, trustee of Americans Concerned About South Africa, published Parker's exposé, describing her as the "female Robert Novak": level-headed, authoritative, and with contacts in all South African parties.[35]

In the aftermath of the Information Scandal—and the revelations about *The Citizen*'s funding from the South African government—the paper's trajectory and reputation shifted away from operating as Pretoria's mouthpiece.[36] Parker left the paper shortly after, reappearing in 1983 with a new project—the *APN*. She struck out on her own at sixty-seven years old, running the *APN* out of her home in Auckland Park, Johannesburg. Throughout the *APN*'s run, Parker bragged about her connections to National Party officials and regularly reported conversations she had with SADF military leadership, Pretoria's securocrats, and midlevel bureaucrats. She possessed close ties with Buthelezi and by extension Inkatha, but when and how that relationship developed remains unclear. Parker visited the United States several times and fostered connections with the conservative intelligencia, specifically with the Conservative Caucus and the International Freedom Foundation. According to one conspiracist and Nazi sympathizer, Parker hosted high-level National Party officials at her Auckland home, and rumors of her connections to National Party officials and SADF generals persist long after her death.[37] Parker was part of Botha's Total Onslaught strategy: according to the South African Truth and Reconciliation Commission, the *APN* was one of the secret projects funded by the SADF between 1978 and 1994, codenamed "Project Villa Marie."[38] Parker's support from the SADF could explain her connections to Buthelezi and Inkatha, which Pretoria also covertly funded.

A single picture of Parker appears in the *APN*—a drawn cartoon of an older, unassuming woman, hardly adorned with makeup or fashionable clothing. There is no record of Parker marrying and no mention of a husband or children. Parker presents herself as an untethered journalist, doggedly focused on exposing South Africa's enemies—nothing more. She does not—in contrast with her counterparts—mask or temper her activism behind a husband. Parker portrayed herself as a lone crusader, with the *APN* as a "citizen's report" speaking bravely from the front lines of the ANC–South African Communist Party–Soviet Union triple alliance. For 89 rand, subscribers would receive twenty-five issues of the *APN* over twelve months, with special rates for seniors, students, and security forces.[39] According to Parker's private correspondence, it cost her almost 365,000 rand annually to run the *APN*, facing almost constant funding challenges.[40] Yet Parker was not without foreign support. She financed the *APN* through generous gifts from Transvaal families, American sympathizers, family trusts in Windhoek, and friends across Cape Town, Stellenbosch, Durban, Johannesburg, Ramsgate, and Natal. Gifts ranged from 10 to 5,000 rand.[41] Parker even found some well-backed American partners. The International Freedom Foundation jointly funded a 1986 *APN* special issue that targeted the ANC, curated for distribution on Capitol Hill and landing amid the congressional debate over passing economic sanctions. Parker fashioned the *APN* as a combination of an intelligence report and a provocateur magazine. Dossiers on "enemies" like Joe Slovo, general secretary of the South African Communist Party, sat side by side with inflammatory headlines like "ANC: 'Freedom Fighters' or Soviet Puppets?" Parker explicitly modeled her efforts after "U.S. groups such as Young Americans for Freedom," the powerful right-wing, grassroots youth organization founded in 1960, creating media to distribute to churches, universities, and speakers.[42]

Parker possessed a unique talent: weaving together far-right writers with distinctly centrist conservative and even neoliberal perspectives against sanctions to create a publication viable for distribution at both the grassroots and national levels. The *APN* included cartoons and reporting from the *Chicago Tribune, Human Events, National Review*, and even the *New York Times* and *Washington Post.*[43] Although based in South Africa, the *APN* relied on US conservative writers, intellectuals, and activists to boost pro-apartheid arguments, and the relationship went both ways—publications like *Conservative Review* commissioned Parker.[44]

Aida Parker and her magazine were a bridge between "real" South Africans and the persuadable American, layering together conservative intellectuals with on-the-ground dispatches. Parker counted some of the most influential figures in the conservative movement among her devotees, such as the conservative writer and member of the John Birch Society Larry Abraham, who called her the "most well-informed and courageous lady I have ever met."[45] On February 15, 1983, Howard Phillips, chairman of the Conservative Caucus, met with Parker in Johannesburg, receiving briefings on politics, communist activity, and the perils of disinvestment.[46] Phillips would meet with Parker on multiple other occasions.[47] Reporting from the *APN* appeared in the Conservative Caucus's monthly magazine *Conservative Manifesto*, and Parker and Phillips—whom she called "Howie"—exchanged writings and speeches. During a visit to the United States in April 1990, Parker met with many influential conservative titans, including Senator Jesse Helms's (R-NC) strategists, American Enterprise Institute and Heritage Foundation analysts, AIM reporters, and George H. W. Bush State Department officials.[48] Throughout the 1980s, Parker's newsletter appeared in the files of conservative intellectuals like William Rusher and Reagan administration officials like Phil Nicolaides and Pat Buchanan.[49] The relationship with Phillips went both ways. Parker reprinted Howard Phillips's 1986 *Issues and Strategy Bulletin* in one *APN* issue attacking Republicans for their growing support for sanctions. Until September 1986, Phillips decried, every prospective candidate for the 1988 Republican presidential nominee went on record against sanctions. If the Senate wanted to be "in step with the party's future," Phillips argued, they ought to support the stance of the Reagan administration and reject economic measures against South Africa.[50] Through Phillips, *Human Events*, and other conservative publications, Parker attacked

Reagan administration "conservatives" as leading the Western stampede toward the ANC.[51] Parker lamented that every conceivable effort was underway by the so-called right wing to rehabilitate the ANC. The *APN* positioned itself as a mouthpiece of the "true" conservative intelligentsia, while Parker positioned herself as an expert outsider on the failings of the US conservative movement to fight back against sanctions.

To Parker and her readers, US and South African antiapartheid activists possessed conspiratorial designs on white South Africans, part of a grand Soviet plot that was not really about apartheid atrocities but instead the imposition of communism through sanctions. Parker claimed access to vast networks of informants reporting on the "true" motives of antiapartheid activists, with a November 1986 issue of the *APN* including a list of those advocating the "demise" of the West. The hodgepodge list included solidarity movements, trade unions, student organizations, churches, heads of state, diplomatic missions, NGOs, and political parties that favored economic sanctions. All of these organizations, Parker insisted, demand that South Africa "negotiate" with the ANC, which "in fact meant surrender."[52] Parker and her associates worked to delegitimize organizing for sanctions as secretly the work of the Soviet Union.

Parker remained relentless, denigrating Black American antiapartheid activists as puppets of international forces, specifically TransAfrica founder Randall Robinson, whom the *APN* called the "ANC's foreign agent in the US."[53] In 1977, Robinson, a civil rights attorney who worked on the staffs of Representatives William "Bill" Clay Sr. (D-MO) and Charles Diggs Jr. (D-MI), founded the TransAfrica Forum in Soweto's aftermath, spurred on by the "intensification of the struggle in Rhodesia, Namibia, and South Africa." Robinson cut his teeth in antiapartheid activism on college campuses, joining a six-day occupation in 1972 of the Harvard president's office to demand divestment. In 1984, TransAfrica launched its direct-action campaign to push Congress to pass economic sanctions. The organization's tactics included the millions-strong prodivestment signature campaign, the "Faces Behind Apartheid" operation that targeted Senators Bob Dole and Jesse Helms for their antisanctions stances, and the organization of thousands from Black middle-class, religious, and political communities.[54] Parker included a six-page spread focusing on Robinson and his "sinister, hidden agenda" of subversion against white South Africans in her "Special ANC Issue." It should be clear to anyone reviewing TransAfrica's record, Parker wrote, that "its concern at the present time is not 'racism' in South Africa but the promotion of radical revolution."[55] Citing reporting from *Human Events*, Parker lamented that Robinson posed a singular threat to Reagan's foreign policy ignored by conservatives.[56] In a continuation of the pro-apartheid strategy, Parker insisted that Robinson did not speak for Black Americans but instead "bamboozled" them with extremism and ignored the "thousands" of Africans fighting to immigrate to a nation "free" of Marxism.[57] Attacking Robinson accomplished two goals for the pro-apartheid movement—denigrating opposition to the apartheid state and insisting that Black activists were inauthentic representatives of South Africa.

The *APN* not only sought to build a case against the ANC but also to build support for the South African government, contrasting the "lies" of antiapartheid activists against the "realities" of quality of life improvements for black South Africans. Thus, Parker and her allies aimed to convince fence-sitting conservatives that radical change was hardly necessary. According to Parker, the regional implications of Washington's "vengeful anti-South African sanctions package" could not be understated. Southern Africa's Frontline States would see sanctions as providing "carte blanche" support of any anti–South Africa actions.[58] Parker mirrored her benefactors' rhetoric: she deployed the Total Onslaught language of the Botha administration, conjuring images of a South Africa surrounded on all sides by vengeful Black communist dictatorships. The actual liberation struggle in southern Africa, the *APN* argued, was freedom from Marxist dictatorship and those who did not want to turn over South Africa to the ANC. Parker remained focused on the ANC, unpacking the effort to "clean up the ANC's image, scrub away its Communist label . . . [and] minimize or even obliterate its frightful record of terrorist violence."[59] She reproduced dozens of articles from the South African Communist Party and *Sechaba*, the ANC's official organ, to illuminate the "many-faceted links" between the ANC and world communist movements.[60] She paired this with a dossier on the "realities" of life in communist-authoritarian southern Africa, which suffered from economic destruction, poverty, civil war, religious repression, and mass killing. In contrast, she highlighted the "freedoms" in South Africa, touting language and ethnic diversity, high enrollment and literacy rates for black children, mineral production, the viability of the bantustans, and South Africa's high quality of life. Parker noted that some changes to apartheid would be necessary, as the National Party committed "the horrendous error of placing the name 'apartheid' on legislation to maintain a divided society."[61] However, she insisted that South Africa should be left alone to solve its racial sins as the nation struggled to manage a level of diversity without parallel. Parker constructed a twofold alternative reality: one where southern Africa's situation demanded total discrediting of the ANC and where the apartheid state—in the process of reforming—should remain untouched by Western sanctions.

For some of her most racially denigrating pieces on black South Africans, Parker also relied on writers who were not South African to make the case for her. It was not just Parker and other white South Africans like her who questioned black South Africans' political and social competency. It was also "neutral" observers—US conservatives simply reporting the "facts"—who questioned black leadership. For instance, Parker excerpted an article titled "American Ignorance: Criminal Neglect?" As the author saw it, white Americans erroneously believed South Africa had a "natural majority of Blacks"—in truth, "pigment" could not overcome destabilizing black tribal politics. Playing into racist tropes of Black disobedience, the writer insisted that black youths in South Africa were out of control, with township streets controlled by "a generation of pubescent Pol Pots." It was an "insane assumption," the article contended, that "black supremacy" would lead to anything but "a boredom with constitutional government and due process, [and] tolerance for body-burning and genocide."[62] These horrifying comments defended white rule and bolstered Parker's message, without her having to make them. The racist tropes did not just come from women like Parker; they also came from the South African government, which openly stated that they could not negotiate with the ANC due to its commitment to armed struggle and covertly circulated reports on necklacing and "black-on-black" violence. Through publications like *APN* and its US partners, a cross-section of conservative writers used overtly racist questioning to challenge black South Africans' "fitness" for governance, citing the very rebellion fueled by the South African government in the townships.

Throughout her pro-apartheid activism, Parker tapped into a discontented populism within the global right, which Nicole Hemmer argued "turn[ed] toward nativism and a more overt racism," "criticism of conservative elites," "wariness about free trade and democracy," and "sharp-elbowed, fact-lite punditry."[63] This discontented populism manifested in the *APN*'s inclusion of writers with a less respectable veneer like John Birchers and Holocaust deniers.[64] Yet Parker's use of extremist and conspiratorial writers remained somewhat limited throughout the mid-1980s, especially in contrast to her postapartheid publications. During the sanctions debates, she actively sought to persuade centrist conservatives of the necessity of working against sanctions, creating a world in which the antisanctions position could remain sustainable for right-wingers of all stripes.

Throughout its existence, the *APN* served as a marketplace of ideas on defending the apartheid state amid the tribulations of the sanctions debates. By denigrating the ANC and curtailing Republican defections to the divestment camp, the pages of the *APN* defended white rule in South Africa. Parker's newsletter offers a window into the antisanction defenses in the mid-1980s as she positioned herself as both an essential tastemaker and truthteller in the pro-apartheid movement. She occupied a unique position within the milieu of pro-apartheid activism. Although she relied on men throughout the *APN*'s run, she served as the *APN*'s sole arbiter, occupying a rare space as an intellectual—with a public role—within white supremacist spaces. Parker proved inspirational to other women; she was cited and read by white women throughout the United States and South Africa, who invoked her advocacy as they began their own. Parker's work had limits, however—she was only the dogged journalist. Others filled out the organizing space opened up by Parker, invoking faith and motherhood to influence the antisanctions debates.

FAITH AND MOTHERHOOD IN GLOBAL ANTISANCTIONS ORGANIZING

In their correspondence and writings, white women working against sanctions used a language of motherhood that questioned the true intentions of the divestment movement vis-à-vis black South Africans. Even if not explicitly leveraging motherhood, white women positioned themselves as the ones who truly cared for black South Africans rather than the "communist terrorists" of the ANC. Their presentation relied on cultivating an air of benevolence that nevertheless remained "predicated upon their position as [one] . . . who possessed the right and power to control."[65] White women positioned themselves as the defenders of black South Africans, weaponizing a rhetoric of "good" or "real" motherhood to discredit black people and to position themselves as true authorities on black experiences.[66]

Cindy Leontsinis of Victims Against Terrorism claimed the spotlight of white motherhood. Although the organization listed Cindy's husband as chairman, United Christian Action, which counted Victims Against Terrorism as one of its member organizations, listed Cindy as the woman in charge. According to Howard Phillips, Cindy and her husband John immigrated to South Africa from Chile to escape "Cuban Communist influence" in the early 1970s.[67] Cindy leveraged her tremendous personality to develop a multiprong activist structure to educate "all South Africans" about the threat of ANC terrorism. Her activism gained traction with US conservative organizations like the Conservative Caucus, the Moral Majority, and the John Birch Society, which supported her accusations against the ANC.[68] She allegedly "enjoyed semi-official propagandist status within the Defense Force [through her] imaginary depiction of an effacing and compliant black society through the use of [black town councilor] puppets."[69] Cindy remains a mysterious figure. Rumors persist that the Leontsinis duo—through their South African security force connections—knew the identity of the assassin who killed Prime Minister Olof Palme of Sweden in 1986, who was allegedly murdered because of his criticism of the apartheid state.[70]

Throughout the 1980s, Cindy positioned herself as a truthteller on the atrocities of the ANC, maintaining that she alone possessed connections with "real" black South Africans who faced the horrors of communism, not apartheid. Cindy leveraged her status as a white "mother figure," insisting that her experiences working as a teacher in the townships uniquely qualified her to comment on the politics of the ANC. She situated herself as an advocate of the "black moderate" who "refused to comply" with the ANC's mandate to be the "sole negotiator" for black South Africans.[71] Cindy was a centerwoman: in her travels throughout Europe and the United States, she appeared with black South African targets of the ANC. Specifically, she worked with a group of black town councilors put into office by the apartheid government as part of the 1982 reforms. They reported their homes firebombed, their children threatened, and their friends murdered by the ANC.[72] Cindy became the nexus point for American conservatives looking for evidence that the ANC was the true terrorist force, using her organization to connect them to the ANC's black South African victims.

Victims Against Terrorism liaised with Western institutions, sharing the effort to undermine South Africa at home and abroad. Cindy held over five hundred seminars, workshops, and lectures on Soviet subversion in southern Africa as part of her "Know Your Enemy" courses.[73] Victims Against Terrorism described their specialization as overseas journeys to "opinion informers" in Britain, France, West Germany, and the United States, conducting radio and television interviews. An organizational brochure included a cartoon of Cindy lecturing an attentive audience about ANC attacks, sanctions terrorism, and psychological and religious warfare. From 1985 to 1987, Cindy crisscrossed the West, agitating against sanctions. She met with Malcolm Rifkind, UK secretary of state for foreign and commonwealth affairs; picketed the Canadian embassy over "Prime Minister Mulroney's advocating and helping terrorism"; and staged protests outside the headquarters of US antiapartheid organization TransAfrica.[74] Where Cindy received her funding for this effort remains unclear, but Victims Against Terrorism allegedly received financial support from the South African Ministry of Foreign Affairs for a significant part of its existence.[75] Whether in her "Know Your Enemy" workshops or in meetings with foreign dignitaries, Cindy positioned herself as an advocate and expert on ANC terrorism that desperately wanted sanctions.

Cindy connected with Phillips and the Conservative Caucus in May 1985. US right-wing organizations like the Conservative Caucus amplified pro-apartheid narratives around black-on-black violence, portraying the ANC as the sole instigator of violence in South Africa. The black-on-black violence narrative took on even greater importance after 1985. As regional civil war broke out in KwaZulu-Natal, global conservatives adopted the narrative of Zulu-ethnic nationalism versus the "Xhosa ANC" to denigrate antiapartheid advocacy.[76] The antisanctions positioning of Inkatha leader Buthelezi was an additional boon to denigrate calls for divestment. But US antisanctions advocates needed South Africans to build their case. In 1985, Cindy's husband wrote an introductory letter to Phillips, stating that he did so "at the suggestion of Aida Parker."[77] Victims Against Terrorism hoped to travel to the United States that year to "cement old friendships and make new ones," spreading the news of black communist organizing in South Africa. After Phillips reviewed some of the materials from Victims Against Terrorism, he hosted the eleven-person delegation as part of the Conservative Caucus's South Africa Project, which he described as a "private interracial group . . . targeted for assassination by Marxist-Leninist forces associated with the ANC."[78] On this trip, Cindy and her group of former black mayors and victims of ANC terrorism appeared as special guests on Jerry Falwell's televised worship service in Lynchburg, Virginia, on May 26, 1985. After an evening meeting with Falwell and Dr. Ron Godwin, executive vice president of Moral Majority, the group appeared on Falwell's *Old-Time Gospel Hour*, which was broadcast on four hundred stations. During the broadcast, Victims Against Terrorism and Phillips railed against disinvestment as a tactic to undermine the reformist apartheid state and support communism. In addition, Phillips and three black representatives of Victims Against Terrorism, Mayor Tamsanqa Linda, Mrs. Joyce Kinkini, and Pastor Ndabezinhle Musa, appeared on *Jerry Falwell Live*, a weekly television program that reached 36 million people. On the program, Phillips and the Victims Against Terrorism representatives emphasized that "while each of us seeks a colorblind society . . . there are issues in addition to apartheid. Communism is a greater evil."[79] By the end of the program, viewers participating in a phone-in survey reported opposition to sanctions by a four-to-one margin.

Throughout the trip, Cindy and her partners met with conservative elites, including National Security African Affairs Directorate specialist Philip Ringdal, Director of Communications Pat Buchanan, Heritage Foundation leaders, and media representatives from *Human Events*, *Washington Times*, and *Nightline*.[80] Perhaps most importantly, Cindy's group met with key strategists of the antisanctions effort in Congress, including Bonnie Borrie of the American Legislative Exchange Council, Paul Weyrich of the Free Congress PAC, and various congressmembers.[81] They rounded out their tour by appearing at the farewell party for the South African ambassador to the United States. Undoubtedly, Cindy made an impression on Phillips, and the two remained in touch.[82] During Phillips's coordination of antisanctions lobbying, he advocated organizing US tours for Victims Against Terrorism, who can "sound the alarm" against the ANC's violence.[83] Phillips highlighted Cindy's status as organizing "moderate blacks" and acting as a foil to the ANC, the centerwoman of a pro-apartheid network only accessible through her.

Women "sounding the alarm" against ANC terrorists emboldened by sanctions included Americans, who wrote to Reagan directly, invoking their status as white women who knew best what black South Africans needed. Throughout the mid-1980s, dozens of women wrote to the Reagan administration to express their opposition to sanctions, many deploying the popular refrain that sanctions would "hurt the very people we seek to help." As Elsa Sandstrom, a longtime friend of Reagan and member of the Federation of Republican Women, put it in July 1985: "Divestiture, as demanded by protesters in this country, would hurt, rather than help."[84] Dr. Vera Von Wiren-Garczynski took a similar tone, writing to Reagan that as an educator of almost twenty-five years with "over half of her students Black," she dealt with "racial education problems." After going on a fact-finding mission to South Africa and meeting with the National Party, she remained convinced that "hostility and sanctions would only hurt the people we are trying to help."[85] Leslie C. Dutton, president and executive director of the American Association of Women, informed Reagan that they did not "intend to sit by on the sidelines while the retirement incomes of American widows are being jeopardized by politicians playing Russian Roulette by imposing sanctions on South Africa."[86] White women also leveraged their platforms to position themselves as the "real" arbiters of black South African suffering. Mary Lee Cake, publisher of the *Bedford Bulletin*, wrote an editorial decrying how "young Blacks get caught in the suicidal trap" of guerrilla propaganda, unaware of what awaited them with an ANC victory.[87] Some women took an even more dramatic stand. Margaret G. Harper, a member of the Republican Presidential Task Force, Senatorial, and National Committees, argued that by empowering the ANC through sanctions, certain destruction awaited South Africa: "all we need to do is look to the black governed nations . . . to see the obliteration of civil rights."[88] Diane Jacobs, vice president of the California Republican Assembly, urged Reagan to hold the line, as she cautioned against sanctions as a tool for freedom.[89] Sanctions, these women argued, would not solve apartheid, invoking a kind of surrogate motherhood in their positioning of fragile black South Africans in contrast to threatening antiapartheid actors who menaced the stability provided by white rule.

The question of stability under apartheid rule and the threat posed to that stability by sanctions also activated Christian sentiments. In South Africa, white women, specifically Afrikaner women, had a particular cultural role as "spiritual soldiers," positioned as the defenders of white Christianity within the home against the black communist threat.[90] Dorothea Scarborough of the Gospel Defense League exemplified efforts to use Christianity to work against sanctions that threatened the heart of the apartheid project. Born on February 14, 1936, in Lübeck, Germany, she married her husband Charles in 1958 before moving to Cape Town. Like Cindy's Victims Against Terrorism, Dorothea's husband was the front for what was likely her operation. Dorothea wrote the Gospel Defense League's monthly newsletter, which targeted North America, and the German-language *Vox Africana*: her readership was over 18,000 and some publications reached over 100,000 prints.[91] In her publications, Dorothea declared her indebtedness to Parker for inspiring her work and providing material for her newsletters. Dorthea was not without her own shadowy symbiosis with the apartheid state. The South African Broadcasting Corporation, the Pretoria-controlled media apparatus, used the Gospel Defense League's programming to critique Bishop Tutu's prodivestment position.[92] Throughout the 1980s, Dorothea advocated to her readers that it was not apartheid that led to the call for sanctions but the spirit of hatred in the church and the erosion of Christianity, family values, and love.

In Dorothea's criticism of the "politics of sanctions," she mirrored the arguments of the wider pro-apartheid movement that tried to denigrate the ANC by targeting black antiapartheid theologians. To the Gospel Defense League, South Africa's liberation theologists, principally Tutu, caused "inestimable suffering to the Blacks" by advocating for sanctions and supporting "radical Blacks," who kill "moderate . . . courageous Black pioneers."[93] In August 1985, Dorothea argued that investment and divestment had become moral and religious issues, with Tutu and Beyers Naudé—whom Dorothea derogatorily called the "Political Preachers"—advocating the use of hunger and deprivation to foment suffering among black South Africans.[94] Quoting an unnamed "Black theologian" in another newsletter, Dorothea charged that the South African Council of Churches "posed as martyrs overseas . . . interpreting Black suffering to the world [and] . . . making decisions from above."[95] South Africa's "Political Preachers" were "false prophets," Dorothea asserted, taking bribes abroad even as they advocated sanctions. These attacks were part of a pattern of violence directed against black antiapartheid theologians by apartheid state security and its surrogates.[96]

Dorothea tried to redraw the lines around acceptable Christian discourse upended by the antiapartheid Kairos theologians who demanded changes to the apartheid theology that dominated South Africa. She stripped down Christianity to simply a love of Jesus, with "true" black and white South Africans standing together in peaceful submission to God—and the apartheid state. This "murderous talk," Dorothea accused, meant that black South Africans would suffer under sanctions, and she reported that over 2,000 of her readers signed a petition rejecting Kairos divestment. As a theological justification, Dorothea cited Sirach 34:21–22: "the bread of the needy is the life of the poor; whoever deprives them of it is a man of blood. To take away a neighbor's living is to murder him; to deprive an employee of his wages is to shed blood."[97] "Invest! Invest! Invest!" Dorothea relayed from her contact with Buthelezi, Lucas Mangope, and other black conservatives. The Gospel Defense League declared that the divestment campaign waged "unabated" economic war on black South Africans and had a second, "more sinister aim" to destroy South Africa's free market system in favor of a communist economic order. Dorothea questioned why the church was seeking to "deny food to the hungry." "What justification [is there] to become economic assassins in the name of God?"[98] South Africa's sanctions agitators needed to focus on the "Bread of Life" rather than listening to an imported Black power theology from the United States.[99] For Dorothea, the "facts" remained unprinted: South Africa's "side"—"medical treatment, education, housing, and low taxes for Blacks"—was ignored by black theologians. Dorothea's readers needed to stand on Jesus's side—the side of reality—with Dorothea calling for her disciples "to not be discouraged by all the violations of the truth, but to stand against it boldly."[100] She drew a line between supporters of sanctions and Christians: "I . . . have not met one Christian who supports divestment. Those who do are not Christians. They are ignorant of the love of Christ and care nothing for their neighbor."[101] In this effort, she spoke not only to white South Africans but also to conservatives across the West as she weaved Christianity into the political question of sanctions.

Other Christians took Dorothea's writings and put them into action in their work against sanctions, specifically two American women, Mary

Ann Gilbert and Anne Shipps. In newsletters, Hammond of Frontline Fellowship specifically named Gilbert, leader of Intercessors for the Suffering Church in Indiana, and Shipps, leader of Unto the Least of These in Texas, as partners in his American lobbying efforts.[102] Beginning in 1982, Gilbert and Shipps coordinated mailing lists, solicited and wrote publications, and sponsored pro-apartheid actors' tours in the United States. Shipps stated that she was "not, ordinarily, too interested in politics . . . but in this case, thinking of all our dear friends in [South Africa] . . . I decided at least to lift my voice in protest."[103] Shipps became connected to the pro-apartheid movement in May 1984 when she invited Arthur Lewis, the pro-Rhodesia pastor, to speak at an interchurch meeting at Hope Chapel in Austin, Texas. At the meeting, Lewis discussed the plight of white Rhodesians and the region's "Marxist takeover."[104] After Lewis's trip, Shipps connected with Hammond and became embedded in the pro-apartheid movement's ephemera network. Gilbert also wrote to Hammond, expressing her fascination with Frontline Fellowship and willingness to awaken the midwestern United States to how sanctions would influence the spiritual battle in southern Africa. Shipps, Gilbert, and Hammond began a monthly correspondence. During the course of their work, Gilbert and Shipps became regular readers of the *APN*—even if they found the tone "a bit harsh"—Inkatha's *Clarion Call*, and the publications of Dorothea's Gospel Defense League and Cindy's Victims Against Terrorism. As the two women became immersed in pro-apartheid organizing, they privately joked that they hoped for a mention in the next edition of Paul Gifford's *The Religious Right in Southern Africa*, which unfavorably documented Hammond's activities.[105]

The "awakening" of Gilbert and Shipps regarding South Africa translated into tangible action and culminated in organizing a multimonth cross-country tour for Hammond in the United States in 1988, leveraging connections with the John Birch Society and the Conservative Caucus. As a result of the advocacy of Gilbert and Shipps, Hammond traveled the country, visiting Virginia, Florida, Texas, Iowa, Washington, DC, and Pennsylvania. He spoke at the National Religious Broadcasters Conference and the Conservative Political Action Conference and conducted interviews with God's News Behind the News, USA Radio Network, Good News Communication, and the In Defense of Liberty Network, among others.[106] Hammond bragged about visiting Congress and conducting "over a hundred and fifty" meetings with pastors, editors, journalists, and military leaders, along with high-profile meetings with the Heritage Foundation, Conservative Caucus, and International Freedom Foundation. Hammond concluded his subscriber letter with hundreds of testimonials of people thanking him for helping them understand the critical position of South Africa. "It was especially moving for me," Hammond concluded, "to see the support of so many Americans for South Africa."[107] The activities of Cindy Leontsinis, Dorothea Scarborough, Mary Ann Gilbert, and Anne Shipps were essential to the pro-apartheid movement's operations in the lead-up to sanctions.

In their efforts to prevent the passage of economic sanctions against the apartheid state, white women took on various roles. South African women like Aida Parker, Dorothea Scarborough, and Cindy Leontsinis provided the intellectual and spiritual arguments against sanctions, making them an indispensable part of the pro-apartheid machine. US women like Anne Shipps and Mary Ann Gilbert curated spaces for pro-apartheid activism to flourish, even as everyday white women wrote to Reagan singing the praises of apartheid rule. As the US congressional-presidential sanctions debate raged on, the pro-apartheid movement became increasingly concerned about the commitment of mainstream conservative parties across the West to defend apartheid. White women were critical organizers of white supremacist actors, who found themselves increasingly excluded from the mainstream Republican Party in 1986. It was the advocacy of these women that brought the antiapartheid, antisanctions position to life throughout the 1980s, as the pro-apartheid movement pushed centrist right-wingers to hold the line against economic coercion. White women's defense of apartheid, which weaponized white benevolence to refashion black South African suffering as emerging not from white rule but from ANC radicalism, became a central pillar of pro-apartheid organizing.

5

BREAKING WITH THE REPUBLICAN PARTY

On February 6, 1985, Pat Buchanan returned to the White House. His last stint saw him serving as an assistant and speechwriter for President Richard Nixon and Vice President Spiro Agnew, and Buchanan's loyalty endeared him to the president during the Watergate scandal. In the last days of Watergate, White House Chief of Staff Alexander Haig offered Buchanan the position of ambassador to South Africa. Buchanan, who had been studying South Africa and writing editorials for the *St. Louis Globe-Democrat* favorable to the apartheid state, promptly agreed, and President Gerald Ford signed off on the post.[1] When news of the appointment reached the press, the diplomatic corps reacted with horror. Ford rescinded the nomination, pushing Buchanan and other Nixon loyalists out of the White House. Buchanan returned in 1985 as the White House communications director, ready to shake up what he saw as a stagnating Reagan administration.

Buchanan's entrance into the Reagan White House in 1985 was a turning point for the administration. Besieged by calls from hardline Republicans that the administration no longer represented real conservative interests, the White House sought to try and win back the base in 1985 and 1986.[2] Part of a great internal shuffle in the White House that saw White House Chief of Staff James Baker swap positions with Secretary of the Treasury Don Regan, Buchanan's hiring appealed to right-wingers. Buchanan, Regan, and others would be true vanguards of conservatism within the White House and push back on weak, centrist policies. In Buchanan's eyes, those weak, centrist policies also included the floundering of constructive engagement. As the White House struggled to fend off sanctions, Buchanan was the conduit of pro-apartheid efforts to mobilize within the Reagan administration, convinced of a right-wing conspiracy to destroy white rule. Buchanan's activism within the pro-apartheid movement was the high-water mark of their infiltration within the Reagan White House and influence in the Republican Party. His activities represented a culmination of almost a decade's worth of organizing by the pro-apartheid movement to gain power within Western conservative movements at one of the highest points of urgency for Pretoria. Buchanan's activism also reveals the limitations of the pro-apartheid movement's vision, which became apparent after the passage of sanctions over Reagan's veto.

As constructive engagement floundered at home and abroad, white power actors worried over the perceived weakened commitment by the Reagan administration to the apartheid state just as Congress was seriously considering passing economic sanctions. As the fight against sanctions continued in the mid-1980s and the apartheid state's abuses continued, centrist Republicans increasingly found constructive engagement untenable. If the apartheid government refused to reform, what policy tools remained for the concerned US politician? Unable to sway centrist Republicans to stick with constructive engagement as Congress moved increasingly to support sanctions, the Reagan administration seemed paralyzed. The failure to build support for constructive engagement created an opportunity for pro-apartheid actors who mobilized within the Reagan White House, persuading officials that they could push Republicans to vote against sanctions. However, pro-apartheid actors felt disappointed in the shallowness of the Reagan administration's antisanctions effort and betrayed by Republicans' eventual support for sanctioning white rule.

By Reagan's second term, the sanctions question became a domestic issue that deeply divided US conservatives and amplified existing conflict over foreign relations, the presidency, free market capitalism, and race.[3] This lightning rod issue divided the right wing, with the far right viewing the center right as not conservative enough. The global conservative support for sanctions intensified far-right, antistate trends, reinforcing the unique place apartheid South Africa held—and continues to hold—in the white power imaginary as betrayed by the mainstream right.[4] The pro-apartheid movement's antisanctions position openly clashed with centrist congressional and White House Republicans who resisted these actors' openly racialized argument, even as they questioned the efficacy of sanctions. The failure to prevent the passage of economic sanctions in 1986 facilitated a greater disillusionment with Reagan, the Republican Party, and global mainstream conservatism. This catastrophe, as it would be described by the pro-apartheid movement over the next decade, pushed white supremacist groups down a more violent, antistate path, mobilizing within South Africa to protect white rule as constructive engagement died.

CONGRESSIONAL REPUBLICANS AND THE FIGHT AGAINST SANCTIONS

Reagan's second term brought dramatic changes for congressional Republicans as they reevaluated imposing economic sanctions against the apartheid state. Democrats and antiapartheid activists initially carried the torch for economic sanctions alone, as Republicans filibustered early attempts at sanctions legislation in support of Reagan's constructive engagement. Centrist Republicans justified their opposition to sanctions in various ways: skepticism of economic coercion as a foreign policy tool, desire to support Reagan's policy, and anticommunist considerations. However, by 1986, constructive engagement's failure to curb the apartheid state's abuses and growing domestic protests against the perceived endorsement of apartheid by the Republican Party demanded a change in strategy.

P. W. Botha's open hostility to any pressure by outsiders to reform apartheid reignited congressional Democrats' efforts to pass sanctions against the apartheid state. On March 7, 1985, Representative William Gray (D-PA) and Senator Edward Kennedy (D-MA) introduced simultaneously sanctions bills with over 175 cosponsors, including both Democrats and Republicans. These sanctions packages prohibited anyone in the US from providing loans to and making investments in South Africa or importing gold coins and computer software.[5] "The broadening bipartisan support for sanctions," Representative Howard Wolpe (D-MI) argued, "testifies to congressional disillusionment with the Reagan administration's policy of constructive engagement," which Democrats critiqued as paying little more than lip service in opposition to white rule.[6] The House passed Gray's bill on June 5, 1985, by a greater than two-to-one margin, while Kennedy's bill languished in committee due to opposition from the Senate's Republican leadership. An alternative emerged from the Senate Foreign Relations Committee, the so-called Lugar Bill after Senator Richard Lugar (R-ID). This bill did not ban new investment and private bank loans to South Africa. Instead, it codified the Sullivan Principles, the then-voluntary corporate contract for South African employees that supported integration and equal pay for workers. Designed as a moderate alternative to Gray's bill, Lugar's version only implemented sanctions after eighteen months instead of the immediate economic punishment the House wanted. Lugar's bill passed the Senate on July 11, 1985, by 80–12, as Congressional Democrats abandoned Kennedy's languishing bill. Two weeks later, the House-Senate conferees met on the competing pieces of antiapartheid legislation as Lugar pushed the House leadership to accept his bill, arguing that the more aggressive bill proposed by Gray would not pass the Senate. After bargaining between Lugar and House leadership, the Senate agreed to accept the ban on gold coins, and house conferees withdrew the immediate ban on new investments in favor of the delayed timetable. A day later, on August 1, the House passed the Conference Report by a vote of 380–48.

The continued opposition to sanctions by congressional Republicans frustrated Democratic legislators, who faced intense pressure from activists to economically hamstring South Africa. The NAACP initiated a letter-writing campaign targeting southern senators that urged passage of the House's version of sanctions. As one NAACP regional director put it, "strong, enforceable economic and political sanctions against the government of South Africa would send a clear and convincing message that apartheid must end now."[7] Religious organizations across faiths and denominations embarked on marches and letter-writing campaigns.[8] Only two weeks after the House passed the Conference Report, the largest antiapartheid demonstration held in the United States occurred at the South African Mission to the United Nations in New York City. Over 60,000 people descended upon the square, bringing together a broad coalition of community and religious organizations, trade unions, student groups, and elected officials.[9] Protestors expressed their anger over the delayed timetable to pressure the apartheid state. Local legislative bodies threatened to take action against South Africa themselves if Capitol Hill refused to act: throughout 1985, twenty-seven state legislatures considered divestiture from firms doing business with South Africa. Nine states and thirty-two cities passed laws divesting nearly $4 billion from firms operating in South Africa, drawing the fury of the White House, which saw these efforts as undercutting executive power.[10] This state-level action—combined with antiapartheid activism—ensured that the sanctions question was not settled.

Although Democrats remained largely unified on the necessity of sanctions, congressional Republicans were split into two camps. The first camp, led by senators like Malcolm Wallop (R-WY), Steve Symms (R-ID), Strom Thurmond (R-SC), and Jesse Helms (R-NC), vigorously defended the South African government. Wallop came to Congress during the "political sea change" of Reagan conservatives, where he joined up with Symms, known for his staunch conservative views and his efforts to "take a bite out of big government."[11] Strom Thurmond, the avowed segregationist, was perhaps best known for conducting Congress's longest-speaking filibuster by a lone senator, speaking against the Civil Rights Act of 1957.[12] Finally, Helms, future chairman of the Senate Foreign Relations Committee and known for his opposition to the 1964 Civil Rights Act and using federal power to integrate, espoused a hard anticommunist line.[13] In debates over sanctions, these senators rallied support through the tried-and-true tactics of the pro-apartheid movement. Throughout the 1985 sanctions debates, Symms insisted that sanctions attacked the strongest African anticommunist nation, cited the Schlemmer Study, and decried Americans as acting like morality police.[14] Wallop took a similar tact, accusing Congress of hypocrisy and ignoring the "black masses who walk thousands of miles to get to South Africa."[15] Helms and Thurmond focused on Pretoria's anticommunism. From the grassroots to Congress, the pro-apartheid message was clear: South Africa was anticommunist, increasingly colorblind capitalist, and pro-Christian and needed American support, not sanctions.

In the second camp, centrist congressional Republicans, led by Lugar, viewed the apartheid state as abhorrent while questioning the efficacy of economic sanctions. Lugar's allies included Chairman of the African

Affairs Subcommittee Nancy Kassebaum (R-KS) and Chairman of the International Economic Policy Subcommittee Charles Mathias (R-MD). Lugar, known as a "master of foreign affairs," served twice as chairman of the Senate Foreign Relations Committee. Committed to bipartisan cooperation, he went against his Republican colleagues on apartheid, arms control, and later the Iraq War.[16] Kassebaum was one of only two women serving in the US Senate during her time in Congress; she was known for her moderacy and working across the aisle on abortion and women's and civil rights.[17] Mathias, known as the "conscience of the Senate," helped draft the 1964 Civil Rights Act.[18] This camp wanted Congress to establish a $15 million monetary fund for black educational programs, mandate that American companies follow the Sullivan Principles, and direct the Export-Import Bank to promote black business.[19] This proposed legislation reflected two Republican assumptions. First, the demands of a modern, capitalist system were incompatible with the arcane system of apartheid, which stymied economic growth under the weight of its oppressive racial system. Second, Republicans viewed capitalism and American businesses as an engine to drive foreign policy change.[20] These assumptions led to the conclusion that the United States needed to foster change and not walk away, which perhaps unwittingly dovetailed with the pro-apartheid attack on sanctions supporters as abandoning South Africa after destroying it.

Both of these camps aligned with the Reagan administration, which adamantly opposed sanctions. In testimony before the Senate Committee on Banking, Housing, and Urban Affairs, Deputy Secretary of State Kenneth W. Dam insisted that moral indignation was "not a substitute for an effective foreign policy."[21] Sanctions, according to Dam, hurt precisely the firms that promote social change in South Africa, freezing the number of black employees benefiting from the Sullivan Principles' antidiscrimination measures. George Shultz echoed Dam's statement. In an address to the National Press Club, Shultz stressed the importance of acting as a positive force in South Africa, insisting that sanctions are ineffectual actions likely to strengthen resistance to change.[22] Chester Crocker summed up Reagan's stance before the House Foreign Affairs Committee's Subcommittee on Africa, stating, "we have no intention of waging economic warfare."[23]

Opposition from the White House to Republican-backed sanctions, even the milquetoast Lugar bill, proved fierce, and Lugar hoped to avoid a direct conflict with the White House over the House Conference Report. In private meetings between Lugar, Senate Majority Leader Bob Dole (R-KS), and administration officials, the White House proposed an executive order to institute some action against South Africa. Republican leadership would kill the sanctions legislation in exchange. Under intense pressure from Pretoria and congressional hardliners to veto the legislation, State Department officials stressed that a presidential veto of sanctions would "destroy any limited credibility U.S. policy still has" in South Africa's black community.[24] Therefore, officials proposed an executive order that included provisions of the sanctions legislation acceptable to the Reagan administration: the ban on loans to Pretoria, computer exports, and Krugerrand gold coin imports and codification of the Sullivan Principles.[25] This option met the centrist Republican need to take punitive action against South Africa while retaining Reagan's total control of the policy, giving constructive engagement more time, and providing Republicans cover to deem the House Conference Report unnecessary. This option proved amenable to Congress's Republican leadership. Helms filibustered bringing the House Conference Report to the floor, giving Senate Republican leadership and Reagan officials time to work out the details. Reagan issued Executive Order 12532 prohibiting trade and certain other transactions involving South Africa on September 9, 1985, and on October 9, 1985, the Senate indefinitely postponed voting on the legislation by unanimous consent. The move infuriated House Democrats, who viewed these tactics as dirty tricks to circumvent the popular sanctions measure.

House Democrats were not the only ones left furious by the Reagan administration's executive order. The same day Reagan announced his executive order, the vice president of the Heritage Foundation, Gordon Jones, fired off a furious letter to Buchanan that included his organization's draft message on sanctions. Needless to say, Gordon wrote, they would not be sending the message out now that Reagan had validated the prosanctions arguments: "he would have ravished her had she not, by her timely compliance, prevented him," insinuating that the United States "raped" South Africa.[26] The cowardly, self-defeating policy proved to Gordon and other defenders of South Africa that the Reagan administration desperately needed political leadership, especially from men like Buchanan. Even milquetoast steps to sanctions were unacceptable.

Unfortunately for the Reagan White House, its sanctions strategy was on borrowed time. The European Economic Community (EEC) imposed sanctions on South Africa just two days after Reagan's executive order. Only Britain abstained from the measure, with the other eleven nations, including West Germany, voting to implement sanctions.[27] Hans-Dietrich Genscher, West Germany's minister of foreign affairs, warned Shultz that his government "[felt] that steps against South Africa [were] unavoidable."[28] Thatcher too eventually caved. Just one month after the EEC imposed sanctions, Thatcher conceded to limited sanctions that banned new government loans; funding for trade missions; computer sales to security forces; cooperation on oil, nuclear, and military technology; and most cultural exchanges.[29] Reagan faced vocal criticism for holding out: the former prime minister of Australia, Malcolm Fraser, assailed Reagan's sanctions holdout and his statements as "deeply disappointing."[30] Fraser also relayed his concerns to Reagan in private. As heads of the Commonwealth Eminent Persons Group, Fraser and the former Nigerian head of state Olusegun Obasanjo wrote to Reagan in 1986 warning that his antisanction stance left South Africa's black leadership to conclude that the West would not support them, leaving only a violent path to end apartheid. In Fraser's and Obasanjo's view, imposing sanctions was the minimum step to make whites feel the impact of apartheid's continued existence and mobilize them to put pressure on their government.[31] The antisanctions stance left the United States increasingly out of step with its Western and African allies.

Reagan's temporary stay of the sanctions debate lasted less than eight months. On June 12, 1986, Botha declared a national state of emergency, holding eight thousand people without charge, an unprecedented crackdown on antiapartheid activists, students, priests, and labor leaders.[32] The state of emergency massively expanded South African police power, imposing curfews and banning television and radio coverage of protests. Within a week of the state of emergency, Pretoria detained over three thousand more people, and the Reagan and Thatcher administrations lodged formal protests.[33] With the apartheid state's abuses on full display, the time for the antiapartheid, antisanctions position seemed to close. In response to Pretoria's crackdown, a bipartisan swath of Congress mobilized to pass sanctions. The House passed H.R. 4868, the Comprehensive Anti-Apartheid Act, on June 18, 1986, just six days after the state of emergency. Congressional frustration over the Reagan administration's continued refusal to act on sanctions included many Republicans who previously supported the executive order. Jim Leach (R-IA) took the administration to task: "All we ask of this Republican administration is that it advances a foreign policy consistent with the views of the first Republican administration, [and] puts the Republican Party on the right side of its heritage [and] our foreign policy on the right side of history."[34] Arlen Specter (R-PA) declared that the time had come for Congress and the House to take a stand.[35] Republican leaders like Dole viewed sanctions as a litmus test of lawmakers' feelings on civil rights as Reagan's antisanctions stance now stood apart from the overall mood of the Republican Party. Nevertheless, Reagan officials made it clear—the president would veto H.R. 4868 if it ended up on his desk. The Republican sanctions showdown had begun.

THE PRO-APARTHEID MOVEMENT'S POINT MAN IN THE WHITE HOUSE

Within the Reagan White House, a cadre of officials, led by Buchanan, carved out pockets of support for white rule, bringing a defense of South African apartheid into the White House as the debate over sanctions raged. Buchanan proved different than many other members of the Reagan administration who—especially in the State Department and the National Security Council—walked the antiapartheid, antisanctions line. Buchanan had a different position and a different goal in mind. Was the apartheid state really that bad, he questioned, and could he move the Reagan White House writ large to his point of view? Throughout his tenure, Buchanan and his allies laid the groundwork of diluting the critiques of white rule, promoting a vision of US-South African relations unconcerned with apartheid and adamantly against sanctions.

Buchanan relied on a group of loyal surrogates in the White House to achieve his goal. Perhaps the most important of Buchanan's confidants was Phil Nicolaides, the conservative media guru who served as the deputy director of special presidential messages from 1986 to 1987. Nicolaides and Buchanan swapped far-right op-eds, intelligence reports, memorandums on State Department endorsements of the ANC, "billion-dollar give-aways" for communist states, and exposés on the real goals of sanctions agitators.[36] Nicolaides forwarded Buchanan evidence of State Department plots against Reagan, insisting that the department covered up evidence of Black support for Reagan's South Africa position. Nicolaides insisted that the objective of the sanctions promoters was war, white collapse, and surrender.[37] In comparison to Soviet atrocities, "Apartheid is a Garden of Eden," argued one editorial Nicolaides shared with Buchanan.[38] Buchanan relied on South Africans as well. In July 1986, John Chettle, director of the South Africa Foundation, wrote to Buchanan, sympathizing with his frustration that constructive engagement had come under fire. To help Buchanan's case, Chettle provided a chart that displayed the success of the Reagan administration in contrast to the aggressive policies of the "barren" Carter years.[39] Chettle recommended that Buchanan send the chart to the White House and congressional allies. A day after receiving Chettle's letter, Buchanan wrote back to him, stating that he would "put [the chart] to good use. Hang in there."[40] Put it to good use he did, sending the chart to Reagan's desk the same day. "As you can see," Buchanan wrote to Reagan, "the most sweeping and dramatic reforms came during the years of 'Constructive Engagement.'"[41]

Buchanan and his partners' efforts to bring Reagan into closer contact with the apartheid state worried members of the administration, even as Buchanan solidified his reputation as a key right-wing power broker within the White House. Five days after Buchanan sent the chart, National Security Advisor John Poindexter intercepted it and Buchanan's note, reprimanding him for sending a document "riddled with overstatements and inaccuracies" to the president. Poindexter tasked his staff to create an accurate chart of the reforms of the South African government and told Buchanan he would get a copy upon its completion.[42] Not all of the recommended readings that Buchanan sent to Reagan were snagged. Just a week after sending the chart, Buchanan sent an editorial from the Information Scandal's Eschel Rhoodie about antiwhite racism blinding US policy toward South Africa, and Reagan read the editorial on Buchanan's recommendation.[43] Buchanan also wrote his own editorials in which he attacked centrist Republican congressmembers who were considering sanctions, to the frustration of National Security Council (NSC) officials.[44] He served as an ally and confidant for the South African government's network of elite lobbyists and academics. Buchanan received telegrams from State Department officials who alleged a grand conspiracy by Shultz: "SOUTH AFRICA IS THE ONLY THING THAT WORKS DOWN HERE," they concluded.[45] Pro-apartheid supporters saw Buchanan's entrance into the White House as the ascent of an essential ally to South Africa amid a hostile State Department that was corrupting Reagan's policies. According to both a retired US Army colonel and a future Washington State Supreme Court justice, Buchanan was the only person with Reagan's ear who had sound judgment and integrity.[46] South Africa's allies implored Buchanan not to abandon the apartheid state.

Buchanan built credibility within the Reagan White House for his pro-apartheid position using his relationships with grassroots conservatives. According to Buchanan, by August 1, 1986, White House mail ran two-to-one in favor of Reagan's South Africa policy.[47] Former ambassadors, retired generals, and local newspaper editors railed against a communist liberal conspiracy against South Africa.[48] Cattle ranchers, insurance agents, and others insisted that white South Africans kept the country economically and culturally updated and were the only stable base for civilization on that "chaotic continent."[49] According to city mayors, business executives, state senators, and investment advisors, black South Africans possessed a uniquely high quality of life as Botha dismantled apartheid.[50] "As odd as it may seem," wrote the Kentucky Senate Republican floor leader, "apartheid is the last, best hope of Democracy on the African Continent."[51] The State Department drew particular ire: it was "in need of a thorough house-cleaning," in league with death-dealing Marxists, and led by the despicable Crocker.[52] These supporters of apartheid found a loyal ally in Buchanan and believed that Reagan would stand against the great moral stampede against South Africa.[53] Buchanan graciously thanked his grassroots supporters, assuring them that they were not alone.[54] In letters between Reagan and founding chairman of the Mississippi Republican Party, Wirt Yerger Jr., Yerger told Reagan, "you need to have Pat Buchanan or some clear thinkers to arm you with the full facts."[55] Reagan assured Yerger that Buchanan and other like-minded folks kept him well briefed. These letters became the justification of Buchanan to convince Reagan to stay the course against sanctions, insisting that the grassroots and Republican elites supported South Africa. Buchanan's fanatic following did not go unnoticed by other members of the Reagan White House.

In 1986, the State Department intervened in some of Buchanan's mail on South Africa, responding directly to notes addressed to Buchanan, and some of Buchanan's staffers tried to "Buchananize" the boiler-plate State Department responses to add Buchanan's unique response style, flair, and content.[56]

Although explicitly brought into the administration to deal with public relations issues, Buchanan had no intention of remaining on the sidelines. He privately lamented that "unfortunately, we do not yet have control of policy [in southern Africa]," as he conspired for a greater role in US-South African relations.[57] In an NSC public diplomacy review, officials hoped to get Buchanan's thinking on the public-facing approach to South African policy. Walter Raymond, NSC intelligence communications and information directorate, mentioned that he and others believed that Buchanan felt he was unnecessarily left out of the US–South Africa diplomacy process. To remedy this, Raymond suggested the NSC work directly with Buchanan to avoid "any unnecessary tension" but, critically, to make sure Buchanan understood that "he [was] to stay clear of policy."[58]

However, Buchanan had no intention of staying clear of policy and instead sought to capitalize on the tense relationship between Shultz and Botha to create a new diplomatic exchange outside of the "toxic" State Department. His fast partner in his schemes was John Sears, whom Pretoria hired after Sears had served as Reagan's campaign manager in the 1980 presidential election.[59] Sears was the highest paid of Pretoria's lobbyists, fetching an annual fee of $500,000.[60] In 1986, Buchanan and Sears tried to use Chief of Staff Don Reagan as the conduit of messages from the Botha administration, rather than the State Department, accusing Shultz of trashing and leaking letters.[61] Regan promptly denied the request, stating that Shultz gave the messages to Reagan and nothing of a derogatory nature occurred. Poindexter even got involved, imploring Buchanan to reassure the South African ambassador that the "State Channel, which is what he ought to use, works fine" for US–South African correspondence.[62] Undeterred, just months later, Botha, through his ambassador, requested that Buchanan deliver Pretoria's messages to Reagan.[63] According to Buchanan, Botha was "extremely exercised" that Reagan seemingly did not want to have a record of communication with the apartheid leader. To resolve this, Buchanan suggested that he should pass on a personal, handwritten note from Reagan to the South Africans indicating that all channels remained open and Reagan wished to continue communication.[64] Incensed, the NSC pegged Buchanan's efforts as part of Botha's "recent practice of bypassing the State Department, apparently to establish a separate channel to the White House."[65] Ultimately, the State Department got Reagan involved to deal with Buchanan's efforts. In a letter to Botha, Reagan wrote that "the U.S. government speaks with one voice—that voice is mine."[66] In the future, Reagan concluded, all correspondence must follow the proper State Department channels.

Buchanan's conniving came at a critical moment for the Reagan White House, as centrist congressional Republicans signaled their willingness to override Reagan's veto to pass economic sanctions against the apartheid state. The Reagan administration's unwillingness to abandon constructive engagement and its inability to shift centrist Republicans away from sanctions created a window of opportunity for Buchanan. Instead of building a veto defense that questioned the efficacy of sanctions, apartheid's defenders pushed Reagan to veto the Comprehensive Anti-Apartheid Act through a dismissal of the seriousness of ending white rule. This veto defense was drawn from the playbook of the pro-apartheid movement, which leveraged its vast network of right-wing media, grassroots organizers, and officials within the United States. Although they promised to reinvigorate a stale US–South African relationship, pro-apartheid actors like Buchanan only drove the Reagan administration into further internal strife and conflict with its Republican allies in Congress who questioned the antiapartheid, antisanctions position.

The Reagan administration's narrow escape from the 1985 sanctions debacle demanded a new strategy in 1986. Initially, the Reagan administration decided not to consider another compromise effort like the 1985 executive order, instead tapping Buchanan and his conservative base to organize the defense. The lynchpin of Buchanan's sanction strategy was to "Reaganize" constructive engagement—essentially, to put Reagan back into South African relations. Buchanan wanted Reagan to "put his personal prestige on the line . . . to turn the stampede and save the policy."[67] In Buchanan's mind, Reagan needed to make the case against sanctions and remind Congress that sanctions would promote a race war and fuel revolutionary violence. To deflect more extreme congressional sanctions efforts, Reagan should indicate the portions of H.R. 4868 that were unacceptable, support Republican senators to stall the legislation, and prepare to fire Crocker. To stave off what he saw as Lugar's "endless appetite for publicity, Buchanan advocated for a new Reagan-led executive order that would also "deny black revolutionaries the chance to claim victory through sanctions."[68] In addition, Reagan should relay to Botha that his administration would stop moving the goalposts on apartheid. This approach ran counter to the State Department and NSC strategy of limiting Reagan's involvement with Botha, instead centralizing Reagan's touch in a sanctions defense and moving the US government away from support for real democratic reform of apartheid.

The importance of putting Reagan at the center of the antisanctions debate was apparent in the strategy laid out by South Africa's lobbyists. Pretoria's consultant, Joan "Jody" Baldwin, sent a memo to the South African ambassador in which she laid out what it would take to sustain Reagan's veto.[69] Buchanan was the most important prong of the attack, Baldwin stated, with his ability to organize all interested outside parties to drum up support for the president's veto and prevent a significant foreign policy defeat for Reagan. Republicans, Baldwin argued, needed more of an out to support the veto beyond Reagan's opposition: Pretoria would provide "the necessary figures to support claims" that sanctions harmed US farmers and caused severe job loss. Reagan also needed to emphasize that the changes made to apartheid by Botha were significant reforms, despite US media coverage. Baldwin pushed to make Reagan a vocal supporter of South Africa, insisting that "the President himself must be actively engaged."[70] Baldwin concluded that the South Africa issue should serve as the last conservative litmus test of the Ninety-Ninth Congress.

Simultaneously, Congress's apartheid defenders sought to delay a vote as long as possible to shore up a veto defense. On Capitol Hill, Buchanan's point person was Paul Weyrich—the conservative activist and founder of the Heritage Foundation and the American Legislative Exchange Council. After consultation with Dole, Huck Walther, president of the US Defense Committee and the National Right to Work Committee, and *Conservative Digest*'s Bill Hoar and William R. Kennedy, a strategy emerged.[71] Buchanan, Weyrich, and Connie Borie of the American Legislative Exchange Council pushed Congress to amend H.R. 4686 to death in committee, using procedural delays to prevent a vote on the bill before the end of the second congressional session on October 18, 1986. Senator Mark Siljander (R-MI) put forth ten different amendments designed to waive provisions of the legislation in the event of a 3 percent increase in black unemployment or terrorist attacks or following a three-year study of the US-South African economic relationship.[72] Representative Philip Crane (R-IL) offered an amendment that would extend sanctions provisions to all communist countries, a massive distortion of the original bill.[73] Dan Burton called for an amendment for a comparative study of human rights between South Africa and other southern African nations. In tandem, Helms, Thurmond, Wallop, and Burton dismissed the seriousness of apartheid through attacks on the Soviet Union and "black mistreatment of blacks" in South Africa.[74] At every point in the bill's lifespan, South Africa's defenders in Congress tried to delay the bill from reaching Reagan's desk.

While Baldwin and Buchanan tried to push Reagan further into US–South African relations, in the administration, Reagan officials admitted that the executive's silence on apartheid played poorly with domestic audiences. A significant foreign policy speech on South Africa could silence doubters on Reagan's commitment to ending apartheid and appease centrist Republicans looking to veto sanctions. A scheduled speaking engagement for Reagan with the World Affairs Foundation and the Foreign Policy Association on July 22, 1986, seemed a perfect opportunity. A who's who of Washington elites and international diplomats received invitations from the White House, whose officials privately promised that the speech would set the record straight on Reagan's stance on apartheid. With the Comprehensive Anti-Apartheid Act expected to move to the Senate for approval after racing through the House in June, officials recognized that they had limited time to shift fence-sitting Republicans to sustain Reagan's veto.

Immediately, the Reagan White House began drafting the speech. In his early drafting, Buchanan sought advice from John Carbaugh, Helms's foreign policy advisor.[75] Carbaugh suggested several themes that he hoped Reagan would stress in his speech. Apartheid was no longer the issue, Carbaugh argued—"a black-on-black" power struggle between factions engulfed the townships in response to white South Africans' rapid dismantling of apartheid. As Carbaugh stated, Reagan needed to stand strong with Thatcher against sanctions and work to "retake the moral high ground, snatching it away from the anti-apartheid lobby," whom he identified as Bishop Desmond Tutu, Oliver Tambo, and Winnie Madikizela-Mandela.

Recommending that Reagan turn the tables on the limousine liberals and yuppie do-gooders, Carbaugh advised Reagan to call for the liberation of the ANC from communist influence, citing Nicolaides's reporting.[76] The NSC took a different view—although Reagan's speech needed to be positive, it needed to mention the ANC, and critically, Reagan needed to underscore his personal dismay over the state of emergency. To give the speech real power, NSC staffers pushed for the speech to unveil a potential new southern Africa strategy that would include personnel throughout the United States and South Africa—like Coretta Scott King or Andy Young.[77] The NSC's draft version of the speech, written on July 10, stressed these themes and included harsh words for the South African government, which was denounced for its "confused vision, lack of compassion, and lack of leadership." Although it dismissed sanctions, the speech set out its expectations for Botha, which included the repeal of all apartheid laws, the unconditional release of Mandela and other political prisoners, negotiations, and an appeal to all southern African leaders to resist calls for divestment.[78] The State Department was largely aligned with the NSC and aimed to use Shultz's upcoming appearance before the Senate Foreign Relations Committee to offer its assessment of the ANC's communist sympathies while calling to increase contact with the ANC.[79]

Although more accurately described as tolerance, the NSC's seeming endorsement of the ANC angered Buchanan and his apartheid state allies. Heritage Foundation decried the review of constructive engagement taking place in the White House, saw the ANC as manipulating Western opinion to hide its allegiance to global communism, and lamented Reagan's blindness on the issue.[80] Buchanan and Nicolaides raged about the efforts to rebrand the ANC by Shultz, who seemingly ignored necklace killings by the ANC as the South African government graciously reformed while fighting off these "terrorist beasts."[81] Mangosuthu Buthelezi even got involved. On July 11, Buthelezi sent a letter to Reagan through Bob Cleaves, alternate ambassador to South Africa, and Senator Paul Laxalt (R-NV), general chair of the Republican National Committee and close friend of Reagan.[82] In the letter, Buthelezi endorsed Reagan's antisanctions stance, stating that Reagan's "humanitarian aid to Black South Africa is the first concrete contribution which the United States has ever made towards the elimination of apartheid." Buthelezi bemoaned that the ANC propaganda machine left world leaders with the false impression that the

ANC was the only negotiating body needed for Pretoria; to Buthelezi, Inkatha was just as important.[83]

South Africa's defenders clearly needed an alternative version of the speech, so Buchanan got more heavily involved because, as one of his surrogates put it, there was "no one in the United States or anywhere else who [knew] this issue better" than him.[84] The first draft of the speech did not exactly meet the standard. This July 11 version did have elements Buchanan seemingly liked: situating the rebellion in South Africa as simply violence from all sides and decrying how the "enemies of freedom" (i.e., the ANC) weaponized restrictions of civil liberties to their advantage. Buchanan crossed off huge swaths of the next few pages: sections that referenced the antiapartheid activism of the 1970s, efforts to organize black unions, and a recognition that Botha "has not yet appreciated that moves to end economic and social apartheid are not enough."[85] The initial speech, although vague on what the Reagan administration saw as its vision for South Africa, offered a more in-depth discussion of apartheid and focused on the apartheid government itself. The next version, written three days, stated that "a major cause of [the] violence [was] the unacceptable policy of apartheid" and that is largely where the discussion of apartheid ended. The speech argued that Americans were "sensitive" because of some "sad and shameful chapters" in US history; although apartheid was odious and disapproved of by bipartisan Americans, Americans "cannot forget South Africa is a friendly nation." The focus then shifted to a defense of the Botha administration as repelling communist invasions and full of courage in its 1982 reforms, as part of eleven changes to phase out apartheid that "received too little attention in our media." In contrast, sanctions would be like "removing doctors, nurses, and medicines from the scene of an accident," citing South African business leaders and Leon Sullivan on how sanctions would lead to the destruction of black South African life. This version of the speech explicitly tied sanctions to empowering the bloodthirsty ANC and the "most radical elements," invoking "killing [of] black moderates, often by the so-called 'necklace' method." Raising the pro-apartheid talking point of an ANC race war waged by brutal necklace killings, the speech ended with Reagan's commitment to not "play in the hands of the extremist and veto any further economic sanctions."[86] This version matched what Buchanan saw as the major goals of the speech, which he relayed to Reagan's chief of staff the same day:

Reagan needed to put his "personal prestige on the line" to powerfully make the case against sanctions. How Buchanan proposed doing that showcased his allegiances: there would be no more "goal post moving" on Pretoria, the United States would support black and white moderates who were against sanctions and against apartheid, and critically, "the President's surrogates—conservatives, Congressmen, press who agree with us" would be given "arguments they [could] use to defend his policy."[87]

The reaction to the speech drafts—and the potential ramifications of Reagan giving it on critical demographics—proved swift. "This speech would be a disaster—RR cannot say the things that are written," wrote the Office of the Chief of Staff, in reference to Buchanan's edits. Regan's office continued, although it "may be true, we will spend the next three months explaining ourselves—it is defensive/apologetic/ and gives the libs who have been waiting for an answer exactly what they want." The office wondered if Reagan should give a speech at all, especially because public attitudes were moving "away from [the administration's] position of using the pressure of quiet diplomacy."[88] Reagan speaking on South Africa "increases the political stakes ten-fold," and those most concerned about the administration's South African policy "are precisely those . . . [needed] in the Fall to hold the Senate."[89] Reagan's team elected to go ahead with the speech, believing that the "combined effect" of Reagan's address on South Africa and Shultz's upcoming testimony before the Senate Foreign Affairs Committee offered "a significant opportunity to influence public and Congressional opinion."[90] To make that influence as powerful as possible, the Reagan administration invited high-profile Black American invitees like members of the Ford Foundation and the NAACP, the president of Howard University, Coretta Scott King, and delegates from the Congressional Black Caucus.[91] The White House also invited a swath of foreign diplomats and prominent Republican congressional leaders, along with grassroots allies like the Heritage Foundation, American Legion, and Conservative Caucus.

Reagan's speechwriters rewrote the speech, which could best be described as a hodgepodge of both Buchanan's and the NSC's versions. Up to the eleventh hour, Buchanan and Nicolaides, with support from the Heritage Foundation, South Africa's US ambassador, conservative allies in Congress, and the Conservative Caucus, pressured the insertion of language that would remove mention of the ANC, specifically stating instead: "the South African government has no obligation to negotiate the future of that country with individuals or organizations who publicly call for a Communist state and use terror tactics to achieve it."[92] Reagan's final version settled on apartheid as a major cause of the violence in South Africa because it treated black people "as third-class citizens in a nation they helped build." He stated that Americans unilaterally believed that if South Africa wanted to be part of the family of Western nations, an end to apartheid was a precondition. Reagan then set out his justification against sanctions, citing the interconnected nature of the southern African economy and the capacity of progressive Western forces to rebuild it after apartheid. Buchanan got his way on the ANC in the speech, which Reagan characterized as engaged in calculated terror and creating the "conditions for racial war" through "necklace" killing of moderate blacks. Reagan used the exact language requested by Buchanan to rule out the ANC in democratic negotiations. Reagan concluded with steps to move toward political peace that mirrored those in the early NSC draft: eliminate apartheid laws on a timetable, release all political prisoners including Mandela, and resist the "emotional clamor" for punitive sanctions. He also tacked on the NSC request to show a positive strategy for southern Africa, offering an additional $45 million to black South Africans to build on almost a billion dollars in aid to the Frontline States.[93] In the final version of the World Affairs Council speech, apartheid took a backseat, with minimal discussion of the horrors of white rule. Instead, Reagan seemingly equated ANC atrocities to those of the apartheid state, focused on Botha's reforms, and chided US businesses—and Congress—to not "cut and run" on South Africa.

The overall reaction to Reagan's speech was adverse. Over 70 percent of US and Western European papers surveyed expressed a widespread negative response, reporting "considerable criticism" in the United States and among African partners.[94] The *New York Times* stated that the "immediate reaction in Congress was negative" and that Republicans and Democrats planned to carry on their push for sanctions.[95] When asked about Reagan's speech, Tutu's reaction was biting: "I am quite angry. I think the West, for my part, can go to hell."[96] Stark condemnation of the speech came from the Democrats' rebuttal to Reagan's speech, which was delivered by Representative Gray. In his opening line, Gray stated "today President Reagan declared the United States and Great Britain co-guarantors of apartheid." Gray dismissed Reagan's arguments about helping black South Africans. "They have suffered for years, not because of sanctions, but because of apartheid," Gray said, "because they cannot vote . . . and they are detained without justification, disappeared by the apartheid government, as part of a modern-day Holocaust." "How can sanctions hurt black South Africans when apartheid is killing them?" Gray questioned. Gray attacked the hypocrisy of Reagan's rejection of economic sanctions for South Africa: if Reagan believed sanctions to be ineffective, "why then have we imposed sanctions against Libya, Nicaragua, Poland, and Cuba, and some 20 nations around the world?"[97]

Reagan's panned speech on July 22 caused serious problems for the administration, which dispatched Shultz to clean up after the president's remarks the next day. Indeed, Reagan's missteps left even less space for antiapartheid, antisanctions Republicans, who did not want to be tied to a White House that seemed hellbent on limiting its critiques of white rule. Before the Senate Foreign Relations Committee on July 23, 1986, Shultz attempted to clarify Reagan's comments while still rejecting sanctions. During his speech, Reagan classified the ANC as "Soviet-controlled," yet Shultz stated that this did not reflect the intelligence of the NSC or State Department and that he actually sought to raise the level and frequency of contact with opposition leadership.[98] Shultz blamed Botha for the slow timetable on apartheid reform and acknowledged that Botha seemed unconcerned with international opinion. Yet even after Shultz's attempted cleanup, Congress seemed unpersuaded by the administration's antisanctions stance.

Apartheid's defenders seethed over Shultz's treasonous testimony and the takeover of Reagan's sound South Africa strategy. In the days after Shultz's testimony, right-wing media attacked the State Department as undercutting Reagan's antisanctions strategy and his policy toward South Africa. In a glossy flyer distributed by the newly formed Coalition Against ANC Terrorism led by Howard Phillips and the Conservative Caucus, the organization attacked Shultz and Crocker. Did these men truly speak for Reagan? "DON'T LET YOUR APPOINTEES TURN OVER SOUTH AFRICA TO THE SOVIET UNION," the leaflet concluded, highlighting inflammatory quotes from the ANC's leadership.[99] Why, Phillips railed, is the second term of the Reagan administration "continuing the policies of the Carter administration?"[100] This "State takeover of Reagan's speech" left the "wizards of foggy bottom" ready to bring down another friendly anticommunist government.[101] Reagan's milquetoast speech left both centrists and right-wingers frustrated, which Buchanan and his allies hoped to capitalize on. Pandering to the center and other leftists had not worked, and the speech cooled no calls for sanctions—a more explicit pro–South Africa strategy could carry the day. In the aftermath of the July 22 speech, Buchanan rejected attempts to temper his support for apartheid South Africa. He took to chastising Republicans holding South Africa to a "different moral standard" than the rest of Africa in a desperate joining of the latest fashionable crusade.[102] In a proposed *Newsweek* editorial, Buchanan railed against "the immaturity of the American Left—a textbook case of arrested development—in a forever re-enactment of the morality play at Selma Bridge," a nasty reference to the "Bloody Sunday" of 1965, when police brutally attacked civil rights activists marching to Montgomery.[103] The chief of staff and NSC opposed Buchanan's editorials.[104] After a copy of one editorial landed in the NSC's office, someone marked it up with underlines and question marks, scrawling at the top "100 percent pure PB—he tried to get all these themes in RR's [July 22] speech."[105] Buchanan was prepared to dial up the temperature of the sanctions debates, building a pro-apartheid defense for resisting them.

Insisting that the Reagan administration had an opportunity to complete an "eminently doable" presidential victory on sanctions that "no one predicted," Buchanan worked his right-wing contacts to drum up support for Reagan's veto.[106] Friendly media like the *Wall Street Journal, Washington Times, Human Events*, and local newspapers ran op-eds calling on Republicans to uphold a likely Reagan veto. Pat Robertson's Christian Broadcasting Network and *Jerry Falwell Live*, with Reverend Jerry Falwell, circulated anti-ANC stories on their channels, urging their viewers to call their senators and demand no sanctions.[107] Buchanan and his team personally called Moral Majority pastor Dr. Adrian Rogers, *Coral Ridge Hour*'s Dr. Jim Kennedy, and National Religious Broadcasting Association president Dr. Ben Armstrong. Public Liaison Director Mari Maseng and Deputy Director Linda Arey drummed up support from Republican women with the aid of conservative media darling and Renaissance Women president Nina May.[108] May privately relayed to Arey that she had South African members in close contact with antisanctions black moderates. Eagle Forum president Phyllis Schlafly issued press releases supporting Reagan's veto and committed to "gin up" enthusiasm against sanctions at the Eagle Forum convention in St. Louis. Joan Heuter—president of the National Association of Pro-America—had her troops "hard at work on South Africa."[109] Buchanan, Maseng, and Arey also tapped into ethnic organizations. They obtained antisanctions endorsements from the League of United Latin American Citizens (LULAC), the nation's oldest Hispanic organization; the US Hispanic Chamber of Commerce and Hispanic-Americana consortiums; Cuban-American leaders; and the Freedom Foundation, an anticommunist coalition of ethnic organizations, and rallied support from twenty-two Eastern European and Southeast Asian American organizations.[110] The thousands of pro-apartheid letters sent to Reagan came to good use. When White House special assistants sent letters to fence-sitting conservative organizations, they emphasized the widespread grassroots antisanctions sentiment.

Enlisting South Africa's black conservatives—principally Buthelezi—proved a lynchpin of Buchanan's antisanctions strategy. Buchanan repeatedly attempted to bring Buthelezi to the United States to directly lobby fence-sitting Republicans against sanctions and drum up support for Reagan's veto. The Heritage Foundation offered to sponsor Buthelezi's trip and set up his itinerary, locking him into meetings on Capitol Hill, Sunday television, religious and radio programs, and the White House press circuit. The pro-apartheid movement's attempts to trot out Buthelezi as a Reagan disciple frustrated the Inkatha leader.[111] Buthelezi rejected the invitation sponsored by the Heritage Foundation, stating that he did "not want to come over . . . as a puppet of any right-wing think tank."[112] He would only come at a presidential invitation and on his own financial and ideological terms to restate his position against apartheid and sanctions. However, the Office of the Chief of Staff and the NSC could not guarantee Buthelezi a visit with Reagan on the Heritage Foundation trip and refused to grant him a presidential invitation.[113] Buthelezi communicated his refusal of Heritage's invitation the day of Reagan's veto, September 26, ensuring that Buchanan would have to make his antisanctions pitch without him.

As Reagan prepared to veto the legislation on sanctions, Buchanan and his partners took an increasingly aggressive line with Republicans who were considering supporting sanctions and clashed over reports that the possibility of sustaining Reagan's veto appeared slim. On September 21,

1986, Buchanan attempted to send a presidential letter to 18,000 Republican fundraisers, asking for their personal intercession to sustain the veto.[114] The letter included pro-apartheid talking points, calling communism the future wave in southern Africa if the United States walks away and attacking sanctions-supporting Republican congressmembers. After reading the letter, Chief of Staff Regan relayed his "real reservations" about asking Reagan to write to contributors for their help sustaining the veto. "God knows I'm not anxious to jump in front of another conservative train," Regan quipped, but he worried the message would ensure that South Africa would be a partisan issue to the White House's detriment.[115] Nevertheless, Buchanan and his partners carried on. On September 15, 1986, Dole held up the Senate's signing of H.R. 4868 to give Reagan until September 26 to veto the legislation, providing Congress only a week to vote to override Reagan's veto before the session adjourned. The time had come for a full-court press from the White House: get Buchanan on the phones to call all interested parties and bill the passage as a "major foreign policy defeat" for Reagan. Republicans needed an "out" to hold up the veto: American job losses in auto, coal, and farming; harm to black South Africans; and the changes to apartheid implemented by Pretoria. According to South Africa's lobbyist Baldwin, Reagan also needed to call Republican House leadership like Bob Michel and conservative Democrats, while also asking Jack Kemp to give a speech against sanctions to keep Dole in line. Baldwin broke down all the congressmembers the administration needed to lock in and how they could do it: pushing the "old wimp Lugar"; galvanizing supporters like Helms, Denton, Symms, and Wallop to feel they are "personally working for Reagan"; bullying Kassebaum to know she "will be fighting Ronald Reagan"; and making Paul Trible "squirm."[116]

Although Buchanan pushed a relentless optimism on the possibility of the Senate sustaining Reagan's veto, doubt emerged among White House officials. After meetings with Dole, Mitch McConnell, and Kassebaum, the outcome of the vote appeared bleak, with prospects dimming by the day.[117] Yet simultaneously, Buchanan pushed the egregiously optimistic vote counts funneled to him from Baldwin and other South African operatives.[118] Buchanan characterized projections of Reagan's defeat on sanctions as "grossly premature" and maintained that the administration could sustain a veto with help from Baldwin and some conservative friends.[119] After Buchanan sent Baldwin's vote count to Chief of Staff Regan, Regan asked William Ball, chief lobbyist and liaison to Congress, to look at Buchanan's count. Ball rejected the numbers, accusing Buchanan of pandering to Botha's cronies.[120] It was not possible, he concluded, to convince twenty additional senators to sustain a veto.

THE DEATH OF THE ANTIAPARTHEID, ANTISANCTIONS POSITION

Amid Buchanan's machinations, White House officials considered how to avoid an embarrassing foreign policy defeat.[121] As Reagan appeared increasingly out of step with Republicans in Congress, officials struggled to devise a new form of the antiapartheid, antisanctions position that could move Republicans away from the veto override. To maintain presidential leadership over South Africa policy, the NSC, led by Walter Raymond, and Chief of Staff Regan proposed a new executive order with provisions from Lugar's bill. Privately, State Department officials expressed that there were no attractive options left and damage control was the only option.[122] State Department and NSC officials urged a realistic reassessment of the sanctions strategy, pointing out that Botha was prepared for a political and economic siege, demanding the preservation of white heritage.[123] The chances of gaining enough Senate support to sustain a veto were nil, as Dole and Lugar appeared convinced that strong sanctions were essential to limit damage to Republicans in November. It was clear, as one official put it, that Lugar and Dole were strong Reagan supporters "trying to cut the President's losses and to persuade him to fill a perceived foreign policy vacuum."[124] Critically, these internal assessments rejected Buchanan's characterization of the congressional Republican leadership.

National Security Advisor Poindexter endorsed a new executive order with minimal changes to H.R. 4868 to sway Republican support. The executive order plan replicated the 1985 strategy: concede to some sanctions to preserve presidential authority. The executive order mirrored three parts of the congressional package. First, Reagan's executive order would comply with Title I, which focused on the general US strategy for the southern Africa region and for South Africa. Second, the White House plan would include all elements of "Title II: Aid Victims of Apartheid"—this included scholarships, agricultural export credits, purchases from victims of apartheid, Export-Import Bank assistance to black firms, fair labor standards by US government and private firms, and prohibition of assistance to groups carrying out "necklacing."[125] Third, in "Title VI: Enforcement Provisions," the White House largely agreed with the enforcement strategy set out by Congress.

However, deviations occurred across the other pieces of H.R. 4868, most significantly under "Title III: Measures to Undermine Apartheid," the economic heart of the sanctions package. The Reagan executive order banned gold coin imports, defense articles, computer exports to security forces, loans to the South African government outside of humanitarian aid, nuclear exports, use of South African bank accounts, munitions exports, and iron and steel imports. However, the administration refused to include key components of H.R. 4868's economic strategy: banning imports or the procurement of goods produced and marketed by parastatals, textiles, uranium, coal, sugar, crude oil, and agriculture and petroleum products. It also refused to terminate air landing rights, the promotion of tourism, US government assistance in trade and investment, and cooperation with South African armed forces. Additionally, the executive order tried to caveat the congressional ban on "no new investments except for black firms" to include American firms that adhered to the Sullivan Principles. The Reagan administration rejected full compliance with "Title IV: Multilateral Measures to Undermine Apartheid." It would only support the White House cutting imports from countries seeking to take "unfair advantage" of sanctions and diluted efforts to seek UN Security Council and multilateral sanctions. Finally, on "Title V: Future Policy," the Reagan administration rejected requirements like additional sanctions if South Africa made no progress on ending apartheid in a year and mandatory reporting on the Bantustans.[126] After reviewing the plan, State Department officials shared with Poindexter that this strategy would be a nonstarter: it would appear "the President is again acting to frustrate the will of large majorities" of Congress.[127]

Meanwhile, tensions between Washington and Pretoria boiled over. Pik Botha chastised US Ambassador to South Africa Herman Nickel over Reagan's communications with Botha. He lamented that Reagan gave no credit for the "positive actions" taken to create a nonracial society, such as abolishing petty apartheid (i.e., public segregation), integrating sports, and repealing legislation on job reservation and mixed marriage regulation.[128] Pik Botha also emphasized Botha's speech before Parliament in February 1986 when he called apartheid "outdated" and shared his principles for a new South African government that respects all human dignity, political aspiration, and elected representation of all South Africans regardless of color.[129] Pik Botha cited "disturbing reports" that the State Department wrote to the European Economic Community urging the adoption of sanctions and ignored these momentous moves from Botha. Pik Botha maintained that this behavior was all part of US refusal to engage in an honest dialogue with the South Africans. Nickel characterized Botha's mood as "testy" and worried that pushing Botha further could result in "another angry outburst and more broken china."[130] Botha did want to be clear on one point, Nickel wrote—the South Africans did not take instructions from the United States or anyone else, with Botha "determined as ever" to demonstrate that he was not acting under foreign pressure. After fights between Shultz and Botha, the Reagan administration suspended dialogue between the two leaders as a result of Botha's tone and behavior toward American intermediaries in mid-1986. A consensus emerged among the State Department that Botha had no intention of instituting reforms pushed by the Americans.

Even as the State Department questioned Botha's commitment to change, Buchanan and his allies brewed dissent against the department's assessments. Buchanan and his allies continued to send inaccurate vote counts to Reagan staffers indicating that the veto could be sustained, tried to facilitate a separate US–South African relationship outside of Shultz's oversight, and began a new prong of their strategy—laying the groundwork for blaming the State Department for the passage of sanctions. Privately, Buchanan and Nicolaides insisted that failure to sustain the president's veto came from the State Department's disapproval of the president's policy, their subtle lobbying for sanctions with legislators, and their undercutting of Reagan in off-the-record media briefings.[131] The issue at hand was Shultz's contradictory testimony after Reagan's July 22 speech and "leaks" from prosanctions White House and State Department members worrying Republicans that Reagan had been "turned."[132] In a memorandum prepared on sanctions scenarios, Buchanan tied any veto override to the State Department's undercutting of Reagan's July 22 speech—specifically, Shultz's "performance" before the Senate Foreign

Relations Committee. To remedy Shultz's treasonous behavior, Buchanan recommended that officials dissolve the State Department's Advisory Committee on South Africa because the committee lacked "real" Reagan supporters. The Advisory Committee, created as part of Reagan's 1985 executive order to stave off the first passage of sanctions, had a broad mandate of "making recommendations on peaceful change in South Africa."[133] The committee would provide advice to Shultz and create a channel of communication between the State Department and various NGOs and private entities in the United States and South Africa, issuing a report every year from the first meeting.[134] The NSC seemed largely skeptical of the Advisory Committee and Buchanan loathed it; Buchanan wrote to Poindexter demanding to know the selection process and successfully struck references to the committee's work from a draft of Reagan's July 22 speech.[135] The Advisory Committee's efforts to meet with the ANC-leadership-in-exile as early as February 1986 likely provoked Buchanan's ire.[136] Buchanan argued that to help stave off a veto override, Reagan should set up an envoy with NSC experience to break the barrier caused by the State Department and discount all recommendations from Shultz's Advisory Committee.[137]

In addition, South Africa's White House allies suggested that Reagan should announce a new South African ambassador, one who "would not await daily orders from confrontationalists in Washington or Embassy staff."[138] Amid discussions about the continued service of the current US ambassador to South Africa, Herman Nickel, Buchanan put forth his candidate—Alan Keyes. A staunch conservative currently serving as assistant secretary of state for international organization affairs, Keyes's status as one of a few Black American political elites who were vigorously against sanctions endeared him to Buchanan.[139] Nicolaides sent Buchanan a transcript of a television debate on *Nightline* between Keyes and TransAfrica director Randall Robinson, noting Keyes's staunch defense of Reagan's policy and insisting he should replace Crocker.[140] It was increasingly clear that State Department "Boer-bashers" wanted Reagan's veto overridden. Shultz's State Department was orchestrating a plan to make Reagan look "irrelevant, incompetent, and immaterial," Nicolaides concluded.[141] This "Boer-basher 180" was a State Department conspiracy to enhance the ANC's reputation.[142] Buchanan and Nicolaides alleged an anti-South Africa conspiracy so insidious that it even included efforts by Shultz himself to suppress news of African support for constructive engagement coming from embassy officials.[143] Egregiously, Crocker, Shultz, and other high-level State Department officials reported a willingness to meet with Oliver Tambo, the ANC president, which was part of a pattern of trying to bring South Africa to its "knees."[144] It was a personnel question, Buchanan and his partners insisted. With the right allies in the State Department, Reagan's veto could be sustained. Instead, Buchanan's efforts suffered at the hands of anti-Reagan officials.

Buchanan and his partners' efforts to put the "right allies" in the US–South African relationship continued throughout August 1986, weeks before the final sanctions vote. On August 22, 1986, Buchanan again battled for Sears and the South Africans to set up a separate channel for Botha. In a memorandum to Regan and Poindexter, Buchanan relayed that the South Africans would be willing to meet with Reagan, Thatcher, and Helmut Kohl. As a carrot to Reagan to hold such a meeting, Sears suggested that Botha would "make [the meeting] a viable 'success.'" Potential options included lifting the state of emergency, releasing Mandela, and negotiating with the ANC—if the organization renounced terror and violence and committed to a democratic future as determined by Pretoria—all demands from Reagan's July 22 speech. However, Sears lamented the tremendous suspicion of the State Department by South Africans and suggested not informing Shultz and his deputies about the potential high-profile summit. Clearly, Pretoria and its US partners hoped to set up the meeting without State Department preconditions of apartheid reform. If Botha could say that he had Reagan's backing for the administration's current course, Sears relayed, it would give him "the support he needs against the South African right-wing."[145] Moving from flattering into warnings, Sears maintained that if the United States hit Botha with sanctions, he would be defenseless against his party's right wing. Again, Sears suggested undercutting the State Department through a private emissary to Pretoria. This emissary, Sears hinted, would have a good chance of success.

Buchanan paired Sears's efforts with his proposal for a new pro-apartheid South Africa policy as a means to sustain Reagan's sanctions veto. Buchanan formally proposed his new approach titled the "Reagan Plan" in a September 10, 1986, memorandum to Regan and Poindexter. According to Buchanan, the Reagan administration needed to "reshuffle the deck—and deal [itself] an entirely new hand—leaving [its] opposition sounding small and petty clamoring for sanctions against Pretoria." Buchanan framed his Reagan Plan for southern Africa around economic progress and security, proposing a ceasefire encompassing Angola, Namibia, Mozambique, and South Africa and legalizing all dissident movements that renounced the use of terror. Buchanan argued that such a plan would be saying "yes to democracy and no to sanctions," with Reagan standing with the Boers. Most importantly, Buchanan stated, all hell would break loose on the Marxist left, who wanted power, "not desegregated lunch counters." Buchanan even created a future headline Reagan could anticipate after implementing this plan: "President Wins Nobel Peace Prize; Bishop Tutu Returns His in Protest."[146]

Furious at the distraction, Raymond, Poindexter, and Shultz rejected the Reagan Plan, as the administration focused its efforts on Reagan's veto message coming only days later. Buchanan prepared an initial draft of the veto message that the Departments of Justice and State rejected.[147] Ultimately, the State Department and NSC's vision for an antisanctions defense won out, and on September 26, 1986, Reagan vetoed the Comprehensive Anti-Apartheid Act, arguing that sanctions would harm black South Africans, offering the promise of future regional aid packages, and announcing the new African American ambassador to South Africa—who was not Buchanan's preferred candidate.[148] Unpersuaded, Congress overrode Reagan's veto just five days later on October 2, 1986, by votes of 313 to 83 in the House and 78 to 21 in the Senate. Mitch McConnell (R-KY) encapsulated Republican frustration with Reagan's continued antisanctions stance, stating, "I think he is ill-advised. I think he is wrong. We have waited long enough for him to come on board."[149] Frustrated by the lack of conservative support within the White House, Buchanan departed the Reagan administration five months after the veto override. The Reagan White House's effort to prevent a veto override offered Buchanan the access he and his compatriots desired—yet they failed to make a lasting mark. However, Buchanan was far from done in his efforts to defend South Africa. After leaving the Reagan White House, Buchanan resumed his media roles on *Crossfire* and *The McLaughlin Group*, and grassroots right-wing demand for him to run for the Republican presidential nominee in 1988 grew. He declined to run, publishing his memoir instead, *Right from the Beginning*, rethinking the trajectory of the right wing in the United States, and keeping his eye—and his pen—on South Africa.[150]

With constructive engagement under assault at home and abroad, apartheid's defenders worried that a weakened commitment to white rule had entered the Reagan White House. The influx of pro-apartheid actors—Buchanan, Sears, Nicolaides, and their compatriots—occurred as Congress seriously considered passing economic sanctions against South Africa, finally gaining Republican supporters in mid-1986. Unable to sway centrist Republicans to stick with constructive engagement, the Reagan administration turned to the more virulent right wing. Buchanan and his partners in the White House, Congress, and the broader pro-apartheid ecosystem built their case that they could get Republicans to vote against sanctions. However, the explicit defense of white rule used in Buchanan's defenses pushed the Republican Party to the brink of crisis as centrist Republicans in the White House and Congress rejected this open endorsement of white rule. The Reagan administration's intransigence, empowered by Buchanan and his partners, coupled with Botha's refusal to reform, finally broke the antiapartheid, antisanctions position among centrist Republicans. Their decision to overwhelmingly support sanctions reflected the recognition, against the best efforts of apartheid's defenders, that it was time to add economic tools to the pressure arsenal against Pretoria. At the end of 1986, supporters of apartheid were ultimately left disappointed in the shallowness of the Reagan administration's antisanctions efforts and betrayed by congressional Republicans' eventual overwhelming support for sanctioning white rule.

The passage of sanctions by the United States against South Africa was the final nail in the coffin of almost a decade's worth of pro-apartheid activism. Throughout the 1980s, South Africa's defenders organized across the West, demanding that conservative leaders not abandon their white ally. In this effort, they relied on a truly global network of men and women, infiltrating governments to try and stave off economic coercion of the apartheid state. Yet they failed. The far right's failure to prevent the passage of economic sanctions in 1986 facilitated a greater disillusionment with Reagan, the Republican Party, and global mainstream conservatism. This failure convinced defenders of white rule to reject conservative politics and instead forge a new path within South Africa. As the conservative government in South Africa under F. W. de Klerk undertook a reformist, democratic path, the pro-apartheid movement confronted a new question. What was white rule in South Africa without apartheid, and who would be their partners if they could not rely on their traditional Western allies who seemed ready to turn them over to the ANC?

III

WHITE POWER WITHOUT APARTHEID

INTERLUDE

Apartheid Theology

In 1989, Bishop Masamba came to town. Driving an American-made Ford Galaxy, he arrived in Victoria West in the Northern Cape and declared the township "filthy with sin."[1] Bishop Masamba went door to door in the township, demanding the residents let him use their homes for worship. He faced resistance when a father refused to let Masamba use the family home. In response, Masamba declared the father a communist who hated white people and the South African Defense Force (SADF). Charging ten rand per household to "purify" the township of the influence of liberation theology, Masamba claimed that he protected God's children from the malign influence of people like the young father. Masamba's schemes continued unchecked without a single improvement to the township until one day a videotape arrived with a recording of a sermon from Archbishop Desmond Tutu. Tutu "spoke of *lekker* things" like peace, justice, and humanity.[2] The son of the man lambasted by Masamba stated that his community was ready for Tutu's preaching, and after seeing the sermon, the citizens ran Masamba out of town. The church was "an exciting place to be," the son concluded.

The story of Bishop Masamba is not real. It came from a pamphlet created by Harold Winkler of the University of Cape Town's Religious Studies Department in collaboration with the Institute for Contextual Theology (ICT), part of the Johannesburg-based South African Council of Churches (SACC). The instructional booklet, created for distribution in South Africa's townships and Bantustans, served as "an introduction and study aid for Christians concerned about the growth of right-wing tendencies in the Christian church."[3] These booklets were circulated because, in 1987, as sanctions fell on South Africa, implemented by the apartheid state's allies in the United States and Europe, General Secretary of the ICT Frank Chikane noted a disturbing trend—the "mushrooming" of right-wing and conservative church groups in black townships and bantustans.[4] Bishop Masamba was not real, but he was a caricature of a growing phenomenon—the metastasizing of what the ICT classified as "right-wing religious groups" that propagated "apartheid theology" in English-speaking, evangelical, and African independent churches. These right-wing religious groups came "in many shapes and sizes" but were highly organized and addressed both black and white South Africans. They were black right-wing leaders like Bishop Isaac Mokoena or white right-wing Christian activists like Dorothea Scarborough. Their goals were twofold according to the ICT—to allay the fears and insecurities of whites and to "pacify Black South Africans or even better, to bring them into 'counter-organizations'; which work against anti-apartheid activists." Their theology was easily digestible: dividing the world into good and evil, Bible literalism, exclusive focus on "souls saved," opposition to liberation theology, and uplifting the prosperity gospel. Some of these organizations were well-funded and well-known US enterprises like Jerry Falwell's *Old-Time Gospel Hour* and Paul and Jan Crouch's Trinity Broadcasting Network, but some were hyperlocal South African varieties like Ed Cain's United Christian Action.[5]

The imposition of sanctions by the United States and Europe changed the trajectory of pro-apartheid activism. Throughout much of the 1980s, a transnational ecosystem of actors pooled their resources to defend the last bastion of white rule from destruction by the West's economic might. They failed. That failure fractured the pro-apartheid movement into an even more disjointed set of actors. For apartheid's defenders, the imposition of sanctions and the concessions of the ruling National Party to reform white rule were enraging—and transformative. As Botha's hold on power weakened and the reformist trajectory of the National Party became clear, apartheid's defenders grappled with what it meant to—and how they could—defend white rule in this next stage. The right-wing religious groups were the front lines of this experimentation, pivoting their work from winning global conservative support for the National Party to defending white hierarchy, power, and the status quo at the local level by appealing to conservative black Christians. This hyperlocal activism acts as a case study for the changes in far-right and conservative thinking in the late 1980s and early 1990s. What did it mean to defend apartheid if apartheid was no more?

The ICT had only begun to scratch the surface of the rapidly evolving on-the-ground activities of pro-apartheid actors in South Africa after the imposition of sanctions in 1986 and the changes in Afrikaner churches. In 1986, the Dutch Reformed Church relayed its new stance toward apartheid—condemn white rule, express regret for the church's role in it, but do not admit guilt.[6] This break matched the tepid reforms put in place by National Party *verligtes* but nevertheless broke from the church's previous role as providing the theological justification for separation that acted as the backbone of apartheid's development. This shift enraged the far right, and in response, three thousand conservative clergy splintered off, forming the Afrikaans Protestant Church, led by Willie Lubbe, theology professor at Stellenbosch University, leader of the Verwoerdian apartheid political party Action Own Future—which later became part of the Conservative Party—and self-styled South Africa's Ronald Reagan.[7]

Lubbe represented the growing far-right challenge to the National Party's claim of a monopoly on the white constituency as the party tried to modify apartheid to survive. In an attempt to stave off sanctions and quell internal rebellion, the Botha administration lifted prohibitions of mixed marriages and sexual relationships, halted forced removals, restored citizenship to some bantustan "citizens," abolished influx control—which restricted black South Africans' movement into urban centers—and desegregated some social amenities.[8] However, these "cosmetic changes" to apartheid did not include the political reforms demanded by activists or sanctions implementors, including lifting the ban on the ANC and free and open elections. The financial constraints imposed by sanctions squeezed the South African economy, with the apartheid state falling into a recession characterized by inflation, unemployment, forced loan repayment, corporate pullout, a bloated apartheid bureaucracy, and falling gold prices.[9]

Economic sanctions laid atop the cross-cutting faction of black South African society that engaged in open rebellion against white rule, demanding an end to the apartheid state. South Africans across race, gender, class, age, and ethnicity engaged in insurrectionary activity that "blurred boundaries of who was regarded as part of the armed struggle," as the ANC called for township-led "people's power."[10] Botha's political crackdown could not stifle the struggle—in 1987, 1,148 strikes occurred, with the National Union of Mineworkers leading over 250,000 miners on a three-week stoppage.[11] By 1987, the broad church of the United Democratic Front (UDF) counted over two million members with seven hundred affiliates, forging formal links with the Congress of South African Trade Unions.[12] South Africa's antiapartheid clergy—specifically Tutu, Allan Boesak, Beyers Naudé, and Chikane—supported widespread defiance of the state of emergency crackdowns of 1986.[13] By 1987, black South Africans worked both locally to improve conditions regarding rent, transportation, and police, and nationally to release political prisoners, end the security regime, and obtain democratic representation.[14]

The South African far right raged over this unstable economic and sociopolitical climate in the 1987 election, amplifying white grievances about apartheid reforms, Western "meddling" in South African affairs, and black resistance to apartheid. The Conservative Party represented a formidable challenge to the National Party's stranglehold on power, with the National Party moving up the election two years to try to weaken the far right. By 1987, Conservative Party strength was concentrated in rural areas in the Transvaal and the Orange Free State and in white working-class suburbs in Witwatersrand, with the Conservative Party claiming upward of 20 percent of white voters.[15] With 166 of 178 seats up for grabs, the campaigning proved fierce. Conservative Party candidates argued that P. W. Botha's reforms put black social and economic advancement before that of lower-income whites, attempting to break the National Party hold on poor Afrikaner voters. The Conservative Party vowed to reinstate abolished apartheid laws and disassemble Botha's Tricameral Parliament that included representation for Indian and Colored South Africans. Crucially for poor whites, Conservative Party head Andries Treurnicht committed to reinstating "labor preference," with Zulus only working in Natal, Xhosas in the Eastern Cape, and Coloreds in the Western Cape.[16] Their strategy worked. The Conservative Party picked up 26.37 percent of the national vote, becoming the official opposition party in the House of Assembly. The 1987 election proved "little short of disastrous" for the National Party, as the Conservative Party pulled half the Afrikaner vote, the National Party's traditional base.[17] Even among the assembly seats where the National Party managed to hold off the "Conservative Party charge," candidates feared the increasingly far-right turn in their constituency. Worryingly, the National Party devoted significant campaign resources to attacking white liberals, but the percentage of the liberal white vote dropped from 27 to 18 percent, showing little white support for even the minimal apartheid reforms proposed by the National Party.[18]

In South Africa, the Conservative Party and National Party trumpeted not only their vision of governance but also their unique understanding of what it meant to protect white rule—with or without the apartheid system. The Conservative Party, now in its role as the official opposition party, had a clear vision of Afrikaner nationalism and preserving white rule through apartheid, in contrast to the National Party's muddled calls for limited reform. Botha's "adapt or die" vision—cosmetic reforms to the apartheid state and the reliance on economic interests to build a black middle class and buttress white capital—bred dissent within white South African society. The Conservative Party had a clear base, advocating specifically for working-class Afrikaners and juxtaposing themselves with the capitalist elites of the National Party's English-speaking whites.[19] However, the split in the Afrikaner vote between the Conservative Party and the National Party reflected more than simple class issues.[20] It also revealed two different approaches to Afrikaner survival and preservation of power. On the one hand, the Conservative Party saw Afrikaner rights as being maintained through explicit, legalized protections for whites. On the other, the National Party increasingly viewed a broader white political survival as only possible through a "color-blind" state apparatus that included some "responsible" black actors in the political system. The National Party's commitment to the Tricameral Constitution and the black local councils reflected this vision of "colorblind" governance, where black South Africans remained trapped within the apartheid bureaucracy. The divisions within white South Africa also hinted at an increasingly caustic conflict over free enterprise and capitalism in South Africa. As the National Party and ANC eventually became locked in a mostly two-way negotiation for apartheid's end, the white far right and its allies positioned themselves as the defenders of capitalism in contrast to the communist ANC. As the ANC moderated its radical class agenda for a distinctly neoliberal economic plan, the far right struggled to convey a unique capitalist vision that could win domestic and international backing. Although refracted through the realities of apartheid rule, the questions of race, capital, and power in the right wing mirrored the debates taking place among its global conservative counterparts.

As the Conservative Party and National Party battled for political control of South Africa, a different, grassroots battle was taking place in South Africa's townships and bantustans. After losing the battle to prevent economic sanctions, right-wing religious groups directed their energy to South Africa's townships, pushing black residents to reject political change in favor of the stability of the apartheid regime. Well-funded, technologically savvy, and singularly focused, right-wing religious groups represented a serious threat to political and religious organizing against white rule in South Africa's townships. As rebellion against the apartheid state spread to nearly every township and bantustan in South Africa, a countereffort emerged to destabilize the churches through right-wing religious movements that reproduced apartheid theology and dismissed agitation against white rule as "black on black violence."[21] Right-wing religious groups pitched a different doctrine to the townships: churches should focus on the Gospel and conversion, leaving "secular aims" to the "secular authorities," a blind obedience to authority akin to, as the South African Council of Churches put it, "Nazism."[22] Although their call was to "depoliticize" the church, the call was still a political statement, just of a different kind. This doctrine called on black and white South Africans to turn away from radical protest and return to the traditional family unit and the "comfort" of the status quo. Preying on the desire of black South Africans for physical, financial, and political safety, these groups again turned the ANC into a boogeyman. This time, however, the activism of the right-wing religious groups focused not on international powerbrokers but on changing local attitudes of black South Africans.

Apartheid theology, as deployed in the immediate aftermath of sanctions, retained many elements of the Dutch Reformed Church's conservative theology. In the 1950s, the Afrikaner-Calvinist Christianity of the Dutch Reformed Church argued that God's will required a separation of the races and that although Scripture teaches the "unity of humanity," apartheid applied to all spheres of life. Each "identity" had a duty toward self-improvement. After the Sharpeville Massacre, the Dutch Reformed Church considered leaving behind its "ghetto theology" but ultimately refused to do so and remained a prisoner of its "apartheid bible" that demanded segregation of the races.[23] In support of this apartheid theology, the Dutch Reformed Church preached the sanctity of the traditional family and the importance of obedience to God's laws. This new version of apartheid theology, curated by the Dorothea Scarboroughs, Ed Cains, and Peter Hammonds of the pro-apartheid movement, stripped out the overt rhetoric of racial segregation. Instead, the apartheid theology of the postsanctions era targeted the ANC's vision of liberation, specifically building a theology around obedience to a benevolent but flawed state, and viewed the SACC as stripped of any real Christianity. As the ANC and their SACC partners called for "Christian participation in the struggle," Dorothea argued that these "ministers" worked for the "love of power," stripping their teachings of any "real Christian doctrine," ignoring the Sacrament, the Lord's Prayer, the Creed, and the Ten Commandments.[24] Kairos theologians presented a vision of South Africa as a "hell on earth," Dorothea contended, but in practice, they "[broke] down all civil authority." The destruction of civil authority broke God's law because man, "obliged to obedience, owes it upwards. . . . It was not a matter of whether individuals are worthy of being obeyed."[25] The Dutch Reformed Church's evolved stance toward apartheid revealed that the church no longer saw the true nature of the ANC-aligned liberation theologists and had lost sight of the true gospel, according to Dorothea and her compatriots.

The apartheid theology of Dorothea decried how Tutu and his followers no longer saw sin as "being in the heart of man, but [rather] in the demolition of the 'sinful structures.' " These false prophets portrayed Jesus Christ as a "rebel against Caesar" and totally ignored that "Christ's Kingdom reign comes from above"—"no man can create Paradise out of (the structures of) this world."[26] Dorothea's apartheid theology took aim at the democratic, multicultural, and pluralistic vision of South Africa proposed by the ANC and its comrades. In a series of publications from 1988 to 1991, the Gospel Defense League took aim at the new South Africa. In "Freedom of Religion: How Vital Is Religion in the New South Africa?," Dorothea declared that South Africa was rooted in reformed Christianity and the law of God, creating an "absolute standard" for the government. The state and its armed and police forces served the common good against a "power theology" that had no regard for the Bible or personal devotion.[27] Dorothea leveled similar critiques at those who advocated for political “pluralism,” which “reduces convictions to convenient opinions and makes dogmatism an outdated approach to life and experience.” Pluralism would move away from Christianity and allow “all lifestyles”—homosexuality, abortionists, and heathenisms—to work within a “secular state” that did not recognize rulers as “ministers of God.”[28] Dorothea had perhaps the harshest words for democracy, which she argued “always equals socialism” and was “nothing less than paganism.” God had “created the languages and peoples of the earth to separate Mankind and decentralize power,” which democracy would upend.[29] In practice, Dorothea said God redeemed mankind in “beautiful diversity” and that God’s law “stress[ed] a decentralized State, local control, and national self-determination” since the postflood scattering, the Babel story, and the call of Abraham.[30] The work of the apartheid theologists in the postsanctions era involved weaponizing biblical principles against those committed to multiculturalism and democracy to instead argue for a reification of segregation and a focus on “God’s law.”

In their focus on what they called a “Battle for a Biblical South Africa,” grassroots right-wing religious groups worked together to “prayerfully and materially help the persecuted Blacks, whose property [had] been taken, whose houses burned down, or whose health [was] destroyed by violence.”[31] The Gospel Defense League operated a vast information library, which distributed booklets, audio tapes, video tapes, magazines, and Christian books to “function as a ‘watchman’ to warn of false teachings, disobedience, and the consequences of rebellion against Almighty God.”[32] The Gospel Defense League recommended booklets published by their authors: reverends, professors, translators, and figures from the pre–Information Scandal Christian League.[33] They also circulated American evangelical materials—Family Protection Scoreboard’s work on liberation theology, work by Christian reconstructionist R. J. Rushdoony, and subscriptions to *Antithesis*, *Chalcedon Report*, and *Counsel of Chalcedon*.[34] These apartheid theologists held seminars, including one that Peter Hammond led that laid out their manifesto for “building a biblical South Africa.”[35] Audio and video recordings of the conference, along with publications, were available for only a few rand.

Right-wing religious groups centralized themselves in South Africa’s black townships, organizing youth groups, choir programs, competitions, and food drives. The ICT uncovered right-wing religious group infiltration into township congregations and parish council leadership. In South Africa's bantustans, right-wing religious groups and apartheid officials established minister fraternal organizations, youth groups, and women's leagues specifically designed to support the bantustan black leaders.[36] Right-wing religious groups organized mandatory personnel training courses to make black South African officials "better Christians and anti-communists." These courses appeared at South Africa's universities as right-wing religious groups took over existing Christian student groups, organizing multiyear trainings and monthly courses to provide a "Christian response" to National Party reforms. Disturbing reports emerged of miners in the Northern Cape continuously exposed to right-wing theology from "conservative ministers who visit compounds."[37] These pro-apartheid churches embarked on a new strategy, moving away from "keeping hearts and minds" in white communities to "winning hearts and minds" in black communities with the promise of religious salvation.[38] Organizations like the Gospel Defense League and Jesus Christ for Peace, familiar faces from the antisanctions campaigns of the 1980s, embarked on massive organizing drives, distributing monthly leaflets to women's groups and spreading anti-SACC and anti-ANC rhetoric. In schools in the North Transvaal, pro-apartheid churches created youth organizations, choirs, and films advertising bible camps for black South African children. Right-wing religious groups offered a gospel that promised financial security, stability, and an end to violence, challenging the "new South Africa" vision put forth by antiapartheid activists.

However, according to journalists and watchdog groups investigating right-wing religious groups throughout the 1980s, these organizations lacked a real constituency among black and white South Africans.[39] What the right-wing religious groups lacked in a vibrant flock, they made up for in resources and support from the Western evangelical machine. The critical tenets of their theology—espoused by Ed Cain, Peter Hammond, and Dorothea Scarborough—of anticommunism, antiliberation theology, biblical fundamentalism, and personal salvation were deeply rooted in apartheid theology. They found a symbiotic partner in US right-wing evangelists, who crafted "an extensive national and international communication network to portray the Republic of South Africa in a positive light as a Christian country, with apartheid virtually dead."[40] This transnational exchange was hardly new, curated and nurtured throughout the

1980s as brokers like the International Freedom Foundation facilitated connections between right-wing religious groups and conservative organizations.[41] US evangelicals represented the next step of this chain, leveraging their massive resources to quickly infiltrate South African churches. For instance, Johannesburg's popular Rhema Christian Church led by Ray McCauley relied on religious literature that was "imported American, bought from Jerry Falwell and Jimmy Swaggart for a pro-Botha line."[42] These US organizations were "obsessed" with "winning souls for Christ" and remained silent on the evils of the apartheid regime and the violence used to maintain it.[43] In this way, these right-wing evangelicals were the perfect partners for the next phase of pro-apartheid activism that was allegedly "apolitical," preaching stability, tradition, and acquiescence to the status quo.

No organization better encapsulated this disturbing collaboration than Trinity Broadcasting Network (TBN). Helmed by Paul and Jan Crouch, TBN, the world's largest religious television network, partnered with the Botha and bantustan governments to deliver a pro-apartheid gospel that emphasized personal responsibility, color blindness, and stability, in opposition to the radical political and social change demanded by the ANC and the SACC. Paul Crouch and his wife Jan formed TBN in 1973 with one low-power station in southern California. Initially getting his start in radio broadcasting, Crouch managed stations in South Dakota and California before creating TBN, which initially only operated in the United States. However, Paul and Jan possessed international ambitions. TBN eventually became the most-watched Christian network in the United States and the world's largest religious broadcaster, maintaining twenty-six global television networks and affiliates, eighty-plus satellites, and over 200,000 television and cable affiliates, including Internet programing.[44] Paul Crouch's TBN retained a single-minded focus on "one crucial goal: to take the love of Jesus to every corner of the earth."[45] The Crouch family's vision for spreading the love of Jesus proved fundamentally different from many liberal and conservative evangelizing efforts at this time—their goals required a direct connection with the apartheid state.

Paul and Jan Crouch proved quite a pair on the air. Paul, relentlessly perky, and Jan, with cotton-candy pink hair, built a religious empire grounded in the Crouches' folksy appeal but on the backs of prosperity gospel rhetoric and small-level donations from Americans. Their humble appearance hid personal extravagance, with TBN's earnings funding his-and-hers mansions in Newport Beach, private jets, ministry homes, and theme parks. Although Paul presented himself as an approachable "friend in Christ," he had a vindictive streak. According to a former TBN producer, Crouch was ruthless and willing to do anything to grow the network, even asking God to kill a man who petitioned the Federal Communications Commission to investigate the network's financial misconduct.[46] Nevertheless, Crouch's theology mirrored much of the "Californian evangelicalism" of the 1980s, fusing Crouch's ambitions with the prosperity gospel of the time. TBN consciously diluted the particularities of any one denomination—Pentecostal in origin, broadcasts included a diverse range of Protestants, Catholics, and Messianic Jews. Crouch valued personal loyalty to TBN over denominational dogmas. Nevertheless, TBN's programming retained many of Pentecostalism's "experiential" characteristics. Programs emphasized a personal and transformative relationship with Jesus Christ, undertook ritualistic performances, and reveled in charismatic experiences like prophecy and healings.[47] Pentecostalism and its associated Charismatic Churches are the "fastest growing churches within Christianity," made up of "600 million adherents worldwide in 2010." Pentecostals also include the African Independent Churches, made up of fifty-five million members across the continent.[48]

TBN's most substantial theological current was the singular certainty of the coming apocalypse. For TBN and its associated evangelicals, proof of premillennial dispensationalism abounded. Humanity was currently living through the last days of history before the second coming of Christ and a millennium of peace. In this, Crouch fixated on the "Great Commission," a mandate to spread the Christian message by whatever means necessary to hurry the world's imminent end.[49] This mandate necessitated international evangelizing—and formed a bridge to the apartheid theologists who also fixated on the "end times." Only once "all people" had the opportunity to hear the gospel could Jesus return, but how to spread the gospel became a point of open debate. Whereas previous efforts at evangelism required physical mobility, Crouch believed that television could create a religious experience without the costs of missionary work.[50] TBN "viewers participate[d] in global evangelism without leaving their living room," teleporting an urgent religious message into previously "inaccessible" nations like South Africa. However, Crouch saw his particular style of television ministry as fundamentally different from that of his predecessors. Only in the twentieth century did evangelicals have the "explosion of knowledge and technology to reach [Africans]."[51]

During the 1980s, Global South states began divesting from Western television imports, but South Africa was a notable outlier. The South African Broadcasting Company (SABC), the state-controlled media apparatus, first launched Radio Bantu to reach African listeners in their native language to spread apartheid propaganda.[52] The apartheid government approved television services through SABC in 1971, maintaining a rigid state monopoly and producing and showing programming that reinforced separate development, launching programming in 1976.[53] Unlike other parts of the African continent, the South African government's active control created favorable conditions for imported Western television. TBN capitalized on this highly restrictive South African television landscape as "TV's final frontier in the industrial world" to supply "essential" religious and political propaganda to the black bantustans.[54] The state monopoly on television paired well with state protection of its private partners—in 1980, the apartheid state enacted the National Key Points Act, which used the state's security apparatus to protect any privately owned "place or area" that was of strategic importance or public interest.[55] This act came in play as Crouch alleged protection of TBN's television stations by SADF, authorized by Botha, against potential saboteurs. However, television remained mostly consumed by white South Africans; in the 1980s, most black South Africans purchased television sets for personal use only as part of the connection of the townships to the electrical grid.[56] From the beginning of TV in South Africa, it retained a "a heavy dose of Calvinist Christianity" and of "stern scripture readings," even as it evolved to include two new channels in 1982 that emphasized the "traditional," "ethnic," and "tribal identity" of black South Africans.[57] As the black middle class grew in South Africa and access to television along with it, consumption habits evolved to viewing American programs like *The Cosby Show*, which depicted a black middle-class family and was the most popular television show among white South Africans during the mid-1980s.[58] Thus, by the mid-1980s, the South African government was searching for more American programming that promoted their worldview of South Africa but that could also reach the emerging black middle class in South Africa.

The black middle class seemed the perfect consumer for TBN's conservative programming. Between 1970 and 2015, the religious tradition with the highest growth rate in South Africa was Pentecostal Christian, which made up almost half of the approximately forty-five million Christians in South Africa by 2015. Additionally, the African Initiated Churches, which shared many of the elements of Charismatic Christianity, comprised nearly 41 percent of all other Christians in South Africa.[59] These churches had a conservative worldview—the Zion Christian Church (ZCC), the largest of the African Initiated Churches with over five million members today, famously hosted Botha in 1985 to address its two million members on the importance of stability and the evils of the ANC.[60] These black Pentecostal leaders "generally show[ed] apathy towards political involvement," with the ZCC as no exception.[61] Pentecostalism, wedded to the resources of the American megachurch-media industrial complex, spread rapidly among African Christians. As the scholar Maria Frahm-Arp argued in her study of three churches founded in 1980 and 1990 and servicing the black middle class in Johannesburg, the churches "critique[d] the present government while at the same time showing little interest in building an alternative state, focusing instead on building lives of success and wellbeing focused around the family and the church community."[62] The conservative Christian worldview of status quo stability and capitalist enrichment could perhaps find an audience in a new black middle class.[63]

It is in this media and emerging middle-class environment that TBN operated. In July 1984, Crouch announced his expansion plans into Ciskei, arranging meetings with the bantustan president Lennox Sebe and the legislative assembly, securing a permit in July 1986. Sebe agreed to build "mighty 100 percent Christian TV stations in their country," with Crouch espousing the "separate nations" rhetoric of the apartheid state.[64] This was not a one-off partnership but part of a formal alliance with the apartheid authorities to provide Christian television for all of South Africa in 1987. South African state and bantustan leaders appeared on TBN fundraising programs, including Ciskei's Lennox Sebe and Reverend V. G. Ntshinga, Transkei's Bantu Holomisa, and Peter van de Venter of South Africa's National Religious Broadcasters.[65] TBN's programming attempted to unmoor viewers from the realities of life in South Africa, fixating instead on the "great haul" of saved Christians reached by TBN. The programming created by TBN conjured the image of South Africa as a place "overrun" by radical communists that demanded intervention by committed evangelicals to proselytize to the heathen masses who were at risk of ultimate corruption by the ANC.[66] In fundraising programs, Crouch condemned "the bloody revolution, totally committed to the overthrow of the legitimate South African government."[67] Throughout TBN's partnership with the South African and bantustan governments, Crouch and his partners positioned the bantustans as independent nations that were positively influenced by the introduction of Christian television.[68] TBN's uniquely symbiotic relationship with the South African state and Bantustan governments paid dividends. Crafting regressive religious programming that deployed a pro-apartheid gospel, US evangelicals bolstered white rule and black bantustan leaders facing a crisis of legitimacy.

Tapping into the fear experienced by everyday South Africans living under despotic rule, TBN tried to offer black South Africans an alternative interpretation of events. TBN also relied on a talented lineup of religious leaders tailored to South Africans. Reinhard Bonnke—a German American Pentecostal famous for his missions throughout Africa—often appeared on TBN's programs and attended meetings in August 1987 between Crouch and South Africa's deputy minister of foreign affairs.[69] TBN's Bophuthatswana station—approved in October 1988—helped Bonnke as he preached to "millions."[70] Crouch's surrogates were not exclusively white people. Beginning in the 1970s, Black preachers hosted *Praise the Lord* and other shows on the network.[71] TBN's relationship with E. V. Hill—the famed pastor of Los Angeles's Mount Zion Missionary Baptist Church and a popular African American preacher—proved essential to the network's credibility in Africa. According to Crouch, Hill's program hit number one in ratings across secular and religious programming in South Africa.[72] By August 1992, E. V. Hill and Jeff and Reeni Fenholt's religious musical show *Highway to Heaven* "competed with secular programs" and appeared consistently on the TBN TV aired by the SABC. Crouch relied on this vast network of African missionaries and African American preachers to dispense a particular brand of theology based on "uplifting the race," dismissing poor, urban Black youth, and accumulating material prosperity within the existing system.[73] Crouch did not keep his congregation only for whites but instead worked with conservative black Christians to combat the moral failings of a world moving away from Christ. TBN could outwardly appear not to hinder racial equality while also tightly controlling a discourse that explained racial inequality as caused by urban violence and moral failings.

Nevertheless, although TBN employed a racially diverse religious lineup, TBN's mailings to its subscribers reveal an organization focused on racial control and minimization of black South African grievances against apartheid. After one of Crouch's pastors, John Jacobs, and the "Power Team" led a religious rally in Ciskei, Crouch commented on how the South African children "went 'bananas' over the Power Team" and how, with Jacobs's firm hand, "ALL listened intently . . . and many were saved!" Crouch's association of black children with bananas was an overt invocation of the racist association of black people with monkeys, with the image of the firm hand as white control. TBN's pastors and leadership insisted that they alone had "the answer to the political, racial, and economic problems of South Africa—NOT Reform, NOT Religion, but JESUS!"[74] The question of the "right kind" of religion dominated TBN's discourse. According to Crouch, it was up to TBN to redeem a "hungry" South Africa. He alone possessed the power to save a violent land.[75] TBN's programming consistently invoked a South Africa in disarray, overrun by communists, radicals, and atheists; conversely, South Africa was still a site of salvation.[76] TBN borrowed its rhetoric from the Botha government, referring to the bantustans as separate "containment" areas outside the white state. Repeatedly, Crouch referred to his expansion efforts in South Africa as "the great haul" and as "religious bodies to be harvested" in the service of Christ.[77] The master control, Crouch stated, must be put into place as Crouch regaled plans to bring a mobile video truck to Ray McCauley's Rhema Bible Church. Unmoored from the realities of life under apartheid, Crouch declared that he was "ON THE WAY to unhinge the very gates of hell in AFRICA."[78]

Crouch's rhetoric of chaos and upheaval abroad tapped into the fears of many US conservatives at home about the state of US race relations in the 1980s and 1990s. TBN's domestic programming mirrored content on South African "black on black violence" and "racial upheaval." Crouch and his team routinely used the language of "riots" to describe civilian rebellions against racist systems in the United States, like the Los Angeles uprisings, and in South Africa, particularly in the Ciskei and Bophuthatswana regions. For instance, in a *Praise the Lord* segment from April 30, 1992, Crouch called for "order through the gospel" in response to the Los Angeles uprisings without commenting on Rodney King's brutal assault by police. According to his guest, Pastor Billy Ingram, the "real tragedy"—property destruction—affected churches and not just South Central Los Angeles. "Black and Hispanic youths," said Ingram, caused "massive pandemonium and totally out of control looting." Black guests Smokey Robinson and Pastor Ed Smith emphasized that the "streets" were teaching Black youths violence and that Black protestors needed churches and elders' influence. Pastor E. V. Hill stated that the uprising "was not really about Rodney King" and was just a tool for "black people to kill black people" and engage in looting and disruption.[79] These domestic and international programs drew a direct link between the causes of Black grievances in the United States and South Africa and a global threat to conservative and religious values. Critically, TBN's South African and US content stressed the overwhelmingly positive influence of the religious network, which was capable of civilizing unruly Black people, particularly youths. However, Crouch's rhetoric on South Africa proved far more explicitly racist and violent than his domestic rhetoric, which often appeared couched in a post–civil rights rhetoric of personal improvement. These two discourses reflected Crouch's savviness about his different audiences and partners. Crouch provided a symbolic link between the threat to white rule in South Africa and the United States while asserting TBN's role as an indispensable, familial stabilizer for black people.

These projects relied on the elevation of black right-wing actors like Bishop Isaac Mokoena and Bishop Mzilikazi Masiya, who advocated for the limited reform agenda of the South African government while questioning the motivations of the ANC. In February 1986, the South African Tourism Board designed an exhibit for the US National Religious Broadcasters annual convention, manned by familiar faces of van de Venter, Mokoena, and Pastor van Kerken. Mokoena, the "most honored guest" of the 1986 convention, was "constantly interviewed on TV and radio and came fully into his own during these interviews, giving the audience a different, positive view of South Africa." The leading figures of the convention—Dr. Ben Armstrong, Jimmy Swaggart, and Reverend Jerry Falwell, "stuck their neck out" for South Africa, supporting the apartheid state for two simple reasons—"we are a Christian nation . . . and we are anti-communists." The organizers of the exhibit hoped to leverage the National Religious Broadcasters' close contact with various right-wing religious groups to coordinate a cross-cultural Christian exchange of gospel musicians and musical festivals. This relationship with US evangelicals, South Africa's organizers argued, might be the "single most important [relationship] . . . worldwide for South Africa."[80] TBN's symbiotic relationship with the bantustan leadership proved essential in this regard. For instance, during an appearance by Transkei head of government Bantu Holomisa on *Behind the Scenes* in March 1989, Crouch said that if he were an American businessman, he would invest in South Africa. Crouch condemned "the bloody revolution, totally committed to the overthrow of the legitimate South African government."[81] In the interview, Crouch repeatedly referred to Transkei as an independent nation, subscribing to the South African state's rhetoric on the bantustans. Although he acknowledged that "there have been wrongs inflicted on the black races," he argued that "things" are changing through "Christian television."[82]

Holomisa, Sebe, and the other black bantustan leaders were in a uniquely precarious situation by the late 1980s. Although nominally "independent," the bantustan leaders relied almost entirely on Pretoria for economic stability and political legitimacy, and rumors of formal reincorporation into South Africa threatened bantustan leaders' power. The Ciskei government—often through South African propaganda networks—touted privatization and deregulation in the region, attempting to attract Western investors and prove the bantustans could remain independent.[83] The KwaZulu, Transkei, and Bophuthatswana bantustan leaders embarked on similar projects, creating industry havens for Western businessmen and promising investment with access to cheap South African labor but outside sanctions policy as "independent states." TBN's programming explicitly enforced their position. Crouch and his team provided a rare defense of the bantustan system while also bringing Western capital into the region. Emboldened by their continued financial growth in South Africa and their subversion of congressional sanctions legislation, Crouch and his family increased their pro-apartheid rhetoric and expansion efforts into the bantustans. Crouch declared, "MISSION ACCOMPLISHED! African Station Number Two," after a meeting with Bophuthatswana's Lucas Mangope in November 1988. Crouch proclaimed that racial unrest and acts of terror "declined significantly" with TBN's presence and that "there is NO APARTHEID."[84] That same week, Crouch met with South Africa's minister of communications and the head of the Dutch Reformed Church to present TBN's plan for "100 percent Christian television." After a two-day rally in Bisho, where TBN and local officials bused in ten thousand black South Africans, Crouch declared the "dark nation had been born in a day."[85] Further encouraged by the South African government's approval for a Christian television network in June 1989, Crouch declared apartheid a secondary issue to Africa's religious salvation and the right of South Africans to hear the gospel.[86] Even after Sebe's overthrow by a military coup on March 4, 1990, and his subsequent charges of corruption and human rights abuses, TBN hardly missed a step. Sebe remained on TBN's Africa board, and Crouch built a relationship with his successor, Oupa Gqozo.

TBN's uniquely symbiotic relationship with the South African state and homeland governments paid dividends for apartheid's supporters. TBN entered 1990 as the world's only international religious network, with 248 broadcasting TV stations, fifteen million homes with cable stations, five satellite stations, and stations in twenty-eight foreign countries. Captivating, regressive religious programming deployed a pro-apartheid gospel in the heart of rebellion against white rule—South Africa's bantustans. This relationship proved profitable not only for TBN and the Botha government but also for black bantustan leaders facing a crisis of legitimacy. Even in the face of congressional sanctions, Crouch and TBN stuck with the apartheid state and the homeland leadership, opposing the radical political and social change demanded by the ANC and SACC.

Chikane noted that the SACC had previously dismissed the right-wing religious groups as simply a lunatic fringe, unworthy of attention. That, he concluded, was a mistake. These organizations were more than propaganda tools of the apartheid state; they also represented a disturbing next phase in white power organizing. Yet, a worrisome knowledge gap existed on the activities of the right-wing religious groups. The SACC decided to undertake a formal study of the right-wing religious groups and their theology through the ICT, which, after its founding in 1981, acted as an incubator of Christian theologizing within the SACC, formulating a doctrine of liberation and reconciliation that would "meet the moment" of the apartheid struggle.[87] But by 1987, the ICT's mission had grown beyond theologizing. Its research and education efforts would thereafter probe the "problematic growth" of right-wing religious groups.[88] Jeff Marishane, an ICT researcher specializing in low-intensity warfare and the interconnections between the South African state and grassroots extremists, took the lead in these efforts.[89] As Marishane's Department of Research Education and Formation envisioned it, their studies of right-wing religion aimed "to provide analysis, to monitor the phenomenon, to assess the impact on public opinion and churches, and to expose the use of right-wing groups by the government to further its political ends."[90] In partnership with the Concerned Evangelicals, a Soweto-based radical Christian theological organization, the ICT embarked on the "Misuse of Religion" series to spread essential information about right-wing religious groups' operations in townships and bantustans. Their first interim report, presented in July 1988, surveyed the state of right-wing religious organizations across South Africa, interviewing leaders and victims of these organizations and examining their material. They concluded that they weaponized Christianity to "bless capitalism," vilify black radicalism, and promote the "emergence of a puppet black moderate" willing to participate in National Party reform through their contacts with the American religious right, business, and government interests. The "Misuse of Religion series" identified several key agents in South Africa, including familiar faces like Aida Parker, Ed Cain, Howard Phillips, Bishop Isaac Mokoena, and Jesus Christ for Peace's Mzilikazi Masiya and David Balsiger. These activists were part of the counterrevolution. They organized social, career, sport, educational, religious, and military activities. Youth events took place in the Gazankulu and Venda bantustans, along with the Vaal Triangle, where John Gogotya, a black antisanctions activist and leader of the military intelligence–funded Federal Independent Democratic Alliance, played host. Mokoena and Mayor Tamsanqa Linda of the South African government-backed town councils ran theological training, aid, and housing programs.[91]

Over the next few years, the ICT assembled a disturbing picture of webs of far-right malaise spreading within black urban and rural communities in South Africa. ICT researchers estimated that pro-apartheid church activism grew by almost 200 percent from 1985 to 1990.[92] The pro-apartheid churches offered a powerful counter-theology—in times of social disorder, the right-wing religious groups' dogmatic, authoritarian formulations provided a firm anchor in the "troubled sea of South African politics."[93] As General Secretary Smangaliso Mkhatshwa of the ICT put it in May 1989, the conflict and divisions among Christians intensified with the introduction of militant right-wing religion amid growing political reforms by the

National Party government. Antidemocratic activism spread fast in South Africa, Mkhatshwa concluded, and "many more of the black oppressed majority [were] beginning to be fooled or confused by it."[94]

Alarmed by this influx of far-right religiosity, the ICT and its partners mustered a challenge to the right-wing religious groups and their US backers. Region by region, the ICT implemented a series of community-based programs to help residents identify right-wing groups and expose congregations spouting far-right ideals in northern and southern Transvaal, the Western Cape, and Natal.[95] The ICT linked local organizations to national resources, sponsoring a Joint Christian Youth Forum to unite all Christian youth structures in Natal to expose the growth of right-wing Christian activists.[96] The "Standing for Truth" campaign linked together different sectors of the church, integrating them into grassroots activism that combated far-right religiosity in urban and rural spaces. In this effort, the ICT tried to build on activism of local African Independent Churches to combat conservative Christianity that left black township residents "frustrated and deserted."[97] Their most ambitious plan was a partnership with the Ecumenical Documentation and Information Center for Eastern and Southern Africa (EDICESA) in Harare, Zimbabwe, in 1988. The ICT, EDICESA, and the Concerned Evangelicals wanted to establish an archive and database on the right-wing religious groups that would contain lists of these groups in southern Africa, along with their leaders, links with each other, international backers, theological and political identities, and social bases. EDICESA also devised plans to train Christians throughout the region to identify and combat the growth of right-wing religious groups. Their first effort at this project came on March 23–30, 1990, with participants from twelve countries trained on how to draw up lists of right-wing religious groups, identify their theology, collect and analyze material, and assess the political and social significance of their activity. After the workshop's success, EDICESA started to prepare Christian literature on the right-wing religious groups to combat their unchallenged influence. "There is a tremendous need," EDICESA concluded, "for popular, socially committed, theologically respectable material that the mainline churches can use in education programs," in contrast to the preponderance of US–South African right-wing material.[98]

The ICT's assessment of black South African Christians as feeling "frustrated and deserted" and facing a "tremendous need" for intervention from their theology reveals an additional challenge faced by the organization—the bedrock of black South African conservative Christianity. The ICT's interpretation of the township theological space was one of black South Africans almost monolithically preyed upon by white right-wingers. Yet in practice, black South Africans tended toward religious conservatism, even amid progressive politics. This reality provided a bastion of potential support for the right-wing religious groups identified by the ICT.[99] The conservative Christian appeals of the right wing, especially through Pentecostals like TBN, served as a proxy for their political agenda that could gain traction with black Christians. The ICT, in its labeling of the "right-wing religious groups," undoubtedly identified a challenge to their theology, operating from an assumption that black South Africans should and would support their vision if not for these outside interventions. The ICT downplayed the "homegrown" elements of the right-wing religious groups, instead insisting that their appeal was from outside Western agitators. The ICT largely rejected that the domestic theology of the right-wing religious groups—Pentecostalism, capitalist materialism, and political conservatism—could appeal to black Christians. The apartheid theologists worked to mobilize black South Africans against the ANC. Their brand of religiosity, which offered a thin veneer of Christianity to cover up extremely reactionary, pro-apartheid views, struggled to gain consistent appeal across South Africa's black townships and bantustans. However, the introduction of American evangelicals, through groups like TBN, acted as an accelerant on the groundwork of the pro-apartheid movement. A cross-ethnic, conservative landscape of Christians existed within South Africa, who were perhaps not as swayed by the apartheid theology of Scarborough and Hammond but were more interested in the conservative anti-ANC Christianity promoted by the Crouches.

In their attempted interventions, the ICT saw firsthand the resiliency and appeals of conservative Christianity. ICT researchers tracked right-wing evangelicalism spreading rapidly throughout southern Africa, through church planting, bible schools, correspondence courses, literature publication, and mass video and cassette distribution.[100] The only stable Christian bookstores, EDICESA lamented, remained evangelical, with many books from right-wing religious groups and other US evangelical organizations. Progressive organizations struggled to keep pace. The on-the-ground programs faced even steeper challenges. Over six months in 1990, the ICT set up crisis ministries in the Odi District of Bophuthatswana at the urging of the Congress of the Traditional Leaders of South Africa, the UDF, and the ANC to support democratization efforts in the bantustans. The crisis ministries faced daily hostility, with open threats made by Bophuthatswana's Mangope to remove the organizations for subverting his regime.[101] Eventually, groups could only hold meetings outside Bophuthatswana. From 1990 to 1991, the ICT expanded these efforts into the Gazankulu, Venda, and Transkei bantustans, setting up a task force to investigate the relationship between the "pro-apartheid churches" and Bantustan leadership.[102]

The massive spread of conservative Christianity did not just come down to right-wingers' organizational and material prowess over their antiapartheid counterparts. This particular theological mixture—Pentecostalism, capitalism, and conservatism—had appeal to black South Africans, which the ICT seemed unable to acknowledge. The decision to tamp down overt support for the apartheid state in favor of conservative Christianity found a base amid black Christians in the townships and bantustans. The grassroots activism of the right-wing religious groups encapsulated the turn taken by the pro-apartheid movement as sanctions fell on South Africa and the Botha regime stumbled. As the apartheid state entered its final years, its defenders evaluated what it meant to defend white rule and how it could do so. The right-wing religious groups represented one direction of that breakaway path, spreading their ideology at the front lines of resistance to the apartheid state, offering an alternative vision of the preservation of white power that also offered an appealing vision to black South Africans. This reconfigured message of the pro-apartheid movement offered conservative black Christians a pathway to material, physical, and social safety previously denied under the apartheid state. The ICT, in their identification of the "enemy" of the right-wing religious groups, correctly identified not only the reactionary, white supremacist power at the grassroots but also just how mainstream many of those actors would become. The right-wing religious groups signified something new that built on traditional Christian values to offer a conservative vision of South Africa for a postapartheid world.

The rise of F. W. de Klerk only hastened these divisions as white paramilitary, political, and religious actors increasingly viewed the ruling National Party not as an embattled ally but as a bitter enemy. How could apartheid's defenders make their case now, with apartheid maligned at home and abroad? The return to the local—as seen through the right-wing religious groups—became the playing field of the white imaginary, as self-defense groups and political organizations offered a contrasting vision of a "new South Africa," one that differed from the ANC's. The white right—and increasingly its black bantustan partners—positioned themselves as the defenders of local control, protecting minority and ethnic rights from the tyranny of national communist, authoritarian power. This partnership, with seeds planted in 1980s antisanctions organizing, emerged anew over shared understandings of ethnicity, territory, political control, and capitalism. In 1990, they sought a new iteration of these shared values—an explicit political alliance, where they, not the ANC, were the defenders of human rights, protectors of tradition, and capitalist titans, crafting a cross-racial alliance that supported ethnic, federal power against the tyranny of an ANC-National Party–dominated democracy. The race to save South Africa was on.

6

HUMAN RIGHTS FOR WHITE POWER

On March 14, 1988, P. W. Botha gave a seventy-five-minute interview with the *Washington Times* during which he declared that the "world should let Pretoria change at its own pace." In his bombastic interview, Botha maligned the United States, stating that the American response to apartheid was "all a function of [its] domestic politics and guilty conscience about [its] racial problems."[1] Botha believed he stood in the position of moderacy, walking the line between left- and right-wing factions who wished to destroy South African society, crafting a new nation for all races and ethnicities. Sanctions only pulled South Africa further away from the West, Botha argued. In the interview, Botha positioned himself as South Africa's leader for the future, managing unrest at home and foreign interference from hypocritical Western allies abroad.

However, increasingly unpopular domestically and reviled internationally, Botha's cabinet pressured him to resign under the guise of health complications related to a stroke, setting off a heated race for party leadership.[2] A seemingly unlikely candidate F. W. de Klerk, minister of national education and planning, jockeyed for the post. During his campaign, de Klerk appeared to take the reformist National Party line, emphasizing the urgent need for National Party–led reform, bashing the ANC, and maintaining apartheid group rights.[3] ANC leadership spoke out against de Klerk's candidacy, viewing him as a continuation of the limited reforms that characterized the Botha administration. However, de Klerk would prove different than his predecessor, committing the South African government to a process of negotiation with the ANC and other liberationist parties that set in motion the end of white rule and the beginning of multiracial democracy in South Africa.

Apartheid's defenders viewed these changes with alarm and recognized that in the aftermath of sanctions, a change of strategy was essential. "The South African Right: Searching for Allies Abroad," declared the 1990 issue of the International Freedom Foundation's *Freedom Bulletin*. Domestic political changes—principally assumption of power by de Klerk and his new reformist agenda—forced the right wing to look beyond the apartheid state for aid. The International Freedom Foundation maintained that this outreach from South African conservatives was not unilateral. International right-wingers saw the "potential gains that ultra-conservatism, as an ethos, could make if the right were to become a dominant political force in South Africa."[4] Yet, the International Freedom Foundation urged caution. The organization noted that the "overtly racist nature" of the apartheid system made them pariahs, susceptible to "overseas conservative fringe elements" masquerading as power brokers in mainstream right-wing circles. The failures of the South African right wing only increased with the collapse of the Soviet Union and the withering of communist ideology, leaving the white right even more isolated and alone.

The International Freedom Foundation incorrectly interpreted the international ambitions of the South African right wing as limited and fringe. However, their assessment of the problems facing the white right in 1990 proved spot on: it was isolated from Western partners in the aftermath of the passage of sanctions, wedded to a declining anticommunist ideology, and disconnected from a defense of white rule that could gain international legitimacy. The end of the Cold War heralded a shift in the pro-apartheid movement's organizing, as white supremacist actors drew on the global human rights movement to defend and reimagine white rule. In a world without the existential threat of the Soviet Union, the pro-apartheid movement's anticommunist rhetoric did not resonate as it had in the 1980s. However, as international concerns about human rights—principally ethnic rights—emerged, apartheid's defenders reimagined themselves as the premier defender of ethnic rights and put themselves in a global story of "liberation" as the Soviet Union collapsed. In doing so, white South Africans built on the foundations of separate development that created the apartheid state to uplift a new version of white rule. It moved beyond positioning South Africa as part of anticolonial Africa to instead put white South Africans as part of liberating ethnic states of the post–Cold War world.[5]

After the passage of sanctions and the assumption of power by de Klerk, transatlantic right-wingers wrestled with what it meant to defend white rule in a world where the apartheid state and the entire Western world seemed to have turned on them. Fearing a permanent shift in the balance of power in South Africa away from whites and toward the black majority, South African far-right parties—backed by their US counterparts—created their vision for white rule. Invoking the historic Boer republics, the self-governing white republics of the late nineteenth century, South African far-rightists demanded the formation of segregated ethno-states or a *volkstaat* under the guise of minority rights protections. However, not all factions the pro-apartheid movement supported the *volkstaat*. Far-right organizations across the United States and South Africa disagreed on the pro-apartheid movement's tactics, strategies, and goals as it faced the reality of a National Party that no longer served exclusively white interests. In their search for a "new South Africa" that could compete with the emerging ANC–South African government vision, the white right eventually coalesced around a rhetoric of ethnic rights in the human rights era.

THE END OF THE COLD WAR AND RESOLUTION IN SOUTHERN AFRICA

After the passage of the Comprehensive Anti-Apartheid Act—and the imposition of sanctions by other Western governments—negotiations in South Africa over democratic transition resumed. The Reagan administration's policy toward South Africa evolved in the two years after sanctions, with State Department officials concentrating on supporting the burgeoning dialogue between the South African government and the ANC.[6] Under the helm of US Ambassador to South Africa Edward Perkins, the Reagan administration increased conversations with the ANC and the United Democratic Front (UDF).[7] Most importantly, Shultz met with the ANC president Oliver Tambo in January 1987, signaling a real—and symbolic—commitment from the US government to engage all political parties in apartheid's end.[8]

After casting off the domestic political leper of Reagan's unwillingness to support sanctions, White House officials focused in earnest on negotiated political settlement to end armed conflict in southern Africa. The weakened position of South Africa in the summer of 1988 pushed Pretoria into honest negotiations to end southern African conflicts, as the South African Defense Force (SADF) took on a "politically sensitive white body count" in Angola and failed to set up a South West Africa People's Organization (SWAPO) alternative in Namibia.[9] Simultaneously, the South African government faced domestic white opposition to the continued expansion of male conscription for the border wars, as it conscripted approximately 600,000 white men in 1992.[10] The End Conscription Campaign, composed mostly of progressive whites, actively sought to influence mainstream white culture in South Africa. The deployment of conscripted troops to quell rebellion in the townships ruptured the "heroic" image of the white soldier, which "was simply not transferable to township duty."[11] Although the National Party demonized the proponents of the End Conscription Campaign as dupes and deviants in thrall to the ANC, Pretoria did halve mandatory service to one year in 1990 in response to increasing turmoil in white society.[12]

However, it was not just South Africans who faced problems in the regional wars. As early as 1986, the leader of the Soviet Union, Mikhail Gorbachev, began to move toward a political settlement in southern Africa, reflecting his aim to reduce confrontation with the West in the Global South.[13] As the Soviet Union deteriorated domestically and Gorbachev managed the fallout of withdraw from Afghanistan, he aimed to settle Namibia and Angola with "as much prestige intact as possible."[14] The reduced capacity of the Soviet Union incentivized political negotiation, especially as a potential full-scale conflict among Cuban, SWAPO, People's Movement for the Liberation of Angola (MPLA), and SADF forces on the Angola-Namibia border loomed. Trying to capitalize on the changing geopolitical circumstances, in May 1988, Assistant Secretary of State Crocker brought the Cuban, Angolan, and South African parties to the negotiating table. The Soviets eventually joined the negotiations in June 1988, pressuring the Cuban and Angolan delegates to accept a political settlement against the backdrop of Gorbachev's rapprochement with

Reagan.[15] Their efforts paid off. In December 1988, Cuba, Angola, and South Africa signed the Tripartite Accord: Pretoria agreed to implement UN Resolution 435, and Havana would withdraw from Angola over twenty-seven months.[16] With the Tripartite Accords, the time of Botha's Total Onslaught policy had seemingly passed.

The collapse of the Soviet Union upended the international system and the dominant capitalist-communist binary. Throughout the 1980s, Gorbachev struggled to save the Soviet Union's economy, attempting to pry apart the old command economy structure in favor of a more liberal economic system, even as it fought off mounting budget deficits. Gorbachev's perestroika efforts also included political reforms designed to break from the bloated bureaucratic influence of the Central Committee of the Communist Party of the Soviet Union. His efforts came to nought after Soviet Russia's president, Boris Yeltsin, defeated a military coup organized against Gorbachev in December 1991. This led to the formal dissolution of the Soviet Union and the declared independence of the Russian, Ukrainian, and Belorussian republics.[17] The collapse of the Soviet Union, the defeat of the ideology of communism, and the victory of the capitalist West upended communism's ideologically aligned movements across the globe. For global conservatives wedded to an anticommunist organizing politics, these arguments became less intelligible after the fall of the Soviet Union. The specter of international communism, the Soviet Union, and its arming of socialist movements around the globe had been seemingly defeated, and thus the urgency of arming its Western-aligned antagonists seemed less urgent. Just as sanctions caused a schism between white supremacists and other conservatives, the fall of the Soviet Union put cracks in the alignment between far-right and centrist conservatives over anticommunism.

De Klerk sought to capitalize on evolving geopolitical and domestic circumstances. The resolution of the Angolan and Namibian conflicts, paired with the Soviet collapse, seemed an opportunity for de Klerk to drive a wedge between the ANC and the South African Communist Party. De Klerk saw himself as a conservative but principally a realist, who recognized that whites needed to make a commitment to fundamental constitutional change and democratic principles in an effort stave off the "tyranny" of a black majority.[18] Although the National Party lost ground to the Conservative Party in 1987, the 1989 electoral gains for the liberal

Democratic Party convinced de Klerk that he had a strong reform mandate from white voters across the National and Democratic Parties.[19] More worrying for de Klerk was the resistance that remained across the country, with black South Africans rejecting the continuation of whites-only elections and demanding quicker, more substantive reforms. The Mass Democratic Movement, which organized members of the UDF, ANC, and Congress of South African Trade Unions (COSATU) into a loose, decentralized coalition to avoid state crackdown, organized election day boycotts that included upward of 75 percent of urban black workers.[20]

By 1989, South Africa was not the only state entering a tumultuous period of democratic transition. The rapid demise of communism in Eastern Europe offered the possibility of a new belt of democratic states, which took place alongside an established international human rights lobby. By the end of the Cold War, Americans on both sides of the political aisle embraced human rights as a driver of US foreign policy—even as they argued over what human rights meant.[21] The institutionalization of human rights in US foreign policy, beginning with Jimmy Carter, continued under Reagan, as he tied anticommunism to international human rights promotion.[22] This bipartisan embrace of human rights opened the door for activists, who built a transnational network that demanded the enforcement of the Helsinki Final Act of 1975.[23] However, human rights was always a nebulous concept, a "compelling, adaptable slogan" acting as the "world's moral *lingua franca*."[24] Throughout the pro-apartheid movement's existence, it dabbled in the tactics and language of international human rights, setting up commissions, fact-finding missions, visits with so-called political prisoners, and witnesses and testimonials on ANC atrocities. These human rights tactics became essential tools of the pro-apartheid movement, who positioned themselves as brave truth tellers in opposition to a global conspiracy against South Africa. The pro-apartheid movement presented itself as a foil to antiapartheid activists—while sharing their language of international human rights—neatly aligning their arguments with the US conservative, anticommunist vision of human rights.

A critical moment of transition in the United States also occurred in 1989, as Reagan's vice president, George H. W. Bush, became president. American right-wingers were not overly enthusiastic about Bush's presidency because the 1990s brought a new style of politics to the Republican

Party that saw the death of Reaganism and the rise of a more grievance-based, populist right.[25] On April 9, 1989, the Bush administration began its National Security Review of South Africa to evaluate US policy priorities in the country and region.[26] Bush opted to continue the dialogue with antiapartheid activists, hosting Bishop Tutu in May 1989, UDF copresident Albertina Sisulu in June 1989, and Nelson Mandela in June 1990 for an official visit and working luncheon.[27] De Klerk and Bush kept up a fairly regular correspondence, exchanging nine calls across Bush's one term. Bush encouraged de Klerk to engage with the ANC, reporting on the positive conversations he had with Mandela, even as de Klerk and Bush repeatedly discussed the affiliations of the ANC with the South African Communist Party (SACP).[28] De Klerk visited Bush in September 1990, after which Bush tasked Secretary of State James Baker III to find ways to support South Africa even within the constraints of sanctions.[29] Despite Pik Botha and de Klerk's attempts to push Bush away from the ANC, Bush retained open lines of communication with Mandela, whom he called after his meeting with de Klerk to offer a summary of their chat.[30] Yet, the meetings gave de Klerk confidence that he was "in step with America now."[31]

Being in step with America also involved having new discussions on human rights. After the end of the Gulf War in 1991, Bush stated that "there is the very real prospect of a new world order . . . a world where the United Nations, freed from cold war stalemate, is poised to fulfill the historic vision of its founders."[32] Bush's "New World Order" speech encapsulated this new vision of international human rights, unmoored from the Cold War and centered on freedom and respect for all individuals. The anticommunist human rights appeals that dominated pro-apartheid organizing in the 1980s looked increasingly untenable. However, the Cold War's end also offered a new opportunity for apartheid's defenders—as human rights activists considered minorities in international human rights.[33] Minorities had long been cast aside in favor of general human rights applicable to all individuals, but in 1990, the Organization for Security and Cooperation in Europe adopted the European Charter for Minorities. This declaration affirmed the rights of individuals in national minorities to express, preserve, and develop their ethnic culture without attempts at assimilation.[34] In this declaration, protecting minority rights would promote equality in multicultural states and prevent the tyranny of the majority, which took on particular urgency for human rights advocates amid rising ethnonationalism in Europe.[35] The language of rights was not new to South Africa either, explored through the African nationalist, liberal, and republican traditions as early as the seventeenth century. As the historian Saul Dubow argued, "if there was one issue uniting Afrikaner and African nationalism through most of the second half of the 20th century, and throughout the Cold War, it was a mutual suspicion of liberal ideology and of an individual-based human rights." The 1980s saw the discovery of human rights simultaneously by both the apartheid government and the ANC. Antiapartheid activists used a language of rights to delegitimize the regime, whereas the apartheid government used an "unusual language" of minority rights that "was deployed not as a *defense* against oppression by a majority, but as a means to *discriminate* against the majority."[36]

For apartheid's defenders, it would be this window—the international recognition of national minorities to be free of attempted assimilation plus existing weaponization of human rights language—that they worked to exploit. The emphasis on ethnic rights was not new in South Africa—the apartheid state's creators premised its existence on ethnic rights to justify segregation. The possibility for a new legitimacy for separate development emerged via the international human rights apparatus. Deploying a language of human rights that focused on ethnic protections not only reforged connections to the transatlantic right wing but also offered a new platform for right-wingers' efforts to preserve white rule as the apartheid state collapsed around them.

THE INTELLECTUAL ORIGINS OF THE *VOLKSTAAT* AND FEBRUARY 2

In the aftermath of the West's passage of sanctions, the pro-apartheid movement's devotees wrestled with the betrayal from their partners at home and abroad. As Aida Parker put it in the April 1987 *Aida Parker Newsletter (APN)*, "picking on Afrikaners, but not on the black African States, will eventually force white South Africa to cut itself off completely."[37] Where did it leave South Africa, Parker questioned, if in the aftermath of sanctions, America seemed content to wage war against South Africans rather than on the perceived sin of apartheid?[38] It was time, Parker concluded, to "stop groveling, to give ourselves a spinal transplant and start hitting back."[39] Parker dedicated her summer 1989/1990 issue, "Racism Around the world: Accusing Our Accusers," to the hypocritical West, as she tackled US slavery, Canadian treatment of Indigenous people, and "apartheid, Australian-style" against the Aborigines.[40] In the "glow of glasnost/perestroika," Donald McAlvany argued, the US and South African governments abandoned anticommunist freedom fighters.[41] Some were even less surprised and less covert in their expressed fears for the white race. The National Association for the Advancement of White People, the white supremacist organization founded by the former Ku Klux Klan grand wizard David Duke, wrote to Botha about the fears induced by sanctions. One of the most infamous white supremacist activists of the twentieth century, Duke established the National Association for the Advancement of White People as a glib refrain on the US civil rights organization the National Association for the Advancement of Colored People. In a newsletter mailed to Botha, Duke's organization argued that the sanctions votes in Congress were nothing more than an attempt to "force the White South Africans into giving up their nation"—an act of treason, infamy, and immorality by the United States.[42] When he sent the newsletter to Botha in 1987, Duke was gearing up for his campaign for the 1988 Democratic presidential nomination before his switch to the Republican Party and his successful campaign for a seat in the Louisiana House of Representatives from 1989 to 1992. Content to turn their backs on the people of South Africa, it was time for the US right wing to reassess South Africa's future and rally for their brothers and sisters in South Africa.

Domestically, the political project of saving apartheid fractured the right, even as it seemingly claimed an even larger share of the white vote. In September 1989, the National Party faced what would become the last whites-only general election. De Klerk and his party released a five-year action plan to create a "new South Africa": a capitalist "democracy" where voters still registered based on racial categories in order to preserve the power of whites. In addition, the National Party continued presenting itself as the only guarantor of white safety, willing to utilize the security state extrajudicially to end the unrest across South Africa. As the historian Christi van der Westhuizen stated, "the message kept the party in power, but 1989 marked its worst showing in thirty years," with the party losing over a dozen seats to the Conservative and Democratic Parties each. The Conservative Party received 31.2 percent of the white vote, campaigning on exclusive white enfranchisement and restricting black movement of ethnic areas. The "shrinking" of the liberal vote, according to Christi van der Westhuizen, "reflected the siege mentality that gripped the white community at large during the 1980s."[43] Yet all was not well among the far-right. The Herstigte Nasionale Party split with the Conservative Party after the 1989 election, demanding the reintroduction of total Verwoerdian apartheid.[44] Herstigte Nasionale Party member Jaap Marais had harsh words for the West and the National Party, zeroing in on Margaret Thatcher, de Klerk, and Botha as backing the ANC out of a secret preference for communism and New World Order.[45] After the 1989 election, some paramilitary activists temporarily broke with the Conservative Party after the Conservative Party refused to resign en mass from Parliament.

The most powerful of the paramilitary activists were those under the banner of the Afrikaner Weerstandsbeweging (AWB), meaning Afrikaner Resistance Movement, a neo-Nazi, Afrikaner nationalist organization led by Eugene Terre'Blanche. Terre'Blanche was known for his flamboyant style and fierce oration, modeling his speeches after Hitler and Mussolini. Born in Ventersdorp, Terre'Blanche served in the South African Police until he left to become a farmer after his disillusionment with the National Party. Terre'Blanche arrived at AWB rallies in the organization's uniform, khakis and a black shirt, and on horseback like a Boer general, surrounded by AWB commandos brandishing their Nazi-adjacent triskelion insignia in black, red, and white.[46] Founded in 1973, the AWB resisted any reform to the apartheid state and infamously targeted black South Africans during the state of emergency in 1984 to 1986.[47] By the late 1980s, the AWB had fixated on the restoration of an independent Afrikaner republic based on the Boer republics, independent states formed in 1795 by Dutch-speaking Boers known as the Afrikaners. These "short-lived mini-states" eventually coalesced into the two independent countries of Transvaal and the Orange Free State, which the Second Boer War of 1899 to 1902 brought to an end. Diamond and gold rushes in the Vaal River and Witwatersrand hills drove British interest in the formerly independent states, forcing the inclusion of the Boer republics into the Union of South Africa.[48]

The AWB possessed the largest private army of the white paramilitaries organized under the Wenkommando. The Wenkommando included a cohesive fighting unit, female fighters, battlefield medical, a youth league, and a military protection wing.[49] Within the ranks of the AWB, former police and SADF commanders served in leadership positions, including at the helm of the Wenkommando.[50] The AWB enjoyed significant support from high-ranking police officers, "a conservative institution even by white South African standards," even though Pretoria had barred police officers from membership in the AWB since 1984.[51] In 1988, the AWB claimed 10,000 active members and 100,000 nonactive members, and in 1989, their planners developed a paramilitary strategy to take control of the traditional Boer republics in Transvaal and the Orange Free State.[52] Right-wingers' easy access to commercial explosives—claymores, dynamite, plastic explosives, and hand grenades—used in bombings of synagogues, newspapers, and union offices, showed a far right with terrorist power. The AWB operated in a commando structure based on the old Boer republics and the existing SADF commandos, operating as a local counterinsurgency force within South Africa. Each Wenkommando unit had a corporal at the head of the team in each town, with commandants who reported to the AWB's generals. The SADF commandos' institutional Afrikaner traditionalist culture, combined with the tight bonds between the commandos and far-right local government, police, and community populaces, left it susceptible to infiltration in conservative rural areas.[53] AWB strongholds also emerged in urban areas with high numbers of white citizens such as Sasolburg, Vaal, Krugersdorp, and Benoi.[54] This infiltration posed a range of problems for the SADF as the AWB launched attacks on black citizens, prevented local elections, and armed sympathetic white vigilante groups. Limitations to this collaboration did exist; the far right did not enjoy widespread support among the SADF officer corps, which disproportionately supported the National Party, whom the AWB attacked as betraying whites.[55]

The AWB and its ideological counterparts increasingly turned to the Afrikaner past to envision its future. On June 10, 1980, H. F. Verwoerd Jr., son of Prime Minister H. F. "Father of Apartheid" Verwoerd, along with Dr. Hercules Booysen and Carel Boshoff, founded the Vereniging van Oranjewerkers out of concern about the position of the Afrikaner nation. Verwoerd Jr., Boshoff, and Booysen represented the "respectable face of the white right wing," a coalition of likeminded thinkers who pushed white South Africans to think about their future beyond apartheid.[56] Verwoerd Jr., born in 1940, spent his days "trying to persuade fellow whites, in essence to cut their losses and establish their own small homeland" after they lost faith in the apartheid dream. He arrived in Morgenzon in 1982 to launch his dream of an all-white Afrikaner homeland.[57] His compatriot, Carel Boshoff, was Verwoerd's son-in-law, a theologian, and a former head of the Afrikaner Broederbond.[58] Booysen, who was vice chairman of Willie Lubbe's Action Own Future political party before joining the Oranjewerkers, was a trained lawyer who focused on building a case for Afrikaners' future in a separate state within international law.[59] These men were not writing in a vacuum; their imagination of what South Africa might look like without apartheid was deeply rooted in long-held white myths about South Africa's past. As Leonard Thompson argued, the Afrikaner nationalist movement's minority status bred two initial themes in the nineteenth and twentieth centuries. First, through the "hallmarks of the nation," Afrikaans language and the Dutch Reformed Church (DRC), Afrikaners and their descendants would fight against the British. Second, the Afrikaners would use those same tools to fight for the racial superiority of Europeans. As the apartheid state came into being, it relied on the myth that black Africans "have no greater historical claim to dominion over the land than whites" because of their alleged arrival in South Africa after the sixteenth-century whites.[60] The historian Shula Marks refers to this conspiracy as the "myth of the empty land," which allowed the apartheid government to justify the creation of the bantustans as necessary for these "recent arrivals" who would destroy each other without state intervention.[61] These myths fueled Afrikaner nationalists' creation of the *volkstaat*, which relied on European ideas of cultural homogeneity through language, territorial integrity for an ethnicity, and separate development within the apartheid system.

Far-rightists relied on these past narratives as they charted the Afrikaners' future. Black domination, the Oranjewerkers, concluded, was inevitable. The Afrikaners needed to create an exclusive white ethno-state exactly like the Bantustans and totally separate from black labor to avoid "accusations of suppression or abuse" and to ensure their survival. In 1986, the Oranjewerkers moved their headquarters to Morgenzon in the Eastern Transvaal to lay claim to the "heart of the Afrikanerstate . . . [in]

the traditional Voortrekker territory, to which no black nation can lay claim."[62] The Oranjewerkers were not alone. In 1982, in the first edition of their newspaper *Sweesplag*, the AWB offered its history of the geography of the "Bantu"—developing separately as tribes, with land free for claiming by the Boers and "ripe for transformation": separation was South Africa's legacy.[63] The Conservative Party struck a similar chord. In a political platform from August 4, 1982, it listed self-determination as its first objective: "integration and power-sharing and/or mixed government in whatever form . . . are irreconcilable with self-determination and are thoroughly rejected."[64] Even though the Conservative Party and the AWB remained fully committed to apartheid in the mid-1980s, the principle of ethnic self-determination was a throughline across right-wing organizing.

For the *volkstaat* enthusiasts, the Afrikaners possessed ambitions not unlike the other powers of the Western world. In their theorizing, organizations like the Oranjewerkers explicitly aligned their vision for a new South Africa to the ethnic rights projects of Europe and the United States. As Verwoerd Jr. stated in 1985, the Afrikaners wanted their own country like "the Germans, French, Japanese, Hungarians, Poles—throughout the world all people have this perfectly natural aspiration." The project of a free and independent existence now captured the imaginations of whites who, to avoid their dispossession of liberty and country, lined up behind the *volkstaat*. This new resolve for the *volkstaat*, Verwoerd Jr. concluded, stemmed from the realization that the Botha government's reform process would only lead to struggle within an artificial unitary state.[65] Nationalism—whether it be Afrikaner or Zulu—could not be ignored., According to Verwoerd Jr., every nation should have their own territory and be free to segregate or integrate as they chose. Verwoerd Jr. concluded that the unwavering determination of the Afrikaner flew in the face of the Reagan government and its support for black governance. How many Afrikaners and their white partners would "take up this task, with self-sacrifice, hard work, and determination," he mused. Boshoff echoed Verwoerd's remarks. Boshoff worked to bring an awakening of the Afrikaner to his undoing: "that he fell afoul of international custom by sharing his country . . . while denying [black South Africans] political rights and by showing no signs of his willingness to exercise his right of self-determination."[66] The right to national self-determination, as recognized by the United Nations, Boshoff concluded, offered a path forward for the Afrikaner, untethered by the troubles of the old order.

In this vision, what Afrikaners needed in their pursuit of a *volkstaat* was a new conservative movement for South Africa. According to Booysen, conservatives, long divided, finally converged by finding a constitutional solution that matched the political aspirations of all ethnic and language groups within South Africa. The cornerstone of the new conservative movement, Booysen argued, was the right to self-determination of peoples. To Booysen, the *volkstaat* was an inclusive whiteness: "the English whites do not at the moment pose a real threat to Afrikaner self-determination. They can, from a constitutional point of view, be included with the Afrikaner. . . . I adhere to the contemporary practice of using Afrikaner and white interchangeably." Tying his theorization to the emerging human rights order, Booysen insisted that human rights are dependent on group relations, with democracy thriving best in homogeneity. As evidence, Booysen cited Bophuthatswana's creation of a bill of rights based on the European Convention for the Protection of Human Rights and Fundamental Freedoms. For the conservative, this approach was decidedly modern, regardless of what the "morally patronizing" Americans and Europeans thought of the Afrikaner. The debate about the morality of separation was superfluous, Booysen argued: the new conservative now focused on separation as protection for ethnic rights. The right of self-determination, "which the Americans and Western Europeans protect by way of nuclear missiles to the point where the existence of the entire world is jeopardized," Booysen now claimed for whites.[67]

Considering these shifts, where did that leave apartheid in the new conservative thinking? The Afrikaner needed to move beyond a crisis mentality and instead look to a future empowered by its vibrancy, population, and economic potential. Booysen and his compatriots sought to rewrite the history of apartheid—separate development now oppressed whites, with Afrikaners unable to gain true self-determination. According to the Oranjewerkers, black South Africans received "two countries, their own homeland and South Africa, the best of two worlds," whereas the whites suffered without a homeland. To Boshoff, the new conservative did not advocate the abolition of apartheid, but instead emphasized how apartheid failed to guarantee Afrikaner self-determination.[68] To *volkstaat* separatists like Booysen, apartheid created an illusion of their own country through influx control. A new vision needed to emerge for an apartheid-free, white homeland. To explore these ideas, Boshoff and a group of Afrikaner intellectuals formed the Afrikaner Freedom Foundation (Avstig) in 1988.[69] Avstig would move beyond the party and parliamentary politics that defined the old problems of the conservative movement to instead focus on the project of Afrikaner survival in a homeland.[70] Boshoff urged caution, though: they could count on no friendship from the Americans. Conservative Party members Clive Derby Lewis and Andries Treurnicht echoed the call for the Afrikaner to stand on principles of separation, but insisted that this vision could win support at the grassroots, both locally and globally.[71] The world of right-wingers abroad—not their treacherous national governments—could act as a boon to this new conservative movement.

This new conservative movement responded to changing political winds in South Africa as de Klerk moved the National Party toward negotiations in the early months of his presidency. His shift stemmed from several factors: Botha's secret engagement with the ANC, specifically Mandela, Thabo Mbeki, and Jacob Zuma; the collapse of the Soviet Union and the subsequent loss of the Total Onslaught and anticommunist justification; a weakened ANC; economic crisis brought on by sanctions; and the problem of legitimacy for the apartheid regime. After the 1989 general election, de Klerk believed he had a mandate for reform and that he had a responsibility to push the *verligte* caucus further, even as he kept conservatives in his cabinet. On February 2, 1990, at the opening of the South African House of Assembly, de Klerk reversed the ban on opposition political parties, repealed the Separate Amenities Act of 1953, unconditionally released Nelson Mandela, and committed the government to negotiations toward a constitutional democracy.[72]

According to de Klerk and his confidants, his rationale for these steps was twofold. First, the de Klerk government believed that freeing Mandela and other ANC figures would weaken the ANC as it made the transition to operating as an open political party. Second, de Klerk saw the changes to the international system—a weak Soviet Union and the decreased threat of communism—as boons to the National Party and not the ANC.[73] As former Inkatha Institute head Schlemmer put it, without Soviet support, the ANC would operate as an internal political actor pressured to concede to a negotiated political settlement that would likely favor the National Party.[74] The de Klerk government's approach to the Tripartite Accord, in contrast with earlier intransigence from Botha, won the apartheid state respect in Western circles, which de Klerk believed he could leverage. As the South African journalist Allister Sparks argued, "de Klerk did not expect his reforms to lead to black-majority rule and the end of Afrikaner nationalism."[75] Indeed, in the address on February 2, 1990, de Klerk upheld group rights and the protection of white rights to maintain the support of conservative ministers and anxious whites as he made the "quantum leap" to end apartheid.[76] De Klerk continued the National Party's modus operandi, which was to try to control the pace and nature of apartheid reforms.

De Klerk underestimated the ANC, even as the ANC trepidatiously engaged in the budding democratic process with the South African government. Famously, Nelson Mandela left a 1989 meeting with de Klerk describing the new prime minister as a "man we could do business with," in stark contrast to Botha.[77] However, the ANC's leadership remained suspicious of de Klerk and his reforms and disagreed on how to engage in any political negotiations process. Mandela did capitalize on the ANC's unbanning and regional legitimization by touring southern Africa and Europe.[78] Simultaneously, the ANC sought to transform from a movement to a political party as it formalized its vision of a democratic, unitary South Africa. The organization initiated its uneven transformation from liberation movement to political party grounded in liberal democratic principles of individual rights in contrast to the radical, ground-up, consensus driven popular politics of its years in exile.[79] Throughout the early 1990s, the ANC developed its vision for South Africa, articulated as wanting "an ordinary democracy as practiced elsewhere in the world."[80]

De Klerk's address on February 2, 1990, catalyzed the urgency of the *volkstaat* question because the National Party's commitment to protecting white rule seemed to be at an end. The speech came to be known in right-wing circles as "Red Friday," seemingly a reference to the unbanning of the red communist-aligned ANC and SACP and the violence they would unleash in South Africa. A host of organizations emerged intent on urban terrorism and a "Third Freedom Struggle" for the Afrikaner, referring to the First and Second Boer Wars.[81] The white far right staged public displays in the aftermath of Red Friday as a show of force and general popularity. On May 27, 1990, far-right activists led a *volksaamtrek*, or people's rally, at the Pretoria Voortrekker Monument, hosting an estimated crowd of between 30,000 and 130,000.[82] Although the Conservative Party hosted the rally, paramilitary movements openly displayed their colors, uniforms, and banners. Khaki-clad horsemen flew the AWB swastika. In his keynote address, Terre'Blanche warned that the Third Freedom Struggle had begun. As the Conservative Party parliamentarian Koos van der Merwe stated, the far right "understands the mood of the people. . . . We could reach a stage where whites would seriously consider resorting to violence."[83] The invocation of the Third Freedom Struggle firmly positioned the far right's fight against apartheid as part of the long struggle for ethnic rights of the white Afrikaner—first against the British empire and now against the South African government.

In the days and months after de Klerk's speech, the far right undertook bombing campaigns and weapons thefts, took public credit for acts of terror, and formed vigilante squads called neighborhood protection groups.[84] In July 1990, white terrorists were responsible for half of the total incidents of terrorism, which followed nearly a dozen bombing attacks since April 1990.[85] Violence in response to the de Klerk reforms specifically targeted black South Africans. One horrific attack occurred in Durban in October 1990, where three AWB members killed seven black people and wounded twenty-seven others after shooting at a bus.[86] Another attack involved the Blanke Veiligheid (White Security) in the Free State mining town of Welkom, who attacked black citizens and stole ammunition under AWB orders as part of a protracted paramilitary conflict against residents of an adjacent black town who boycotted white businesses. Other neighborhood protection groups popped up in Brits, Klerksdorp, and Virginia, with one AWB-backed self-protection committee forcibly removing black South Africans found in Belfast after dark.[87] In December, police arrested twelve white men believed to be affiliates of the Afrikaner vigilante group Bureau for White Liberation who attacked several hundred black children at a school picnic with whips, automobile fans, and clubs.[88] US media followed the rise in terror, regaling readers with "blood-curdling names like the Order of Death, the White Wolves, and the White Liberation Army," led by notorious underground leaders who declared open war on de Klerk, black people, and white liberals.[89] "I promise you my friend," one AWB member said in an interview with the *New York Times*, "we'll fight to the last drop of blood for a white South Africa."[90]

The National Party tried to control the paramilitary right. On May 14, 1990, Minister of Law and Order Adriaan Vlok met with a Terre'Blanche-led delegation.[91] The three-hour meeting concluded with a joint statement from Terre'Blanche and Vlok affirming their shared commitment to the security of the South African people.[92] However, the AWB refused to halt its military preparations and expanded its targets beyond black citizens and liberal whites to include National Party officials. This program of fear, crafted in the weeks after the *volksaamtrek*, aimed to push the National Party to reconsider negotiations, terrorize South Africa's population, and artificially inflate the reach of the far right. Additionally, far-right leaders sought to reestablish links with the SADF and police to rupture the National Party's hold on power. Conservative Party leadership called on the military and police to become part of the Boers' independence struggle as the natural allies of the right-wingers. Reinvigorating the relationship between the paramilitary right and the SADF and police tapped into traditional Afrikaner self-defense committees organized during the Boer Wars, invoking the Third Freedom Struggle.

The invocation of the Third Freedom Struggle became an essential marker of the shift of the white right from preserving the apartheid state to advocating for a *volkstaat*. Following de Klerk's speech on February 2, 1990, the AWB combined its paramilitary activity with vocal support for creating the *volkstaat* through a justification of minority rights, joining other right-wing organizations. Terre'Blanche and top AWB officials insisted that they were not racist but instead were protecting the rights of the white minority from the black majority.[93] Right-wingers stepped up their attacks on the negotiations process, as police and SADF officers uncovered plots to kill Mandela and National Party leadership.[94] Simultaneously, the Conservative Party leveraged its position in Parliament to organize in favor of a *volkstaat*, crafting the "Freedom's Manifesto of Our People" on May 26, 1990, which announced their commitment to not rest until their "freedom in [their] own fatherland [was] assured."[95] In early 1991, the Conservative Party announced Operation Strongarm, which detailed how to use force if the government refused to call for a white election. Members planned to issue identity documents for white citizens in conjunction with other far-right parties for "all those who support the restoration of the Boer Republics."[96] Through political and violent means, the South African far right increased the tension with the National Party, demonstrating a cohesive evolution of a pro-apartheid movement that was now focused on white minority rights.

BETRAYAL AT VENTERSDORP

"Now is the time to know thine enemy," Parker declared in her first *APN* of the year after de Klerk's Red Friday speech. Parker viewed de Klerk's announcement with suspicion, arguing that the speech unequivocally put black and white South Africans alike onto uncharted seas of a new South Africa, spelling the end of 338 years of white supremacy in Africa.[97] The traps were set against them, Parker insisted, as a global propaganda campaign worked to make democratic reforms a one-on-one affair between the National Party and the ANC. McAlvany took a similar tune in the winter of 1990, writing in his newsletter that de Klerk had "plung[ed] down the slippery slope of surrender."[98] Howard Phillips agreed with McAlvany's assessment, arguing that de Klerk had committed to South Africa's "future in collaboration with a gang of Marxist-Leninist thugs."[99] History's most dangerous era, claimed Parker and her compatriots, had begun.[100] After de Klerk's betrayal, Parker traveled to the United States, meeting with her prime contacts—the Heritage Foundation, Howard Philips, and congressmembers—and expressing rage about "how [their] entire propaganda effort had ground to a dismal, disgraceful halt."[101]

As Parker traveled, negotiations began. On May 4, 1990, the ANC and the South African government agreed to resolve existing political violence and commit to a peaceful process of negotiations.[102] Just over a month later, de Klerk lifted the four-year-old state of emergency imposed by Botha in the three provinces of Transvaal, Cape Province, and the Orange Free State; he later lifted it in Natal in October, citing the "factional fighting" between Inkatha and the UDF-ANC forces.[103] On September 14, 1991, South African political parties signed the National Peace Accord, which developed a path toward multiparty democracy, peaceful power sharing, and social and economic reconstruction. The National Peace Accord, with twenty-four signatories, required all participating political parties and organizations to condemn violence while calling on the SADF and police to protect all people from criminal acts and violence without bias.[104] Most importantly, the National Peace Accord paved the way for the Convention for a Democratic South Africa (CODESA), which, after its December 1991 launch, created a governing forum to work out the democratic transition.

Against the backdrop of the peace accords, the South African government was still operating a covert war domestically that fueled the so-called black-on-black violence that the National Party weaponized abroad to prove that black South Africans were unable to govern. In 1990, political violence increased in South Africa by 136 percent, "the worst year of political violence in modern South African history," leaving 3,693 dead.[105] In conversations between de Klerk and Bush in 1991, de Klerk repeatedly maligned the ANC's ability to govern, saying that the organization had "some pretty wild elements."[106] Black right-wingers like Buthelezi fueled these narratives in partnership with the state. In his conversations with Bush in June 1991, Buthelezi stated, "Violence now in South Africa is endemic. It is very worrying. A culture of violence is being created by the ANC focus on the armed struggle. Some of them think they can shoot their way into power." Throughout his conversations with Bush, Buthelezi argued that all South Africans, including black residents, were frightened by the ANC-led violence: "We, the Blacks, must get our act together and negotiate."[107]

The urgency of solidifying group rights as part of a new South Africa only grew as the ANC–South African government domination of the negotiations process loomed. The chairman of the Pretoria Bar Council, I. W. B. de Villiers, perhaps best encapsulated the thinking of these new conservative activists, who looked to move the case for group rights away from apartheid rationales to one that could match the emerging global human rights order. In 1991, de Villiers maintained that the recognition of group rights, beyond simple individual rights, was one of the most important developments in international law. Citing the 1966 International Covenant on Civil and Political Rights, de Villiers argued that the debates of the Third Committee of the UN General Assembly solidified the concerns over minority protection. The dignity of the human person and their rights within their group were the key pieces of the Draft International Convention on the Protection of National or Ethnic Groups of Minorities, which was presented by the Minority Rights Group to the UN Human Rights Commission over a decade ago. Self-determination of peoples, de Villiers concluded, is not only a genuine right but also a peremptory norm of international law. De Villiers took it further, arguing that the San Jose Declaration of December 1981 enshrined ethno-development, meaning the state had a sovereign obligation to establish an institutional framework for and guaranteed survival of that development against outside interference. By this logic, de Villiers insisted that human rights "would not be worth anything if they were left to the discretion of the majority," arguing for group rights in micro-states within a federal system.[108]

This logic appeared across right-wing efforts. The Conservative Party dedicated a subcommittee to exploring the *volkstaat* by reviewing international examples of ethnic divisions and the terms of secession, as in Yugoslavia and a future Kurdistan. A prominent example was Israel, which in the Conservative Party's interpretation "purified" Palestine from "foreign tribes," noting favorably how the Israeli government restricted socialization, housing, and property to segregate Israeli and Palestinian societies. In reference to Europe, the Conservative Party argued that the homogenous division of states and borders within the continent came at the expense of two world wars, thus validating the need to create ethnic states before conflict broke out. The Conservative Party explicitly described its work as building on other far-right intellectuals in the South African Bureau of Racial Affairs and the Oranjewerkers to theorize different visions of a Boerestaat or Afrikanerland.[109] What united each organization, in the Conservative Party's estimation, was a shared commitment to a homeland for Afrikaners and a need to mobilize the grassroots.

The National Party fought back against the burgeoning *volkstaat* agenda of the far right, critiquing the Conservative Party's extensive effort to mask the reality of apartheid's end. By 1990, the Conservative Party—led by Andries Treurnicht—proved an existential threat to the reformist vision of the National Party. Born in 1921 in the Cape Province, Treurnicht was a hardcore Afrikaner nationalist ministering through the DRC and a founding editor of *Die Burger.* Treurnicht entered politics in 1971, becoming chairman of the Afrikaner Broederbond in 1972 and earning the nickname "Dr. No" because of his ardent rejection of any apartheid modifications. After his expulsion from the National Party and the formation of the Conservative Party, Treurnicht took on an almost mythic quality, known as the "Lion of the North." However, according to the scholar F. A. Mouton, his "imposing and confident appearance provided only a thin cover for someone who was not equipped to be an efficient political leader."[110] The National Party attacked Treurnicht as having no alternative to reform, resisting negotiation because of Conservative Party weakness as its leadership knew that "the possibility of creating one consolidated continuous fatherland for a people [was] highly unlikely."[111]

The conflict between the South African government and the white far right came to a head on August 9, 1991, after a violent confrontation between the police and AWB supporters during a speech given by de Klerk in the AWB stronghold of Ventersdorp. Following a pattern of disrupting the speeches of National Party officials, the AWB had announced their intention to disrupt the speech before de Klerk's arrival in Ventersdorp. As the speech began, Terre'Blanche gathered hundreds of khaki-clad AWB members brandishing the group's swastika-like insignia, but police officers barred them from breaking into the venue hosting de Klerk's speech. "Hundreds of policemen and white protestors battled with guns and tear gas," the Associated Press reported, as "pitched battles raged through the main street" and white militants opened fire on black civilians.[112] The police removed the protestors after about fifteen minutes of violence and arrested six AWB members, including Terre'Blanche. In his remarks, de Klerk chastised the AWB as "looking for trouble."[113]

Shockingly for the far right, the police used lethal force against right-wing supporters for the first time under the apartheid state.[114] Known as the "Battle of Ventersdorp" among the far right, police forces killed at least three AWB members and injured fifty-eight others before arresting AWB leadership. In a speech to the assembled crowd, AWB General Secretary Piet Rudolph declared, "What we have seen here tonight is the start of the Boer uprising."[115] After Ventersdorp, Pretoria's National Intelligence conducted an investigation into the potential threat of the far right. It concluded that the *volkstaat* offered a means to pull the far right into the negotiations process if an ethno-state could be guaranteed, but if the far right believed the *volkstaat* was unachievable, terror, instability, and obstruction of negotiation seemed likely.[116] Ventersdorp proved to be a turning point in the relationship between the white far right and the South African government. After Ventersdorp, Frontline Fellowship's Hammond invoked the shared heritage of the United States and South Africa, drawing parallels between George Washington and Paul Kruger, the Afrikaner's tragic hero. Hammond explicitly connected the Afrikaner's Lost Cause to Confederate heroes Robert E. Lee and Stonewall Jackson. Hammond, tying together two lost causes for whites, compared the heroism of Custer's Last Stand with the heroism of white South Africa, which remained valiant in the face of destruction by the National Party.[117] Ventersdorp reaffirmed the "inclusive white supremacy" possible in a white ethno-state for English and Afrikaners. In a letter of application to the Oranjewerkers, one English-speaking white South African stated that he refused to live under a black-dominated government and hoped to learn more about the *volkstaat*. In his reply, the Oranjewerker director wrote that it was "encouraging to know" of English speakers who wished to join the cause of Afrikaner freedom: any person who identified with the nation was welcome to join the struggle.[118]

US pro-apartheid organizations saw Ventersdorp as clear proof that the South African government no longer represented white interests. The Council of Conservative Citizens echoed the AWB's calls to attack National Party officials and explicitly described Ventersdorp as a turning point in the pro-apartheid movement's relationship with the state. In their August 1991 edition of *Citizens Informer*, Robert Slimp wrote that Ventersdorp proved that the South African government was losing its grip, as the AWB derailed de Klerk's plans to run South Africa into the ground. Ventersdorp would erode support among Afrikaners for the National Party, Slimp predicted, with right-wing commandos attracting thousands of battle-hardened whites; Slimp ended the article by stating that he "believe[d] the right-wing whites [would] win."[119] According to apartheid's defenders, the greatest insult was the West's betrayal of its natural allies, with the Bush administration selling out South Africa and refusing to protect white minority rights. The Virginia-based American-Afrikaner Union backed the Conservative Party plans for a white homeland. Led by Robert J. Hoy—an active neo-Nazi and staffer for David Duke—the American-Afrikaner Union accused the Bush administration of pushing de Klerk to reform.[120] In the April 1990 issue of the John Birch Society's *New American*, McAlvany railed against the sellout of South Africa. South Africa had an American gun to its head, forcing it to surrender power to the ANC. The return of Jesus Christ would not be greeted with as much joy as Mandela, McAlvany wrote bitterly, with Mandela's release a "psychological defeat for millions of South African whites and moderate Blacks."[121] McAlvany insisted that globalists had infiltrated the National Party and the Republican Party as part of an unholy alliance to destroy the Conservative Party, part of a grand conspiracy to prevent a white homeland. Indeed, the white nationalist magazine *The Instauration* targeted Bush and de Klerk for rolling out the red carpet for black terrorists.[122] Slimp went on speaking tours of Mississippi and Arkansas, reminding his listeners that "further reform is white surrender" and only the Conservative Party guaranteed justice for all racial groups through their plan for a white homeland.[123]

The pro-apartheid movement's factions recognized that they needed to embrace a new vision of white rule that could gain national and international legitimacy. After Ventersdorp, apartheid's defenders aligned behind the far-right vision of South Africa, viewing the National Party as no longer representative of white interests. As one of Mary Ann Gilbert's pro–South Africa pen pals put it, South Africa now moved in a direction that needed careful handling. It was up to US partners to "spell out to as many people as possible in the halls of power" the need to work out a solution that prevented the birth of a one-party Marxist, anti-Christian state.[124] The invocation of Christian arguments in defense of white power was no accident: Christianity would be critical glue between white Americans and South Africans and black conservative and bantustan leaders. Their shared language of Christianity would be a bridge to build to a new South Africa as part of this new human rights rhetoric. In a September 1991 document produced by the Conservative Party titled "South Africa: The State of the Nation," the party laid out its new base of support and political vision after Ventersdorp. Whites, in the Conservative Party vision, would not consent to rule in a unitary state, explicitly aligning with "the new found freedom which the former Iron Curtain countries now enjoy." The Conservative Party insisted that they represented the anticolonial history of all forced into arbitrary boundaries, with democracy and human rights impossible until a nation remained free within its own territory. In its vision for the future, the Conservative Party insisted that tens of thousands of English accepted their hand of friendship, taking as many white people as possible. According to the Conservative Party, it addressed all of South Africa's problems by creating a system that acknowledged both black and white ethnopolitical aspirations.[125]

"THE YES VOTE IS A BLANK CHECK": THE MARCH 1992 REFERENDUM

In her September-October 1991 issue of *APN*, Parker broke down the "blockbuster global problem"—a world "seething with secessionist, separatist groups who have had enough of the 'ties that bind.' "[126] It was time to consider radical surgery in the face of the possibility of black-ANC domination of South Africa. According to Parker, whites finally seemed to recognize that they could—like black South Africans—claim a homeland in the face of de Klerk's power-sharing illusions.[127] However, in an analysis prepared by Major General Tienie Groenewald, a former SADF and military intelligence chief and far-right activist, all was not lost for the white South African. The National Party, with the support of the ANC, planned to hold an all-white referendum on the transitional government constitutional process. The white electorate effectively held veto over this process. Groenewald warned of returning a "yes" result: "Once the transitional government is imposed, there will be no turning back."[128] March 17, 1992, would be South Africa's last chance. In the last all-white referendum in South Africa, the de Klerk government posed one question: "Do you support continuation of the reform process which the State President began on February 2, 1990 and which is aimed at a new constitution through negotiations?" The government, Parker concluded, botches everything it touches, and no white South African should give the National Party a signed blank check.[129] Treurnicht and the Conservative Party struck the same tune. Two weeks before the referendum, Treurnicht told his supporters that if they truly believed in freedom of choice, they would not give de Klerk a blank check.[130] According to Treurnicht, common sense dictated looking at the end result of negotiations, which would bring only oppression under a one-man-one-vote system. Treurnicht pleaded that de Klerk's threats should be ignored, insisting that the "awesome" resistance of whites and Zulus to "Xhosa/ANC rule" was far more fearsome than any ANC mass action. Catastrophe awaited with this vote, Treurnicht concluded, pleading for whites to not give their country away.

Unfortunately for apartheid's defenders, their calls proved unpersuasive to the majority of South African whites. Of the 2.8 million whites who voted, 1.9 million supported de Klerk's reform process and just over 875,000 voted no, corresponding to 68.6 percent in favor and 31 percent against among the 88 percent of registered voters who cast a ballot (some districts had over 96 percent turnout). De Klerk's reforms won in fourteen of fifteen electoral regions—with the Afrikaner bedrock of Northern Transvaal holding out at 57 percent against the reforms. De Klerk's strongest support came from English-speaking whites, especially in urban areas—85 percent in Durban and Cape Town and 75 percent in Johannesburg voted yes.[131] Even more worryingly for the white right, the National Party carried majorities in districts helmed by Conservative Party candidates, revealing the shallowness of the antireform position.[132] Companies like Anglo-American, B.P. Shell, Standard Bank, Toyota, and Delta Motor Corporation urged their employees to vote yes, citing a potential end to sanctions and the financial devastation that could come with a vote of no.[133] The ANC, UDF, Democratic Party, and Inkatha (reorganized in 1990 as the Inkatha Freedom Party) urged whites to vote yes.[134]

Unsurprisingly, far-right whites called foul. Parker derided the insolent manner in which foreign and domestic money bought the landslide through coercion, subversion, and stampeding voters. The relentless use of the "Big Lie technique would have turned Hitler, Goebbels and Mao green-eyed with envy," Parker whined, with the Conservative Party collecting affidavits of whites fed yes-vote propaganda. In Parker's telling, the time came to align fully behind the *volkstaat* and allow white and black supremacy "to exist side by side in different parts of the country" in response to the "over-hyped referendum."[135] Drastic action was now the order of the day. In her June 1992 issue of *APN*, Parker announced the formation of Action Save South Africa (ACTSA)—a "desperate group" of ex-ANC, former SADF, black and white, Christian and Muslim, all held together by the psychological glue of South Africa's imminent demise. ACTSA's formal objective was to "train and mobilize all freedom-loving forces in South Africa," and after its formation in September 1991, it set up working groups, trainings for Inkatha and youth leaders, political branches, and propaganda and information campaigns in order to "shake the masses from their present lethargy."[136] ACTSA members worked hard to offset the "shamefully-rigged media blitz for a Yes vote in the referendum," Parker claimed, as now it was time to join forces with all those who opposed de Klerk's agenda. In her next issue in July 1992, Parker laid out strategies to conserve food, energy, and medical supplies and instructions on how to harden home defenses in the face of an inevitable civil war.[137] Parker's apocalyptic tone was echoed by apartheid's defenders, who wrung their hands over the ruin of South Africa at the hands of the ruling National Party and their Western partners, who were not content to let sanctions alone crush whites. The Conservative Party prepared to respond to the referendum failures in their October 1992 plan for mobilizing the Afrikaner volk. They needed to fight back by building political propaganda, developing the economic research to support the *volkstaat*, and organizing among the grassroots, middle, and top tiers of the volk. However, the referendum failure needed to be reckoned with by Conservative Party leadership: the party needed to rebuild its structure and popular confidence and find new allies.[138] In their effort, they would find their allies—the black bantustan leadership.

The end of the Cold War heralded a shift in the pro-apartheid movement's organizing, as white supremacist actors drew on the global human rights movement to defend and reimagine white rule in South Africa. In a world without the existential threat of the Soviet Union, the pro-apartheid movement's anticommunist rhetoric did not resonate as it had in the 1980s. As international concerns about human rights emerged in the 1990s, the pro-apartheid movement positioned itself as the premier defender of ethnic rights for whites. After de Klerk reversed the ban on the ANC on February 2, 1990, South African white paramilitary and political actors organized across the nation, insisting that the National Party no longer represented white interests. The National Party and the ANC's formal process of negotiating toward a democratic transition galvanized far-right violence in South Africa. In response to de Klerk's betrayal, the acceptance of the *volkstaat* became shared across the white right as a remarkable cohesiveness emerged among its leadership in favor of white ethno-states.[139] However, far-right organizations across the United States and South Africa disagreed on whether and how they could achieve a *volkstaat* as they faced the reality of a National Party that no longer exclusively served white interests.

The renewed focus on national and ethnic minority rights within democratic states provided the ideal mechanism for pro-apartheid activists to continue using human rights rhetoric to defend white rule while building a bridge to South Africa's black conservative leaders. These black nationalists, including bantustan leaders like Mangosuthu Buthelezi, feared their loss of status as a result of the free and fair elections that the ANC would likely dominate. Using a language of human rights that focused on ethnic protections reforged connections built in the early 1980s pro-apartheid movement. The *volkstaat* shift proved critical to winning the partnership of black bantustan leaders and developing a shared vision of a new divided South Africa, even as it would become its undoing.

7

THE COLORBLIND FAR RIGHT AT APARTHEID'S END

On October 6, 1992, the newly formed Conference for Concerned South Africans, helmed by the KwaZulu, Bophuthatswana, and Ciskei governments, sent out an invitation for a convening of like-minded people. Their heads of state—Mangosuthu Buthelezi, Lucas Mangope, and Oupa Gqozo—invited all who questioned the wisdom of the agreements set out in the September 26, 1992, Record of Understanding between F. W. de Klerk and the ANC president Nelson Mandela.[1] At the conference, black bantustan leaders and white rightists from the Conservative Party and the Afrikaner-Volksunie—an Afrikaner separatist schism of the Conservative Party—denounced the bilateral government-ANC negotiations. They pledged to oppose any attempt to make South Africa a unitary state via a transitional government fueled by the oppressive tactics of the ANC.[2] In the weeks following this initial meeting, the conference formalized into the Concerned South Africans Group (COSAG), which was styled as neither a negotiating body nor an alliance but rather a collection of "true democrats insistent upon . . . an all-inclusive vision for Southern Africa."[3] The *Aida Parker Newsletter (APN)* cheered the announcement of COSAG, calling it a "development long in the making," and Aida Parker attended the first meeting.[4]

This chapter discusses the coalescing of two alliances—the black bantustan leaders and the white right on one side and the ANC and the South African government on the other—and their shifting strategies in the battle for the future of South Africa. The black-white, self-described "unholy alliance" was a determined and intransigent spoiler of the ANC–South African government negotiations as both alliances spent the early 1990s trying to outmaneuver each other.[5] However, the alliance between the black bantustan leaders and the white right was more than just a roadblock to the eventual triumph of the neoliberal new South Africa envisioned by the ANC and South African government negotiators. The black-white conservative alliance represented a new post–Cold War right wing that emphasized divestment from federal power, ethnic rights, and a skepticism of representative democracy. The alliance responded to the shifting winds of the Cold War's end with a renewed focus on ethnic rights and the emerging global neoliberal order. Yet, the ANC's move toward neoliberalism weakened the free market positioning of the black-white alliance, diluting one of its strongest avenues for legitimacy. The pro-apartheid movement cheered COSAG's development, viewing it as South Africa's savior and a model for the West. Conceding apartheid's formal end did not mean abandoning its tenets—separate development lived on.

The unbanning of the ANC did not just transform the landscape of the white right—it also challenged black bantustan leadership, who fell under almost immediate threat from ANC mass action. Amid the political violence that gripped South Africa during the transition, Buthelezi's position as a South African government partner and the West's preferred successor to the apartheid state eroded. Allegations of collaboration between Inkatha and Pretoria were eventually substantiated in 1991 and 1992, ostracizing Inkatha. Abandoned by Western and South African governments, Inkatha doubled down on its rhetoric on the minority rights of Zulus against the tyranny of the majority Xhosa ANC. Simultaneously, Bophuthatswana wrestled over how it could present itself as a legitimate state. A shared emphasis on minority rights fostered a connection between black and white nationalists, who tried to gain national and international legitimacy by presenting a vision for a postapartheid—yet still divided—South Africa. From COSAG's formation to its final form as the Freedom Alliance, its members navigated an uneasy tension. Desperate to gain legitimacy as independent states in a post–Cold War and post–white rule South Africa, each of its member organizations remained inescapably tied to their particular challenges—bantustan dependence on

Pretoria, the unacceptability of a white ethno-state, and Inkatha's drive to be seen as separate from its unsavory partners.[6] Even as COSAG gained the backing of far-right players, it struggled to gain traction with centrists and to cast off the realities of its apartheid origins. Although COSAG eventually rebranded as the Freedom Alliance, the coalition proved too tenuous to hold together. At its core, this uneasy partnership signified an evolving form of conservative organizing that used a shared language of ethnic rights to reach across the color line. The black-white conservative alliance fiercely held, but thinly envisioned, a new South Africa built on the rewriting of separate development in the language of the neoliberal New World Order.

A CRISIS OF LEGITIMACY AND THE FORMATION OF COSAG

As the South African far right mobilized, a different battle waged between the ANC and the Inkatha Freedom Party (IFP). When the ANC ban was lifted in February 1990, it set off an upsurge in political violence that lasted until 1994, with an estimated 14,000 deaths. The unbanning of political organizations unleashed a race for power within South Africa's black communities between the National Party, the ANC, and the IFP. The violence centered in the Vaal Triangle and the Rand's Greater Johannesburg as pro-IFP hostel dwellers clashed with the ANC-dominated townships to win over black South Africans.[7] Throughout the 1980s, the IFP political machine controlled land, public services, education, and security throughout KwaZulu and Natal. After the ANC ban was lifted, the IFP expanded its operations outside of KwaZulu, contesting the ANC's image as the "government in waiting" and positioning Buthelezi as a moderate alternative to the popular Mandela. In practice, the IFP operated in this period as a "syndicate" of rural Zulu chiefs and urban bosses, backed by the coercive KwaZulu Police, which functioned as Buthelezi's personal militia. After the unbanning of the ANC and Mandela's release from prison, Buthelezi's Inkatha rebranded as the Inkatha Freedom Party in July 1990 in a bid to compete for black voters outside the traditional Inkatha strongholds of Natal and KwaZulu. Inkatha's origins as a Zulu movement and its persistent ties to Zulu nationalism, monarchy, and traditionalism limited recruitment to Zulu migrant laborers living in the Rand and won over few converts.[8] Buthelezi and his partners' explicit use of Zulu identity stood in contrast to the ANC, United Democratic Front (UDF), and Congress of South African Trade Unions (COSATU), which rejected ethnic divisions as having no place in a new, multiracial, and democratic South Africa.

In the Rand, the IFP clashed with the ANC, which was building up its base of support in multiethnic communities with large numbers of isiXhosa speakers. The IFP positioned the Zulus, South Africa's largest ethnic group, against the Xhosas, the second largest group, portraying the ANC as a "Xhosa-dominated organization, ready to usurp the Zulu nation, kingdom and way of life."[9] In practice, the ANC and its UDF and COSATU partners were multiethnic movements, even if the ANC did have a high number of isiXhosa speakers in leadership positions. Rumors and fear of ethnic violence fueled conflict in the Vaal Triangle, including the creation of ethnically based self-defense groups. In July 1990, residents in the East Rand and Vaal townships reported constant attacks by people claiming IFP membership. Rumors of a Third Force—a South African government–backed, extrajudicial body driving the violence in the townships to intimidate the ANC and support the IFP—emerged.[10] But the reports were more than mere rumors. Throughout the transition, the apartheid government overtly and covertly backed the IFP, fueling violence throughout South Africa in an effort to delegitimize the ANC as incapable of governing. Between July 1990 and June 1991, almost 2,000 violent incidents occurred, mostly in the Vaal area.[11] According to Franziska Rueedi, this deeply personal violence included "massacres, IFP-aligned hostel dweller attacks on train commuters, drive-by shootings, public ANC-IFP violence, and necklacing killings of perceived *izimpimpi* (sellouts)."[12] The civil war in KwaZulu-Natal pitted the IFP against the UDF and COSATU, leading to the death of at least 12,000 people, thousands of arson and petrol attacks, and hundreds of stonings. It created between 200,000 and 500,000 refugees.[13]

The massacre in Sebokeng on July 22, 1990, encapsulated the emerging dynamics within South Africa. In March 1990, Buthelezi and his allies spoke against "the disbanding of the homeland system and the erosion of traditional Zulu values," including the power of the *amakhosi*, the traditional chiefs.[14] Inkatha feared for its place in a new South Africa, as the

ANC made it clear that their vision had no bantustans, and Buthelezi tied the survival of the Zulu kingdom and the KwaZulu bantustan together. COSATU engaged in mass action for an entire week across South Africa after Buthelezi's remarks, and one of Inkatha's most notorious warlords staged a bloody invasion of Natal that forced 20,000 people from their homes. Days later at an ANC rally in Sebokeng on July 4, speakers allegedly demanded the removal of all IFP members from the Vaal, and ANC youth left the rally to attack IFP supporters' homes and businesses.[15] The IFP formally launched a week later, holding a rally for peace in Sebokeng on July 22, 1990, during which ANC supporters hurled abuse, stones, and petrol bombs at arriving IFP members.[16] As they marched through Sebokeng, IFP hostel dwellers, armed with assegais, pangas, knobkerries, and other weapons, clashed with ANC youths and COSATU supporters, leaving over thirty people dead. According to COSATU and township residents, the police refused to disarm the IFP, even though they were prewarned about weapons; the police "watched Inkatha attack without intervening; then, when residents fought back, police moved in with teargas and rubber bullets to disperse the residents."[17]

Violence continued in the Vaal throughout 1990 and 1991. The Human Rights Commission reported "no fewer" than forty-nine massacres occurring over two years, with the IFP being the assailant in thirty-four, the ANC in six, security forces in four, and "unidentified whites" in many others. In their analysis of the massacres, the Human Rights Commission identified common drivers: the IFP's violent political mobilization, the use of "extreme terror tactics" to "immobilize, disorganize, and paralyze township communities," the centrality of hostels, police and security force complicity in massacres committed by "unidentified whites" and the IFP, and "retaliation."[18] After Sebokeng, the IFP launched aggressive recruitment campaigns in the Vaal. Observers argued that these recruitment campaigns falsely inflated the IFP's support numbers and that the organization used violence and "ethnicity as a calculated ploy to disguise political motives" and gain national recognition.[19] Buthelezi, once lionized by white South Africans and Western conservatives as a moderate alternative to the ANC, faced an unfavorable domestic landscape as the IFP moved to become a national party. According to some activists, Buthelezi weaponized the Vaal violence to force a high-level meeting with Mandela out of fear of being left out of the negotiations for a democratic transition.

The ANC and IFP also clashed over allegations of a Third Force, with Buthelezi arguing that the violence was black-on-black ethnic conflict and the ANC focusing on allegations of IFP–security forces collaboration.

A historic meeting between Mandela and Buthelezi occurred on January 29, 1991, their first face-to-face meeting in twenty-eight years, resulting in a pledge of coexistence and an end to political violence.[20] From July 11 to September 14, 1991, the National Peace Convention brought together the National Party, the IFP, and the ANC. The convention focused on four issues: "(1) a Code of Conduct for political parties, to include stay-aways and boycotts; (2) a Code for the security forces, to include 'self-defense committees'; (3) socio-economic development to include 'youth and training' . . .; and (4) monitoring and implementation mechanism to include peace secretariats at the national, regional, and local levels." After months of negotiations, the parties reached an agreement, signing the National Peace Accord in September 1991, the first stepping stone on the way to constitutional talks at the Convention for a Democratic South Africa (CODESA) in December 1991.[21]

Buthelezi's supporters crowned him the "prince of peace" after the National Peace Accord, and IFP supporters flooded its signing in "an intentional show of strength" by Buthelezi.[22] However, amid these steps toward peace between the IFP and the ANC, disturbing evidence of Pretoria-IFP collaboration emerged. In 1991, explosive revelations emerged of "Operation Marion," a 1986 effort by the South African Defense Force (SADF) to train two hundred Inkatha members at a military base in Caprivi, Namibia. SADF trainers subjected Caprivi cadets to extensive anti-ANC education courses and training on kidnapping, surveillance, demolitions, interrogations, bombings, and countermobilization.[23] Caprivi cadets identified their trainers as white SADF men and stated that they saw IFP leadership in the camps, specifically M. Z. Khumalo, then-secretary-general of the IFP, and Buthelezi.[24] Although forced to admit the existence of Caprivi, the IFP and SADF maintained that this was a one-off program, concealing that Caprivi was only one part of the SADF's efforts to build a black political alliance to counter the ANC.[25] In 1998, the South African Truth and Reconciliation Commission concluded that the SADF "conspired with Inkatha to provide [them] with a covert, offensive paramilitary unit (hit squad) to be deployed illegally against persons and organizations perceived to be opposed to or enemies of both the South African government and Inkatha."[26] The Inkathagate scandal, broken by the *Weekly Mail*, ended Pretoria and IFP's insistence that Caprivi was isolated, revealing the de Klerk government's support for the IFP and proving collaboration was not isolated to the Botha era.[27] The exposé uncovered over 250,000 rand of government funding for IFP rallies designed to show the "strong base" of Buthelezi and gain the "upper hand against the ANC."[28] Furthermore, the *Weekly Mail* quoted Minister of Law and Order Adriaan Vlok admitting that these IFP funding efforts emerged from the government's interest in supporting a black leader promoting an antisanctions message in the United States and Europe.[29] Buthelezi vigorously denied that he or the IFP Central Committee knew about these funds. "The money was not," Buthelezi stated, "I repeat not, used to further an IFP alliance to smash the ANC"; instead, Buthelezi alleged a conspiracy to prevent IFP democratic participation.[30]

The credibility of de Klerk, who was coming off a wildly successful nine-nation summer tour of Western Europe to build support for the negotiations process, suffered enormously.[31] He went into a three-day retreat after Inkathagate.[32] Western media reacted unfavorably to the revelations; the *Guardian* and *Toronto Star* lay the blame firmly at the feet of de Klerk.[33] De Klerk's efforts to restore his "shattered credibility," according to the *Christian Science Monitor*, did not convince Western diplomats of his commitment to rooting out state elements provoking violence.[34] The *Los Angeles Times* took a similar tone, stating that the Inkathagate scandal revealed what many had suspected—Pretoria had backed up its known fondness for Inkatha with secret payments, and de Klerk was not yet committed to democracy.[35] The *Wall Street Journal*, which covered the IFP favorably, reacted to Inkathagate with irritation, calling de Klerk's behavior "stupid," giving a "sheen of legitimacy" to allegations that Buthelezi was a lackey of the regime.[36] The Western reaction proved resounding—de Klerk's funding of the IFP needed to end. The Inkathagate revelations proved a dangerous turning point as the IFP's support dwindled among Western centrist power brokers. Yet after Inkathagate, pro-apartheid organizations supported Buthelezi, reigniting tried-and-true rhetoric around anticommunism, ANC terrorism, and ethnic rights. As United Christian Action put it, Buthelezi's exclusion signaled the "death knell" for all black moderates.[37] The organization, along with the Conservative Party and the Afrikaner Weerstandsbeweging (AWB), argued that Inkathagate prompted an overreaction from de Klerk.[38] Defenses of Buthelezi appeared in US magazines like *Conservative Review*, where pro-apartheid writers like Parker accused the West of ignoring the "clear threat" to Mangope, Buthelezi, and Gqozo from the terrorist ANC.[39] Parker was not incorrect—ANC organizing did threaten the legitimacy of the IFP, and the loss of Pretoria's patronage sent Buthelezi down a dangerous path.

This clear evidence of collaboration between the South African government and the IFP was revealed amid the negotiations at CODESA I, which began in December 1991. At CODESA I, all the major parties, except the Conservative Party and the Pan Africanist Congress (PAC), signed a Declaration of Intent to create a new constitution, but divisions quickly appeared between the National Party and the ANC. The National Party pushed for a national election of a constitution-making body and an interim government, recognizing that the longer they delayed an election, the more unfavorable the result would be.[40] In addition, Buthelezi declined to attend CODESA, fueling a perception and, increasingly, the reality that the democratic transition required only two players: the National Party and the ANC.[41] Discussions ground to a halt at CODESA over the "geographic distribution of power," including whether South Africa would be a federal or unitary state, how much power states should have, and how much of a majority would be required for final constitutional decisions. The ANC had the support of more than half the bantustan leadership by the time they walked out in May 1992, leaving Ciskei, Bophuthatswana, and KwaZulu on the outskirts.[42]

As 1992 began, the violence in the Vaal Triangle and the destruction of the IFP's legitimacy abroad pushed the IFP toward its other bantustan holdouts. The other bantustan holdouts, principally Bophuthatswana, were making plans of their own. Mangope's refusal to sign the Declaration of Intent in 1991 and commit to a single South African state and citizenship drew the ANC's attention to the bantustan's reincorporation to the alarm of Mangope's strategic planners.[43] Throughout 1992, in public and in private, the Bophuthatswana government reiterated its commitment to remain a fully independent nation with close economic ties to the new South Africa. Only a confederal association—with strong economic ties but limited political control—could be an alternative. Mangope's government worked to position Bophuthatswana's "ethnic identity" even as it recognized the fraught, uphill battle of ethnic-based identification. Repeatedly, the Bophuthatswana government cited the Keate Award of 1871 from the British government as proof of the viability of a Tswana ethnic territory that "prevailed before colonization and apartheid."[44] The use of the Keate Award, and not the actual creation of an "independent" state in 1977, highlighted a problem identified in a commissioned report for the Mangope administration. The South African public largely viewed a federal or confederal state with suspicion, echoing the ANC view of such a state as a means to ensure "domination and entrenchment of racial and ethnic privileges."[45] Bophuthatswana needed a new origin story: "South Africa is in the unfortunate position that this concept of cultural homogeneity has been contaminated by an unfair association with apartheid. This has caused accessory factors such as economic viability to be considered decisive because of 'political correctness.'"[46] Bophuthatswana, its fellow bantustan holdouts, and those demanding a *volkstaat*, needed to assert the value of a culturally homogenous, regional government outside of apartheid origins.

Bophuthatswana and the other bantustans also needed to prove their economic viability. Throughout 1991 and 1992, Bophuthatswana officials commissioned a series of studies on the economic viability of the bantustan from the African arm of the consulting firm Deloitte, Pim Goldby, internal think tanks, and the Human Sciences Research Council. The results were not positive. The Human Sciences Research Council report put it bluntly—Bophuthatswana would face an "extremely difficult political and economic situation if it should remain independent," isolated politically and internationally, with no economic support from the state.[47] In the bantustan's internal summary of the Deloitte economic report, officials acknowledged that "it would appear" that Bophuthatswana lagged behind South Africa's socioeconomic development.[48] Yet officials insisted on the viability of their ethno-state. Mangope launched the SATSWA (South African-Tswana) Regional Initiative in 1991, a fantasy socioeconomic development plan that tried to build bridges to Orange Free State and Northern Cape Afrikaners through Christian values, free enterprise, and mother tongue education.[49] SATSWA could theoretically make Bophuthatswana viable without Pretoria's support. In a scenario-planning report on possible reincorporation of Bophuthatswana into South Africa, Bophuthatswana's head of strategic planning D. W. Schoeman argued that the bantustan already proved "beyond any doubt" its ability to take charge of its future, meeting all "basic criteria" for an independent state, with the only obstacle being a lack of international recognition.[50] Bantustan officials acknowledged privately that the prospect of ending development assistance could cause major problems. Therefore, a federal option where the bantustans retained their sovereignty while cooperating on economic and security issues could be a "win-win," but this option was in direct opposition to the ANC's goal of creating a unitary state.[51]

The vision of Bophuthatswana as an independent state needed to come alive. Its leaders needed to find alternative financial streams, and they did so through the SunBop casinos, valued at almost $1 billion. In 1992, SunBop hosted the Miss World pageant, part of an agreement between the British pageant producers, Eric and Julia Morley, and Sol Kerzner's Sun International.[52] The 1992 Miss World pageant hosted an array of American talent, including, as judges, African American actor Billy Dee Williams, best known for his role as Lando Calrissian in the *Star Wars* franchise; American model Jerry Hall, partner of Mick Jagger and wife of Rupert Murdoch; and former Miss USA of 1970 Deborah Shelton.[53] The first Miss World event held in Africa "formed part of the glittering events marking the opening of the $300 million African theme fantasy resort, The Lost City, at Bophuthatswana's lavish gambling resort Sun City, 80 miles northwest of Johannesburg." The event included over 6,000 guests, including actresses Joan Collins and Brigitte Nielsen, socialite Ivana Trump, and writer Sidney Sheldon, and was televised in seventy-one countries, reaching over 400 million viewers. Russia's Julia Kurochinka, an "18-year-old blue-eyed brunette from Moscow, dressed in a black outfit trimmed in gold," took the title, with the first runner-up hailing from the United Kingdom.[54] Camera shots panned the Lost City resort throughout the pageant, lingering on the "African" décor—elephants and other animals, along with unidentified "tribal" patterns and shields. Upon Kurochinka's crowning, four men dressed in "tribal" attire carried her on a throne of zebra skin, flanked by statues of elephants. According to the pageant's organizers, proceeds would go to "help feed starving children through the UN-sanctioned Operation Hunger, a relief organization operating in South Africa."[55] But not every review of the 1992 Miss World pageant was glowing. In the *New York Times* coverage of the pageant, the paper noted that armed Bophuthatswana Defense Forces soldiers put up roadblocks on the road leading to Sun City and African dancers and attendants wore clothes "drawn from a make-believe tribe that favored leopard skin and white boas."[56]

The glittery resort and its Miss World pageant stood in stark contrast to the reality of life in South Africa as violence rocked the Vaal, KwaZulu, Natal, and the bantustans. Efforts to quell the violence took on particular urgency with the collapse of CODESA II in response to the Boipatong massacre on June 17, 1992, and the ANC decision to use mass action to target the bantustans. At Boipatong, hundreds of IFP-aligned hostel dwellers, armed with pangas, assegais, guns, and knives, attacked ANC-supporting township residents, killing forty-five people.[57] "An orgy of slaughter" took place as a gang of armed warlords "hacked, stabbed, and killed" township residents, including a nine-month-old baby, a four-year-old child, and twenty-four women, one of whom was pregnant.[58] Victor Khethisi Kheswa, who was known as the "Vaal Monster" and had connections to the World Preservatist Movement (formerly the World Apartheid Movement), played a central role. Police branded him and his aligned hostel KwaMadala as "enemies of peace" for their engagement in "intimidation, abduction, assault, rape, and murder."[59] For the ANC, the events of Boipatong, rumors of Zulu impis fighting alongside vigilante white men, and evidence of security force negligence and collaboration with armed IFP hostel dwellers provided an unacceptable basis to continue democratic negotiations. ANC leaders Cyril Ramaphosa and Joe Slovo toured Boipatong in the aftermath of the massacre, which Slovo described as a war zone. "People have been murdered in their beds, not by people in uniform," Slovo stated, "but we have absolutely no doubt that those who sent them wore police uniforms."[60] According to Franziska Rueedi, although the extent of security force complicity with the Boipatong massacre remains unknown due to evidence tampering and record destruction, it is clear that the Vlakplaas covert police unit armed IFP strongmen in the Vaal throughout the transition.[61]

The day after the Boipatong massacre, Mandela declared that "Mr. de Klerk and his regime bear full responsibility for the violence in the country and these townships in particular."[62] In response, the ANC withdrew from CODESA II, declaring August a month of "rolling mass action" of strikes, civil disobedience, and direct action—South Africa's largest since the 1950s.[63] The ANC specifically targeted Bophuthatswana and Ciskei because of their refusal to integrate into a unitary South Africa. These efforts came to fruition on September 7, 1992, in Ciskei's capital Bisho. ANC leadership sent a memorandum to the South African government demanding that Gqozo step down and an interim government step in and bring Ciskei into the democratic transition.[64] De Klerk refused, citing Ciskei's independent status, and the ANC responded by mobilizing 80,000 marchers led by the ANC and South African Communist Party (SACP) members Chris Hani, Cyril Ramaphosa, Steve Tshwete, and Ronnie Kasrils. The Ciskei Defense Forces opened fire on the marchers, who were attempting to walk into Ciskei and occupy Bisho, firing bullets and throwing grenades, killing at least twenty-eight unarmed demonstrators with automatic weapons, and injuring hundreds. The *Sun* described Gqozo's troops firing into the crowd indiscriminately as joining "a South African tradition: that of Sharpeville, Soweto, and Boipatong."[65] Eleven days later, King William's Town hosted 70,000 mourners for the mass funerals held for the victims of the Bisho massacre, and the ANC's Walter Sisulu doubled down on the liberation movement's commitment to mass action and to make the bantustans ungovernable.[66] A judicial investigation condemned the bantustan security force's conduct as a violent overreaction to the only form of peaceful political activity open to disenfranchised South Africans.[67] The investigation led by the Ciskei High Court, in contrast, concluded that the massacre should be described as the "mass invasion of Bisho" as part of a master plan to bring down the bantustan.[68] Frustratingly for the bantustan holdouts, the ANC refused to back down from testing their leadership, and de Klerk appeared indifferent to raising security and political support for the Ciskei administration.[69] This indifference signaled the apartheid state's recognition that the bantustans were not functional, independent states but weak entities dependent on the white government.

The events at Bisho not only terrified bantustan leadership but also highlighted the urgency for the major players to return to the negotiating table to avoid outright civil war. As the *Nation* put it, Gqozo's intransigence and the desire for revolution by the SACP have "had precisely the opposite effect. . . . [They have] jolted the ANC and the government back to the negotiating table." The events at Bisho "showed both sides the potential for anarchy," and de Klerk and the ANC agreed to a summit on violence as the ANC reduced its demands to return to negotiation from fourteen to three.[70] This reality catalyzed the signing of the Record of Understanding between the ANC and the South African government just a little under three weeks after the Bisho massacre.[71] The Record of Understanding laid out the basis of resuming negotiations, through bilateral communication, a democratic constitution assembly or constitution-making body, a fixed time frame, and a transitional government of national unity.[72] Buthelezi's IFP was left out of the Record of Understanding; Buthelezi "warned" de Klerk that the democratic negotiations were not bilateral and that "he was waiting for an answer on the question of KwaZulu's involvement in the negotiations process."[73]

The urgency of the bantustan survival project after the Record of Understanding, which Buthelezi called "the ultimate betrayal of the negotiating process," drove COSAG's formation.[74] The COSAG approach to negotiations rested on two contradictory premises—first, that the bantustans were independent, viable states that should not be incorporated into a new South Africa and, second, that any negotiations to create a new "internal" South Africa demanded the perspective of any interested, external "southern African" parties. This ouroboros reasoning drove COSAG's demand for a new multilateral forum outside the ANC–South African government domination of negotiations and laid the intellectual foundations for the one unifying principle that pulled COSAG's disparate parties together—self-determination for ethnic groups in a decentralized state, or the federalist project.

For the ostensibly independent Transkei, Bophuthatswana, Venda, and Ciskei, the beginning of the democratic transition posed a problem and a threat to their federalist project. Bophuthatswana found powerful allies in Gqozo and Buthelezi by demanding "true southern African" negotiations and a federal state, in contrast to the unitary state desired by the ANC. In a series of 1992 position papers presented to CODESA before the Bisho massacre, Bophuthatswana and Ciskei officials argued that the bantustan would not give up its sovereignty and independent status and any constitution negotiated without its involvement could not be enforced.[75] The IFP concurred; the CODESA framework was ill-equipped to regulate any constitution-making process because ethnic violence made any election "at best a charade and at worst a propaganda-and-intimidation competition."[76] As the IFP put it, until all parties—not just the ANC and the South African government—reached agreement on a new federal South Africa, there could be no change in the bantustan's self-governing status.[77] It was time, COSAG argued, to create a "new inclusive and totally Southern African negotiating forum" that recognized the independence of the bantustans and the white right's self-determination.[78] By calling for southern African negotiations, the newly formed COSAG attempted to set themselves up as the true democratic negotiators. In this federalist project, the exclusionary ANC–South African government eroded the possibility for a regional constellation of peaceful democratic states.

This federalist project was not only for South Africans but also for Western partners because this "rebranding" created a different "new South Africa" out of bantustan fear of integration and with formal *volkstaat* partners. The federalist project proved persuasive. The tenth anniversary edition of *APN* announced COSAG's arrival as South Africa's "Key to Freedom." COSAG drew in every "concerned and thinking South African," Parker crowed, "united" in its one determination to keep South Africa habitable from the de Klerk wreckage.[79] Parker attended COSAG's meetings via Action Save South Africa and corresponded with their members, precirculated her articles, connected COSAG with other right-wing groups, and offered suggestions on their communication strategy.[80] According to Parker, COSAG was a "tremendous learning experience for Black and White delegates alike: a great leap forward in understanding and perceptions on both sides, giving us a glimpse of what a magnificent country we could have in the hands of reasonable, realistic men."[81] Parker, as per usual, had her finger on the pulse of the pro-apartheid movement, which greeted the formation of COSAG and its federalist project with enthusiasm. As South Africa's holdouts lined up behind COSAG, the global pro-apartheid movement echoed the call, wildly supporting this "alliance of saviors" against the New World Order conspiracy to destroy South Africa as the Cold War ended.[82] To apartheid's defenders, the New World Order pushed forth by Bush and sanctions advocates, in cahoots with the South African government, targeted South Africa's black and white ethnic groups. According to this vision, South Africa moved into a new dispensation, no longer a bulwark against communism, as "global powers" now supported the ANC, forcing the Zulus to engage in self-defense.[83] South Africa was at a crossroads, reported United Christian Action, as the ANC took over the foreign governments of Ciskei, Transkei, and Venda through coups, engaged in secret arms dealings, and declared war on Buthelezi.[84] Despite communist systems collapsing in Eastern Europe and Africa, the "South African communists march[ed] on undeterred," spurred on the SACP and its ANC front organization.[85] The ANC simply weaponized "the issue of political prisoners and exiles to apply great pressure on the government," according to Ed Cain's United Christian Action. United Christian Action also challenged Chris Hani at a televised press conference at the National Press Club in Washington, DC, in May 1991, declaring the ANC a party of violent attackers who use necklaces to assassinate moderate black leaders.[86] United Christian Action concluded that Mandela was "simply not his own boss" and subject to the ANC's violent "political, military network," hellbent on "reducing the nation to ungovernability."[87]

South Africa's right-wing religious groups distributed this message to its pro-apartheid partners abroad. In 1992, Ed Cain launched the *Roca* (Review of Current Affairs) *Report* to keep Western readers up to date on developments in southern Africa. In the *Roca Report*'s first edition, Cain accused the National Party of abandoning Venda, Ciskei, and KwaZulu, with the "real political heavyweights" of Mangope, Buthelezi, and Andries Treurnicht standing against CODESA.[88] It was abundantly clear why the Conservative Party refused to be part of CODESA—it was, as Cain put it, a travesty of democracy. Cain later became connected to and corresponded with COSAG's black bantustan and white right leadership.[89] The *Roca Report* also supported the increasing violence of the Afrikaner far right as indicative of the level of rejection of the government's reforms and the deep anger in large sections of the white community at their inability to alter the process.[90] US pro-apartheid groups echoed these sentiments, viewing political violence in South Africa as caused by the ANC and supported by Washington and part of a conflict that put South Africa's bantustans at risk. As the *Conservative Review* questioned, was it "fair to rival, non-terrorist blacks, including the Zulus and the self-governing homelands," to legalize the ANC?[91] Reed Irvine's Accuracy in Media brought out familiar faces to combat "Mandela mania," including Cindy Leontsinis who promised subscribers secret footage of Winnie and Nelson Mandela taking part in "necklacing moderate Blacks."[92] Pat Buchanan also entered the fray, accusing Mandela of reeking of terrorism and the ANC of igniting a race war between Zulu and Xhosa.[93] According to apartheid's defenders, the executive and congressional leadership of the

US government ought to "hang their heads in shame for the mess they created in South Africa" and for putting the very foundation of Western civilization at stake.[94] The Bush and de Klerk administrations' betrayal of minority whites and black bantustan leaders in favor of the tyranny of the ANC demanded a rejection of the ongoing negotiations process and support for the emerging COSAG and its federalist project.

COSAG's federalist project rested on a bedrock of paramilitary and grassroots support that was local and global. Ciskei established financial links with the AWB, holding private meetings between Gqozo and Eugène Terre'Blanche.[95] Gqozo brought in former SADF and military intelligence chief and far-right paramilitarist Tienie Groenewald to consult for the Ciskei government; Gqozo had met Groenewald through his *volkstaat* advocacy in COSAG.[96] Investigations into the Khumalo gang—an IFP hit squad implicated in arson, murder, and sexual assaults—revealed that gang members used AWB homes as safehouses.[97] Buthelezi's calls for Zulus to arm themselves in self-protection units drew support from the pro-apartheid movement.[98] For six months, *APN* ran a relief fund for the IFP, asking for secondhand SADF or military-style fatigues, military boots, ammunition pouches, sheets, tents, medical supplies, and meals.[99] In partnership with Action Save South Africa, Parker raised over 60,000 rand, with donations from the United States, Britain, and Australia, by running ads in right-wing US magazines like *Soldiers of Fortune, Larry Abraham's Insider Report*, and the *Moneychanger*.[100] For its supporters, COSAG represented the last, best hope for the pro-apartheid movement and its emerging federalist project.

THE UNHOLY ALLIANCE LOBBIES FOR ITS FEDERALIST, NEW SOUTH AFRICA

By 1992, one critical avenue for COSAG lobbying the South African government and the wider Western world narrowed: the black-white alliance's position as the preferred free market partner to the West. From 1990 to 1992, the ANC's economic strategy evolved toward the importance of protecting private property and neoliberalism and away from its previous focus on economic redistribution.[101] As early as 1987, business leaders began meeting with the ANC-in-exile in Lusaka.[102] The rise of neoliberalism, "a political ideology that uses markets to increase the free flow of goods and capital across state borders . . . and limit the state's role in the provision of economic and social security for its citizens," aligned with the transformations within South Africa.[103] According to Roger Southall, "South African capitalism had begun to lose faith in the capacity of the National Party. . . . Therefore, it looked for an accommodation with the ANC."[104] In the early 1990s, white capital, mirroring its involvement in the creation of the black middle class in South Africa, "became heavily involved in courting the ANC"; for example, Mandela, Walter Sisulu, and Tokyo Sexwale launched the Batho Batho Trust in 1992 to unofficially operate as the ANC's investment arm.[105] These investments were based on the relationships Mandela had made with white capital while he was in prison, including Harry Oppenheimer and Bophuthatswana casino mogul Sol Kerzner, who partially paid for the honeymoon of Mandela's daughter. This represented, as Roger Southall states, the connection building between "the 'old guard' and the incoming political elite."[106]

In addition, the rise of social neoliberalism in the 1990s saw a unification around the economics of neoliberalism but with its left and right factions diverging on social issues like racial equality.[107] In South Africa, this social neoliberalism facilitated a partnership between the ANC and the National Party, which moved away from state interventionist policies for whites toward a market economy. This approach allowed the de Klerk administration to hold "a market-friendly economic line while ensuring that they [kept] Mandela on-side politically through resolving 'massive problems of social justice and inequity.' "[108] The social neoliberal alignment between the ANC and the South African government reinforced their shared commitment to a unitary South Africa. It maximized their political power without compromising on neoliberalism, while also committing to reconciliation and national healing.[109] As Robert van Niekerk and Vishnu Padayachee argue, the ANC's move toward neoliberalism reflected the collapse of the socialist model of the Soviet Union and Eastern Europe and the seduction of "market-friendly policy pragmatism espoused by . . . late apartheid economic bureaucrats as well as big business interests."[110] Mandela shared his support for free enterprise in his meeting with Bush on December 5, 1991: "We need a climate to inspire investors. . . . We have declared our support for free enterprise. . . . We are keen to have investors, and we want them not to think they'll lose their property."[111] Mandela hoped to assuage Bush on the ANC's economic policy.

This social neoliberal orientation that emerged between the South African government and the ANC countered a key prong of the bantustan–white right strategy to gain international legitimacy in 1992. Before the formation of COSAG, the black bantustans and the white right positioned themselves, both domestically and internally, as capitalism's defenders, in contrast to the communist economic policies of the ANC. By 1992, the ANC's neoliberal overtures limited the space for COSAG's capitalist vision. Globally, center-right governments increasingly backed the ANC. As a result, the best option for COSAG was to present itself as the defender of ethnic rights within a federal South Africa. Bolstered by a groundswell of pro-apartheid support, COSAG member parties agreed to a three-pronged lobbying approach against CODESA: demanding an end to violence, specifically the ANC's mass action campaigns; insisting on the right to self-determination in a federal not unitary South Africa; and demanding the disbanding of private armies, principally the ANC's uMkhonto we Sizwe and the Pan Africanist Congress's Azanian People's Liberation Army. Those prongs represented the end of the consensus within COSAG. From the outset, the IFP, the bantustans, and the white right resisted the creation of a unified platform that would limit the individual autonomy of each party to negotiate with the South African government. This fracturing represented more than simple collective action failures but rather deep-seated divisions within this conservative alliance over race and state power.

The IFP's desire to set the organization apart from its COSAG partners began at the second meeting. On December 7, 1992, IFP national chairman and delegate to COSAG, Dr. Frank Themba "F. T." Mdlalose presented an assessment of the organization. Mdlalose noted the origins of COSAG in its objections to the Record of Understanding but, with alarm, described two months of inertia after the conference, during which it abandoned working groups, recruited no additional members, and arranged no follow-up meetings. Action, Mdlalose argued, was necessary for COSAG's legitimacy as a true counter body to the ANC–South African government alliance. However, Mdlalose couched his call for COSAG action in a demand for maximum autonomy for its members. Mdlalose argued that the Steering Committee needed to avoid the "premature adoption of COSAG documents which could be prescriptive for political parties." Specifically, Mdlalose, speaking in his capacity as the IFP's chairman, stated that any attempt by COSAG to prescribe the form, content, or timetable of the negotiations would be dangerous. COSAG should focus its efforts on waging the "battle for human minds and souls" and achieve solidarity on constitutional principles.[112] The IFP remained firm on this issue throughout COSAG's existence—in March 1993, the IFP stated that COSAG "should not take or negotiate on behalf of its members any unified political position so as to transform itself into a political alliance."[113] Rather, COSAG would exist as a "clearing house of information" and as a point of convergence for constitutional strategies to eventually create a federalized South Africa.

In remarks on December 7, 1992, Mdlalose articulated the challenges faced by the IFP in its alliance with COSAG and its approach to negotiations. For the IFP, COSAG was a means to an end. The IFP represented the largest constituency of any of the COSAG parties, and although ostensibly acting as the political party representative of the Zulu people, the IFP operated in concert with the KwaZulu government, also part of COSAG. As the IFP and the KwaZulu government envisioned the negotiations process, a new constitution for South Africa would emerged out of a Multi-Party Negotiating Forum that South Africans would ratify by referendum. Most importantly, this process would lead to "ground-up democracy building," by which each federal state would craft its own constitution, explicitly empowering the existing KwaZulu/Natal Constitution adopted in 1992.[114] The KwaZulu/Natal Constitution emerged out of the KwaZulu/Natal *indaba* (meaning conference or matter of discussion) and the work of the Buthelezi Commission of 1982 and "was prepared as a model for regional government in a single South African state."[115] Two Americans in Buthelezi's inner circle with ties to the US right wing, Albert Blaustein and Mario Oriani-Ambrosini, crafted a constitution that "would debilitate the central government of future South Africa." Described by the legal scholar Stephen Ellmann as "riddled with bizarre typographical and stylistic errors," the KwaZulu/Natal Constitution "outline[d] a relationship between state and nation in which state sovereignty is intensely and repeatedly insisted on" and argued that a "Federal Republic of South Africa . . . does not, and may never, exist."[116] As the IFP saw it, the KwaZulu/Natal Constitution would become the model for other states to choose their own form of government without a unitary state.[117] In contrast to other federalist models, the KwaZulu/Natal Constitution rejected the supremacy of national law, instead declaring that each state was imbued with that power. More specifically, the constitution empowered existing regional militias to essentially operate as armies, severely limited national taxation power, and "convert[ed] all property held by the national government in KwaZulu/Natal into property of KwaZulu/Natal."[118] Buthelezi explicitly used the constitution to counter the idea of an ANC–South African government bilateral negotiations process.[119] For the IFP, COSAG proved the popular demand for a federal South Africa and validated the ground-up approach already in place in KwaZulu/Natal.

Thus, throughout COSAG's early efforts, IFP and KwaZulu government leadership sought to limit the organization's ability to dictate to individual parties. After Mdlalose presented his "Way Forward" document to the rest of the Steering Committee in December 1992, COSAG descended into disarray. As justification for his statement, Mdlalose noted that there was "already a fear" at the IFP's Central Committee that COSAG had gone too far in calling for a multiparty negotiating forum in 1993. The white right dismissed the IFP's concerns. The Conservative Party's delegates argued that the IFP's objectives were misleading and there was no fundamental difference between COSAG and KwaZulu's constitutional aims, with Groenewald "despairing" about the IFP's need to distance itself already from COSAG.[120] In a pattern that would become familiar to COSAG, Bophuthatswana's delegates became frustrated by the delays. Bophuthatswana's Rowan Cronjé, future chairman of COSAG, expressed his and the Ciskei delegates' discomfort that Mdlalose had drafted a "Way Forward" document ostensibly from COSAG but really representing the IFP.[121] Cronjé has an interesting—if not surprising—history. The son of Afrikaner parents who immigrated to southern Rhodesia, Cronjé served in the Rhodesian cabinet in various roles from 1966 to 1979, including overseeing the expansion of the Rhodesian security forces in the fight against Robert Mugabe.[122] After his efforts to "entrench white property rights and control of the armed forces and bureaucracy for at least 10 years," in the cabinet, Cronjé was a delegate for the conservative Rhodesia Front from 1979 to 1985.[123] He returned to South Africa in 1985 after a brief stint as an advisor to Ciskei's Lennox Sebe and joined the Bophuthatswana government. Yet again, Cronjé wore many hats for the executive he served, holding roles as minister of aviation, defense, and foreign affairs concurrently throughout his service from 1986 to 1994.[124] The *Washington Post* called Cronjé "the most powerful figure in Bophuthatswana after Mangope."[125]

The dynamic of the IFP withdrawing, the white right pulling in, and Bophuthatswana trying to create unity repeated throughout COSAG's internal and external debates, despite the IFP's designs to pull other members of COSAG toward its position. In confidential discussions with Mangope and Gqozo, Buthelezi tried to draw a distinction between the three bantustan leaders and the rest of the COSAG coalition. As Buthelezi put it, each man represented existing states with constitutions and power structures, contrasting with the white right.[126] They should work together to advocate for federalism, human rights, the removal of social apartheid, full protection of cultural and political minorities, and free enterprise. After these discussions, a consensus seemed to emerge, with the three men meeting with de Klerk on December 10, 1992, and planning a meeting between COSAG and the government.[127] These meetings—between the bantustan holdouts and de Klerk—reveal a core issue at the heart of COSAG. Each party, in its belief in a federalized South Africa, hoped to preserve as much of their own power as possible and resented their partners. Buthelezi and Mangope both hoped to be viewed as the true leader of black South Africa, not Mandela's ANC, and constantly sought to leverage their positions to make that possible through bilateral conversations with the South African government. In addition, the bantustan leaders had long been the partners of the South African government: a National Party pulling toward the ANC was an entirely new and unfamiliar dynamic.

COSAG's first test negotiating as a cohesive body came on January 8–9, 1993, in its initial meetings with the South African government. While COSAG's chairman Cronjé (Bophuthatswana) sought to promote the organization as a coherent alliance, gripes of individual group members derailed the discussions. IFP delegates moved up in the agenda a discussion of reported slights made by Pretoria officials against the IFP. Conservative Party representatives demanded written transcriptions of discussions and agreements between the ANC and the South African government. However, eventually COSAG members moved on to their main demand: ensuring a multiparty negotiating forum that was fundamentally different from CODESA and free of the taint of ANC–South African government bilateral agreements. In a seeming betrayal of his bantustan allies, Vincent Joseph Gaobakwe "Joe" Matthews (IFP) noted the impracticality of "cutting up" South Africa, even as Chris de Jager (Afrikaner Volksunie) disagreed and Cronjé (Bophuthatswana) constantly insisted that his bantustan had not committed to reentering South Africa.[128] Despite these divisions, in the COSAG postmortem discussion, Groenewald praised Cronjé for managing COSAG and putting on a "unanimous front" and emphasized the organization's diversity as a "point of strength." Yet in the face of South African government commitment to a unitary state, COSAG divisions wasted precious time. To the ire of COSAG members, the IFP quietly pursued its own, unapproved bilateral agreements with the South African government in late January 1993 and Bophuthatswana officials responded with private bilateral agreements of their own.[129] Some cheered the divisions. Parker applauded all the "powerful separatist/dissolution movements" that had sprung up across South Africa and that all "want[ed] to go it alone, free from the tyranny of a strong central government in a unitary state."[130] She cheered the headline-snatching efforts of Buthelezi and Mangope and the multiplicity of proposals for the *volkstaat* as part of an impulse for self-determination as old as humanity.

In committee meetings after the January 8–9 meeting, Bophuthatswana's delegates insisted on a reframing of COSAG, attempting to modernize and refashion its alliance and its presentation to the world in the post–Cold War era. COSAG "did not, in fact represent South Africa, but part of Southern Africa, with the countries represented . . . being Bophuthatswana, Ciskei, and South Africa" and a yet-to-be-determined Afrikaner and KwaZulu-Natal territory.[131] Throughout the spring of 1993, Mangope affirmed Bophuthatswana's commitment to staying independent, proposing various models for cooperation, like the European Economic Community or a reconstructed federal arrangement like Germany, the United States, or Australia.[132] Throughout the spring and summer of 1993, Bophuthatswana officials refused to be "lumped in with the other TBVC [Transkei, Bophuthatswana, Venda, and Ciskei] states," insisting on their viability as an economic and cultural state and positioning themselves at home and abroad as truly independent.[133] Mangope's efforts paid off on April 19, 1993, when Buthelezi and Mangope met with the secretary-general of the United Nations Dr. Boutros Boutros-Ghali. At the meeting, Mangope discussed COSAG's value, addressed the merits of federalism and multiparty negotiations, and received an invitation from Boutros-Ghali to meet again in May or June.[134] Mangope coupled these efforts with a June 7, 1993, SATSWA meeting that included more than 1,500 delegates as Mangope wooed Afrikaner conservatives with his Afrikaans and his right-wing political agenda. This new region would be a chance to reestablish the old Tswana nationhood while also committing to nonracialism and act as "antidote to Conservative Party racism."[135] In an attempt to leverage their successes, Gary Dixon, head of Bophuthatswana's Information Services, tasked the US lobbying firm Szlavik, Hogan & Miller to set up a meeting between COSAG and the Clinton White House in August 1993. Joe Szlavik, the "devils' advocate" lobbyist for corrupt elites across the globe, cautioned the Mangope administration, deeming Clinton a "domestic" president less concerned about foreign policy, even as the firm set up meetings with Congress, media, and academics.[136] For Bophuthatswana, this newfound legitimacy seemed proof of their ability to rewrite their origins.

However, Bophuthatswana was still fragile at home, and its officials forged partnerships with a newly reorganized white right. In an attempt to provide a broad platform to contest electoral discussions, the white right launched the Afrikaner Volksfront (Afrikaner People's Front) in May 1993 to ensure the protection of white minority rights. This organization linked most of South Africa's right-wing organizations together to push the South African government–ANC alliance to heed demands for Afrikaner self-determination in a *volkstaat*. The Afrikaner Volksfront emerged from a group of retired SADF and police generals: Constand Viljoen; Lieutenant General Koos Bischoff, former SADF chief of operations; Lieutenant General Cobus Visser, former South African Police head of investigations; and Groenewald. The Afrikaner Volksfront proved a crucial development for the white right's political organizing, operating as an umbrella organization to unite the far right.[137] The newly formed Afrikaner Volksfront met with Bophuthatswana's Cronjé and J. J. Ferreira on May 12, 1993, to shore up their alliance. Cronjé shared his appreciation for Viljoen's efforts while lambasting the de Klerk government's efforts to "discredit the rightists."[138] Increasingly, the holdout bantustan state of Bophuthatswana tied its fate to the power of the far right even as it searched for legitimacy abroad.

Black bantustan leaders found a new basis of legitimacy on a platform of federalism that allowed for the rewriting of the history of separate development, even as it tied them closer to the reactionary far right. This paradigm became clear after the assassination of beloved antiapartheid activist and militant leader Chris Hani on April 10, 1993, by white extremist Janusz Walus. Walus was a member of the AWB with links to the World Apartheid Movement, and Clive Derby-Lewis, the Conservative Party parliamentarian who armed Walus, was well-known among international far-right groups.[139] Hani's assassination revealed the collaboration between the political Conservative Party and paramilitary AWB, part of a sophisticated web of almost two hundred far-right groups.[140] In the aftermath of Hani's assassination, Conservative Party members offered to protect properties that lined Hani's funeral route. White paramilitary groups threatened to embark on a cleansing of black agitators, and Ventersdorp's factions of the AWB told black residents that they would meet the same fate as Hani. According to Terre'Blanche, Hani's death was "inevitable," but Hani's assassin had not acted on AWB instructions.[141] An AWB newsletter published after Hani's assassination included editorials from the McAlvany Intelligence Advisor and reporting from Buchanan on the "big lie" of whites committing crimes against black South Africans. Other organizations took a similar tone: Frontline Fellowship viewed Hani's murder as the "natural culmination" of white rage in the face of the ANC's terrorist attacks.[142] In Peter Hammond's eyes, Buthelezi, Mangope, Gqozo, and white-right groups were protecting white rights after universal betrayal from the West.[143] Although divisions remained, after Hani's assassination, the far right largely lined up with its bantustan partners.

The Afrikaner Volksfront tried to position itself as a legitimate political force committed to enshrining minority constitutional rights in the aftermath of Hani's assassination, demanding a *volkstaat* comprising 15 percent of South Africa. They forged a relationship with the Conservative Party and its new leader, Ferdinand "Ferdi" Hartzenberg, joining the Afrikaner Volksfront's executive council. Hartzenberg left the National Party along with Treurnicht in 1982, and upon Treurnicht's death in 1993, he took control as head of the Conservative Party and leader of the opposition in the whites-only South African Parliament from 1993 to 1994. Unanimously elected by six hundred members of the Conservative Party, Hartzenberg pledged to "negotiate for a future, not a funeral" and declared that the "party would not compromise on its demand for self-determination for the Afrikaner."[144] Under his leadership, Hartzenberg helped bridge the Afrikaner Volksfront to the Conservative Party–controlled city councils and agricultural unions, traditional right-wing strongholds.[145] Viljoen connected with black bantustan leadership, meeting with Gqozo on June 4, 1993, to obtain his support for a *volkstaat* and pledging closer links with the Bophuthatswana and KwaZulu homelands out of their "shared opposition to a unitary state."[146] The US pro-apartheid movement greeted these developments with delight. Neo-Nazi groups sent bulletins on supporting the Conservative Party, which had "finally moved to militancy."[147] The Council of Conservative Citizens warned that Hani's assassination was the natural culmination of the "wimpish government of President de Klerk," viewing the Afrikaner Volksfront as conservative organizing against the "sellout of whites."[148] Council of Conservative Citizens officials met with Groenewald, who confirmed that a strong "White People's Army" would form to fend off multiparty negotiations that would rob the Afrikaner of a viable homeland. For those interested in learning more about the Afrikaner Volksfront, the organization recommended subscribing to Frontline Fellowship, indicative of the continued salience of the organization and its partners who organized against sanctions.

The paramilitary far right continued to target the South African government–ANC negotiations, emboldened by Hani's murder and their reorganization under the Afrikaner Volksfront. This came to a head on June 25, 1993. In what the *Los Angeles Times* described as a "brazen attempt to thwart constitutional negotiations," approximately 3,000 armed right-wingers stormed the site of the multiparty negotiations. Armed with shotguns and led by Terre'Blanche's AWB, the paramilitary right-wingers engaged in a two-hour siege of the World Trade Center, ramming an armored truck through the glass doors, sending the negotiating delegates scrambling for cover, and effectively holding the negotiators hostage as they "assaulted black and white delegates."[149] "Police stood idly by" as AWB members, armed and in uniform, "roamed the halls and occupied the main debating chamber, where they sang hymns and painted '*Eie Volk, Eie Land*,'—One People, One Land—on the walls."[150] According to black police officers on duty, white commanders ordered them to keep out of the way as white police mingled with right-wingers and refused to arrest them as a result of a prior agreement made between the police and the AWB. Some police even changed into AWB uniforms. Police arrested only twenty-one rioters four days after the attack.[151] Delegates hid for several hours until the white supremacist rioters left, but thousands of right-wingers remained outside cheering and shouting slogans: "stop phony negotiations; no to socialist slavery, and de Klerk is *'n verraier*—a traitor." One of the AWB's leaders delighted in the attack, stating that the "idea was to get in there. We have got home to people inside that talking isn't enough. This showed we mean business."[152]

Although the AWB and its Afrikaner Volksfront partners insisted they had not planned violence, investigators concluded that the "conduct of members of the AWB was anything but spontaneous."[153] Publicly, Viljoen stated that the World Trade Center attack proved that a bloodbath would be unavoidable "if the government does not recognize the demands of COSAG." Yet, Viljoen tried to distance the Afrikaner Volksfront from the World Trade Center invasion, framing the attack as the work of fanatical AWB fringe members.[154] Although Viljoen attempted to portray the Afrikaner Volksfront as a unified front, serious divisions existed between the Afrikaner Volksfront and the AWB over how to best protect minority rights and contest the 1994 elections. The Afrikaner Volksfront seemed willing to engage with the electoral process, whereas the AWB insisted only paramilitary violence could protect the white right.

Divisions among the South African far right paralleled those among their US counterparts, who had a mixed response to the AWB's takeover of the World Trade Center. Writers for the neo-Nazi newsletter *Resistance* wrote they awoke "to the news coverage of Land Rovers battering through yuppie palaces where the traitor de Klerk conspired with the ANC to destroy the Afrikaner."[155] White men with guns proved glorious, as Boers rediscovered the courage to drag the National Party to the gallows, *Resistance* crowed. However, the newsletter also claimed that the AWB and Conservative Party flubbed it and that cowardly and incompetent fools ran the organization just like the US white resistance. Nevertheless, organizations like the Friends of White South Africa remained committed to supporting the AWB as the "true defenders of white self-determination."[156] Centrist US conservatives panned the AWB. The *Economist* lambasted the "zealots" who damaged the credibility of COSAG and "made trouble" for Mangope's "genuinely independent country."[157] Parker did note a "terrible travesty at the World Trade Center" in her Christmas 1993 issue of

APN: not the attacks led by the AWB, but rather the wider negotiations, a "charade staged by the National Party at a cost of some R70 million to the taxpayer and endlessly presenting the most shameless political gerrymandering South Africa has ever witness[ed]."[158]

The decision to organize the disparate black bantustans and the white right parties within COSAG offered a new legitimacy to its vision of federalism, both domestically as it sought to influence CODESA and abroad with potential international partners. However, COSAG suffered from its internal divisions, as each party disagreed on the trajectory, platform, and tactics of the organizations. Perhaps even more troubling for the black bantustan leadership, principally Buthelezi's IFP, white fanaticism reigned unchecked. In response to the World Trade Center attack, COSAG dissolved, yet the circumstances that drove its parties together persisted.

EMERGENCE OF THE FREEDOM ALLIANCE

In the aftermath of the embarrassing World Trade Center attack, COSAG disbanded, but it remerged as the Freedom Alliance on October 7, 1993, encompassing the familiar faces of the Afrikaner Volksfront, the IFP, Ciskei, Bophuthatswana, and the Conservative Party. Buthelezi, Gqozo, Viljoen, and Hartzenberg agreed that the time had come for a more powerful front that fixated on self-determination and regional states, the next phase in their federalism project. They feared disinformation campaigns designed to drive wedges between their members, pleading for trust and loyalty among members.[159] COSAG, in their eyes, floundered in its limited opposition to the Record of Understanding, divided by bilateral negotiations between each member party and the South African government. This new formation under the Freedom Alliance offered a more comprehensive approach to negotiations, with subcommittees and open solicitations of other groups rights organizations like the Free Cape Movement, Solidarity, and the Venda bantustan.[160] The Freedom Alliance, in their eyes, now operated as a true alliance, with each member committed to God, self-determination, law and order, and the free market, outside the confines of a racist, totalitarian unitary state. Through free elections, cultural diversity, and maximum devolution of power to the member states, the Freedom Alliance could create a new South Africa.[161] Unsurprisingly, Parker cheered the formation of the Freedom Alliance as South Africa's only real hope, even as she pushed the organization to enter the elections or it "will be history."[162] Nevertheless, Parker insisted that all eyes needed to turn to Freedom Alliance, citing coverage from *Southern African Update*, a new newsletter from the Council of Conservative Citizen's Bob Slimp, which hosted a "Freedom Alliance Update" from Groenewald himself.

COSAG's reorganization elevated the possibility of a cross-racial destabilization campaign. Although incapable of winning a conventional conflict, the black-white alliance could embark on a terrorist program of sabotage and assassinations. The AWB high command boasted its ability to mobilize an estimated 4,000 to 10,000 followers toward a civil war, which, backed by the war planning of the Afrikaner Volksfront and its estimated additional 5,000 forces, could draw in 10,000 to 25,000 white police officers.[163] Buthelezi could lead a boycott alone or, even more worryingly, with the white right's backing. The Vaal Triangle IFP and the East Rand AWB signed a cooperation pact on November 27, 1993, stating "that no one will govern without the Boer and the Zulu," and reports of joint IFP-AWB trainings emerged in 1994.[164] The Freedom Alliance could make good on this threat through their connections to the South African military and the robust South African arms industry crafted in the wake of sanctions. By 1991, South Africa claimed the "largest arms industry in the southern hemisphere and [was] the world's fifth largest arms exporter."[165] As Hennie van Vuuren argued, the apartheid war machine funded destruction within South Africa, "enmeshing" the National Party and its allies "in a sinister world governed by the interests of right-wing forces, neoconservatives, and anti-democratic regimes."[166] The access to these weapons by the Freedom Alliance proves this threat was not just political but also militant.

The Freedom Alliance hashed out its new organizing principles in a Bosberaad from November 2–4, 1993, focusing on self-determination, phased negotiations, demarcation of regions, taxation, and constitutional courts, tying their efforts to federal states like Israel and Eritrea.[167] COSAG's problems remained within the Freedom Alliance: Bophuthatswana and Ciskei insisted on their independence, KwaZulu on recognition of its constitution, and the white right on the *volkstaat*.[168] It was the *volkstaat* that ultimately derailed the Freedom Alliance's vision, as the IFP's palpable disdain for a white ethno-state emerged.[169] Would the Freedom Alliance actually agree to create a white ethno-state that would exclude and repress black South Africans? The Alliance wrestled over whether the *volkstaat* would be for Afrikaners or "all whites," concluding that it did not want to "demarcate a white state" but rather one for the "Afrikaner people."[170] Yet, no "natural majority" of Afrikaners existed in a geographically defined region, and the endless machination of the white right crafted an octopus-like shape to grab as many Afrikaners as possible. These were not new questions for white South Africans. The question of Afrikaner versus English whites drove apartheid legislation and crafted the "inclusive white nationalism" of the 1970s in response to mass resistance to apartheid, and now the far right wrestled with the question again as part of their federalism project. To Parker, the term "Afrikaners" was used "as a generic term for all patriotic South African whites."[171] Throughout October and November 1993, the Freedom Alliance debated internally, finally proposing on November 15 two means of building the *volkstaat*: either adjust the existing state boundaries to have Afrikaner subregions to make a future *volkstaat* possible or delay the final approval of the *volkstaat* until after national elections and only approve of the possibility of the ethno-state.[172] An uncomfortable question sat at the debate's heart: For whom was the white state?

The October 1993 establishment of the Transitional Executive Council acted as the first real grasp of parliamentary power held by antiapartheid forces, accelerating the urgency of the Freedom Alliance project. With one representative from each of the nineteen parties participating in the Multi-Party Negotiating Forum, the Transitional Executive Council would be a "quasi-government" as South Africa moved to democracy through free and open elections administered by the Independent Electoral Commission on April 26–28, 1994.[173] The Transitional Executive Council also controlled the bantustans. For the far right, the Transitional Executive Council was an existential threat to the minority rights approach of the Freedom Alliance, committing South Africa to a unitary, not federal, future. Furthermore, the Transitional Executive Council affirmed its commitment to neoliberal economic principles, limiting the possibility of the Freedom Alliance positioning itself as the preferred capitalist partner to the Western world. In 1993, the International Monetary Fund and the Transitional Executive Council, backed by the South

African Finance Ministry, agreed to an $850 million loan, tying the future government to austerity and the willing sell/buyer land reform model.[174] The Transitional Executive Council posed a literal and existential threat to the Freedom Alliance, challenging the bantustan leadership and their ability to propose a future vision for South Africa.

In response, the Freedom Alliance redoubled its commitment to a political vision of South Africa, as their economic vision of free market capitalism had largely been subsumed within the Transitional Executive Council's neoliberal agreements. In the Freedom Alliance's negotiations with the ANC and the South African government, it demanded a national leaders summit representing "all" political parties, with an "all-inclusive" discussion of issues: federalism, violence, transitional government, and constitution, among others.[175] According to the Freedom Alliance's logic, this approach could weaponize the collective power of each member organization to enshrine their regional demands in a constitution before competing in a free and open election where they would likely lose to the ANC. In addition, the Freedom Alliance focused on two sections of the ANC–South African government draft constitution, sections 118 and 121, which placed the regional government as "the secondary rather than the primary government of the people," falling far below the "federalist standard" of states.[176] In contrast, the Freedom Alliance envisioned regional states with original and residual taxing powers standing on equal footing with the national state. Until the South African government met their demands, the Freedom Alliance insisted on preserving the autonomy of self-governing territories and TBVC states. The Freedom Alliance hoped to freeze apartheid South Africa's state boundaries before national elections, where they would undoubtedly lose out.

The Freedom Alliance also worked to change its image in the aftermath of Hani's assassination and the attack on the World Trade Center. On October 11, 1993, Freedom Alliance communications specialists Suzanne Vos and Gary Dixon excavated the key "image issues" of the organization: Conservative Party and Afrikaner Volksfront racism, the lack of constituent support for the alliance, the IFP's "jumping into bed with Fascists and Neo-Nazis," and rumors of right-wing paramilitary mobilization.[177] The executive committee struck a similar chord in its October 11 meeting, noting that the "perception of self-determination as racism" hindered the possibility of public support for the Freedom Alliance.[178] These concerns were not just image. The Freedom Alliance recognized its fragile position, privately admitting that if Ciskei "tumbled" it could have a domino effect on the other bantustans, exposing the organization as having limited support.[179]

The Freedom Alliance went on the offensive, hosting sixty-five diplomats, twenty of whom were heads of mission, in late October 1993 and had ambitious plans for a tour of the United States, United Kingdom, United Nations, and Western Europe to counter the ANC and build foreign support.[180] In January 1994, the Freedom Alliance planned this Western trip to "introduce, inform, and advise leaders and opinionmakers on the Freedom Alliance, its history, policy and aims and to canvas as much as possible support from them for it" while also raising funds. The trip would include one member each from Bophuthatswana, KwaZulu, the Afrikaner Volksfront, and Ciskei and would likely cost around 130,000 rand.[181] The Freedom Alliance planned outreach to the chairman of the European Economic Community, the Belgian ambassador to South Africa, and a consulate offensive in Japan, Australia, Zambia, and the Ivory Coast.[182] Bophuthatswana continued its solo campaign, with Bophuthatswana's bureacrats lauding its self-determination efforts in the *Washington Post* and local U.S. publications.[183]

The race to rebrand the Freedom Alliance occurred as its members privately recognized that elections would likely go ahead with or without them. Notably, internal documentation argued that unless the Freedom Alliance participated in the Transitional Executive Council and the 1994 election, "there [was] no possibility of international recognition" for separate states.[184] Any violent action—such as a seizure of power under a coup d'état—would lead to sanctions and isolation, with the Freedom Alliance not able to govern South Africa alone. Critically, the Freedom Alliance's threat assessment analysts identified that its war talk and its perception as a group of spoilers alienated potential supporters, specifically the middle class who supported the IFP's peace and stability agenda. Ciskei's Gqozo verbalized these concerns at the Freedom Alliance's meeting in January 1994. According to Gqozo, the Freedom Alliance "continuously and repeatedly fail[ed] to make the impact which [was] necessary to sway the process" after Ciskei lost its independent status.[185] Although he viewed the negotiations as a "farce," Gqozo declared it was time to enter the Transitional Executive Council—which Ciskei did on January 12, 1994—and transform into an alliance capable of contesting the elections.[186] In the days after Ciskei's entrance, the Freedom Alliance decided that the "differences in the policies of the member organizations [were] too great" to form a political alliance.[187] The Freedom Alliance leaders agreed that Gqozo's decision brought "embarrassment" to the organization, with Walter Felgate of the IFP reinforcing that the leadership needed to remain unified on staying outside the Transitional Executive Council.[188] Privately, Felgate relayed to Buthelezi in February 1994 that he was "no longer sure" of the mandates of the other Freedom Alliance members, privately pegging the Afrikaner Volksfront as next to cave.[189] The IFP noted the "political costs" of further association with the *volkstaters*, who refused to enter the election.[190] Yet, the Afrikaner Volksfront and the IFP agreed that Bophuthatswana's ability to remain outside negotiations, as "the most independent" of the bantustans, would be the key to the Freedom Alliance's survival.[191] If it remained free, the federalism project could stay alive.

MANGOPE'S FALL AND THE FREEDOM ALLIANCE'S END

Even as the Freedom Alliance worked to preserve political power, it cracked down on those within their territory who tried to force democratic participation. In a democratic organizing workshop across the Transvaal, participants viewed the Freedom Alliance, Buthelezi, and Mangope as "desperate and dangerous" to stall elections, subjecting organizers to detention as part of a well-planed, professional campaign of violent intimidation.[192] International observers raised the alarm that these conditions reflected a "capitulation" of Pretoria to the Freedom Alliance.[193] As Peter Harris described in *Birth: The Conspiracy to Stop the '94 Elections*, the months leading up to the elections were a time of fear and oppression. Election officials recognized that even if the bantustans agreed to participate in the elections, the extent of repression was so severe that fair results would be impossible. Rumors of weapons buildups in KwaZulu and Natal, under the control of IFP gangsters and right-wing vigilantes primed to start a civil war, horrified officials. In conversations with election officials, Harris recalled the description of KwaZulu as a "nightmare" and that "Inkatha [would] make it very difficult, if not impossible to run an election there."[194]

This preelection organizing tested the hold Mangope had over Bophuthatswana. After civil servants went on strike and Mangope launched a crackdown, Terre'Blanche pledged his support for Mangope and offered armed assistance "to quell the communist invasion."[195] On March 11, 1994, armed right-wing convoys drove into Mmabatho. Thousands of right-wing paramilitary forces flooded into Bophuthatswana from northern white farming communities. Flowing into Bophuthatswana in cars and trucks, armed and angry white militants, numbering between 1,500 and 5,000, "fired indiscriminately at blacks on the street," "parading" through town with "guns whistling." Far-right whites beat reporters, cutting them with knives and stealing their cameras at gunpoint.[196] Viljoen and Mangope later exclusively blamed the trigger-happy AWB. Yet on March 10, armed supporters of the Afrikaner Volksfront entered at the request of Mangope after Viljoen issued a rallying call through the right-wing station Radio Pretoria.[197] Afrikaner Volksfront forces slaughtered black civilians, attacked foreign journalists, and assaulted Bophuthatswana police officers. Bophuthatswana Defense Forces finally drove the paramilitary whites out, executing three of them and causing Mangope to flee. In one of the most infamous images of the violence of the transition era, three white men in torn AWB uniforms lay "sprawled . . . beside their bullet-riddled blue Mercedes-Benz. One man was dead, his head in a pool of gore, while the other two bled slowly." A *Los Angeles Times* reporter who had interviewed two white paramilitarists watched as a black Bophuthatswana Defense Forces soldier shot one in the face and one in the back of the head. The image of the dead white soldiers executed by a black South African soldier circulated around South Africa and the world, jolting white South Africans. Police confirmed the deaths of twenty-two people, as a reporter described the scene: "gunfire echoed throughout the hot, still air, and barricades of burning tires sent plumes of acrid black smoke billowing into the air near the charred hulks of burned-out cars and trucks."[198]

The pro-apartheid movement reacted with horror to Mangope's ouster. The attacks on the Afrikaners who rushed to aid the people of Bophuthatswana were wildly misplaced, Hammond wrote. According to Hammond, these were not neo-Nazis but brave fighters trying to create a multiracial alliance of Zulus and Afrikaners who were attempting to "remain free from the Marxist madness."[199] After Mangope's ouster on March 13, the Transitional Executive Council officially took control over

Bophuthatswana. Just two days later, SADF forces drove out thousands of white militants, announcing a state of emergency in fifty-three towns and cities "mainly in the white right-wing strongholds of Transvaal and Orange Free State provinces."[200] Mangope's call to arms to the white right served as a test case regarding whether the bantustans could exist independently and whether the white far right commanded the forces it claimed. The answer proved to be a resounding no. Mangope's removal sent shockwaves through the Freedom Alliance—both to the resistant bantustan leaders and its white supremacist partners. The AWB army's defeat by the Bophuthatswana Defense Forces proved a complete political embarrassment and military failure, puncturing the façade of a robust, ready, right-wing army. For KwaZulu and Ciskei, the Bophuthatswana case revealed the unsustainability of the bantustan model without Pretorian financial and military support. Mere weeks after Mangope's ouster, Ciskei government workers and police went on strike, fearful of job and pension loss in a postapartheid South Africa if Ciskei remained separated and forcing Gqozo's resignation on March 22, 1994. Disturbingly to the Freedom Alliance, Gqozo's resignation came after asking for the South African government to intervene to restore order.[201] The Transitional Executive Council swiftly blocked Pretoria from deploying paramilitary stability units and appointed two administrators to secure the bantustan for its reincorporation after the April elections. This reincorporation alarmed factions of the IFP, which demanded that Buthelezi enter the Transitional Executive Council or risk political irrelevancy, as the elections, scheduled for a little over a month away on April 26–29, loomed.

The Bophuthatswana fiasco and the public humiliation of the Afrikaner Volksfront provided an out for Viljoen, who broke with the paramilitary right to participate in the election. The personal intercession of Mandela proved essential.[202] Viljoen's resignation to participate in the election decimated the Freedom Alliance, which now only included the Conservative Party and the IFP. With Viljoen's resignation, nine of the Conservative Party's thirty-four parliamentary members resigned and participated in the elections under the banner of the Freedom Front. Standing outside the elections seemed to only lead to political irrelevancy.

With the Freedom Alliance hemorrhaging support, the IFP found itself backed into a corner, as unrest by residents demanding to participate in the national elections rocked KwaZulu and Buthelezi reiterated his commitment to staying out. In a seeming last-ditch effort on April 8, de Klerk, Mandela, Buthelezi, and Zulu king Goodwill Zwelithini met to come to an agreement that would bring the IFP into the election. The outlook was not positive. The IFP demanded a delay in the elections—a nonstarter for both de Klerk and Mandela—so it remained unclear precisely what concessions the Transitional Executive Council could offer. In the week leading up to the election, chaos reigned within the IFP. Senior IFP members threatened to resign rather than join Buthelezi in the "political wilderness," with factions attempting to register for the elections without Buthelezi's approval.[203] Yet, on April 20, 1994, a mere week before the election, de Klerk and Mandela reached a deal with Buthelezi and the IFP agreed to participate in the election. This decision did not reflect a great rapprochement between the ANC and the IFP. Rather, Buthelezi found himself backed into a corner by the undeniable momentum of the national election process. Furthermore, the creation of the Ingonyama Trust, which reserved 2.8 million hectares of land under the control of the Zulu monarch, facilitated the participation of the IFP in the elections. This land not only preserved the monarchy and the *amakhosi* who backed the IFP but also "shield[ed] KwaZulu from the transformative ambitions of the central government."[204] However, this deal almost did not come to pass. Walter Felgate, one of Buthelezi's closest confidants and speechwriters, later testified to the Truth and Reconciliation Commission about the relationship between Buthelezi and Bureau of State Security agents, whom he said met monthly for decades. Indeed, in the weeks leading up to the IFP's election entry, the Transitional Executive Committee instituted a state of emergency, and dozens of arms caches were seized, confiscating weapons from Inkatha's main training camp in Mlaba.[205] Felgate testified in 1998 that these efforts were part of a secret plot to disrupt the 1994 elections by far-right whites through paramilitary violence that only collapsed once Buthelezi entered the election.[206]

After Buthelezi's entrance, the only spoilers remained the paramilitary right wing. Just two days before the election, far-right-wing resistance escalated, with sixteen bombing attacks in Western Transvaal, Ventersdorp, Bloemfontein, and Pretoria. These right-wing attacks followed nearly thirty bombings in early 1994 that targeted ANC and trade union offices and government installations, causing millions of rand in damage. This violence continued in the three days leading up to the election.

On April 24, 1994, a ninety-kilogram car bomb exploded in central Johannesburg, with a second massive bomb ripping apart Germiston the next day and a final bomb at the airport. Known as the "Bree Street Bombings," the attacks remain the largest act of bombing terrorism in Johannesburg's history, with twenty-one people killed and over a hundred wounded. Police arrested thirty-four AWB members in connection with the bombings.

Pro-apartheid groups greeted the April 26–29 elections with undisguised horror. In the days of the election, police scrambled from voting station to voting station responding to bomb threats that risked shutting down polling stations. "The lights are going out in South Africa and the last vestige of Western civilization is vanishing and Africa is truly the Dark Continent. . . . Shed a tear for that lost civilization and another one for ours that is also being lost," wrote the editor-in-chief of the *Citizens Informer*.[207] However, there were a "few heroes" worth mentioning, reminded the *Chalcedon Report*—Hammond, Parker, and the United Christian Action, for organizing them all.[208] Parker concluded that South Africa had self-destructed and the April 1994 elections would not, by any standard, be free and fair, but she urged her readers to cling to remnants of the Freedom Alliance. The cataclysmic events of the last month—the illegal removal of bantustan leadership—finally betrayed South Africa. However, Parker knew where it all started—1978, the Information Scandal, where "everything possible had been done to . . . destroy the conservative leadership," altering the course of South African history, forever cowering to American blackmail.[209]

South Africa's first free and open elections brought a resounding victory for Mandela's ANC—the remnants of the Freedom Alliance fared far worse. The Freedom Front's efforts to contest the election using a *volkstaat* platform with an Afrikaner homeland paid little dividends, securing a little over 2 percent of the national poll and nine representatives in the National Assembly.[210] Although the Freedom Front—and its earlier iteration, the Afrikaner Volksfront—claimed that several hundred thousand people wanted a *volkstaat*, polling revealed that even in areas of its most substantial support, over 75 percent of voters voted for the ANC. The IFP fared far better, mustering 10.3 percent of the vote, entitling them to three cabinet positions and forty-three representatives in the National Assembly. However, the elections in KwaZulu were contentious—IFP supporters hacked to death distributers of voting instructions, and the organization's late entry meant an additional 35,000 poll workers need to be "recruited, trained, and paid" in a matter of days. Inefficiencies in voting station management led to reduced service in KwaZulu and Natal and allegations of unfairness from the IFP, even as reports reached the Independent Electoral Commission of the IFP setting up illegal voting stations to inflate their counts.[211] Nevertheless, the IFP, ANC, and National Party formed the Government of National Unity, with Buthelezi appointed as minister of home affairs. The ANC dominated the cabinet, holding sixteen of twenty-three seats.

Throughout the 1990s, a far-right alliance emerged between South Africa's black bantustan leaders and white political and paramilitary parties. An ending Cold War pushed pro-apartheid activists away from defending white rule under the guise of anticommunism and toward a rhetoric of minority rights and protections. This rhetoric of minority rights facilitated a partnership with black bantustan leaders, who expressed their opposition to the CODESA negotiations by demanding protection for ethnic minorities. In response to the South African government–ANC domination of the talks, South Africa's black bantustan leaders and their white supremacist partners tried to gain national and international legitimacy by presenting a vision for a postapartheid—but still segregated—South Africa. This uneasy alliance of convenience against the ANC signified an evolving—if fragile—form of white supremacy that used a shared language of ethnic rights to reach across the color line to create a new vision of racial hierarchy in South Africa. The alliance between white and black nationalists proved challenging, as US and South African far-right groups reimagined white rule at apartheid's end.

CONCLUSION

In the November/December 1994 issue of the *Aida Parker Newsletter (APN)*, Parker reflected on the wrenching, painful aftermath of apartheid's end. We got *Uhuru* (Swahili for freedom), Parker bitterly commented, and South Africa is "now like Humpty Dumpty. It can't be put back together again; because no one now ruling has the faintest idea of how to set about it."[1] Others shared Parker's unfavorable postmortem, refusing to acknowledge the legitimacy of the 1994 elections. Far-rightists spread conspiracies in their circles, alleging thousands of murdered white voters, missing ballots, inadequate security, and the switching and tampering of voting boxes that left the Inkatha Freedom Party (IFP) entirely off the ballot.[2]

To apartheid's defenders, the darkest warnings of white South Africans had come to pass. Whites fled in mass, targets of avaricious redistribution by the state and brutal looting by black South Africans, a land of no police protection and a collapsing economy. The Truth and Reconciliation Commission forced whites to "hand everything over," leaving no facet of life untouched by those that use "apartheid and White racism as an excuse for their complete lack of initiative."[3] Just months after the 1994 election, the editors of the Afrikaans-language far-right newspaper *By Die Vlagpaal* included a special invitation to English-speaking South Africans to join their organization. "Anyone with roots in Europe and committed to the ideals of the Christian Boere-Afrikaner" could join, fighting shoulder to shoulder against ungodly, anti-Christian atheism, liberalism, and internationalism.[4] In 1996, Ed Cain and Peter Hammond, now director of United Christian Action, filed a formal objection to the certification of South Africa's new constitution, deeming it anti-Christian and antifamily.[5] After 1994, the paramilitary white right formed new partnerships across the United States and Europe, including with Britain's Western Goals Institute, France's National Front, the Flemish Vlaams Blok, the United States' SS Action Group, and Germany's International White Power Network.[6] South Africa's white supremacist right continued to frame Afrikaner nationalism as a question of ethnic rights protected by international law after 1994, invoking issues of land redistribution, education, and language.

Parker published monthly editions of her newsletter until she died in 2003, reserving particular ire for the National Party, which she decried as throwing South Africa to the "political wilderness," as de Klerk left "destruction for ordinary people in [his] wake."[7] She was not alone in her anti–National Party stance. A new class of right-wing Afrikaners emerged, implementing an aggressive, hardline strategy against the ANC and National Party leadership. Led by Theo de Jager, leader of the Ruiterwag—the secret junior Broederbond—and Dr. Isak de Villiers, editor of *Rapport*, the two men openly criticized de Klerk's sellout strategy and openly conflicted with the ANC. South Africa's young Afrikaners must realize that "the borderline between reconciliation and grovel has already been reached," De Villiers insisted, as the Ruiterwag called for a rollback of the Truth and Reconciliation Commission tribunals and affirmative action programs.[8] These continued attacks on not only the ANC but also de Klerk revealed that the National Party no longer served as the torchbearer of Afrikaner nationalism. Throughout the 1994 campaign, the National Party leadership believed it could win black South African voters by weaving together a platform of nonracial democracy, free market economics, and law and order, yet the party's thrashing at the hands of the ANC quickly disabused National Party leadership of that notion.[9] The National Party formally dissolved in 1997 and sought to reinvent itself as the New National Party, which failed to make a legislative impact. White South Africans supportive of apartheid reform flocked to either the ANC or the Democratic Party. It seemed that for white South Africans—both those holding on to and those rejecting apartheid—the National Party no longer represented white interests.

Other visions of white protection emerged in the aftermath of apartheid's fall. Some white South Africans believed that the "Boer people [would] not survive liberal democracy" and would only survive through "concentrating demographically in those strongholds where [they could] start building the New Christendom on a local level."[10] That "dream" would not be realized through a *volkstaat*, which failed to come to fruition after the post-1994 Volkstaat Council failed to agree on a single proposal.[11] Instead, what was left of the *volkstaat* became Orania, an all-white town in South Africa's Northern Cape controlled by Boshoff's descendants. Monuments to Afrikaner leaders decorate the town of around 3,000, Afrikaans is the only language spoken, and no black South African is permitted to live or work in the town.[12] As Carel Boshoff Jr. stated in a presentation at the 2014 Property and Freedom Society conference—the "white nationalist friendly" gathering that later included Richard Spencer of the alt-right and billionaire Peter Thiel—Orania was unique[13]: "Orania is the first ever community of Afrikaners that jealously [does] its own work. . . . [They have not] built their property and wealth on other people's labors," which makes it a "third Afrikaner, a mutation of our modern and unsustainable predecessors."[14] Not everyone proved so enthusiastic about Orania—as one academic argued, "unless significant numbers of Afrikaners are convinced of accepting the *volkstaat* ideal and move to Orania," a "full-fledged Volkstaat will not become a reality," particularly considering the "negative perceptions of Afrikaners in the rest of South Africa."[15] Parker and her compatriots raised funds to establish orphanages for impoverished white children. One of her charities, Mission Rescue, joined with the Mine Workers Union, which later became Solidarity, a community-based organization that helped poor whites "left out" by affirmative action in the new South Africa.[16] Out of Solidarity emerged AfriForum, a "chauvinist, narrow, white nationalist organization" opposed to land redistribution.[17] As of 2024, AfriForum, part of the Greater Solidarity Movement, includes 350,000 members across its various organizations, which include trade unions, media, education, and civic groups.[18]

The far right mourned the lost opportunities of a Buthelezi-led South Africa. In a March 1996 report titled "The New Right-Wing," the Independent Board of Inquiry concluded that the nature of South Africa's right wing fundamentally changed in the lead-up to the 1994 democratic elections. The right wing was no longer "confined to white fringe groupings but [had] grown to include a number of homeland leaders and their followers" as part of a new black right wing.[19] Although Buthelezi's IFP participated in the 1994 elections, winning 50.3 percent of the KwaZulu-Natal regional vote and claiming forty-one seats in the provincial assembly, political violence had an incalculable effect.[20] The Independent Electoral Commission designated seventy-nine voting zones of KwaZulu-Natal as "no-go" areas where one or more parties could not campaign freely, affecting 6,030,219 potential voters.[21] Although Buthelezi and the IFP entered into an uneasy alliance with the ANC, Buthelezi would spend the rest of his political career trying to hide his collaboration with the apartheid state. However, Buthelezi's inner circle made this task impossible by revealing to the Truth and Reconciliation Commission that Buthelezi collaborated with the South African security apparatus.[22] Ultimately, the IFP and Buthelezi were relegated to play second fiddle to Mandela and his successors, solidified by Buthelezi's retirement from political life in 2017. Lucas Mangope, Bantu Holomisa, and Oupa Gqozo all formed independent political parties that failed to make an electoral mark while the Truth and Reconciliation Commission investigated human atrocities committed by bantustan leaders.[23] Transkei's Holomisa fell out with ANC leadership after he aired allegations of corruption between the ANC and Sun City's Sol Kerzner. The corruption and bureaucratic bloat of North West province, formerly Bophuthatswana, saw scandals of its own; Rowan Cronjé "found himself under public pressure to return a government-issued Mercedes-Benz car he had received during his final years in office." Mangope formed his own political party, under which he engaged in "historical revisionism" about the "successes" of his bantustan regarding tourism, civil service, investment, and public transit.[24]

South African right-wingers were not the only ones who mourned apartheid's end. US white supremacist groups moved even further away from political solutions after apartheid. South Africa's omen loomed large, argued the Council of Conservative Citizens (CofCC), which accused the US government of refusing to acknowledge its shameful role in creating a hell on earth for all God-fearing South Africans. As Slimp put it in 1996, "If our great American Republic is going to survive, we must see that our would-be rulers of the New World Order are using South Africa as a blueprint for ourselves."[25] To the CofCC, the blame rested solely on the shoulders of the Bush and Clinton administrations, which destroyed the "freest" nation in Africa.[26] As a *Conservative Review* writer put it in the article, "Suppressing the 'White Tribe:' The War Against South Africa," resistance was futile. Whites needed to accept their diminished status, as the architects of the New World Order looked forward to a "complete sweep" of the United States and South Africa.[27] Once whites gave up power to "satisfy the priests of political correctness," they could not regain their sovereignty.[28] The lessons of South Africa should be lessons for Americans. One writer cautioned that South Africa's violent fate could happen in "every other African country where Black majority rule replaced ruling white minorities" and could become reality in the United States.[29] In 1998, the CofCC organized sponsors for white South African refugees to the United States, insisting that white women and girls were the targets of brutal black violence.[30] The message to far-right Americans was clear—the US and South African governments no longer represented white interests. White citizens had to take matters into their own hands.

American far-right actors enraged by the US government's betrayal of South Africa reflected more significant antistate trends emerging in the mid-1990s among the right wing. White power activists across the United States, Europe, and South Africa came to view the state as a hindrance—rather than an aid—to white power.[31] This antistate trend fueled the militia movement in the United States, which, at its peak in the mid-1990s, included nearly five million members and sympathizers.[32] The most violent example of this US far-right, antistate terrorism occurred on April 19, 1995, in Oklahoma City. Two antigovernment, white supremacist terrorists detonated a bomb in the Alfred P. Murrah Federal Building, killing 168 people and injuring 680 others.[33] The bombers cited their anger at the US government's handling of Ruby Ridge in 1992 and the Waco siege in 1993 as motivation for carrying out the attacks. They positioned themselves as part of a broader social movement but were only one aspect of the antistatism of the 1990s.[34] Fueled by the end of apartheid and the Cold War, conspiracies of a "New World Order" rapidly gained momentum in the far right of the 1990s.[35] As stated in 2001 in a reproduced editorial from Dr. Susan Huck's monthly *APN* column "Letter from America," "the talking heads are in a twist about Timothy McVeigh," part of a "heavy-handed effort at actual demonization of McVeigh."[36] Huck got her start in southern Africa working with Rhodesia's former foreign minister and defense minister before joining up with Ted Shackley, the infamous deputy director of operations for the CIA.[37] By the mid-1990s, the far right saw the US government not as an ally but as an enemy worth resisting.

That enemy worth resisting included a moderate Republican Party that seemed to win out. Bush fended off an early charge from Pat Robertson in the Republican presidential primary in 1988, defeating Senator Bob Dole of Kansas with 67.9 percent of the vote, trouncing Dole's 19.2 percent. Bush could have potentially faced Donald Trump in the Republican primary, who "briefly hinted at a run in 1987 when he took out newspaper advertisements against Reagan-era foreign policy."[38] In the presidential election, Bush handily defeated Democratic Party challenger Michael Dukakis by a margin of 426 to 111 in the Electoral College vote, carrying 53.4 percent of the national vote and solidifying Republican control of the White House through the end of the Cold War. However, Bush's presidency was not the resounding victory for the moderate Republican Party that many hoped. Although Bush handily won the presidency, grassroots conservative activists—long suspicious of Bush—appeared lukewarm about his candidacy and unenthusiastic about his record while in office.[39] Discontent bubbled at the margins of what was once the Reagan coalition, best encapsulated by Pat Buchanan's 1992 primary challenge to Bush. In September 1991, Buchanan laid out his plan for "America First—A Foreign Policy for the Rest of Us." Buchanan explicitly positioned his America First ideology—advanced by an alliance of paleo-libertarians and Old Right traditionalists—in opposition to Bush's New World Order. Invoking thinly veiled racial coding, Buchanan insisted that the "incivility and brutality" of US cities and the "rise of ethnic hatred" compelled Americans to put "our family first, our people first, our country first."[40] Although Buchanan lost his primary challenge, the incumbent's defeat at the hands of Democrat Bill Clinton only fueled critique among the right of the "Bush Republican Party."

As the historian Nicole Hemmer argues, "as militia membership grew, the lines between the conservative movement and these far-right groups blurred . . . [giving] shape to the dominant political type of the 1990s: the angry white male." Buchanan joined a cadre of "angry white men"—Rush Limbaugh, militias, and Klansmen—along with the right-wing think tank complex that "believed the colorblind racism of the Reagan era was ill-suited to both the realities and the mood of the 1990s."[41] The 1990s saw the rise of contemporary conservative darlings like Dinesh D'Souza and

Laura Ingraham, who helped the Republicans rebound in 1994 with a landslide congressional victory. In this new 1990s Republican Party, the House Republican caucus reemphasized cultural conservatism and took an even more confrontational stance with their party and its executives.[42] The "insurgency" within the party seemed to be paying off: in his 1996 presidential run, Buchanan set off to a blistering start, eventually winning Alaska, New Hampshire, Louisiana, and Missouri. "Pitchfork Pat" raged against globalism, the New World Order, immigrants, and women, as he "blurred lines between the far right and the Buchanan movement" within the Republican Party. Buchanan eventually lost to Dole, but he nurtured the conspiratorial streak that would dominate the anti-Clinton activities of the Republicans in Congress and the party throughout much of the early 2000s. Buchanan's departure from the Republican Party in 1999, along with the War on Terror and the disputed victory of George W. Bush in 2000, kept the far-right insurgency contained within the party.[43] That changed after the 2008 election of the first African American president of the United States, Democrat Barack Obama. Even as the *New York Times* trumpeted, "Obama Elected President as Racial Barrier Falls," Obama's election catalyzed a landscape of US far-right activism, encapsulated by the emergence of the Tea Party and the proliferation of racist conspiracies, stereotypes, and slurs directed at the Obama family.[44] For white supremacist activists, Obama's victory signaled not only unacceptable changes in American society but also a general weakness within the Republican Party and its leadership. Throughout the Obama presidency and in the lead-up to the 2016 presidential election, moderate and far-right visions of US conservatism struggled for dominance.

South Africa's right wing received new life of its own, gaining power from the failings of the ruling ANC, specifically around the economy. The thirtieth anniversary of apartheid's end in 2024 brought forth a flurry of reflections about the state of South Africa, and the diagnosis was not pretty. The *Economist* reported that just 29 percent of South Africans thought "their life will get better over the last five years" and 79 percent believed that "political leaders cannot be trusted." Unemployment in South Africa reached a whopping 32 percent, the GDP per person was lower in 2024 than in 2008, and South Africans grapple daily with a crumbling infrastructure and record-high rolling blackouts. South Africa remains one of the most economically unequal countries in the world, as black South Africans make up a disproportionate share of the chronically poor, transiently poor, and vulnerable. In contrast, white South Africans, who compose only 7 percent of the population, "make up more than a fifth of the middle class and about two-thirds of the elite."[45] This economic malaise combined with revelations of widespread corruption within the ANC party apparatus and the national government culminated in the 2021 arrest of former president Jacob Zuma on corruption charges.

The colorblind far right in South Africa has sought to capitalize on this economic malaise. In 2018, the Gospel Defense League published a pamphlet titled "Farms and Freedom Under Fire in South Africa," which attacked the ANC and the communist Economic Freedom Fighters (EFF) for their efforts to transfer over four thousand farms from white South African farmers. Pushing the conspiracy of a genocide against white Afrikaner farmers, the Gospel Defense League argued that these efforts to attack white South African farming were part of a "smokescreen to distract from corruption and failure" and one of the "racist policies" of Mandela's Black Economic Empowerment program. "Farm attacks in South Africa are 700 percent higher than any country in the world," the Gospel Defense League argued, and an act of "war against whites," part of a program of "farm terror" and "farm torture" where families are "tied up, cut with machetes and pitchforks, burned with boiling water or hot irons, dragged behind vehicles, raped and mutilated in incomprehensible savagery."[46] Although farm murders have increased in South Africa, according to one fact-checking article, "there are no reliable statistics to back up claims that white farmers are more likely to be killed than either black farmers or the general population."[47]

The former bantustans play a critical role in the colorblind far right. KwaZulu-Natal continues to struggle with political violence—from 2000 to 2021, 418 political hits took place and 118 were in KwaZulu Natal, part of a "layer upon layer of violence that involves thugs, mafia, drug dealers, corrupt politicians, and taxi hitmen. . . . In KZN, might is right."[48] One scholar argued that this violence can be traced back to the "spiral of the war between Inkatha and the ANC . . . [spawning] complex networks of complicity that stretch from the lowest forms of organized crime to the highest echelons of the state."[49] Mangope's son, retired brigadier general Kgosi Kwena Mangope, was elected chairperson of North West province's party ActionSA in 2021 and ran for North West premier in 2024.[50]

He served in the Bophuthatswana Defense Force from 1981 to 1994, becoming a colonel before joining the South African National Defense Force, one of many former bantustan security personnel who found their way into the military and private security.[51] As the historian Laura Phillips contends, the "ANC brought many of the bantustan leaders and chiefs into the fold," propping up chiefs through the Communal Land Rights Act and reinforcing a "nostalgia" around the bantustans as spaces of "law and order," "ethnic nationalism," and incubation of the "black middle class."[52]

The growth of the black middle class is changing the fabric of South African society.[53] As Roger Southall argued, it is essential to move away from the image of the black African middle class as "black diamonds": "parasitic" consumers of goods, a one-dimensional vision of this dynamic group shaped by globalization and democratization.[54] In his analysis, Southall credits the growth of the black middle class to the ANC's black empowerment programs that filled out governance, often relying on an influx of black professionals from the bantustans as a "petty bourgeoisie" of "chiefs, politicians, civil servants, teachers, and traders."[55] This group has a growing affinity with black Pentecostalism, part of a larger rise of charismatic African Pentecostal pastors across the continent.[56] These churches have come under fire for their "authoritarian governance structure built around . . . a personality cult," where pastors wield control through "spiritual, symbolic, human, political, and economic" capital to cover up sexual abuse and corruption.[57] The Charismatic African Pentecostals retain their links to the US Christian right, which through groups like Focus on the Family, Alliance Defending Freedom, Trinity Broadcasting Network, and others lobbied governments in Kenya, Tanzania, Nigeria, Uganda, South Sudan, and Zimbabwe to pass anti-LGBTQ+ and antiabortion laws.[58] In South Africa, Jacob Zuma's presidency "laid the groundwork for a resurgent fundamentalism with unprecedented social and political influence" due to his "robust Christianity" and his favoritism of "Evangelical-Pentecostal-Charismatic forms of Christianity," best exemplified in his relationship with Ray McCauley's Rhema Bible Church. Kingdom Now and the New Apostolic Reformation fuel megachurches in South Africa that "have a close resemblance to their American founders" and reject the "imposition" of liberal values on society by a flawed state.[59]

A new multiracial, federalist, conservative coalition could be emerging today. In 2018, Hammond argued that a new landscape of potential allies could be mobilized into their coalition: "the Coloured, Malays, and all Afrikaans speakers in the Western Cape should be attracted by the possibility of regaining control over their own communities and respect for their language."[60] As Ismail Lagardien wrote in the *Daily Maverick* in 2024, Colored South Africans "were active in the various permutations of 'collaboration and democracy' during the apartheid era . . . with more conservative elements finding a home in the Minority Front, the Freedom Front Plus or the Patriotic Front."[61] These conservative elements fuel a contemporary call for secession from the Western Cape via the fringe right-wing civil group Cape Independence Advocacy Group. According to their polling, one in three residents of the Cape support independence, including 65 percent of the centrist Democratic Alliance (DA) and 89 percent of the Freedom Front Plus, citing independence as "improving governance and escaping ANC misrule."[62] As the scholar Oscar van Heerden argued, "at the core of the arguments for secession of the Western Cape is racism, nothing else," built on two "fallacies" of a "well-governed province" able to function with economic independence.[63] The ANC's Yonela Diko insists that these secessionists "converge on federalism," appear "to be triggered by what they called 'successive waves of immigrants arriving' in the Western Cape," and hope to create a "quasi-federalist country split along ethnic and racial lines."[64]

The failure of South Africa after apartheid continues to draw Americans into its web, even those at the highest echelons of power. The election of Donald Trump in 2016—and his brand of racist authoritarianism—revealed that far-right ideas had gained significant traction within the right wing. As Buchanan put it in an interview with *Politico* in 2017, his greatest achievement was being the proto Trump: " 'The ideas made it,' Buchanan tells [the *Politico* reporter], letting out a belly laugh, 'But I didn't.' "[65] In May 2019, members of AfriForum toured the United States, meeting with Congress and conservative media outlets to spread conspiracies of white attacks on farmers, despite the fact that by 2010 farm murders had "declined even more quickly than that of other contact crimes across South Africa" and sat well below the national murder rate of 35.8 murders per 100,000, at only 5.7. Furthermore, a global network of white rightists—Peter Dutton in Australia, Vladimir Putin in Russia, and Tucker Carlson and Donald Trump in the United States—all engaged in these conspiracies.[66] As the journalist Simon Kuper wrote in a 2024 edition of the *Financial Times*, "four of Maga's [Donald Trump's Make America Great Again] most influential voices"—Peter Thiel, venture capitalist David Sacks, Tesla founder and X's Elon Musk, and QAnon conspiracy creator Paul Furber—"are fiftysomething white men with formative experiences in apartheid South Africa." These men believe "inequality is natural and [live] in fear of a race war," drawing them "towards a certain type of American politics."[67] Upon Trump's reelection, Musk became a key advisor to Trump, and the two of them began trafficking in conspiracies of antiwhite genocide. Trump offered Afrikaners refugee status in March 2025 and stopped all aid to South Africa over a land expropriation law that he alleged constituted a human rights violation against white minority Afrikaners.[68]

The rise of the global far right—and the particularities of its manifestations in South Africa and the United States—shows the importance of the pro-apartheid movement. In the 1980s, the pro-apartheid movement signified an evolving form of US and South African white supremacy that proved far reaching, organized, and innovative in its ability to graft onto existing mainstream right-wing ideas. These discourses supporting white rule evolved throughout the 1980s in response to US conservative political thought. In particular, the pro-apartheid movement latched onto Cold War ideas about anticommunism, emerging racially "colorblind" policies, and Christian activism to justify white rule. Centrist conservatives found themselves under pressure from the far right to take a less confrontational posture toward South Africa, even as they simultaneously faced pressure from the global antiapartheid movement to reject white rule. Although the pro-apartheid movement operated in its own far-right spaces, its ability to graft onto existing discourses present in US right-wing media and cooperate with political organizations defined and grew its influence. These US conservative networks acted as critical conduits of defenses of white rule, pushing the Republican Party closer to the apartheid government using ideas about race and global order that right-wingers already possessed. As the power of the right wing grew in politics—best encapsulated by the election of Ronald Reagan in 1980—transatlantic far-right activists mobilized these pro-apartheid discourses to shore up conservative support for apartheid South Africa. Initially, this right-wing pressure seemed to pay dividends, as the first term of Reagan's constructive engagement catered to the apartheid state's interests when executing the policy. Yet, the pro-apartheid movement in both the United States and South Africa remained frustrated by the tepid nature of the relationship, with each pushing their conservative leadership for a closer partnership.

Pro-apartheid disenchantment with mainstream conservative leadership only grew in the United States after the Comprehensive Anti-Apartheid Act of 1986. Reagan's second term and the floundering of constructive engagement pushed pro-apartheid actors into the policymaking process of the White House. Leveraging the internal disruption of the Reagan White House—as every faction of the administration worked to sustain the president's sanctions veto—pro-apartheid actors gained influence over US–South African relations. Yet, even as white rule's defenders infiltrated the White House, mainstream US conservatives—led by Republicans in Congress—shunned open support for South Africa. Mainstream conservatives broke with the far right, pushing the pro-apartheid movement down an antistate path, as congressional Republicans chose to support economic sanctions and defied their president's veto.

When the South African government entered negotiations with the ANC in 1990, white power organizations operated in South Africa's bantustans and townships to drum up support for white rule. These far-right activists increasingly deployed Christianity as a mechanism of control against black South Africans as the end of the Cold War diminished the importance of anticommunism. Individual pro-apartheid churches entered South Africa's black communities, preaching a gospel of stability, colorblindness, and personal responsibility in defense of white governance. Simultaneously, white South Africans increasingly deployed a rhetoric of ethnic rights and minority protection to justify forming segregated ethno-states in response to ANC–South African government negotiations. This focus on ethnic rights created an additional bridge to South Africa's black nationalist leaders in KwaZulu, Ciskei, and Bophuthatswana, building on over a decade of collaboration against Western sanctions in the 1980s. This uneasy alliance of convenience against the ANC signified an evolving—if fragile—form of white supremacy that used a shared language of ethnic rights to reach across the color line to defend racial hierarchy.

On the surface, the story of the pro-apartheid movement appears to be one of failure. South Africa became a multiracial democracy with a liberal constitution. The Western powers—principally the United States—explicitly supported South Africa's move toward democracy, greeting the election of the ANC's Mandela with enthusiasm. Conservative governments, in their refusal to defend South Africa to their fullest extent, pushed the far right to work against them in both the United States and South Africa, questioning the mainstream right-wing project and working openly against the state. However, the rise of the far right since 2016 reveals that the black-white conservative vision—of the Concerned South Africans Group, the CofCC, and Frontline Fellowship—might have survived after all. As the scholar Siphiwe Dube argues, a New Right has emerged in South Africa, oriented around economic neoliberalism, political conservatism, and religious Pentecostalism and appealing to an "undeclared coalition" that includes the black middle class and aspiring middle class. The transition from apartheid to postapartheid is a rightward turn, with the "right-minded citizen who is disgruntled . . . and seeks to escape this condition by instituting a new form of domination."[69] These cross-cutting capitalist and Christian discourses are not unique to South Africa: Republican pollster Patrick Ruffini argued in 2023 that the new "Party of the People" in the United States would be right-leaning, populist Black, Hispanic, Asian American, and mixed-race voters invigorated by messages of the free market, faith, family, and a rejection of "diversity politics."[70] This conservative political messaging, tied to Christian religiosity and capitalist empowerment, appeals across and beyond racial identity and was seemingly solidified in 2024, as Trump saw significant gains among Black, Latino, Asian American, and immigrant voters.[71] Far-right political actors across India, Brazil, and Hungary found electoral success through an authoritarian, racialized agenda that relies on but also moves beyond white supremacy. This begs the question: Is the "antistate turn" for the far right over? Perhaps the better questions are: How real was the antistate turn of the 1990s? Was it merely a blip in the overall trajectory of a far-right wing recalibrating its plan to take back a state that betrayed them temporarily?

Perhaps the pro-apartheid movement's failure lies in the reality that the ANC and the South African government coopted the movement with a capitalist, neoliberal message that was ready for the emerging economic era. Maybe it lies in their defense of and open association with a system of brutal white supremacist hierarchy and oppression that seemed dated as the Cold War ended and the New World Order emerged. Undoubtedly, their failure is in no small part a result of the bravery and resistance of antiapartheid activists in South Africa who refused to settle for a piecemeal ending of white rule. What is clear is that pro-apartheid's coalition of black and white conservatives and far-right activists straddled different eras—Cold War and post–Cold War, civil rights and post–civil rights, apartheid and postapartheid—and could not survive the vortex of those competing winds. Perhaps their message of colorblindness, Christianity, political conservatism, and the free market did not have the space to be successful in 1994. Maybe it has the space now.

ACKNOWLEDGMENTS

How does one write a book? Six years later, I have come to my answer: slowly, then all at once. Then slowly again, and then all at once. Again and again. Until one day, the book is miraculously done, and all that remains is gratitude for the community that sustained this work.

First, at the University of Texas (UT) at Austin: My indefatigable advisor, Jeremi Suri, encouraged me to think bigger, argue bolder, and never doubt myself. My incredible mentors—Mark Lawrence and Will Inboden—nurtured this project at its various stages of infancy. The wider UT community—specifically the Clements Center for National Security and the History Department—hosted the most brilliant people who filled those early years with joy. Jackie Jones, Neil Kamil, Peniel Joseph, and Aaron O'Connell—thank you for helping me grow into the scholar I am today.

This project would not have been possible without generous institutional support. Early research support came from the University of Texas at Austin History Department and the graduate school, the Clements Center for National Security, and the Society for Historians of American Foreign Relations. Special thanks to the Ronald Reagan Presidential Library archivists, especially Ray Wilson. The bulk of this research was only possible with the incredible support of the Social Science Research Council's Mellon International Dissertation Research Project. Special thanks to the

University of Witwatersrand's Historical Papers Research Archive and the amazing archivists Gabriele Mohale, Elizabeth Marima, and Mphonyana Taulela. Thanks to the Billy Graham Center Archives for their support via the Torrey M. Johnson Research Grant and Bob Shuster and Katherine Graber for their enthusiasm for this work. Thanks to the Tamiment Library's Cold War Center at New York University with support from the Agnes N. Haury Travel Grant, Michael Koncewicz, and Becky Schulte, curator of the Wilcox Collection at the University of Kansas. I had the generous support of the Harvard Kennedy School's Belfer Center as an Ernest May Predoctoral Fellow in History and Policy—many thanks to Fred Logevall—the PEO International Sisterhood, and the American Council of Learned Societies. I returned to South Africa in the summer of 2023 and had the pleasure of completing my fieldwork. Many thanks to Atline Maluleke at the University of Johannesburg, Sherian Latif at the Alan Paton Centre, and Lwazi Mestile, Freddy Sentso, and Thabang Khanye at the Archive of Contemporary Affairs at the University of the Free State. To Lloyd Roberts and Ruhan Fourie—you made my research so much better.

I spent the last two years as a postdoctoral fellow at the Center for Presidential History (CPH) at Southern Methodist University. This book would never have made it out of the doldrums if not for my incredible community in Dallas. To Jeff Engel, Brian Franklin, and Ronna Spitz, getting to be part of CPH was the best experience a new scholar could ask for; thank you for always encouraging me, laughing with me, and helping me do whatever I wanted to do. Thank you for keeping me on as a senior fellow as I brought this book across the finish line and made it exactly what I wanted it to be. Jill Kelly—your mentorship and friendship have meant so much to me, and I loved working on the Global Oral History of Pepfar together. To Nicole Hemmer, Christi van der Westhuizen, and Jill Kelly—again!—I am so grateful for your feedback during my manuscript workshop run by CPH. Your feedback helped me bring my vision of this book to life.

To the incredible team at Columbia University Press, thank you for marshaling me through this work, especially the series editors, Sarah Snyder and Jay Sexton. Stephen Wesley, thank you for loving this project first and getting me through all the hurdles that come with publishing. Any views or errors in this work are mine and mine alone.

To my dear friends: How drab my life would be without all of you. To Katie Bennett, Raymond Blackwell, John Carranza, Natalie Cincotta, Erica Davanian, Andrew Erhardt, Alexandra Evans, Mark Hand, Chamara Fernando, Teo Gonzalez, Carolyn Levy, Jasmine Martin, Theo Milonopolous, Mina Mitreva, Madeleine Olson, Chichi Orji, Sarah Nelson, Jonathan Ng, Lukas Schmelter, Akash Shah, Graeme Thompson, Kim Turner, Emily Whalen, Tiana Wilson, and Cecily Zander—your friendship has brought so much joy and laughter to my life. To Ash Hand—there is no one I would rather share an office with, and this book would not exist without you. Thank you, my dear friend.

Last, thank you to my family. To my grandmother, Diane Kulik, who, as soon as I told her I was publishing a book, wanted to preorder it for her public library, and my grandfather, Leonard Kulik, who would have read it cover to cover the day it came out, thank you for your love. To my brother, Canyon—your relentless march to the beat of your own drum inspires me every day. I feel so lucky to be your sister. To my fiancé, Julian Cowell, thank you for loving me exactly as I am and being my favorite conversation partner. Finally, to my mother, Heather, and father, John. This dream began because you gave me the freedom to be exactly who I wanted to be. Thank you for being my greatest champions. Everything I am and will be is because of you.

GLOSSARY

"Nothing is covered up that will not be revealed, or hidden that will not be known." Luke 12:2

PEOPLE

ABRAMOFF, JACK: Leader of the International Freedom Foundation, an anti-communist, far-right organization financed by the South African government.

BALDWIN, JOAN "JODY": Well-known lobbyist with the United International Consultants, paid over $100,000 a year for her expertise as a former staffer with the Senate Republican Policy Committee and former Nixon administration aide.

BALSIGER, DAVID: Producer of Biblical News Service and *Family Protection Scoreboard.*

BENSON, IVOR: Fanatical white supremacist born in South Africa living in the United Kingdom.

BOOYSEN, HERCULES: Founder of the *Vereniging van Oranjewerkers.*

BOSHOFF, CAREL: Founder of the *Vereniging van Oranjewerkers.*

BOTHA, P. W.: Sixth state president of South Africa and proponent of the Total Onslaught strategy, coordinating military, political, and social policies supporting white rule.

BOTHA, PIK: South African foreign minister from 1977 to apartheid's end.

BROWNFELD, ALLAN: Journalist, writer, and publisher of the *AIM Report*, produced by Accuracy in Media, which reported on the US media's negative coverage of apartheid South Africa.

BUCHANAN, PAT: Director of communications and special assistant to the president for communications in the Reagan White House.

BURTON, DAN: Republican congressman from Indiana.

BUTHELEZI, MANGOSUTHU: Chief minister of the KwaZulu bantustan and Inkatha Freedom Party leader.

CAIN, EDWARD: Head of United Christian Action.

CHETTLE, JOHN: Director of the South Africa Foundation.

CRANE, PHILIP: Republican congressman from Illinois.

CRONJÉ, ROWAN: Chairman of Concerned South Africans Group and advisor to the Ciskei and Bophuthatswana governments.

CROUCH, JAN: Wife of Trinity Broadcasting Network founder Paul Crouch.

CROUCH, PAUL: Founder of Trinity Broadcasting Network.

DE KLERK, F. W.: Seventh state president of South Africa and the last head of state of the apartheid government.

DE WET, SERVAAS: Retired police colonel and head of the AWB's *Wenkommando*, the white paramilitary commando forces.

DENTON, JEREMIAH: Republican senator from Alabama.

FALWELL, JERRY: Right-wing evangelical and host of *Jerry Falwell Live*. Infamous for his 1985 "fact-finding mission" to South Africa, after which he declared Reverend Desmond Tutu a "phony."

GILBERT, MARY ANN: Led Intercessors for the Suffering Church, which brought South African right-wing religious groups like Frontline Fellowship to the United States.

GQOZO, OUPA: Last leader of the Ciskei bantustan.

GROENEWALD, TIENIE: Former SADF military intelligence chief and formed the Afrikaner Volksfront as one of the four founder-generals.

HAIG, ALEXANDER: Secretary of state under Ronald Reagan from 1981 to 1982 and directed constructive engagement policy in southern Africa.

HAMMOND, PETER: Chairman of Frontline Fellowship, a right-wing religious group operating in Mozambique and Zimbabwe. Hammond remains active, posting videos on X of his sermons and appearing on far-right European radio shows and American programs railing against "woke ideology," transgender rights, and "globalist conspiracies" targeting white South Africa; he took over United Christian Action after Cain's retirement and eventual death in 2002.

HELMS, JESSE: Republican senator from North Carolina.

HLAPANE, BARTHOLOMEW: Killed by the ANC after becoming an *askari*.

HOAR, BILL: Vice president of *Conservative Digest* and author of *Architects of Conspiracy: An Intriguing History*, which promotes the far-right conspiracy of one-world government.

HOLOMISA, BANTU: Leader of Transkei bantustan.

KENNEDY, WILLIAM R., JR.: Publisher of *Conservative Digest*. Kennedy acquired *Conservative Digest* from Richard Viguerie, the "conservative mailing-list guru," for $300,000 in 1985, operating a "die-hard conservative" tastemaker until federal investigators charged him with a $40 million fraud scheme in 1992.

KEYES, ALAN: Staunch African American conservative who served in the Reagan administration as assistant secretary of state for international organization affairs.

LEONTSINIS, CINDY: Helmed Victims Against Terrorism, a South African right-wing religious group, and part of United Christian Action.

LEWIS, ARTHUR: South African pastor who fled Zimbabwe after the fall of Rhodesia.

LINDA, THAMSANQA: Former mayor of Ibhayi township near Port Elizabeth, elected as part of the 1982 Black Local Authorities Act.

MAHLATSI, ESAU: Black South African mayor of Sebokeng. Killed by the ANC in 1992 for his participation in the Pretoria-created city council system.

MANGOPE, LUCAS: Leader of the Bophuthatswana bantustan.

MARAIS, JAAP: Leader of the Herstigte Nasionale Party.

MASIYA, MZILIKAZI: Leader of the Balsiger-backed Jesus Christ for Peace.

MCALVANY, DONALD: Editor of the *McAlvany Intelligence Advisor*, a monthly geopolitical and financial newsletter. McAlvany's son-in-law is the far-right filmmaker and former politician Curtis Bowers, who produced the documentary *Agenda: Grinding America*

Down on the "communist, socialist, progressive attempt to take over America."

MCCAULEY, RAY: Leader of Rhema Christian Church in South Africa that partnered with the Jerry Falwell and Jimmy Swaggart ministries.

MOKOENA, ISAAC: Bishop of the Reformed Independent Churches Association (RICA).

NICOLAIDES, PHIL: Conservative media guru and deputy director of Special Presidential Messages from 1986 to 1987.

NÖFFKE, CARL: Former head of the South African Information Services and director of the Institute of American Studies at Rand University.

PARKER, AIDA: Created the *Aida Parker Newsletter* in the aftermath of the Muldergate scandal.

PHILLIPS, HOWARD: Chairman of the Conservative Caucus and grassroots mobilizer against the Comprehensive Anti-Apartheid Act of 1986.

REAGAN, RONALD: Fortieth president of the United States.

RUSHER, WILLIAM: Founder of the US conservative movement and publisher of *National Review*.

RYSKIND, ALLAN: Editor of *Human Events: The National Conservative Weekly*.

SCARBOROUGH, CHARLES: Along with wife Dorothea Scarborough, ran the Gospel Defense League after the collapse of the Christian League of Southern Africa during the Muldergate Scandal.

SCARBOROUGH, DOROTHEA: Along with husband Charles Scarborough, ran the Gospel Defense League after the collapse of their Christian League of Southern Africa during the Muldergate scandal.

SEARS, JOHN: Former campaign manager for Reagan's 1980 presidential bid. Paid lobbyist for the apartheid government throughout the 1980s.

SEBE, LENNOX: Leader of Ciskei bantustan.

SHIPPS, ANNE: Head of Unto the Least of These, which brought South African right-wing religious groups like Frontline Fellowship to the United States.

SILJANDER, MARK: Republican representative from Michigan.

SLIMP, BOB: Reverend of the Calvary Presbyterian Church in Columbia, South Carolina, and columnist for the Council of Conservative Citizen's newspaper *Citizens Informer*.

SWAGGART, JIMMY: US televangelist and host of the weekly *Jimmy Swaggart Telecast.*

SYMMS, STEVE: Republican senator from Indiana.

TERRE'BLANCHE, EUGENE: Infamous leader of the Afrikaner Weerstandsbeweging (AWB).

THURMOND, STROM: Republican senator from South Carolina.

TREURNICHT, ANDRIES: Founder and leader of the Conservative Party, nicknamed "Dr. No." Treurnicht led the official opposition in the National Assembly in 1987 and opposed F. W. de Klerk's negotiations with the ANC.

VERWOERD JR., H. F.: Son of Prime Minister H. F. Verwoerd and founder of the *Vereniging van Oranjewerkers*

VILJOEN, CONSTAND: Chief of the South African Defense Force beginning in 1980. Formed the Afrikaner Volksfront, an umbrella group for far-right organizations in South Africa, along with Major General Tienie Groenewald, Lieutenant General Koos Bischoff, and Lieutenant General Cobus Visser.

WALLOP, MALCOLM: Republican senator from Wyoming.

WEYRICH, PAUL: Founder of the Heritage Foundation and the American Legislative Exchange Council.

ORGANIZATIONS

ACCURACY IN MEDIA (AIM): US conservative organization founded by Reed Irvine that tracked liberal bias in media. AIM remains active, engaging in conspiracies about Vince Foster, President Barack Obama, the COVID-19 pandemic, and climate change, among other issues. In 2023, AIM sponsored a series of trucks at Harvard, Yale, and the University of Colorado Boulder displaying the names, images, and personal information of college students involved in pro-Palestinian activism.

AFRICAN DEMOCRATIC MOVEMENT (ADM): Formed by Gqozo and backed by the SADF as a merger of "moderate" Black leaders. Styled as an ethnic-cultural movement like Buthelezi's Inkatha.

AFRIKANER BROEDERBOND: Secret organization dedicated to the preservation of Afrikaner rights. Strong links to the Dutch Reformed Church and the National Party.

AFRIKANER VOLKSFRONT (AVF): Formed by General Constand Viljoen; Major General Tienie Groenewald, former chief of military intelligence; Lieutenant General Koos Bischoff, former SADF chief of operations; and Lieutenant General Cobus Visser, former head of investigations for South African police. Acted as an umbrella group for far-right organizations in South Africa, formally proposing the creation of a *volkstaat* for white South Africans.

AFRIKANER WEERSTANDSBEWEGING (AWB): Translates as Afrikaner Resistance Movement. Violent Afrikaner, nationalist, neo-Nazi arm of white resistance in South Africa.

BIBLICAL NEWS SERVICE: Produced by David Balsiger and published *Family Protection Scoreboard*. Distributed over 525,000 copies of "South Africa: A Nation on Trial" to American opinion makers.

COALITION AGAINST ANC TERRORISM: Formed during the 1986 veto debates by Howard Phillips and the Conservative Caucus.

CONCERNED SOUTH AFRICANS GROUP (COSAG): Formalized in April 1993 after the IFP withdrew from the Multi-Party Negotiating Forum. Included the IFP, the Ciskei and Bophuthatswana homelands, the CP, and various far-right political and paramilitary organizations. Rejected the National Party–ANC domination of the negotiations and dismissed the ANC's proposed unitary South Africa.

CONSERVATIVE CAUCUS: Chaired by Howard Phillips and organized against sanctions. Research and Education Foundation arm produced monthly publications on conservative issues.

CONSERVATIVE PARTY (CP): Far-right political party that challenged South Africa's ruling National Party. Broke away from the National Party in 1982.

COUNCIL OF CONSERVATIVE CITIZENS (COFCC): Successor to the anti-integration Citizens Councils that predominantly existed in the US South and Midwest. Published the newspaper *Citizens Informer*.

DUTCH REFORMED CHURCH (DRC): Christian denomination representing 37 percent of white South Africans and 65 percent of Afrikaners.

FREEDOM ALLIANCE (FA): Formed in December 1993 out of the Concerned South Africans Group. Included the AVF, the IFP, Ciskei and

Bophuthatswana homelands, and the CP. Rejected a unitary South Africa in favor of self-determination and limited central government.

FREEDOM FRONT (FF): Formed by Viljoen after leaving the AVF. Participated in the 1994 election under a *volkstaat* platform.

FRONTLINE FELLOWSHIP: Right-wing religious group operating in Mozambique and Zimbabwe chaired by Peter Hammond under the United Christian Action umbrella.

GOSPEL DEFENSE LEAGUE: Run by Charles and Dorothea Scarborough and under the United Christian Action umbrella.

HERITAGE FOUNDATION: US right-wing think tank active in the antisanctions movement and the 1986 sanctions debates.

HERSTIGTE NASIONALE PARTY (HNP): One of the oldest far-right parties in South Africa. Limited electoral presence throughout the 1980s due to its total commitment to Verwoerdian apartheid.

INKATHA FREEDOM PARTY (IFP): Zulu ethnic and nationalist organization helmed by Mangosuthu Buthelezi. Predominant political party in KwaZulu and Natal homelands.

INTERCESSORS FOR THE SUFFERING CHURCH: Helmed by Mary Ann Gilbert.

INTERNATIONAL FREEDOM FOUNDATION: Anticommunist, far-right organization founded by Jack Abramoff and financed by the South African government.

INTERNATIONAL SOCIETY FOR HUMAN RIGHTS (ISHR): Nonprofit based in Europe with financial and political connections to the US conservative movement.

JESUS CHRIST FOR PEACE —US right-wing-backed collective of black South Africans supporting P. W. Botha led by Mzilikazi Masiya.

NATIONAL CENTER FOR PUBLIC POLICY RESEARCH: Organized the International Strategy Symposium with the Jefferson Education Foundation. Founded by College Republican National Committee Organizer Amy Moritz in 1982. The group now sits on the advisory board of Project 2025, the far-right proposal for the second Donald J. Trump presidency by the conservative think tank Heritage Foundation, and organizes Project 21, a network of Black conservatives.

NATIONAL PARTY: Ruling party of South Africa beginning with apartheid's formation in 1948.

NATIONAL SOCIALIST VANGUARD: US neo-Nazi organization that supported an alliance between Buthelezi's Zulus and white Afrikaner nationalists.

NATIONAL STUDENT FEDERATION: Pro–National Party student group active in South African universities in the 1980s.

REFORMED INDEPENDENT CHURCHES ASSOCIATION: Led by Bishop Isaac Mokoena. Alleged over 4.5 million members and part of the United Christian Action umbrella network.

RHEMA CHRISTIAN CHURCH: Led by Ray McCauley.

SOUTH AFRICA FOUNDATION: Directed by John Chettle in the 1980s. Represented South African business interests in the United States and worked closely with South Africa to develop an anti-sanctions strategy.

SOUTH AFRICAN DEFENSE FORCE (SADF): South African armed forces from 1957 to 1994.

TRINITY BROADCASTING NETWORK: A global religious television network founded by Paul Crouch.

UNITED CHRISTIAN ACTION (UCA): Helmed by Ed Cain and one of the most influential right-wing religious groups in South Africa. Coordinated fourteen organizations, including the *Aida Parker Newsletter*, Frontline Fellowship, and Gospel Defense League.

UNTO THE LEAST OF THESE: Helmed by Anne Shipps, and brought South African right-wing religious groups like Frontline Fellowship to the United States.

VERENIGING VAN ORANJEWERKERS: Translates as Organization of Orange Workers. Formed in 1980 and acted as an early supporter of the *volkstaat* plan, later founding Orania.

VICTIMS AGAINST TERRORISM: South African right-wing religious group and part of United Christian Action. Helmed by Cindy Leontsinis.

PUBLICATIONS

AIDA PARKER NEWSLETTER: Created by former journalist Aida Parker in the aftermath of the Muldergate scandal, under United Christian Action.

DIE BEELD: Afrikaans-language daily newspaper launched in 1974 and based in Johannesburg.

DIE BURGER: Afrikaans-language daily newspaper launched in 1914 and based in Cape Town. Actively supported the National Party, often serving as a mouthpiece for the party.

THE CITIZEN: South African newspaper founded in 1976. Revealed that funding came from the South African government during the Muldergate scandal.

CITIZENS INFORMER: Newspaper for the Council of Conservative Citizens.

CONSERVATIVE DIGEST: Right-wing magazine published by William R. Kennedy and Bill Hoar.

CONSERVATIVE REVIEW: Semi-regular magazine published by the Council for Social and Economic Studies, created by Roger Pearson, the eugenicist and extreme right-winger.

FAMILY PROTECTION SCOREBOARD —The fall 1987 edition, "South Africa: Nation on Trial, Is It a Black-White Conflict?," circulated over 525,000 copies.

HUMAN EVENTS: *The National Conservative Weekly:* Conservative weekly newspaper edited by Allan Ryskind.

IVOR BENSON'S BEHIND THE NEWS: Monthly newsletter produced by Ivor Benson, a fanatical white supremacist born in South Africa and living in the United Kingdom.

MCALVANY INTELLIGENCE ADVISOR: Monthly geopolitical and financial newsletter produced by Donald McAlvany.

NATIONAL REVIEW: Semi-monthly conservative magazine founded by William Rusher.

RAPPORT: Afrikaans-language daily newspaper launched in 1970 and based in Johannesburg.

ROCA REPORT: Created by Ed Cain in 1992 to keep Western readers up to date on negotiations in South Africa.

SIGNPOSTS: *A Digest of Researched Information for Concerned Christians:* Publication produced by United Christian Action and Ed Cain.

SOUTH AFRICA DIGEST: Weekly news aggregate produced by South Africa's Department of Information.

SWEEPSLAG: Translates as Crack of the Whip. AWB promotional magazine.

DIE TRANSVALER: Afrikaans-language newspaper established in 1947 that explicitly supported the Transvaal branch of the National Party.

WASHINGTON TIMES: US conservative daily newspaper founded by Sun Myung Moon's News World Communications. Part of an orchestrated plot by the South African government to buy the paper to act as a propaganda mouthpiece for the apartheid state. Continues to traffic in birtherism, COVID-19, and climate change conspiracy theories.

DIE VADERLAND: Afrikaans-language daily newspaper launched in 1936 and based in Johannesburg until 1988.

ARCHIVES

Alan Paton Centre and Struggle Archives, University of KwaZulu-Natal (APC)
Archive of Contemporary Affairs at the University of Free State (ARCA)
Bancroft Library Manuscripts Collection at the University of California at Berkeley (BLMC)
GALE: Political Extremism and Radicalism: Far-Right Groups in America
George H. W. Bush Presidential Library
Jerry Falwell Library at Liberty University (JFL)
Hall-Hoag Collection at Brown University (HHC)
Kenneth Spencer Research Library at the University of Kansas (UKL)
Michigan State University Special Collections
Ronald Reagan Presidential Library (RRPL)
South African Historical Archive
Trinity Broadcasting Network Thirtieth Anniversary Collection
Truth and Reconciliation Commission (TRC)
United States Congressional Record
United States Library of Congress (LOC)
United States National Archives and Record Administration (NARA)
University of Johannesburg Archival Collections (UJAC)
University of Witwatersrand Historical Papers (UWHP)
Wheaton College Special Collections (WCSC)
Yale University Library

NOTES

INTRODUCTION

1. Letter from Donald E. deKieffer to L. E. S. deVilliers, Re: American Legion, March 24, 1977, C4/2 CSR&E, South Africa/ deKieffer's Correspondence; Correspondence/ [South Africa, 1977]; Donald E. deKieffer's Correspondence with the Department of Information (DOI), Officials (Rhoodie, deVilliers, Retief, etc. during 1977); through 1977, University of Johannesburg Archival Collections (UJAC), Johannesburg, South Africa.
2. Memorandum from Donald E. deKieffer to L. E. S. de Villiers, RE: American Legion Project, May 26, 1977, C4/15—S.A. Correspondence 5-18-77 to 8-31-77, UJL. Memorandum to L. E. S. de Villiers from Donald E. deKieffer RE: American Legion, August 24, 1977, C4/15—S.A. Correspondence 5-18-77 to 8-31-77, UJAC.
3. From Donald E. deKieffer to Gerbie Grobler, RE: Slie Presentation and the American Legion, December 29, 1977, C4/15—S.A. Correspondence January 1, 1978–March 31, 1978, UJAC.
4. From Donald E. deKieffer to Gerbie Grobler, RE: American Legion Slide Show/Logistics, January 3, 1978, C4/15—S.A. Correspondence January 1, 1978–March 31, 1978 UJAC.
5. Report from Joe L. Matthews, October 31, 1978, C4/16—South Africa Correspondence 9/5/78-12/14/78, UJL. Dr. Robert Foster, "South Africa Speech and Slide Presentation," 1978, C4/16, UJAC.
6. Letter from Alvis Carver to Donald E. deKieffer, November 3, 1978, C4/16, UJAC.
7. From Donald E. deKieffer to L. E. S. deVilliers, RE: U.S. Effort, November 8, 1977, C4/2 CSR&E, South Africa/ deKieffer's Correspondence; Correspondence/ [South Africa, 1977]; Donald E. deKieffer's Correspondence with the Department of Information (DOI), Officials (Rhoodie, deVilliers, Retief, etc. during 1977); through 1977, UJL.
8. Ron Nixon, *Selling Apartheid: South Africa's Global Propaganda War* (Pluto, 2016), 59.

9. Mervyn Rees and Chris Day, *Muldergate: The Story of the Info Scandal* (Macmillan South Africa, 1980), 45–58.
10. "The Principle Goal of This Office in Three words, viz. Lobbying the U.S.A. Congress," C4/17—So. Africa—Corres.—July to——, 1974, UJAC.
11. "Friends Returning" and "Friends Not Returning," C4/2 CSR&E, South Africa/ deKieffer's Correspondence; Correspondence/ [South Africa, 1976]; Donald E. deKieffer's Correspondence with the Department of Information (DOI), Officials (Rhoodie, deVilliers, Retief, etc. during 1976); through 1976, UJAC; Patrick Andelic, *Donkey Work: Congressional Democrats in Conservative America, 1974–1994* (University Press of Kansas, 2019), xxiv; Eric M. Uslaner et al., "Interpreting the 1974 Congressional Election," *American Political Science Review* 80, no. 2 (June 1986): 591–96.
12. Letter from Donald E. deKieffer to John P. McGoff, December 12, 1974, Grand C4/7—Jury Exhibits/DEK 40 through 50 (h), Vol. IIGJ #2/80-11/Ex #309(e), 309(g), 309(k), 309(e), Reintroduced GJ #3 (83–2)/DEK #40, 41, 42, and DEK #43, UJAC. Letter from John P. McGoff to Ned S. Arbury, March 7, 1975, C4/4—deKieffer Correspondence/John Peter McGoff, Documents obtained from Collier, Shannon/ dek Assoc., UJAC; letter from Donald E. deKieffer to L. E. S. de Villiers, June 15, 1976, C4/2 CSR&E, South Africa/ deKieffer's Correspondence; Correspondence/ [South Africa, 1976]; Donald E. deKieffer's Correspondence with the Department of Information (DOI), Officials (Rhoodie, deVilliers, Retief, etc. during 1976); through 1976, UJAC.
13. "The Principle Goal of This Office in Three Words." Young Americans for Freedom was *the* US conservative youth organization for over thirty years. Founded in 1960, it gave conservative youth organizing a "permanent framework," a "training ground in political action, public relations, and education methods," and "the development of a leadership cadre that . . . helped produce the election of Ronald Reagan as President in 1980." Wayne Thorburn, *A Generation Awakes: Young Americans for Freedom and the Creation of the Conservative Movement* (Jameson, 2010), 31; Letter from Carl E. O'Brien to John Vorster, August 5, 1976, C4/20—South Africa—Correspondence 9-1-76, UJAC.
14. Letter from Carl E. O'Brien to John Vorster, August 5, 1976, C4/20—South Africa—Correspondence 9-1-76, UJAC.
15. Letter from Donald E. deKieffer to Sydney S. Baron, January 12, 1977, C4/2 CSR&E, South Africa/ deKieffer's Correspondence; Correspondence/ [South Africa, 1977]; Donald E. deKieffer's Correspondence with the Department of Information (DOI), Officials (Rhoodie, deVilliers, Retief, etc. during 1977); through 1977, UJL; memorandum from Donald E. deKieffer to Marsja Retief, RE: Paul Scott, January 4, 1978, C4/3, UJAC; letter from John P. McGoff to Donald E. deKieffer, April 18, 1977, C4/8—Grand Jury Exhibit/ 80-11/ Exhibit Nos. 332, 332 (a) through 332 (j), [Introduced 2/3/81], #dek #67-75, #75(a) and 75 (b) and #76, 76(a), 7/5/84 M., UJAC.
16. Letter to John McGoff from Jeffrey St. John, March 30, 1977, C4/8, UJL.
17. Donald E. deKieffer to L. E. S. deVilliers and Sydney Baron, Re: "Pro-South African Groups," August 26, 1977, C4/2 CSR&E, South Africa/ deKieffer's Correspondence; Correspondence/ [South Africa, 1977]; Donald E. deKieffer's Correspondence with the

Department of Information (DOI), Officials (Rhoodie, deVilliers, Retief, etc. during 1977); through 1977, UJAC.

18. Rees and Day, *Muldergate*, xv.
19. Nixon, *Selling Apartheid*, 100.
20. Mayeni Jones and Nobuhle Simelane, "Race Policies or Israel—What's Really Driving Trump's Fury with South Africa?," BBC, February 23, 2025.
21. Saul Dubow, *Apartheid, 1948–1994* (Oxford University Press, 2014), 2, 5.
22. Roger Southall, *Whites and Democracy in South Africa* (James Currey, 2022), 33.
23. William Beinart, *Twentieth-Century South Africa* (Oxford University Press, 2001), 145, 148.
24. This number would balloon to over 1,300 by 1987. Uma Shashikant Mesthrie, "Tinkering and Tampering: A Decade of the Group Areas Act (1950–1960)," *South African Historical Journal* 28 (1993): 178.
25. Beinart, *Twentieth-Century South Africa*, 153.
26. Alex Lichtenstein, "Making Apartheid Work: African Trade Unions and the 1953 Native Labour (Settlement of Disputes) Act in South Africa," *Journal of African History* 46 (2005): 313; Beinart, *Twentieth-Century South Africa*, 159.
27. Technically, Minister of Colonies O. H. Morris of Great Britain first used the phrase. Crawford Young, *The Postcolonial State in Africa: Fifty Years of Independence, 1960–2010* (University of Wisconsin Press, 2012), 3; Katherine Everett, Emily Hardick, and Damarius Johnson, "The Year of Africa," *Origins: Current Events in Historical Perspective* (December 2020), https://origins.osu.edu/article/year-of-africa-1960-rumba-pan-africanism-Kariba; James H. Meriwether, *Tears, Fire, and Blood: The United States and the Decolonization of Africa* (University of North Carolina Press, 2021), 3; Piero Gleijeses, "Africa in the Cold War," *African Studies* (October 2021); Frank Gerits, *The Ideological Scramble for Africa: How the Pursuit of Anticolonial Modernity Shaped a Postcolonial Order, 1945–1966* (Cornell University Press, 2023); Ryan Irwin, *Gordian Knot: Apartheid and the Unmaking of the Liberal World Order* (Oxford University Press, 2012); Corrie Decker and Elisabeth McMahon, "From Modernization to Structural Adjustment," in *The Idea of Development in Africa* (Cambridge University Press, 2020); Jeffrey Byrne, "Africa's Cold War," in *The Cold War in the Third World*, ed. Robert J. McMahon (Oxford University Press, 2013), 101–23; Andrew DeRoche, *Kenneth Kaunda, the United States and Southern Africa* (Bloomsbury, 2016); Piero Gleijeses, *Conflicting Missions: Havana, Washington, and Africa, 1959–1976* (University of North Carolina Press, 2003); and Odd Arne Westad, *The Global Cold War: Third World Interventions and the Making of Our Time* (Cambridge University Press, 2003).
28. Beinart, *Twentieth-Century South Africa*, 146; T. Dunbar Moodie, *The Rise of Afrikanerdom: Power, Apartheid, and the Afrikaner Civil Religion* (University of California Press, 1975), 257; Christoph Marx, "Verwoerdian Apartheid and African Political Elites in South Africa, 1950–68," in *A History of South Africa*, ed. Leonard Thompson (Yale University Press, 2001), 189. Throughout *Saving Apartheid*, "black" will be both capitalized and lowercase depending on the context. When referencing South Africa and discussions

within South Africa, I lowercase "black" to reflect the Black Consciousness denotation that referred to all people of color "subject to the oppression of apartheid." Natasha Erlank, *Convening Black Intimacy: Christianity, Gender, and Tradition in Early Twentieth-Century South Africa* (Ohio University Press, 2022), ix; and Jill Kelly, *To Swim with Crocodiles: Land Violence and Belonging in South Africa, 1980–1996* (Michigan State University Press, 2018), xxi. In contrast, when referring to the United States and wider transnational Blackness, I capitalize "Black." See Mke Laws, "Why We Capitalize 'Black' (and Not 'White')," *Columbia Journalism Review*, June 16, 2020, https://www.cjr.org/analysis/capital-b-black-styleguide.php.

29. "Sharpeville Massacre, 21 March 1960," South African History Online, https://www.sahistory.org.za/article/sharpeville-massacre-21-march-1960.
30. Beinart, *Twentieth-Century South Africa*, 167.
31. Jamie Miller, *An African Volk: The Apartheid Regime and Its Search for Survival* (Oxford University Press, 2016), 2–22; Daniel Conway and Pauline Leonard, *Migration, Space and Transnational Identities: The British in South Africa* (Palgrave Macmillan, 2014), 39. For more, see James Barber and John Barratt, *South Africa's Foreign Policy: The Search for Status and Security, 1945–1988* (Cambridge University Press, 1990); Tom Lodge, *Sharpeville: An Apartheid Massacre and Its Consequences* (Oxford University Press, 2011), 182; and Laura Evans, "Contextualizing Apartheid at the End of Empire: Repression, 'Development' and the Bantustans," *Journal of Imperial and Commonwealth History* 47, no. 2 (2019): 383.
32. Ashley Parcells, "'The Empire That Shaka Zulu Was Unable to Bring About': Ethnicizing Sovereignty in Apartheid South Africa, 1959–1970," *Journal of Social History* 56, no. 1 (2022): 195–225.
33. Evans, "Contextualizing Apartheid at the End of Empire," 393–94.
34. Lodge, *Sharpeville*, 167, 172.
35. "Military Service Becomes Compulsory for White South African Men, 9 June 1967," South African History Online, https://sahistory.org.za/dated-event/military-service-becomes-compulsory-white-south-african-men.
36. Stewart Lloyd-Jones and António Costa Pinto, eds., *The Last Empire: Thirty Years of Portuguese Decolonization* (Intellect, 2003); Raquel Varela, *A People's History of the Portuguese Revolution* (Pluto, 2019); and Gleijeses, *Conflicting Missions*, 230–45.
37. Odd Arne Westad, "Moscow and the Angolan Crisis, 1974–1976: A New Pattern of Intervention," *Cold War International History Project Bulletin*, nos. 8–9 (Winter 1996–1997): 21–37.
38. André Wessels, "Half a Century of South African 'Border War' Literature: A Historiographical Exploration," *Journal for Contemporary History* 42, no. 2 (December 2017): 24.
39. Richard Dale, *The Namibian War of Independence, 1966–1989: Diplomatic, Economic and Military Campaigns* (McFarland, 2014); Vilho Shigweda, *Enduring Suffering: The Cassinga Massacre of Namibian Exiles in 1978 and the Conflicts Between Survivors' Memories and Testimonies* (University of Western Cape, 2011); and Sisingi Kamongo and Leon Bezuidenhout, *Shadows in the Sand: A Koevoet Tracker's Story of an Insurgency War* (30° South, 2011).

40. William Finnegan, *A Complicated War: The Harrowing of Mozambique* (University of California Press, 1992); Éric Morier-Genoud, Michel Cahen, and Domingos M. do Rosário, *The War Within: New Perspectives on the Civil War in Mozambique, 1976–1992* (James Currey, 2018); Stephen A. Emerson, "The Battle for Mozambique: The South African Factor," *Journal of the Middle East and Africa* 5, no. 1 (2014): 61–82.
41. Eddie Michel, *The White House and White Africa: Presidential Policy Toward Rhodesia During the UDI Era 1965–1979* (Routledge, 2020), 1; Luise White, *Unpopular Sovereignty: Rhodesian Independence and African Decolonization* (University of Chicago Press, 2015).
42. Rob Skinner, *The Foundations of Anti-Apartheid: Liberal Humanitarians and Transnational Activists in Britain and the United States* (Palgrave Macmillan UK, 2010), 2; Seane Mabitsela, "Impact of United Nations' Anti-Apartheid Regimes on South African Race Relations, 1952–1974," *Journal of Nation-Building and Policy Studies* 8, no. 1 (April 2024): 94.
43. Mabitsela, "Impact of United Nations' Anti-Apartheid Regimes," 95, 99.
44. Mabitsela, "Impact of United Nations' Anti-Apartheid Regimes," 100–101; Rodrigo Fracalossi de Moraes, "Transnational Activism and Domestic Politics: Arms Exports and the Anti-Apartheid Struggle in the UK–South Africa Relations (1959–1994)," *Foreign Policy Analysis* 17, no. 4 (2021): 1–21.
45. Irwin, *Gordian Knot.*
46. Kenneth S. Broun, *Saving Nelson Mandela: The Rivonia Trial and the Fate of South Africa* (Oxford University Press, 2012).
47. Stephen Ellis, *External Mission: The ANC in Exile, 1960–1990* (Oxford University Press, 2013); Emma Elinor Lundin, "'Now Is the Time!' The Importance of International Spaces for Women's Activism Within the ANC, 1960–1976," *Journal of Southern African Studies* 45, no. 2 (2019): 323–40; Colin Bundy, "South Africa's African National Congress in Exile," *Oxford Research Encyclopedia of African History*, April 26, 2018.
48. Rob Skinner, "Humanitarianism and Human Rights in Global Anti-Apartheid," in *A Global History of Anti-Apartheid: "Forward to Freedom" in South Africa*, ed. Anna Konieczna and Rob Skinner (Palgrave Macmillan, 2019), 35.
49. De Moraes, "Transnational Activism and Domestic Politics," 1.
50. Daniel Magaziner, *The Law and the Prophets: Black Consciousness in South Africa, 1968–1977* (Ohio University Press, 2010), 20; Ofole Mgbako, "'My Blackness Is the Beauty of this Land': Racial Redefinition, African American Culture, and the Creation of the Black World in South Africa's Black Consciousness Movement," *Safundi: The Journal of South African and American Studies* 10, no. 3 (2009): 304–5.
51. Tendayi Sithole, *Steve Biko: Decolonial Meditations of Black Consciousness* (Lexington, 2016), 3, 12.
52. Francis Njubi Nesbitt, *Race for Sanctions: African Americans Against Apartheid, 1946–1994* (Indiana University Press, 2004); Brenda Gayle Plummer, *In Search of Power: African Americans in the Era of Decolonization* (Cambridge University Press, 2012); Keisha N. Blain, *Set the World on Fire: Black Nationalist Women and the Global Struggle for Freedom* (University of Pennsylvania Press, 2018); and Tiana U. Wilson, "The Making of *Triple Jeopardy*," *WSQ: Women's Studies Quarterly* 51 nos. 1–2 (Spring/Summer 2023): 201–7.

53. Tiana U. Wilson, "The Third World Women's Alliance and Anti-Apartheid Organizing," *Black Perspectives*, May 3, 2024, https://www.aaihs.org/the-third-world-womens-alliance-and-anti-apartheid-organizing/; Peter Limb, Richard Knight, and Christine Root, "The Global Antiapartheid Movement: A Critical Analysis of Archives and Collections," *Radical History Review* 119 (2014): 161–77; and William Minter, Gail Hovey, and Charles Cobb Jr., *No Easy Victories: African Liberation and American Activists Over a Half Century, 1950–2000* (Africa World Press, 2008).
54. "The June 19 Soweto Youth Uprising," *South African History Online*, https://www.sahistory.org.za/article/june-16-soweto-youth-uprising; and Julian Brown, *The Road to Soweto: Resistance and the Uprising of 16 June 1976* (Boydell & Brewer, 2016).
55. Noor Nieftagodien, "Black High School Students and the Overthrow of Apartheid," *Black Perspectives*, https://www.aaihs.org/black-high-school-students-and-the-overthrow-of-apartheid/.
56. "Special Issue: Anti-Apartheid Movements on Campus," *Safundi* 23, nos. 1–2 (2002); Amanda Joyce Hall, "Students Are the Spark: Anti-apartheid in the Long 1980s," *Journal of African-American History* 108, no. 3 (Summer 2023): 369–97; and *The Road to Democracy in South Africa*, vol. 3: *International Solidarity* (South African Democracy Education Trust, 2008).
57. Jessica Ann Levy, "Black Power, Inc.: Global American Business and the Post-Apartheid City," *Enterprise and Society* 21, no. 4 (2020): 866–74; Mattie C. Webb, "'An Exercise in the Art of the Possible': Waging a Battle Against Apartheid in the South African Workplace," *Enterprise and Society* 25, no. 2 (2024): 329–57; and Saul Dubow, "New Approaches to High Apartheid and Anti-Apartheid," *South African Historical Journal* 67, no. 2 (2017): 304–29.
58. Thomas Borstelmann, *Apartheid's Reluctant Uncle: The United States and Southern Africa in the Early Cold War* (Oxford University Press, 1993) and *The Cold War and the Color Line: American Race Relations in the Global Arena* (Harvard University Press, 2003).
59. Gleijeses, *Conflicting Missions*.
60. Nancy Mitchell, *Jimmy Carter in Africa: Race and the Cold War* (Stanford University Press, 2016); and Andy DeRoche, *Kenneth Kaunda, the United States and Southern Africa* (Bloomsbury, 2016).
61. Piero Gleijeses, *Visions of Freedom: Havana, Washington, Pretoria, and the Struggle for Southern Africa, 1976-1991* (University of North Carolina Press, 2013); Alex Thomson, *U.S. Foreign Policy Towards Apartheid South Africa, 1948–1994* (Palgrave Macmillan, 2008); Simon Stevens, "'From the Viewpoint of a Southern Governor': The Carter Administration and Apartheid, 1977–81," *Diplomatic History* 36, no. 5 (November 2012): 843–80; Raymond Paretzky, "The United States Arms Embargo Against South Africa: An Analysis of the Laws, Regulations, and Loopholes," *Yale Journal of International Law* 12, no. 133 (1987): 133–57.
62. Southall, *Whites and Democracy in South Africa*, 33.
63. Barber, *South Africa in the Twentieth Century*, 173.
64. Southall, *Whites and Democracy in South Africa*, 35.
65. Christi van der Westhuizen, *White Power and the Rise and Fall of the National Party* (Zebra, 2007), 112–17.

66. Douglas Booth, "Hitting Apartheid for Six? The Politics of the South African Sports Boycott," *Journal of Contemporary History* 78, no. 3 (July 2003): 477–93; and Mychal Matsemela Odom and Daniel Bankole Widener, "From South Africa to South Central L.A.: Transnational Black Protest, Celebrity, and the Cultural Boycott," *Critical Arts* 34, no. 1 (2020): 99–115.
67. Alan Posner, "Imagining Total Onslaught: South African Military Threat Scenarios and Doctrinal Change, 1953–1975," *Journal of Strategic Studies* 46, no. 2 (2023): 378–403.
68. F. A. Mouton, "'Dr No': A.P. Treurnicht and the Ultra-Conservative Quest to Maintain Afrikaner Supremacy, 1982–1993," *South African Historical Journal* 65, no. 4 (2013): 577–95; Daniel Conway, *Masculinities, Militarization, and the End Conscription Campaign* (Manchester University Press, 2012), 40.
69. Mouton, "'Dr No'; Conway, *Masculinities, Militarization, and the End Conscription Campaign*; Barber, *South Africa in the Twentieth Century*, 247.
70. Barber, *South Africa in the Twentieth Century*, 40.
71. Van der Westhuizen, *White Power*, 121–23.
72. Van der Westhuizen, *White Power* 133–34; and Annette Seegers, "South Africa's National Management System, 1972–90," *Journal of Modern African Studies* 29, no. 2 (June 1991): 10.
73. Bernard Magubane, "The Crisis of the Garrison State," in *The Road to Democracy in South Africa*, vol. 4: *Part II [1980–1990]* (Unisa, 2010), 10.
74. Van der Westhuizen, *White Power*, 131.
75. Sifiso Mxolisi Ndlovu and Jabulani Sithole, "Trade Union Unity Summits and the Formation of COSATU, 1980–1990," in *The Road to Democracy in South Africa*, vol. 4: *Part II [1980–1990]*, 916, 930
76. Eddy Maloka, "The South African Communist Party in the 1980s," and Mbulelo Vizikhungo Mzamane and Bavusile Maaba, "The Azanian People's Organization, 1977–1990," in *The Road to Democracy in South Africa*, vol. 4: *Part II*, 1179–82, 1299–303.
77. Chris Saunders, "Liberal Democratic Anti-Apartheid Activity Within South Africa," in *The Road to Democracy in South Africa*, vol. 4: *Part II [1980–1990]*, 1605–19.
78. Monica Ferro Gameiro Fernandes, "Beyond Borders: A Transnational History of the Black Sash and Fedsaw, c1952–62" (PhD diss., Brunel University, 2019).
79. Ronald Kasrils, *The Unlikely Secret Agent* (Monthly Review, 2012); and David Everatt, *The Origins of Non-Racialism: White Opposition to Apartheid in the 1950s* (Wits University Press, 2018)
80. F. A. Mouton, "'One of the Architects of Our Democracy': Colin Eglin, the Progressive Federal Party and the Leadership of the Official Parliamentary Opposition, 1977–1979 and 1986–1987," *Journal for Contemporary History* 40, no. 1 (June 2015): 1–22.
81. Magubane, "The Crisis of the Garrison State," 38.
82. Evans, "Contextualizing Apartheid at the End of Empire," 391–93.
83. Daniel Douek, "'They Became Afraid When They Saw Us': MK Insurgency and Counterinsurgency in the Bantustan of Transkei, 1988–1994," *Journal of Southern African Studies* 39, no. 1 (2013): 207; and Allister Sparks, *Tomorrow Is Another Country* (Penguin, 1994).

84. Shula Marks, *The Ambiguities of Dependence in South Africa: Class, Nationalism, and the State in Twentieth-Century Natal* (Johns Hopkins University Press, 1986), 6; Daniel Branch, *Defeating Mau Mau, Creating Kenya: Counterinsurgency, Civil War, and Decolonization* (Cambridge University Press, 2009); and Jacob Dlamini, *Askari: A Story of Collaboration and Betrayal in the Anti-Apartheid Struggle* (Oxford University Press, 2015).
85. Dlamini, *Askari*, 10–12.
86. Parcells, " 'The Empire That Shaka Zulu Was Unable to Bring About,' 198.
87. Parcells, " 'The Empire That Shaka Zulu Was Unable to Bring About"; Kelly, *To Swim with Crocodiles*; Douek, " 'They Became Afraid When They Saw Us' "; Sasha Polakow-Suransky, *The Unspoken Alliance: Israel's Secret Relationship with Apartheid South Africa* (Knopf Doubleday, 2011); Andrew Manson and Bernard Mbenga, "Bophuthatswana in the 1980s and the UDF in the Western Transvaal," in *The Road to Democracy in South Africa*, vol. 4: *Part II [1980–1990]*, 669–704; and Christian M. Rogerson, "Tourism Evolution in Rural South Africa: From Native Reserve to Apartheid Bantustans c 1920–1994," *Geo Journal of Tourism and Geosites* 40, no. 1 (2022): 120–28.
88. Laura Phillips, "History of South Africa's Bantustans," in *Oxford Research Encyclopedia of African History* (Oxford University Press, 2017); Saul Dubow, *Racial Segregation and the Origins of Apartheid in Twentieth Century South Africa, 1919–1936* (Macmillan, 1989); Gerard Mare, "Class Conflict and Ideology Among the Petty Bourgeoisie in the 'Homelands': Inkatha—A Study" (African Studies Institute Seminar, University of the Witwatersrand, Johannesburg, 1978); and Robert Morrell, ed., *Political Economy and Identities in KwaZulu-Natal: Historical and Social Perspectives* (Indicator, 1996).
89. Roger Southall, *South Africa's Transkei: The Political Economy of an Independent Bantustan* (Heinemann, 1982); Linda Chisholm, "Late-Apartheid Education Reforms and Bantustan Entanglements," *African Historical Review* 50, nos. 1–2 (2018): 27–45; Timothy Gibbs, "Apartheid South Africa's Segregated Legal Field: Black Lawyers and the Bantustans," *Africa* 90, no. 2 (2020): 293; Anne Heffernan, "The University of the North and Building the Bantustans, 1959–1977," *South African Historical Journal* 69, no. 2 (2017): 195–214; and Sekibakiba Peter Lekgoathi, " 'You Are Listening to Radio Lebowa of the South African Broadcasting Corporation': Vernacular Radio, Bantustan Identity and Listenership, 1960–1994," *Journal of Southern African Studies* 35, no. 3 (2009): 575–94.
90. Kelly, *To Swim with Crocodiles*; Siphiwe Ignatius Dube, "The New Religious Political Right," *Religion and Theology* 28 (2021): 153–78; Mzala (Jabulani Nxumalo), *Gatsha Buthelezi: Chief with a Double Agenda* (Zed, 1988); Gerhard Maré and Georgina Hamilton, *An Appetite for Power: Buthelezi's Inkatha and South Africa* (Raven, 1987); Shireen Hassim, "Reinforcing Conservatism: An Analysis of the Politics of the Inkatha Women's Brigade," *Agenda* 2, no. 2 (1988): 3–16.
91. Allan Anderson, "New African Initiated Pentecostalism and Charismatics in South Africa," *Journal of Religion in Africa* 35, no. 1 (2005): 66–92; Joel Cabrita and Natasha Erlank, "New Histories of Christianity in South Africa: Review and Introduction," *South African Historical Journal* 70, no. 2 (2018): 307–23. This growth of Pentecostalism is part of a larger surge in southern and eastern Africa.

92. Kathleen Belew, *Bring the War Home: The White Power Movement and Paramilitary America* (Harvard University Press, 2019).
93. Kyle Burke, *Revolutionaries for the Right: Anticommunist Internationalism and Paramilitary Warfare in the Cold War* (University of North Carolina Press, 2018), 8, 55.
94. Terence Ball and Richard Dagger, "Inside *The Turner Diaries*: Neo-Nazi Scripture," *PS, Political Science and Politics* 30, no. 4 (1997): 717–18; Renee Brodie, "The Aryan New Era: Apocalyptic Realizations in *The Turner Diaries*," *Journal of American Culture* 21, no. 3 (1998): 13–22; Belew, *Bring the War Home*; Maria Paula Meneses, Celso Braga Rosa, and Bruno Sena Martins, "Colonial Wars, Colonial Alliances: The Alcora Exercise in the Context of Southern Africa," *Journal of Southern African Studies* 43, no. 2 (2017): 397–410; Burke, *Revolutionaries for the Right*; Niels Boender, "From Federation to 'White Redoubt': Africa and the Global Radical-Right in the Geographical Imagination of UDI-Era Rhodesian Propaganda, 1962–1970," *Journal of Imperial and Commonwealth History* 51, no. 6 (2023): 1200–28; and Martin Durham and Margaret Power, eds., *New Perspectives on the Transnational Right* (Palgrave Macmillan, 2016).
95. Jefferson Cowie, *Stayin' Alive: The 1970s and the Last Days of the Working Class* (New York, 2010), 15.
96. Kevin Kruse, *White Flight: Atlanta and the Making of Modern Conservatism* (Princeton University Press, 2005); Joseph Crespino, *In Search of Another Country: Mississippi and the Conservative Counterrevolution* (Princeton University Press, 2007); and Matthew D. Lassiter, *The Silent Majority: Suburban Politics in the Sunbelt South* (Princeton University Press, 2006).
97. Darren Dochuk, *From Bible Belt to Sunbelt: Plain-Folk Religion, Grassroots Politics, and Evangelical Conservatism* (Norton, 2011), xxiii.
98. Richard Johnson, "The 1982 Voting Rights Act Extension as a 'Critical Juncture': Ronald Reagan, Bob Dole, and Republican Party-Building," *Studies in American Political Development* 35, no. 2 (2021): 223–38; Gyung-Ho Jeong et al., "Cracks in the Opposition: Immigration as a Wedge Issue for the Reagan Coalition," *American Journal of Political Science*, 55 (2011): 511–25; Jane Mayer and Doyle McManus, *Landslide: The Unmaking of the President, 1984-1988* (Houghton Mifflin, 1989); Kevin M. Kruse and Julian E. Zelizer, *Fault Lines: A History of the United States Since 1974* (Norton, 2019); and Gillian Peele, "American Conservatism in Historical Perspective," in *Crisis of Conservatism? The Republican Party, the Conservative Movement, and American Politics After Bush*, ed. Joel D. Aberbach and Gillian Peele (Oxford University Press, 2010).
99. William Finnegan, "Coming Apart Over Apartheid: The Story Behind the Republicans' Split on South Africa," *Mother Jones* (April–May 1986): 42.
100. Chester A. Crocker, "South Africa: A Strategy for Change," *Foreign Affairs* 59, no. 2 (1980): 324.
101. Gleijeses, *Visions of Freedom*, 178. For transcripts of Reagan's separate development defense, see Ronald Reagan, July 6, 1977 broadcast, Pre-Presidential Papers, series 1A, Box 11, RRPL and Ronald Reagan, March 3, 1981, interview with Walter Cronkite of *CBS News, Public Papers of the Presidents of the United States*, General Services Administration of the United States, 1981, 97.

102. Alex Thomson, "Incomplete Engagement: Reagan's South Africa Policy Revisited," *Journal of Modern African Studies* 33, no. 1 (1995): 86.
103. Chester A. Crocker, Mario Greznes, and Robert Henderson, "Southern Africa: A U.S. Policy for the '80s," *Africa Report* 26, no. 1 (January/February 1981): 7–14; Gleijeses, *Visions of Freedom*, 181.
104. Chester Crocker, *High Noon in Southern Africa: Making Peace in a Rough Neighborhood* (Norton, 1993), 67; Zachary Kagan-Guthrie, "Chester Crocker and the South African Border War, 1981–1989: A Reappraisal of Linkage," *Journal of Southern African Studies* 35, no. 1 (2009): 69.
105. Evan D. McCormick, "Beyond Revolution and Repression: U.S. Foreign Policy and Latin American Democracy, 1980–1989" (University of Virginia, 2015), 39.
106. Beth A. Fischer, *The Reagan Reversal: Foreign Policy and the End of the Cold War* (University of Missouri Press, 1997); and Alexander M. Haig Jr., *Caveat: Realism, Reagan, and Foreign Policy* (Scribner, 1984).
107. Ramón Sánchez-Parodi Montoto, "The Reagan-Castro Years: The 'New Right' and Its Anti-Cuban Obsession," in *Fifty Years of Revolution: Perspectives on Cuba, the United States, and the World*, ed. Soraya M. Castro Mariño (University Press of Florida, 2012), 261; and Jonathan C. Brown, *Cuba's Revolutionary World* (Harvard University Press, 2017).
108. Chester Pach, "The Reagan Doctrine: Principle, Pragmatism, and Policy," *Presidential Studies Quarterly* 36, no. 1 (March 2006): 75–88; and James M. Scott, "Reagan's Doctrine? The Formulation of an American Foreign Policy Strategy," *Presidential Studies Quarterly* 26, no. 4 (Fall 1996): 1047–61.
109. Burke, *Revolutionaries for the Right*, 119; Ariel Armony, *Argentina, the U.S., and the Anti-Communist Crusade in Central America, 1977–1984* (Ohio University Center for International Studies, 1997); Christopher Dickey, *With the Contras: A Reporter in the Wilds of Nicaragua* (Touchstone, 1987); Gerald Horne, *The Color of Fascism: Lawrence Dennis, Racial Passing, and the Rise of Right-Wing Extremism in the United States* (New York University Press, 2006); and Gerald Horne, *From the Barrel of a Gun: The United States and the War Against Zimbabwe, 1965–1980* (University of North Carolina Press, 2001).
110. Victoria Brittain, "Jonas Savimbi: Angolan Nationalist Whose Ambition Kept His Country at War," *The Guardian*, February 24, 2002, https://www.theguardian.com/news/2002/feb/25/guardianobituaries.victoriabrittain.
111. William Charles Inboden, "Ronald Reagan, Exemplar of Conservative Internationalism?," *Orbis* 62, no. 1 (2018): 43–55.
112. Kim Phillips-Fein, *Invisible Hands: The Businessmen's Crusade Against the New Deal* (Norton, 2009); Jennifer Burns, *Goddess of the Market: Ayn Rand and the American Right* (Oxford University Press, 2011); Jonathan Davis, "Thatcher, Reagan, and Free Markets: Ghost Towns, Rust Belts and a New Individualism," in *The Global 1980s: People, Power, and Profit*, ed. Jonathan Davis (Routledge, 2019); Bethany Moreton, *To Serve God and Wal-Mart: The Making of Christian Free Enterprise* (Harvard University Press, 2010); and Angus Burgin, *The Great Persuasion: Reinventing Free Markets Since the Depression* (Harvard University Press, 2012).

113. Jessica Levy, "Black Power in the Board Room: Leon Sullivan and the Corporate Anti-Apartheid Response," *Enterprise and Society* 21, no. 1 (March 2020): 170–209; Zeb Larson, "The Sullivan Principles: South Africa, Apartheid, and Globalization," *Diplomatic History* 44, no. 3 (2020): 479–503; Robert Massie, *Loosing the Bonds: The United States and South Africa in the Apartheid Years* (Doubleday, 1997); and Lester K. Spence, *Knocking the Hustle: Against the Neoliberal Turn in Black Politics* (Punctum, 2015). For more on the free market aspect of antisanctions advocacy by Reagan officials, see chapter 3.
114. Borstelmann, *Apartheid's Reluctant Uncle* and *The Cold War and the Color Line*; and Mitchell, *Jimmy Carter in Africa.*
115. On constructive engagement, see J. E. Davies, *Constructive Engagement? Chester Crocker and American Policy in South Africa, Namibia and Angola, 1981–1988* (Ohio University Press, 2007); Thomson, "Incomplete Engagement"; and Christopher Coker, *The United States and South Africa, 1968–1985: Constructive Engagement and Its Critics* (Duke University Press, 1986).
116. Marilyn Lake and Henry Reynolds, *Drawing the Global Colour Line: White Men's Countries and the International Challenge of Racial Equality* (Cambridge University Press, 2008), 4; Daniel Immerwahr, *How to Hide an Empire: A History of the Greater United States* (Macmillan, 2019); Eliga H. Gould, *Among the Powers of the Earth: The American Revolution and the Making of a New World Empire* (Harvard University Press, 2014); and Andrew Zimmerman, *Alabama in Africa: Booker T. Washington, the German Empire, and the Globalization of the New South* (Princeton University Press, 2012).
117. John W. Cell, *The Highest Stage of White Supremacy: The Origins of Segregation in South Africa and the American South* (Cambridge University Press, 1982); William Minter, *King Solomon's Mines Revisited: Western Interests and the Burdened History of Southern Africa* (Basic, 1986); and Horne, *From the Barrel of a Gun.*
118. Plummer, *In Search of Power*, 10–15.
119. Miller, *An African Volk*, 18. On domestic politics in US foreign relations, see Daniel Bessner and Fredrik Logevall, "Recentering the United States in the Historiography of American Foreign Relations," *Texas National Security Review* 3, no. 2 (Spring 2020): 38–55. For multidimensional studies of modern US foreign relations, see Salim Yaqub, *Imperfect Strangers: Americans, Arabs, and U.S-Middle East Relations in the 1970s* (Cornell University Press, 2016).
120. Carol Anderson, *Eyes Off the Prize: The United Nations and the African American Struggle for Human Rights, 1944–1955* (Cambridge University Press, 2003); Jonathan Rosenberg, *How Far the Promised Land? World Affairs and the American Civil Rights Movement from the First World War to Vietnam* (Princeton University Press, 2005); and Penny Von Eschen, *Race Against Empire: Black Americans and Anticolonialism, 1937–1957* (Cornell University Press, 1997).
121. Mary L. Dudziak, "Desegregation as a Cold War Imperative," *Stanford Law Review* 41, no. 1 (1988): 61–120; Chad L. Williams, *Torchbearers of Democracy: African American Soldiers in the World War I Era* (University of North Carolina Press, 2013); and David K. Johnson, *The Lavender Scare: The Cold War Persecution of Gays and Lesbians in the Federal Government* (University of Chicago Press, 2004).

122. "Special Issue: Anti-Apartheid Movements on Campus," *Safundi* 23, nos. 1–2 (2002); *The Road to Democracy in South Africa*, vol. 3: *International Solidary* (South African Democracy Education Trust, 2008); Douglas Booth, "Hitting Apartheid for Six? The Politics of the South African Sports Boycott," *Journal of Contemporary History* 38, no. 3 (2003): 477–93; Douglas Booth, "The South African Council on Sport and the Political Antinomies of the Sports Boycott," *Journal of Southern African Studies* 23, no. 1 (1997): 51–66; Michael Bueckert, "Boycotts and Backlash: Canadian Opposition to Boycott, Divestment, and Sanctions (BDS) Movements from South Africa to Israel" (PhD diss., Carleton University, 2020); Derek Catsam, *Flashpoint: How a Little-Known Sporting Event Fueled America's Anti-Apartheid Movement* (Rowman & Littlefield, 2021); Jonathan R. Freeman, "Artists and Activism: Black Voices of Resistance and the Cultural Boycott of South Africa" (PhD diss., Purdue University, 2018); Limb et al., "The Global Anti-apartheid Movement"; and Anne Konieczna and Rob Skinner, eds., *A Global History of Anti-Apartheid: "Forward to Freedom" in South Africa* (Palgrave Macmillan, 2019).
123. Van der Westhuizen, *White Power*; Hermann Giliomee, "Constructing Afrikaner Nationalism," *Journal of Asian and African Studies* XVIII, nos. 1–2 (1983): 83–98; Hermann Giliomee, *The Afrikaners: Biography of a People* (University of Virginia Press, 2003); James Barber, *South Africa in the Twentieth Century* (Blackwell, 1999); Nigel Worden, *The Making of Modern South Africa: Conquest, Segregation and Apartheid* (Blackwell, 1994); Sampie Terreblanche, *A History of Inequality in South Africa, 1652–2002* (University of Natal Press, 2002); Nancy L. Clark and William H. Worger, *South Africa: The Rise and Fall of Apartheid* (Pearson Education, 2004); and William Beinart, *Twentieth Century South Africa* (Oxford University Press, 2001); Verne Harris, " 'They Should Have Destroyed More': The Destruction of Public Records by the South African State in the Final Years of Apartheid, 1990–1994," *Wired Space*, University of Witwatersrand, 2002; and Verne Harris "The Archival Sliver: A Perspective on the Construction of Social Memory in Archives and the Transition from Apartheid to Democracy," *Refiguring the Archive* (2002): 135–60.
124. Miller, *An African Volk*, 6.
125. Accounts of South African government-directed propaganda abroad run into this particular challenge, such as Hennie van Vuuren, *Apartheid, Guns, and Money: A Tale of Profit* (Hurst, 2019), and Nixon, *Selling Apartheid*.
126. Bongani Ngqulunga, "The Changing Face of Zulu Nationalism: The Transformation of Mangosuthu Buthelezi's Politics and Public Image," *Politikon* 47, no. 3 (2020): 287–304; Ben Temkin, *Buthelezi: A Biography* (Frank Cass, 2003); Laura Evans, *Survival in the "Dumping Grounds": A Social History of Apartheid Relocation* (Brill, 2019); Leo Barnard and Gert van der Westhuizen, "Die 'Slag van Mmabatho': die einde van regse weerstand teen die nuwe Suid-Afrika? Deel I: die val van Lucas Mangope se tuislandregering in Bophuthatswana," *Journal for Contemporary History* 31, no. 2 (January 2006): 163–77; Michael Lawrence and Andrew Manson, "The 'Dog of the Boers': The Rise and Fall of Mangope in Bophuthatswana," *Journal of Southern African Studies* 20, no. 3 (September 1994): 447–61; Laura Evans, "The Bantustan State and the South African Transition: Militarization, Patrimonialism and the Collapse of the Ciskei Regime, 1986–1994," *African*

Historical Review 50, nos. 1–2 (July 2018): 101–29; and Cindi Fezile, "The Rise and Fall of the Ciskei Homeland and Bantustan Leadership, 1972–1994," *Oral History Journal of South Africa* 6, no. 2 (December 2018): 1–8.

127. Peter Eisenstadt, ed., *Black Conservatism: Essays in Intellectual and Political History* (Garland, 1999), ix; David Henry Anthony, *Max Yergan: Race Man, Internationalist, Cold Warrior* (New York University Press, 2006); Sabelo J. Ndlovu-Gatsheni, "Black Republican Tradition, Nativism and Populist Politics in South Africa," *Transformation* 68, no. 1 (2008): 53–86; Jessica Anne O'Conner, "Black Conservatives and the Policy of Constructive Engagement, 1981–1989" (PhD diss., Australian Catholic University, 2022); Preston H. Smith, "'Self-Help,' Black Conservatives, and the Reemergence of Black Privatism," in *Without Justice for All: The New Liberalism and Our Retreat from Racial Equality*, ed. Adolph Reed (Westview, 1999); Deborah Toler, "Black Conservatives Part One" and "Black Conservatives Part Two," *The Public Eye Newsletter* (1993); and Angela K. Lewis, "Black Conservatism in America," *Journal of African American Studies* 8, no. 4 (2005): 3–13.

128. Sara Diamond, *Spiritual Warfare: The Politics of the Christian Right* (Black Rose, 1990).

129. Dube, "The New Religious Political Right," 157; Roger Southall, *The New Black Middle Class in South Africa* (Jacana Media, 2016); Geoffrey Modisha, "A Contradictory Class Location? The African Corporate Middle Class and the Burden of Race in South Africa," *Transformation: Critical Perspectives on Southern Africa* 65 (2008): 120–45.

130. On the Ku Klux Klan, see Kelly J. Baker, *Gospel According to the Klan: The KKK's Appeal to Protestant America, 1915–1930* (University of Kansas Press, 2011); Kathleen M. Blee, *Women of the Klan: Racism and Gender in the 1920s* (University of California Press, 1991); Nancy MacLean, *Behind the Mask of Chivalry: The Making of the Second Ku Klux Klan* (Oxford University Press, 1994); Wyn Craig Wade, *The Fiery Cross: The Ku Klux Klan in America* (Simon and Schuster, 1987); and Michael Zatarain, *David Duke: Evolution of a Klansman* (Pelican, 1990). On the white power movement in the 1990s, see Sara Diamond, *Roads to Dominion: Right-Wing Movements and Political Power in the United States* (Guilford, 1995); Betty A. Dobratz and Stephanie L. Shanks-Meile, *The White Separatist Movement in the United States: "White Power, White Pride!"* (Twayne, 1997); Raphael S. Ezekiel, *The Racist Mind: Portraits of American Neo-Nazis and Klansmen* (Penguin, 1995); Mattias Gardell, *Gods of the Blood: The Pagan Revival and White Separatism* (Duke University Press, 2003); Michael Kimmel and Abby L. Ferber, "'White Men Are This Nation': Right-Wing Militias and the Restoration of Rural American Masculinity," *Rural Sociology* 65, no. 4 (2000): 582–604; and Robert Futrell, *American Swastika: Inside the White Power Movement's Hidden Spaces of Hate* (Rowman and Littlefield, 2010).

131. Belew, *Bring the War Home*, 3.

132. Burke, *Revolutionaries for the Right.*

133. Matthew Karp, *This Vast Southern Empire: Slaveholders at the Helm of American Foreign Policy* (Harvard University Press, 2016); Matthew Frye Jacobson, *Barbarian Virtues: The United States Encounters Foreign People at Home and Abroad* (Hill and Wang, 2001); Paul Kramer, *The Blood of Government: Race, Empire, the United States, and the Philippines* (University of North Carolina Press, 2006); and Mary A. Renda, *Taking Haiti: Military*

Occupation and the Culture of U.S. Imperialism, 1915–1940 (University of North Carolina Press, 2001).

134. Daniel Geary, Camilla Schofield, and Jennifer Sutton, eds., *Global White Nationalism: From Apartheid to Trump* (Manchester University Press, 2020), 2.

135. Elizabeth Gillespie McRae, *Mothers of Massive Resistance: White Women and the Politics of White Supremacy* (Oxford University Press, 2018), 7.

136. Christopher S. Browning and Matt McDonald, "The Future of Critical Security Studies: Ethics and the Politics of Security," *European Journal of International Relations* 19, no. 2 (2011): 235–55; and Keith Krause and Michael C. Williams, *Critical Security Studies: Concepts and Cases* (University of Minnesota Press, 1997).

137. As Margaret E. Keck and Kathryn Sikkink argue in *Activists Beyond Borders: Advocacy Networks in International Politics* (Cornell University Press, 1998), what makes these transnational networks unique is their ability to promote causes, ideas, and norms that often involve individuals advocating policy changes that "cannot be easily linked to a rationalist understanding of their interests."

138. Scholars of white supremacy have long recognized the critical interplay between violent and nonviolent means of preserving racial hierarchy. See McRae, *Mothers of Massive Resistance*; Anders Walker, *The Ghosts of Jim Crow: How Southern Moderates Used Brown v. The Board of Education to Stall Civil Rights* (Oxford University Press, 2009); George Lewis, *The White South and the Red Menace: Segregationists, Anti-Communism and Massive Resistance, 1945–1965* (University of Florida Press, 2004); Tom Sugrue, *The Origins of the Urban Crisis: Race and Inequality in Postwar Detroit* (Princeton University Press, 2005); and Lisa McGirr, *Suburban Warriors: The Origins of the New American Right* (Princeton University Press, 2015).

139. Burke, *Revolutionaries for the Right*; Susan Williams, *Who Killed Hammarskjold? The UN, the Cold War and White Supremacy in Africa* (Oxford University Press, 2014).

140. Seymour Martin Lipset and Earl Raab, *The Politics of Unreason: Right Wing Extremism in America, 1790–1970* (Harper & Row, 1970), 19; and John Kekes, *Moderate Conservatism: Reclaiming the Center* (Oxford University Press, 2023).

141. Noam Gidron and Daniel Ziblatt, "Center-Right Political Parties in Advanced Democracies," *Annual Review of Political Parties Science* 22 (2019): 23.

142. Gidron and Ziblatt, "Center-Right Political Parties in Advanced Democracies," 24; Eviane Leidig, *The Women of the Far Right: Social Media Influencers and Online Radicalization* (Columbia University Press, 2023), 24.

143. Geary et al., *Global White Nationalism*, 10.

144. Lake and Reynolds, *Drawing the Global Colour Line*; Gerald Horne, *White Supremacy Confronted: U.S. Imperialism and Anti-Communism vs. the Liberation of Southern Africa from Rhodes to Mandela* (International, 2019); and Cell, *The Highest Stage of White Supremacy.*

145. Danelle van Zyl-Hermann and Jacob Boersema, "Introduction: The Politics of Whiteness in Africa," *Africa* 87, no. 4 (2017): 651–61.

146. I elected not to conduct interviews with far-right activists as a result of logistical (the bulk of this research was conducted during the COVID-19 pandemic) and ethical concerns.

For more on the ethics of interviewing far-right activists, see Kathleen M. Blee, "Methods, Interpretation, and Ethics in the Study of White Supremacist Perpetrators," *Conflict and Society* 1, no. 1 (2015): 9–22.

1. TELLING THE STORY OF WHITE POWER

1. David Otto, "Advertisement," *Citizens Informer* 24, no. 1 (1993), CofCC, Folder HH 365C/22—Tri State Informer Inc., Part II, Box T-23, Hall Hoag Collection (HHC), Brown University, Providence, Rhode Island.
2. "Council of Conservative Citizens," SPLC, accessed July 30, 2024, https://www.splcenter.org/fighting-hate/extremist-files/group/council-conservative-citizens.
3. "Council of Conservative Citizens," *All Things Considered*, NPR, February 23, 1999, and "Council of Conservative Citizens," SPLC.
4. Andrew Kaczynski, "Nikki Haley Defended Right to Secession, Confederate History Month and the Confederate Flag in 2010 Talk," CNN, February 21, 2023, https://www.cnn.com/2023/02/21/politics/nikki-haley-secession-confederate-history-month-flag-kfile.
5. Otto, "Advertisement."
6. Robert L. Slimp, "Will Bill Clinton Invade South Africa?," *Citizens Informer* 24, no. 1 (1993), CofCC, Folder HH 365C/22—Tri State Informer Inc., Part II, Box T-23, HHC.
7. Slimp remained active until 2010, when he appeared in a video produced by Palmetto Patriots, a group that "fights attacks against Southern culture," questioning then–South Carolina gubernatorial candidate Nikki Haley about her Christian faith. Kaczynski, "Nikki Haley Defended Right to Secession"; Peter Wallsten and Valerie Bauerlin, "Haley Keeps Taking the Southern Test," *Wall Street Journal*, June 22, 2010; Benjamin J. Young, "Soldiers of Fortune, Soldiers of God: Evangelical Mercenaries and the Making of the Rhodesian-American Religious Lobby, 1965–1980," *Cold War History* 24, no. 3 (2024): 379–400.
8. "My Racial 'Epiphany,'" Earl P. Holt III in *Citizens Informer*, Council of Conservative Citizens, December 2021.
9. Slimp, "Will Bill Clinton Invade South Africa?"
10. Jeffrey D. Howison, *The 1980 Presidential Election: Ronald Reagan and the Shaping of the American Conservative Movement* (Routledge, 2014); Andrew Busch, *Reagan's Victory: The Presidential Election of 1980 and the Rise of the Right* (University of Kansas Press, 2005); Jack Germond and Jules Witcover, *Blue Smoke and Mirrors: How Reagan Won and Why Carter Lost the Election of 1980* (Viking, 1981); and Rick Perlstein, *Reaganland: America's Right Turn, 1976–1980* (Simon & Schuster, 2020).
11. Meg Heckman, "The New Hampshire Publisher Who Became the 'Political Godmother' of the Modern Right," *Politico*, February 7, 2020.
12. Ronald Reagan, "Transkei: Alive and Well," *Manchester (N.H). Union Leader*, November 19, 1976.
13. Ben Bradford, "The Republican National Convention That Changed the GOP," *Time*, July 16, 2024.

14. Christi van der Westhuizen, *White Power and the Rise and Fall of the National Party* (Zebra, 2007), 113–14, 122.
15. De Wet Potgieter, *Total Onslaught: Apartheid's Dirty Tricks Exposed* (Zebra, 2007), 94.
16. Bernard Magubane, "The Crisis of the Garrison State," in *The Road to Democracy in South Africa*, vol. 4, part 1 [1980–1990] (Unisa Press, 2010), 16, 30.
17. "With Reagan, SA, and the USA Will Benefit," *Die Vaderland*, February 1, 1980, Folder: Feb. 1980, Box 5, Jan.–Apr. 1980, A1597—Doreen Nussey trans., "From the Afrikaans Press," University of Witwatersrand Historical Papers (UWHP), Johannesburg, South Africa; Hannes de Wet, "SA Could Win in This Way," *Die Transvaler*, November 6, 1980, Folder: Nov. 1980–Dec. 1980—last summaries for the year, Box 7, Sep.–Nov. 1980, A1597—Doreen Nussey trans., "From the Afrikaans Press," UWHP.
18. "Oh America!," *Die Beeld*, March 21, 1980, Folder: Mar 1980, Box 5, Jan.–Apr. 1980, A1597—Doreen Nussey trans., "From the Afrikaans Press," UWHP.
19. "Grounds for Discussion in Haig's Realism—Premier," *Die Beeld*, January 16, 1981, and "Reagan Man Working for S.A.," *Die Vaderland*, January 14, 1981, Folder: Jan. 1981, Box 8, Jan.–Apr. 1981, A1597—Doreen Nussey trans., "From the Afrikaans Press," UWHP.
20. "Thus Talks a Leader, Says PW," *Die Beeld*, March 5, 1981, Folder: Mar. 1981, Box 8, Jan.–Apr. 1981, A1597—Doreen Nussey trans., "From the Afrikaans Press," UWHP.
21. "Our Choice," *Die Beeld*, September 2, 1981, Folder: Sep. 1981, Box 10, Sept.–Dec. 1981, A1597—Doreen Nussey trans., "From the Afrikaans Press," UWHP.
22. "SA's Ties with USA Firmer," *Die Beeld*, May 7, 1981, Folder: May 1981, Box 9, May–Aug. 1981, A1597—Doreen Nussey trans., "From the Afrikaans Press," UWHP. For more on the differences between the Afrikaans language presses, see F. A. Mouton, " 'Survival in Justice': Apartheid and the Schalk Pienaar—Dr. A.P. Treurnicht *broedertwis*, 1968–1978," *South African Historical Journal* 69, no. 3 (2017): 452–67; and Johannes D. Froneman and Christo J. Lombaard, "Peace-Seeking Afrikaans Editors in the Apartheid Era: Journalistic Perspectives in a Theological Framework," *Verbum et. Ecclesia* 41, no. 1 (2020): 1–9.
23. "Angolan Incursion 'Is Exploitation,' " *Die Beeld*, September 4, 1981, Folder: Sep. 1981, Box 10, Sept.–Dec. 1981, A1597—Doreen Nussey trans., "From the Afrikaans Press," UWHP.
24. Letter to president-elect Ronald Reagan from Richard A. Allen, December 12, 1980, WHORM Subject File (016900-023819), Box 163, CO 141 (South Africa), Collection: CO Countries, Ronald Reagan Presidential Library, RRPL, Simi Valley, California.
25. Letter to Edwin Meese III from William P. Hanson, March 23, 1981, WHORM Subject File (016900-023819), Box 163, CO 141 (South Africa), Collection: CO Countries, RRPL. Hanson's letter came after his trip to South Africa, where he also visited a bantustan, writing to Reagan that he would assess "a Black fresh out of the Bush to have the mentality of a four to five year old." Although it is unclear why or how Hanson visited, it is likely he went on a trip paid for by a South African NGO or business group. For more on these organizations, see chapter 2.
26. Rotary International is a global service network that currently numbers over 1.4 million members.
27. Letter to Ronald Reagan from John H. Ewing Jr., November 11, 1981, WHORM Subject File (050000-074999), Box 164, CO 141 (South Africa), Collection: CO Countries, RRPL.

28. Magubane, "The Crisis of the Garrison State," 41–42.
29. Nigel Worden, *The Making of Modern South Africa: Conquest, Segregation and Apartheid* (Blackwell, 1994), 134; Leonard Thompson, *A History of South Africa* (Yale University Press, 2001), 226–28.
30. Saul Dubow, *Apartheid, 1948–1994* (Oxford University Press, 2014), 226–66.
31. Gregory Houston, "The ANC's Internal Underground Political Work in the 1980s," in *Road to Democracy in South Africa*, 133.
32. Rob Skinner, *The Foundations of Anti-Apartheid: Liberal Humanitarians and Transnational Activists in Britain and the United States* (Palgrave Macmillan, 2010), 2; Steven Gish, *Alfred B. Xuma: African, American, South African* (New York University Press, 2000); Amanda Joyce Hall, "Students Are the Spark: Anti-apartheid in the Long 1980s," *Journal of African-American History* 108, no. 3 (Summer 2023): 369–97; Amanda Joyce Hall, "Struggle for Another World: Movements Against South African Apartheid and the Global Challenge to Anti-Black Racism, 1971–1991" (PhD diss., Yale Graduate School of Arts and Sciences, 2022); Wanda Hendricks, *The Life of Madie Hall Xuma: Black Women's Global Activism During Jim Crow and Apartheid* (University of Illinois Press, 2022); Iris Berger, "An African American 'Mother of the Nation': Madie Hall Xuma in South Africa, 1940–1963," *Journal of Southern African Studies* 27, no. 3 (2001): 547–66; Francis Njubi Nesbitt, *Race for Sanctions: African Americans Against Apartheid, 1946–1994* (Indiana University Press 2004); Brenda Gayle Plummer, *In Search of Power: African Americans in the Era of Decolonization* (Cambridge University Press 2012); Robert Trent Vinson, *The Americans Are Coming! Dreams of African American Liberation in Segregationist South Africa* (Ohio University Press, 2012); and Nicholas Grant, *Winning Our Freedoms Together: African Americans and Apartheid, 1945–1960* (University of North Carolina Press, 2017).
33. Tomas D. Schuman, "Disinvestment Movement in the U.S.: A Proven Soviet Measure," in "South Africa: Nation on Trial, Is it a Black White Conflict?," *Family Protection Scoreboard*, 1987, Folder: Jr, Right-Wing Religion, AG2843—Institute for Contextual Theology, "Right-Wing Religion," UWHP.
34. Phoebe Courtney, "The Truth About South Africa," *The Independent American*, 1985, BX6.N2 C687 1985, Radicalism, Michigan State University Special Collections, Lansing, Michigan.
35. Jamie Miller, *An African Volk: The Apartheid Regime and Its Search for Survival* (Oxford University Press, 2016), 18.
36. Donal Lowry, "The Impact of Anti-Communism on White Rhodesian Political Culture, ca. 1920–1980," *Cold War History* 7, no. 2 (May 2007): 169–94.
37. Thomas Borstelmann, *Apartheid's Reluctant Uncle: The United States and Southern Africa in the Early Cold War* (Oxford University Press, 1993), 4.
38. There is a clear rhetoric parallel to the "containment" rhetoric deployed by the US foreign policy apparatus throughout the Cold War. See Paul Rich, "United States Containment Policy, South Africa and the Apartheid Dilemma," *Review of International Studies* 14, no. 3 (1988): 179–94.
39. "Who Is Promoting Revolution in South Africa . . .?," United Christian Action, 1986, Box 9, United Christian Action (UCA), Correspondence and Brochure, Mary Ann Gilbert,

Serials Correspondence, SC 79, Intercessors for the Suffering Church Collection, Wheaton College Special Collections (WCSC), Wheaton, Illinois.

40. South Africa would back Renamo until the Nkomati Accord of 1984, a nonaggression pact between the apartheid state and Mozambique. The Nkomati Accord was the high-water mark of constructive engagement's success. The view of Renamo as nothing more than a proxy of the white regimes in South Africa and Rhodesia continues today, even as historians challenge this reductionist rendering. In the 1980s, US conservatives enthusiastically backed Renamo and pushed the Reagan administration to openly back them. "Why Won't Administration Get Behind RENAMO?," *Human Events*, vol. XLVI, no. 45, November 8, 1986, and Frederick Kempe, "GOP Right Wing Hinders Reagan Bid to Woo Mozambique from the Soviets," *Wall Street Journal*, June 1, 1987.
41. "Tribute to Dr. Ed Cain," Frontline Fellowship, April 11, 2002.
42. "Tribute to Ed Cain," *Frontline Missions SA*, November 4, 2002.
43. "Welcome to the Fellowship," Frontline Fellowship, Peter Hammond, 1984, Box 3, Frontline Fellowship, News/Prayer Letters, 1984–1995, SC 79, Intercessors for the Suffering Church Collection, Mary Ann Gilbert, Serials Correspondence, WCSC.
44. "Introducing Peter Hammond," Frontline Fellowship, February 15, 2019, https://www.frontlinemissionsa.org/uploads/1/0/4/1/104153586/introducing_peter_hammond_lh__15feb2019_.pdf.
45. On the legacy of Robert Mugabe, see Sue Onslow and Martin Plaut, *Robert Mugabe* (Ohio University Press, 2018).
46. "Prayer and Praise Newsletter, July 1984," Peter Hammond, Frontline Fellowship, 1984, Folder 3, Southern Africa, carton 43 BANC MSS 98/70, Collection on the US Right [ca. 1950s–1997], Sara Diamond Papers, UC Berkeley Bancroft Library Manuscripts Collection (BLMC), Berkeley, California.
47. Daniel Conway, *Masculinities, Militarization, and the End Conscription Campaign* (Manchester University Press, 2012).
48. Korbus du Pisani, "Puritanism Transformed: Afrikaner Masculinities in the Apartheid and Post-Apartheid Period," in *Changing Men in Southern Africa*, ed. Robert Morrell (Zed, 2001), 158. On contemporary muscular Christianity in South Africa, see Siphiwe Dube, "Muscular Christianity in Contemporary South Africa: The Case of the Mighty Men Conference," *Hervormde Teologiese Studies* 71, no. 3 (2015): 1–9.
49. "Introducing Peter Hammond," Frontline Missions.
50. "44 Years Ago—Conversion to Christ," *Frontline Missions SA*, April 4, 2020, https://www.frontlinemissionsa.org/dr-peter-hammond/43-years-ago-conversion-to-christ.
51. "Do You Support Apartheid Racism?," *Frontline Missions SA*, October 10, 2017.
52. Conor Heffernan, "Representations of Hulk Hogan in the 1980s: Christianity, Masculinity, Xenophobia," *Arts (Basel)* 12, no. 1 (2023): 22.
53. James H. Meriwether, *Tears, Fire, and Blood: The United States and the Decolonization of Africa* (University of North Carolina Press, 2021), 138.
54. Elizabeth Schmidt, *Cold War and Decolonization in Guinea, 1946–1958* (Ohio Univesity Press, 2007), 183, and Muna Ndulo, "Constitutions and Constitutional Reforms in African Politics," *Politics*, July 29, 2019.

55. "Prayer Report: Black Africa (Africa South of the Sahara)," Peter Hammond, Frontline Fellowship, 1986, Box 3, Frontline Fellowship, News/Prayer Letters, 1984–1995, SC 79, Intercessors for the Suffering Church Collection, Mary Ann Gilbert, Serials Correspondence, WCSC.
56. "Prayer Report: Mozambique," Peter Hammond, Frontline Fellowship, 1986, Box 3, Frontline Fellowship, News/Prayer Letters, 1984–1995, SC 79, Intercessors for the Suffering Church Collection, Mary Ann Gilbert, Serials Correspondence, WCSC.
57. "God's Plan for South Africa," Frontline Fellowship, July 1985, Box 3, Frontline Fellowship, News/Prayer Letters, 1984–1995, SC 79, Intercessors for the Suffering Church Collection, Mary Ann Gilbert, Serials Correspondence, WCSC.
58. "Blacks Alarmed by Lifting of State of Emergency," March 5, 1986, United Christian Action, Box 9, United Christian Action, UCA News 1986–1992, South Africa, SC 79, Intercessors for the Suffering Church Collection, Mary Ann Gilbert, Serials Correspondence, WCSC.
59. Maurice C. Fleming, "What Is Wrong with Apartheid?," *Citizens Informer*, vol. 17, no. 4, CofCC, Fall 1985, Folder HH328A:124—Tri-State Informer, Part II, Box T-23, HHC.
60. "Facts About Southern Africa the International Media Will Not Give You," *Aida Parker Newsletter*, Issue 109, August 1987, Folder 16, Aida Parker, carton 42, Sara Diamond Papers, BANC MSS 98/70, Collection on the US right [ca. 1950s–1997], BLMC.
61. Matthew D. Lassiter, *The Silent Majority: Suburban Politics in the Sunbelt South* (Princeton University Press, 2006), 2–4.
62. For more on mainstreaming, see Marcus A. Brooks, "It's Okay to Be White: Laundering White Supremacy Through a Colorblind Victimized White Race-Consciousness Raising Campaign," *Sociological Spectrum* 40, no. 6 (2020): 400–416.
63. Darren Dochuk, *From Bible Belt to Sunbelt: Plain-Folk Religion, Grassroots Politics, and Evangelical Conservatism* (Norton, 2011), xxiii.
64. Justin Gomer, *White Balance: How Hollywood Shaped Colorblind Ideology and Undermined Civil Rights* (University of North Carolina Press, 2020), 102, 130.
65. van der Westhuizen, *White Power*, 115, 116.
66. Philip I. Levy, "Sanctions on South Africa: What Did They Do?," Economic Growth Center Discussion Paper No. 796, Yale University, February 1999, 3.
67. "Mandela's Release Would Trigger the First Stage of Marxist Revolution in SA," United Christian Action, October 1, 1986, United Christian, Box 9, United Christian Action, UCA News 1986–1992, South Africa, SC 79, Intercessors for the Suffering Church Collection, Mary Ann Gilbert, Serials Correspondence, WCSC.
68. "Why United Christian Action Opposes the Mamelodi Christian Encounter," United Christian Action, March 18, 1988, Box 9, United Christian Action, UCA News 1986–1992, South Africa, SC 79, Intercessors for the Suffering Church Collection, Mary Ann Gilbert, Serials Correspondence, WCSC.
69. For more on Mokoena, see chapter 2.
70. "Divest from the Politicized Gospel, Support United Christian Action," United Christian Action, 1987, Folder 19, NRB 87 South Africa, Carton 42, Sara Diamond Papers, BANC MSS 98/70, Collection on the US Right [ca. 1950s–1997], BLMC.

71. "The Soviets Anti-South Africa Juggernaut: Moving Into High Gear," *African Intelligence Digest*, July 30, 1985, Folder H226A:3—African Intelligence Digest, Box A-9, Part II, HHC.
72. "A Personal Message on South Africa (for Overseas Friends): An Urgent Call to Prayer," Frontline Fellowship, 1986, Box 3, Frontline Fellowship, News/Prayer Letters, 1984–1995, SC 79, Intercessors for the Suffering Church Collection, Mary Ann Gilbert, Serials Correspondence, WCSC.
73. "A Personal Message on South Africa (for Overseas Friends)."
74. William Murchison, "Will Ciskei Show South Africa How It's Done?," *Washington Times*, 1986, Box 2, History of South African Movement, N.D., V. 1 I, Personal Papers of Chris Bunker, Series No. PP/329, University of Kansas Library Archives (UKL), Lawrence, Kansas; Elizabeth Flock, "Sun Myung Moon's Death Leaves Conservative Newspaper at a Crossroads," *US News & World Report*, September 4, 2012, https://www.usnews.com/news/blogs/washington-whispers/2012/09/04/sun-myung-moons-death-leaves-conservative-newspaper-at-a-crossroads.
75. Murchison, "Will Ciskei Show South Africa How It's Done?"; Flock, "Sun Myung Moon's Death Leaves Conservative Newspaper at a Crossroads." For more on the libertarian response to the bantustans, see Quinn Slobodian, *Crack-Up Capitalism: Market Radicals and the Dream of a World Without Democracy* (Metropolitan, 2023), 81–98.
76. John Blundell, "Tell America to Come and See for Itself What Is Happening Here in Ciskei," *Reason*, undated, Box 2, History of South African Movement, 3/22/85-4/12/85, V. 2 II, Personal Papers of Chris Bunker, Series No. PP/329, UKL.
77. "A Personal Message on South Africa (for Overseas Friends)."
78. James Barber, *South Africa in the Twentieth Century* (Blackwell, 1999), 251, 255, 257.
79. Ruhan Fourie, "'Angels and Demons'? The Dutch Reformed Church and Anticommunism in Twentieth Century South Africa" (PhD diss., University of the Free State, Bloemfontein, 2021), 200, citing J. H. P. Serfontein, *Apartheid, Change, and the NG Kerk* (Taurus, 1982), 91.
80. T. Dunbar Moodie, "Confessing Responsibility for the Evils of Apartheid: The Dutch Reformed Church in the 1980s," *South African Historical Journal* 72, no. 4 (2020): 630.
81. Tracy Kuperus, "Resisting or Embracing Reform? South Africa's Democratic Transition and NGK-State Relations," *Journal of Church and State* 38, no. 4 (Autumn 1996): 842, and T. Dunbar Moodie, *The Rise of Afrikanerdom: Power, Apartheid, and the Afrikaner Civil Religion* (University of California Press, 1975).
82. Hermann Giliomee, *The Afrikaners: Biography of a People* (University of Virginia Press, 2003), 462.
83. Fourie, "'Angels and Demons'?," iii.
84. Thomas Resane, "The Church's Prophetic Role in the Face of Corruption in the South African Sociopolitical Landscape," *Pharos Journal of Theology* 98, no. 1 (2017): 2.
85. On Kairos, see Peter Walshe, "Christianity and the Anti-Apartheid Struggle: The Prophetic Voice Within Divided Churches," in *Christianity in South Africa: A Political, Social, and Cultural History*, ed. Richard Elphick and Rodney Davenport (University of California Press, 1997), 383–99.

86. "The Kairos Document: Its Origins and Concerns," The Kairos Theologians, August 1985, Folder: G2, ICT, Kairos Doc. History, KAIROS Document, G1–G8, AG2843—Institute for Contextual Theology, UWHP.
87. "Challenge to the Church: A Theological Comment on the Political Crisis in South Africa," The Kairos Theologians, February 1986, Folder: G1, ICT, Kairos Doc. Text (+ Manuscripts), KAIROS Document, G1–G8, AG2843—Institute for Contextual Theology, UWHP.
88. "The Kairos Document: Its Origins and Concerns."
89. Demaine Solomons, "On Re-Membering Reconciliation and the Black Theological Impulse Embedded in the Kairos Document," *Ecumenical Review* 74, no. 4 (October 2022): 519. Kairos's legacy continued far beyond South Africa, with the Kairos Document serving as inspiration for calls for "discernment, decision, and action" against apartheid around the world, specifically in Palestine in 2009. Allan Aubrey Boesak, *Kairos, Crisis, and Global Apartheid: The Challenge to Prophetic Resistance* (Palgrave Macmillan, 2015), 1.
90. "Divest from the Politicized Gospel, Support United Christian Action."
91. Patrick J. Buchanan, "Bishop Tutu, the Liberals and Apartheid," *Washington Inquirer*, November 9, 1984, Folder 8, Buchanan, carton 45, Sara Diamond Papers, BANC MSS 98/70, Collection on the US Right [ca. 1950s–1997], BLMC.
92. John Allen, *Rabble-Rouser for Peace: The Authorized Biography of Desmond Tutu* (Simon & Schuster, 2006), 217–18, 265.
93. Gospel Defense League Newsletter, Gospel Defense League, July 1986, Folder 19, NRB 87 South Africa, carton 42, Sara Diamond Papers, BANC MSS 98/70, Collection on the US Right [ca. 1950s–1997], BLMC. Ed Cain, "Liberation Theology," July 25, 1986, Folder 4, Southern Africa, carton 43, Sara Diamond Papers, BANC MSS 98/70, Collection on the US Right [ca. 1950s–1997], BLMC.
94. Ivan Petrella, *The Future of Liberation Theology: An Argument and Manifesto* (Routledge, 2016), vii. For more on liberation theology, see Christian Büschges, Andrea Müller, and Noah Oehri, eds., *Liberation Theology and Others: Contextualizing Catholic Activism in 20th Century Latin America* (Lexington, 2021); Ghirmai Negash, *African Liberation Theology: Intergenerational Conversations on Eritrea's Futures* (Red Sea, 2018); Lilian Barger *The World Come of Age: An Intellectual History of Liberation Theology* (Oxford University Press, 2018); and Peter Walshe, *Prophetic Christianity and the Liberation Movement in South Africa* (Cluster, 1995).
95. "About Us," Gospel Defense League.
96. "A Tribute to Mrs. Dorothea Scarborough," *Frontline Missions SA*, May 27, 2022, accessed January 16, 2023, https://www.frontlinemissionsa.org/in-memorium/a-tribute-to-mrs-dorothea-scarborough.
97. "Evaluating the Legacy of Archbishop Desmond Tutu," Gospel Defense League, 2021, accessed January 16, 2023.
98. "The Kairos Document—A Document Against the Athentic (sic) Teaching of Christ Since It Speaks for Sanctions," 1985, Folder: G9, ICT, Kairos Doc., Translations—Foreign/International Response, G9, AG2843—Institute for Contextual Theology, Kairos Document—Response, UWHP.

99. "Liberation Theology," Frontline Fellowship, 1987, Box 3, Frontline Fellowship, News/Prayer Letters, 1984–1995, SC 79, Intercessors for the Suffering Church Collection, Mary Ann Gilbert, Serials Correspondence, WCSC.
100. Gospel Defense League Newsletter, Gospel Defense League, December 1985, Folder: G9, Kairos Document Responses—Negative, G9, AG2843—Institute for Contextual Theology, UWHP.
101. Publishing in both Afrikaans and English, Christian Mission International directed most of its energy to exposing the evils of communism to Christians around the world. The organization remains based in Germiston, South Africa, now renamed as The Voice of the Martyrs. "When God Is Replaced: A Response to the Kairos Document," Christian Missions International, 1986, Folder: Kairos Document Responses—Negative, G9, AG2843—Institute for Contextual Theology, UWHP.
102. Melani McAlister, *The Kingdom of God Has No Borders: A Global History of American Evangelicals* (Oxford University Press, 2018), and Lauren Turek, *To Bring the Good News to All Nations: Evangelical Influence on Human Rights and U.S. Foreign Relations* (Cornell University Press, 2020).
103. "SACC: A Revolutionary Club," "The Enemies Within—Part I: The Priests Take on Pretoria, 'Comrade Jesus' and the SA Revolution," *Aida Parker Newsletter*, APN Special Issue 1987, Folder: J1, Right-Wing Religion, AG2843—Institute for Contextual Theology, UWHP.
104. "It's Not Murder, It's a Political Statement," "The Enemies Within—Part I."
105. Gospel Defense League Newsletter, June 1985, Box 3, Gospel Defense League Newsletters, 1985–1995, SC 79, Intercessors for the Suffering Church Collection, Mary Ann Gilbert, Serials Correspondence, WCSC.
106. "The All-Powerful Mind Police," Student Moderate Alliance, Third Quarter 1985, Box 5, National Student Federation (NSF), Pamphlets, handouts, info, SC 79, Intercessors for the Suffering Church Collection, Mary Ann Gilbert, Serials Correspondence, WCSC.

2. THE ONLY TRUE FRIENDS SOUTH AFRICA HAS

1. "Opening Statement of Senator Jeremiah Denton," Hearings Before the Subcommittee on Security and Terrorism of the Committee on the Judiciary United States Senate Ninety-Seventh Congress Second Session on the Role of the Soviet Union, Cuba, and East Germany in Fomenting Terrorism in Southern Africa (hereafter cited as the Denton Hearings), March 22, 1982, 3.
2. "Closing Remarks of Senator Jeremiah Denton," Denton Hearings, March 31, 1982, 705.
3. George Lardner Jr., "Assault on Terrorism: Internal Security or Witch Hunt?," *Washington Post*, April 20, 1981.
4. Steve Chawkins, "POW Who Blinked 'Torture' in Morse Code," *Los Angeles Times*, March 29, 2014, https://www.latimes.com/archives/la-xpm-2014-mar-29-la-me-jeremiah-denton-20140329-story.html.

5. Jacob Dlamini, *The Terrorist Album: Apartheid's Insurgents, Collaborators, and the Security Police* (Harvard University Press, 2020), 235–38.
6. "The Denton Hearings," *TransAfrica Forum: A Research and Educational Affiliate of TransAfrica Issue Brief*, TransAfrica, October 1982, African Activist Archive, https://africanactivist.msu.edu/recordFiles/210-849-26728/taforum1982opt.pdf.
7. Arthur Lewis, "The Valley of the Shadow," Rhodesia Christian Group, March 1983, Box 8, Rhodesia Christian Group Newsletter, 1982–1990, SC 79, Intercessors for the Suffering Church Collection, Mary Ann Gilbert, Serials Correspondence, Wheaton College Special Collections (WCSC), Wheaton, Illinois.
8. Aziz Choudry, *Learning Activism: The Intellectual Life of Contemporary Social Movements* (University of Toronto Press, 2015); Donatella della Porta and Sidney Tarrow, eds., *Transnational Protest and Global Activism* (Rowman & Littlefield, 2004), 21; Sidney Tarrow, *Power in Movement: Social Movements and Contentious Politics* (Cambridge University Press, 1998); and Paul Almeida, *Social Movements: The Structure of Collective Mobilization* (University of California Press, 2019), 66–74.
9. Michael Ondaatje, *Black Conservative Intellectuals in Modern* America (University of Pennsylvania Press, 2011), 5.
10. Leah Wright Riguer, *The Loneliness of the Black Republican: Pragmatic Politics and the Pursuit of Power* (Princeton University Press, 2016), 8.
11. Phil McCombs, "Alan Keyes: The Question of Justice: State's Point Man on South Africa, His Battles and His Sudden Resignation," *Washington Post*, September 17, 1987, https://www.washingtonpost.com/archive/lifestyle/1987/09/18/alan-keyes-the-question-of-justice/f791ffff-57d8-4243-aada-5aef73597bcd/.
12. Louis G. Prisock, *African Americans in Conservative Movements: The Inescapability of Race* (Springer, 2018), 3.
13. McCombs, "Alan Keyes."
14. Franziska Rueedi, *The Vaal Uprising of 1984 and the Struggle for Freedom in South Africa* (James Currey, 2021), 23, 2, 3.
15. Christi van der Westhuizen, *White Power and the Rise and Fall of the National Party* (Zebra, 2007), 143–44.
16. Rueedi, *The Vaal Uprising of 1984*, 20.
17. Karin Johansson, "South Africa: Independent Black Churches on Their Own Again," *Christianity Today*, February 6, 1981, https://www.christianitytoday.com/ct/1981/february-6/evangelist-and-pope-confer-privately-in-rome.html.
18. Press Statement of the African Spiritual Churches Association (ASCA) on Bishops Isaac Mokoena and Mzilikazi Masiya, Sanctions, Election, Bannings, and Restrictions, African Spiritual Churches Association, 1989, Folder: H5, ICT, Personal Files, Mokoena. I, H4–H5, Staffing & Admin, Personal Files, AG2843—Institute for Contextual Theology, UWHP. Broadcasters to Receive Awards at NRB '86, National Religious Broadcasters, February 2–5, 1986, Folder 11, NRB Press Releases, carton 23, Sara Diamond Papers, BANC MSS 98/70, Collection on the US Right [ca. 1950s–1997], UC Berkeley Bancroft Library Manuscripts Collection (BLMC), Berkeley, California.

19. Larry Kickham, "How U.S. Evangelicals Bless Apartheid," 1987, Folder: Jr, Right-Wing Religion, AG2843—Institute for Contextual Theology, University of Witwatersrand Historical Papers (UWHP), Johannesburg, South Africa.
20. "Mokoena Abducted, Assaulted, and Robbed Following His Plea to be Heard," United Christian Action Press Release, November 26, 1986, Box 9, United Christian Action, UCA News 1986–1992, South Africa, SC 79, Intercessors for the Suffering Church Collection, Mary Ann Gilbert, Serials Correspondence, WCSC.
21. "Mokoena Abducted, Assaulted, and Robbed," WCSC.
22. Kickham, "How U.S. Evangelicals Bless Apartheid."
23. "Picket Against Apartheid Collaborators," Capital District Coalition Against Apartheid and Racism, March 25, 1991, http://kora.matrix.msu.edu/files/50/304/32-130-168-84-african_activist_archive-a0a703-b_12419.pdf.
24. Nina Easton, *Gang of Five: Leaders at the Center of the Conservative Ascendancy* (Simon & Schuster, 2002).
25. "Have Sanctions Worked? An International Conference of the Effects of Sanctions on the Process of Peaceful Reform in South Africa," Jefferson Educational Foundation, October 21, 1987, South Africa Sanctions, October 1987—January 28, 1988, RAC Box 16, African Affairs Directorate, NSC: Records, Collection: African Affairs Directorate, RRPL; Rueedi, *The Vaal Uprising of 1984*, 169.
26. Richard H. Schmidt, "South Africa Update," About My Father's Business, Inc., 1986, Folder 20, South Africa, carton 42, Sara Diamond Papers, BANC MSS 98/70, Collection on the US Right [ca. 1950s–1997], BLMC.
27. From 1989 to 1993, the US government registered About My Father's Business as a foreign agent of the GMR Group, a South African company assisting Pretoria in subverting global sanctions run by the Italian Mario Ricci. US Department of Justice, "Foreign Agents Registration Act," https://efile.fara.gov/ords/fara/f?p=1381:136:7586627165327:::136:P136_DATERANGE:N, accessed January 31, 2023; Martin Bailey, "Spy Hired to Bust Sanctions," *Observer*, April 26, 1987, 4. For the GMR Group's involvement in the corruption and subversion of the Seychelles government—Ricci's home base—see Stephen Ellis, "Africa and International Corruption: The Strange Case of South Africa and Seychelles," *African Affairs* 95, no. 379 (1996): 165–96.
28. "Have Sanctions Worked?"
29. IMDB, "David Balsiger Biography," https://www.imdb.com/name/nm0051142/bio/.
30. "The Odd History of Sanctions Busting Bishop," *Mail and Guardian*, July 21, 1989, https://mg.co.za/article/1989-07-21-00-the-odd-history-of-sanctions-busting-bishop/.
31. Stephen Ellis, "Mbokodo: Security in ANC Camps, 1961–1990," *African Affairs* 93, no. 371 (April 1994): 283, 289.
32. Stephen Ellis, *External Mission: The ANC in Exile, 1960–1990* (Oxford University Press, 2013), 154, 176; Paul Trewhela, *Inside Quatro: Uncovering the Exile History of the ANC and SWAPO* (Jacana Media, 2009).
33. "Denton Hearings," 349.
34. Dlamini, *The Terrorist Album*, 240.
35. Denton Hearings, March 22, 1982, 386, 463.

36. "ANC Says It Assassinated Top Impimpi and Other Informers," *Sapa*, May 12, 1997, https://www.justice.gov.za/trc/media/1997/9705/s970512e.htm.
37. "The Media Target South Africa," *AIM Report*, Accuracy in Media, October, 1986, Box 1, AIM Report (Accuracy in Media Reporting), C 79, Intercessors for the Suffering Church Collection, Mary Ann Gilbert, Serials Correspondence, WCSC.
38. Joseph Lelyveld, "Bombs Damage Atom Plan Site in South Africa," *New York Times*, December 20, 1982.
39. Ellis, *External Mission*, 209
40. Shireen Hassim, "Family, Motherhood and Zulu Nationalism: The Politics of the Inkatha Women's Brigade," *Feminist Review*, no. 43 (1993): 2.
41. Thembisa Waetjen, "The 'Home' in Homeland: Gender, National Space, and Inkatha's Politics of Ethnicity," *Ethnic and Racial Studies* 22, no. 4 (1999): 655.
42. Waetjen, "The 'Home' in Homeland," 659; Michael MacInnes, "Inkatha, Propaganda, and Violence in KwaZulu-Natal in the 1980s and 1990s" (PhD diss., Chapman University, 2022), 7; Gerhard Maré and Georgina Hamilton, *An Appetite for Power: Buthelezi's Inkatha and South Africa* (Indiana University Press, 1988).
43. Mxolisi R. Mchunu, *Violence and Solace: The Natal Civil War in Late-Apartheid South Africa* (University of Virginia Press, 2021) 2.
44. Gerhard Maré, "Review of *Violence and Solace: The Natal Civil War in Late-Apartheid South Africa*," *South African Historical Journal* 73, no. 2 (2021): 545; and De Wet Potgieter, *Total Onslaught: Apartheid's Dirty Tricks Exposed* (Zebra, 2007), 6.
45. van der Westhuizen, *White Power*, 145.
46. "Marxist Violence in the Black Townships," by Don Tanner and Kirk Kidwell in "South Africa: Nation on Trial," *Family Protection Scoreboard*, 1987, Folder 20, South Africa, carton 42, Sara Diamond Papers, BANC MSS 98/70, Collection on the US Right [ca. 1950s–1997], BLMC.
47. van der Westhuizen, *White Power*, 144–45.
48. "Power-Sharing—When and How?," *Clarion Call*, Special Edition, "Inkatha and the Struggle for Liberation in South Africa," 1987, Kwazulu Bureau of Communications, Michigan State University Special Collections.
49. Jill E. Kelly and Liz Timbs, "The Rise and Fall of Mangosuthu Buthelezi," *Africa Is a Country*, December 11, 2017, https://www.sahistory.org.za/sites/default/files/archive_files/The%20rise%20and%20fall%20of%20Mangosuthu%20Buthelezi.pdf.
50. "Summary of 'South Africa's Champion of Nonviolence'" and "The South African Disinvestment Question in the Light of South and Southern African Realities," Mangosuthu Buthelezi, March 9, 1984, Box No. 15: South Africa, House Foreign Affairs Committee—Minority—General Files: South Africa—Soviet Union, RG 233—Records of the United States House of Representatives, Ninety-Ninth Congress, United States National Archives and Record Administration (NARA), Washington, DC.
51. Jill Kelly, *To Swim with Crocodiles: Land Violence and Belonging in South Africa, 1980–1996* (Michigan State University Press, 2018), 170.
52. Doug Tilton, "Creating an 'Educated Workforce:' Inkatha, Big Business, and Educational Reform in KwaZulu," *Journal of Southern African Studies* 18, no. 1 (March 1992): 167, 171.

53. Ben Temkin, *Buthelezi: A Biography* (Routledge, 2003), 251.
54. "Investment in SA—A Strategy for Liberation," *Clarion Call*, vol. 1, 1985, Kwazulu Bureau of Communications, vol. 1–4, Michigan State University Library Special Collections.
55. "The Recommendations," *Clarion Call*, vol. 2, 1985, Kwazulu Bureau of Communications, vol. 1–4, Michigan State University Special Collections.
56. Jabulani Sithole, "Neither Communists nor Saboteurs: KwaZulu Bantustan Politics," in *The Road to Democracy in South Africa, Volume 2 [1970–1980]* (Unisa Press, 2007), 823.
57. Kelly, *To Swim with Crocodiles*, xxix.
58. William R. Kennedy Jr., "America Lasters Are Making War on South Africa," *Conservative Digest*, August 1986, Box 2, South Africa, Background Information, re Sanctions (7 of 12), Series I: Subject File, Communications, Office of, Buchanan, Patrick: Files, RRPL.
59. Erik von Kuehnelt-Leddihn, "South Africa-Yesterday and Today," *Chronicles: A Magazine of American Culture*, May 1988, Folder 16, Paleoconservatives Chronicles, 1988–1990, carton 45, Sara Diamond Papers, BANC MSS 98/70, Collection on the US Right [ca. 1950s–1997], BLMC; Stephen Piggott, "Meet Jessica Vaughan, the Anti-Immigrant Movement's Representative at Tomorrow's Senate Judiciary Committee Hearing on DACA," *Southern Poverty Law Center*, October 2, 2017, https://www.splcenter.org/hatewatch/2017/10/02/meet-jessica-vaughan-anti-immigrant-movement%E2%80%99s-representative-tomorrow%E2%80%99s-senate-judiciary.
60. William A. Rusher, "Final Copy of 'A Short Course on South Africa,'" *National Review*, 1988, Folder 3: Books, A Short Course on South Africa, 1987–88, Box 184, William A. Rusher Papers, 1940–2010, Library of Congress (LOC), Washington DC.
61. Howard Ruff, *Financial Success Report* XII, no. 28 (August 4, 1986), WHORM Subject File (434700-435499), Box 171, CO 141, South Africa, RRPL.
62. "South Africa: Nation on Trial."
63. Robert Webb, "Zimbabwe Offers Ray of Hope for a Tired, Frightened World," *Cincinnati Inquirer*, December 7, 1980; Eric Brodin, "Policies in Review: A Fact-Finding Tour of Southern Africa," *Daily Record*, March 12, 1987.
64. Letter to Ronald Reagan from Frank Reilly, October 8, 1986, WHORM Subject File (428400-429999), Box 170, CO 141, South Africa, RRPL.
65. John Browne, "Visit to South Africa, 1–14 March 1986, Outline Assessment, General Observations," March 18, 1986, WHORM Subject File (383000-390999), Box 168, CO 141, South Africa, RRPL.
66. Christian M. Rogerson and Jayne M. Rogerson, "Racialized Landscapes of Tourism: From Jim Crow USA to Apartheid South Africa," *Bulletin of Geography: Socio-economic Series* 48 (2020): 7–21; Christian M. Rogerson, "Tourism Evolution in Rural South Africa: From Native Reserve to Apartheid Bantustans c. 1920–1994," *Geo Journal of Toruism and Geosites* 40, no. 1 (2022): 120–28; and D. H. Alderman and J. Inwood, "Towards a Pedagogy of Jim Crow: A Geographic Reading of the Green Book," in *Teaching Ethnic Geography in the 21st Century*, ed. L. E. Eastaville, E. J. Montalvo, and F. A. Akiwumi (National Council for Geographic Education, 2014), 68–87.
67. "Doing Well—Mangope," *SA Digest*, September 9, 1983, 5, Box VI A1.5 (19), South Africa Digest, 1983, SC #65, David O. Moberg, WCSC.

68. Ron Nixon, *Selling Apartheid: South Africa's Global Propaganda War* (Pluto, 2016), 17, 96.
69. See James Sanders, *South Africa and the International Media, 1972–1979: A Struggle for Representation* (Taylor & Francis, 2012); John Siko, *Inside South Africa's Foreign Policy: Diplomacy in Africa from Smuts to Mbeki* (I.B. Tauris, 2014); and Walter Pincus, "South Africa's Lobby," *Washington Post*, January 29, 1977, https://www.washingtonpost.com/archive/politics/1977/01/29/south-africas-lobby/31658102-763a-4811-8a3f-8fd4951566bc/.
70. Nixon, *Selling Apartheid*, 96.
71. Shiri Krebs, "The Legalization of Truth in International Fact-Finding," *Chicago Journal of International Law* 18, no. 1 (June 2017): 83–163.
72. Toby Rider and Matthew P. Llewellyn, "Barbarians, Bridge Builders, and Boycott: The British Sports Council's Fact-Finding Mission to South Africa," *International Journal of the History of Sport* 36, no. 1 (January 2019): 24–47.
73. George Bryant, "Fact-Finding Tour to South Africa," *Toronto Star*, February 14, 1987.
74. "Special Report: The Untold Story of South Africa," *Fundamentalist Journal*, 1985, Box 2, History of South African Movement, N.D., V. 1 I, Personal Papers of Chris Bunker, Series No. PP/329, UKL.
75. Alan Cowell, "Botha Sees South African Churchmen and Falwell," *New York Times*, August 20, 1985.
76. "Jerry Falwell: Champion of Apartheid?," *Congressional Record* 131, no. 111 (September 10, 1985): E3956.
77. James R. Dickenson, "Tutu a 'Phony,' Falwell Says: Moral Majority Leader Boosts South Africa," *Washington Post*, August 1985.
78. Augusta Dell'Omo, "Infernal Handiwork: Trinity Broadcasting Network Aids Apartheid South Africa, 1980–1994," *Diplomatic History* 45, no. 4 (2021): 779–80.
79. Memo for Peter Gemma from Howard Phillips, February 18, 1983, Folder 7A; CC 1:2 Box 63, CC 1-2-4 The Conservative Caucus, Jerry Falwell Library (JFL) at Liberty University, accessed online.
80. "The Donald McAlvany Story: Anti-Communism, Precious Metals, and the Globalist Agenda—Part I," *Faith, Family and Freedom with Curtis Bowers*, July 12, 2024, https://podcasts.apple.com/us/podcast/the-donald-mcalvany-story-anti-communism-precious/id1758382642?i=1000662769056.
81. David Corn and Jefferson Morley, "Beltway Bandits," *The Nation*, September 26, 1988, 288; Donald McAlvany, "Soviet Strategy for Conquest of South Africa," 1987, uploaded to YouTube January 10, 2012, accessed August 12, 2024, https://www.youtube.com/watch?v=-4vPgeKBh8s.
82. "13th Annual Geopolitical/Financial Tour of South Africa, Nov. 9–26, 1988," *McAlvany Intelligence Advisor*, n.d. 1990 + 1991, Box 5, SC 79, Intercessors for the Suffering Church Collection, Mary Ann Gilbert, Serials Correspondence, WCSC.
83. Nicola Sarah Van der Merwe, "Gambling in the Bophuthatswana Sun: Sun City and the Political Economy of a Bantustan Casino: 1965–1994" (thesis, University of the Witwatersrand, Johannesburg, 2017), 1–2.
84. Martin Bailey, "UK Firm Stakes a Claim in Sun City," *Observer*, September 13, 1987.

85. Christopher Connelly, "Apartheid Rock," *Rolling Stone*, June 10, 1982, https://www.rollingstone.com/music/music-news/apartheid-rock-108260/2/.
86. Martin Chilton, "'Sun City': How Little Steven Took on Apartheid, Opened the World's Eyes," *UDiscoverMusic*, October 25, 2023, https://www.udiscovermusic.com/stories/little-steven-sun-city-protest-song/.
87. Allen Palmeri, "Pastor Feels Empathy for South Africa, Country's Apartheid Doesn't Compare to American Segregation, Slimp Says," *Sun Herald*, April 24, 1993.
88. "South Africa Tour 'October 90," *Citizens Informer* 20, no. 2 (Winter 1989), CofCC, Folder HH167.47—Tri-State Informer, Box T-23, Part II, HHC.
89. "Metro—South Citzen's Council Places South Africa Ad," *Citizens Informer* 18, no. 4 (Fall 1986), CofCC, Folder HH334C:5—Tri-State Informer, Box T-23, Part II, HHC.
90. Robyn Kimberley Autry, "The Monumental Reconstruction of Memory in South Africa: The Voortrekker Monument," *Theory, Culture and Society* 29, no. 6 (2012): 146–64.
91. "St. Louis Group Finds Media Distorts South Africa's Image," *Citizens Informer* 16, no. 3 (Summer 1984), CofCC, Folder HH328A:124—Tri-State Informer, Box T-23, Part II, HHC.
92. Stephen A. Emerson, "The Battle for Mozambique: The South African Factor," *Journal of the Middle East and Africa* 5 (2014): 66; Stephen R. Davis, *The ANC's War Against Apartheid: Umkhonto We Sizwe and the Liberation of South Africa* (Indiana University Press, 2018), 9, 16, 22, 213.
93. Constitution of the Frontline Fellowship, Frontline Fellowship, undated, Box 3, Frontline Fellowship, News/Prayer Letters, 1984–1995, SC 79, Intercessors for the Suffering Church Collection, Mary Ann Gilbert, Serials Correspondence, WCSC.
94. "Mozambique Report: Eyewitness Testimonies of Persecution and Atrocities," Frontline Fellowship, 1986, Box 3, Frontline Fellowship, News/Prayer Letters, 1984–1995, SC 79, Intercessors for the Suffering Church Collection, Mary Ann Gilbert, Serials Correspondence, WCSC.
95. "Mozambique Report," International Society for Human Rights, September 1986, and Robert Chambers, "Invitation to Attend Human Rights in Southern Africa Meeting," International Society for Human Rights, March 29, 1986, Folder 4, Southern Africa, carton 43, Sara Diamond Papers, BANC MSS 98/70, Collection on the US Right [ca. 1950s–1997], BLMC.
96. "West German Day of the Churches: Only the ANC Can Abolish Apartheid," Gospel Defense League, Box 9, United Christian Action, UCA News 1986–1992, South Africa, SC 79, Intercessors for the Suffering Church Collection, Mary Ann Gilbert, Serials Correspondence, WCSC; "Our Path," Kirchentag, https://www.kirchentag.de/en/about-kirchentag.
97. For more on Cindy and Dorothea, see chapter 5. "South African Public Responds Magnificently to UCA's Call for Help," United Christian Action Press Release, June 5, 1987, Box 9, United Christian Action, UCA News 1986–1992, South Africa, SC 79, Intercessors for the Suffering Church Collection, Mary Ann Gilbert, Serials Correspondence, WCSC.
98. "Special Report," Kirchentag 1987, Frontline Fellowship 1987, Box 3, Frontline Fellowship, News/Prayer Letters, 1984–1995, SC 79, Intercessors for the Suffering Church Collection, Mary Ann Gilbert, Serials Correspondence, WCSC.

99. Letter from David Martin of the Southern Africa Research and Documentation Centre to Tore Hem, NORAD, July 23, 1987, Folder 4, Southern Africa, Sara Diamond Papers, carton 43, BANC MSS 98/70, Collection on the US Right [ca. 1950s–1997], BLMC.
100. "Revolutionaries in South Africa Strengthen Their Power," United Christian Action March 19, 1986, Box 9, United Christian Action, UCA News 1986–1992, South Africa, SC 79, Intercessors for the Suffering Church Collection, Mary Ann Gilbert, Serials Correspondence, WCSC.
101. "Information for Intercessors," Frontline Fellowship, May 16, 1987, Wheaton College Special Collections, SC 79, Intercessors for the Suffering Church Collection, Mary Ann Gilbert, Serials Correspondence, Box 3, Frontline Fellowship, News/Prayer Letters, 1984–1995, WCSC.
102. "America in Decline: Debt: Democrats, Astrology, and Sanctions," *The McAlvany Intelligence Advisor*, May 1988, Folder: Jr, Right-Wing Religion, AG2843—Institute for Contextual Theology, UWHP.
103. Arthur Lewis, "The Night Is Far Spent," Rhodesia Christian Group, February 1982, Box 8, Rhodesia Christian Group Newsletter, 1982–1990, SC 79, Intercessors for the Suffering Church Collection, Mary Ann Gilbert, Serials Correspondence, WCSC.
104. "The Valley of the Shadow," Rhodesia Christian Group.
105. "Information for Intercessors," Frontline Fellowship.
106. Jane Mayer and Doyle McManus, *Landslide: The Unmaking of President Reagan* (Fontana/Collins, 1989).
107. Edmund Fawcett, *Conservatism: The Fight for a Tradition* (Princeton University Press, 2020), 330.
108. van der Westhuizen, *White Power*, 88.
109. "African Elections Database," last updated February 24, 2011, accessed August 12, 2024, https://africanelections.tripod.com/za.html.
110. Letter from America, United Christian Action Press Release, October 29, 1986, Box 9, United Christian Action, UCA News 1986–1992, South Africa, SC 79, Intercessors for the Suffering Church Collection, Mary Ann Gilbert, Serials Correspondence, WCSC.
111. "Tread Safely Into the Unknown," Good Hope Christian Group Newsletter, December 1988, Box 3, Good Hope Christian Group Newsletter, 1988–1991, SC 79, Intercessors for the Suffering Church Collection, Mary Ann Gilbert, Serials Correspondence, WCSC.
112. Parker quoted in "UNISA Professor of Theological Ethics on Negotiations with the ANC," United Christian Action, February 8, 1988, Box 9, United Christian Action, UCA News 1986–1992, South Africa, SC 79, Intercessors for the Suffering Church Collection, Mary Ann Gilbert, Serials Correspondence, WCSC.
113. "Truth out of South Africa," *Ivor Benson's Behind the News*, February 1985, Folder 3, Ivor Benson, carton 31, Sara Diamond Papers, BANC MSS 98/70, Collection on the US Right [ca. 1950s–1997], BLMC.
114. "Terrorism: The Rhetoric and the Reality," *Ivor Benson's Behind the News*, August 1985, Folder 3, Ivor Benson, carton 31, Sara Diamond Papers, BANC MSS 98/70, Collection on the US Right [ca. 1950s–1997], BLMC.

115. Stephanie Schoeman, "Undermine Their Culture and a People Perishes in South Africa . . . and Everywhere," DT 1971.S35 1987, Radicalism, Michigan State University Special Collections.
116. Letter from America, United Christian Action.
117. "The Kingdom Way," from Christian Biblical America, April 1985, Folder 437A: Christian Biblical America, Box C-49, Part II, HHC.
118. "South Africa and the U.S.A.," National Socialist Vanguard Report, April/June 1986, Folder 19, National Socialist Vanguard, carton 31, Sara Diamond Papers, BANC MSS 98/70, Collection on the US Right [ca. 1950s–1997], BLMC.
119. The Southern National Newsletter, the Southern National Party, Volume 9, No. 3, Spring 1987, Folder 20, Neo Nazis, carton 31, Sara Diamond Papers, BANC MSS 98/70, Collection on the US Right [ca. 1950s–1997], BLMC.

3. MAKING AND BREAKING CONSTRUCTIVE ENGAGEMENT

1. "UCA Thanks US President Reagan for His Stand Against Sanctions," United Christian Action, July 23, 1986, Box 9, United Christian Action, UCA News 1986–1992, South Africa, Serials Correspondence, SC 79, Intercessors for the Suffering Church Collection, Mary Ann Gilbert, Wheaton College Special Collections (WCSC), Wheaton, Illinois.
2. See Christabel Gurney, "In the Heart of the Beast: The British Anti-Apartheid Movement, 1959–1994"; William Minter and Sylvia Hill, "Anti-apartheid Solidarity in the United-States-South African Relations: From the Margins to the Mainstream"; Joan Fairweather, "Canadian Solidarity with South Africa's Liberation Struggle"; Peter Limb, "The Anti-apartheid Movements in Australia and Aotearoa/New Zealand"; and Hans-Georg Schleicher, "The German Democratic Republic and the South African Liberation Struggle," in *The Road to Democracy in South Africa, Volume 3, International Solidary* (Unisa Press, 2003).
3. Dylan Valley "Spike Lee, *Do the Right Thing* and the Cultural Boycott of Apartheid South Africa," *Safundi* 20, no. 4 (2019): 404–6; and Jane Duncan, "Cultural Boycotts as Tools for Social Change: Lessons from South Africa," *Transformation (Durban, South Africa)* 92, no. 1 (2016): 60–83.
4. Letter from P. W. Botha to Ronald Reagan, May 12, 1981, South Africa: Presidential Correspondence (5/21/1981–11/23/1983), RAC Box 16, Collection: African Affairs Directorate, NSC, Box 8, African Affairs Directorate, National Security Council (NSC): Records, RRPL.
5. Letter from Ronald Reagan to P. W. Botha, June 11, 1981, South Africa: Presidential Correspondence (5/21/1981–11/23/1983), RAC Box 16, Collection: African Affairs Directorate, NSC, Box 8, African Affairs Directorate, NSC: Records, RRPL.
6. Pik Botha has no relation to P. W. Botha. For clarity, I will always use Pik when referring to Pik Botha. Memorandum for the President from Alexander M. Haig, Jr., Subject: Summing up of Pik Botha Visit, May 20, 1981, Volume I, 1/20/81–12/31/82, Box 4, South Africa, NSC: Country File: Records, NSC Staff and Office Files, Executive Secretariat, RRPL.

7. Cable from American Consulate Cape Town to Secretary of State Washington D.C., Subject: Meeting with Prime Minister P.W. Botha/Ambassador Nickel, April 22, 1982, Vol I 1/20/81–12/31/82 [1 of 7], Box 4, South Africa, NSC: Country File: Records, NSC Staff and Office Files, Executive Secretariat, RRPL.
8. *South African Digest* for Week Ended March 20, 1981 and *South African Digest* for Week Ended April 17, 1981, Box VI A 1.4. (13), *South African Digest*, January–June 1981, SC 65, David O. Moberg, WCSC.
9. *South African Digest* for Week Ended May 22, 1981, Box VI A 1.4. (13), *South African Digest*, January–June 1981, SC 65, David O. Moberg, WCSC.
10. *South African Digest* for Week Ended June 26, 1981, Box VI A 1.4. (13), *South African Digest*, January–June 1981, SC 65, David O. Moberg, WCSC.
11. *South African Digest* for Week Ended November 6, 1981, Box VI A 1.4. (13), *South African Digest*, July–November 1981, SC #65, David O. Moberg, WCSC.
12. The Reagan administration developed this particular structure, which included the vice president, the secretary of defense, the secretary of state, the assistant for national security affairs, and the director of the Central Intelligence Agency.
13. National Security Planning Group, March 24, 1981, from Richard V. Allen, NSPG 0003, 24 March 1981 [South Africa; Nicaragua], Box 91305, NSC: NSPGs, Box 1, Records, Collection: Executive Secretariat, Executive Secretariat, NSC: National Security Planning Group (NSPG): RRPL.
14. "National Security Council Meeting on Poland; Nicaragua/Central America; Southern Africa," NSC, March 26, 1981, NSC 00006, 26 March 1981, Box 91282, NSC: Meeting Files, Executive Secretariat, RRPL.
15. Joseph Lelyveld, "Reagan's Views on South Africa Praised by Botha," *New York Times*, March 5, 1981, https://www.nytimes.com/1981/03/05/world/reagan-s-views-on-south-africa-praised-by-botha.html.
16. "National Security Council Meeting on Poland; Nicaragua/Central America; Southern Africa," NSC.
17. Letter from Ronald Reagan to P. W. Botha, November 23, 1983, Memorandum for Robert C. McFarlane from Charles Hill, Subject: Suggested Letter to South African Prime Minister Botha, November 18, 1983, South Africa: Presidential Correspondence (5/21/1981–11/23/1983), RAC Box 16, Collection: African Affairs Directorate, NSC, Box 8, African Affairs Directorate, NSC: Records, RRPL.
18. Letter from P. W. Botha to Ronald Reagan, December 1, 1983, South Africa: Presidential Correspondence (12/01/1983–05/18/1984), RAC Box 16, Collection: African Affairs Directorate, NSC, Box 8, African Affairs Directorate, NSC: Records, RRPL.
19. Cable from American Consulate Cape Town to Secretary of State, Subject: Namibia's South African Response to Contact Group Message, September 30, 1981, South Africa—Working File [08/01/1981—03/31/1981], Box 9, Collection: African Affairs Directorate, NSC, Box 1, African Affairs Directorate, NSC: Records, RRPL. For more on the HNP and its ultraconservative counterpart, the Conservative Party, see F. A. Mouton, "'Dr No': A.P. Treurnicht and the Ultra-Conservative Quest to Maintain Afrikaner Supremacy, 1982–1993," *South African Historical Journal* 65, no. 4 (2013): 577–95.

20. Cable from American Consulate Cape Town to Secretary of State, Subject: Namibia: Pik Botha's Comment on Press Leaks About Zurich Talks, September 30, 1981, Box 4, South Africa Vol I 1/20/81–12/31/82 [2 of 7], NSC: Country File: Records, NSC Staff and Office Files, Executive Secretariat, RRPL.
21. Cable from American Consulate Cape Town to Secretary of State, Subject: P.W., Pik, and Malan in Windhoek: Pik Briefs Charged, November 10, 1981, Vol I 1/20/81–12/31/82 [2 of 7], Box 4, South Africa NSC: Country File: Records, National Security Council (NSC) Staff and Office Files, Executive Secretariat, RRPL.
22. Cable from American Embassy Cape Town to Assistant Secretary of Crocker in Dakar, October 23, 1981, Subject: Pik and the Prospects of a SWAPO Victory, Vol I 1/20/81–12/31/82 [1 of 7], Box 4, South Africa NSC: Country File: Records, National Security Council (NSC) Staff and Office Files, Executive Secretariat, RRPL.
23. Matthew P. Llewellyn and Toby C. Rider, "Sport, Thatcher, and Apartheid Politics: The Zola Budd Affair," *Journal of Southern African Studies* 44, no. 4 (2018): 575–92; E. H. H. Green, *Thatcher* (Hodder Education, 2006), 151; R. Hyam and P. Henshaw, *The Lion and the Springbok: Britain and South Africa Since the Boer War* (Cambridge University Press, 2007), 18.
24. Shirdath Ramphal, "Mandela's Freedom, the Commonwealth and the Apartheid Axis," *The Round Table* 106, no. 6 (2017): 620.
25. Hallvard Kvale Svenbalrud, "Apartheid and NATO: Britain, Scandinavia, and the Southern Africa Question in the 1970s," *Diplomacy and Statecraft* 23 (2012): 746–62.
26. Saul Dubow, "New Approaches to High Apartheid and Anti-Apartheid," *South African Historical Journal* 67, no. 2 (2017): 316, 321–22; Sam Matthews Boehmer, "Questionable Allies: British Collaboration with Apartheid South Africa, 1960–90," *International History Review* 46, no. 1 (2024): 102–19; and Josiah Brownell, "'One Last Retreat': Racial Nostalgia and Population Panic in Smith's Rhodesia and Powell's Britain," in *Global White Nationalism: From Apartheid to Trump*, ed. Daniel Geary, Camilla Schofield, and Jennifer Sutton (Manchester University Press, 2020).
27. Rob Skinner, "The Moral Foundations of British Anti-Apartheid Activism, 1946-1960," *Journal of Southern African Studies* 35, no. 2 (2009): 399–416; Roger Fieldhouse, *Anti-Apartheid: A History of the Movement in Britain: A Study in Pressure Groups* (Merlin, 2005); and "How ANC/Swapo use London's 'Red Ken,'" *Aida Parker Newsletter*, February 16, 1984, *Aida Parker Newsletter*, No. 1 March 1983—No. 32 May 1984 + No. 71 (incomplete), APC Periodicals, Alan Paton Centre and Struggle Archives (APC), University of KwaZulu-Natal, Pietermaritzburg, South Africa.
28. Katharina Karcher, "Violence for a Good Cause? The Role of Violent Tactics in West German Solidarity Campaigns for Better Working and Living Conditions in the Global South in the 1980s," *Contemporary European History* 28, no. 4 (November 2019): 566–80; and Heike Hartmann and Susann Lewerenz, "Campaigning Against Apartheid in East and West Germany," *Radical History Review* 119 (Spring 2014): 193.
29. Daniel Manulak, "'An African Representative': Canada, the Third World, and South African Apartheid, 1984–1990," *Journal of Imperial and Commonwealth History* 49, no. 2 (2021): 370.

30. Daniel Manulak, "A Marathon, Not a Sprint: Canada and South African Apartheid, 1987–1990," *International Journal* 75, no. 1 (March 2020): 85.
31. Michael Bueckert, "Boycotts and Revolution: Debating the Legitimacy of the African National Congress in the Canadian Anti-Apartheid Movement, 1969–94," *Radical History Review* 134 (May 2019): 107.
32. Gareth Evans, "Commonwealth Diplomacy and the End of Apartheid," *Round Table* 106, no. 1 (2017): 61–69.
33. "Let's Be Hawkish with the Aussies," *Aida Parker Newsletter*, October 13, 1983, *Aida Parker Newsletter*, No. 1 March 1983—No. 32 May 1984 + No. 71 (incomplete), APC Periodicals, APC.
34. Memorandum of Conversation, Subject: Summary of the Vice President's Meeting with Chancellor Helmut Schmidt of the Federal Republic of Germany, May 22, 1981, Box 47, Memorandums of Conversation—Vice President Bush (04/29/81–7/82), NSC: Subject File, Executive Secretariat, RRPL.
35. Memorandum of Conversation, Subject: Summary of the President's Meeting with Prime Minister Malcolm Fraser of the Commonwealth of Australia, June 30, 1981, Box 49, Memorandums of Conversation—President Reagan [July 1981], NSC: Subject File, Executive Secretariat, RRPL.
36. Cable from American Embassy in Cape Town to Secretary of State, June 20, 1981, Subject: Namibia: Is South Africa Emphasizing USG Differences with Rest of the Contact Group?, vol. I 1/20/81–12/31/82 [2 of 7], Box 4, South Africa, NSC: Country File: Records, National Security Council (NSC) Staff and Office Files, Executive Secretariat, RRPL.
37. Cable from American Embassy in Cape Town to Secretary of State, September 30, 1981, Subject: Namibia: Pik Botha's Comment on Press leaks about Zurich talks, vol. I 1/20/81–12/31/82 [2 of 7], Box 4, South Africa, NSC: Country File: Records, National Security Council (NSC) Staff and Office Files, Executive Secretariat, RRPL.
38. Cable from American Embassy in Cape Town to Secretary of State, October 9, 1981, Subject: Pik/Charge Conversations, vol. I 1/20/81–12/31/82 [2 of 7], Box 4, South Africa, NSC: Country File: Records, National Security Council (NSC) Staff and Office Files, Executive Secretariat, RRPL.
39. Cable from American Embassy in Cape Town to Secretary of State, January 30, 1982, Subject: USG-SAG Bilaterals, South Africa vol. I 1/20/81–12/31/82 [1 of 7], Box 4, NSC: Country File: Records, NSC Staff and Office Files, RRPL.
40. Cable from American Consulate Cape Town to Secretary of State, Subject: Second Constitutional Report: A Preliminary Appreciation, November 29, 1982, South Africa—Working File: [02/13/1982–12/31/1982], Box 9, Collection: African Affairs Directorate, NSC, Box 2, African Affairs Directorate, NSC: Records, RRPL.
41. Craig Charney, "Class Conflict and the National Party Split," *Journal of Southern African Studies* 10, no. 2 (April 1984): 275.
42. "Stop ANC Terrorism . . . Reform Don't Deform," and "Support Freedom and Security in S.A.," National Student Federation, Box 5, National Student Federation (NSF), Pamphlets, handouts, info, SC 79, Intercessors for the Suffering Church Collection, Mary Ann Gilbert, Serials Correspondence, WCSC.

43. Cable from American Consulate Cape Town to Secretary of State, Subject: REDACTED discusses regional situation, November 17, 1982, Box 4, South Africa, vol. I 1/20/81–12/31/82 [1 of 7], NSC: Country File: Records, National Security Council (NSC) Staff and Office Files, Executive Secretariat, RRPL.
44. *South African Digest* for the week ended July 2, 1982, Box VI A1.5, *South Africa Digest*, 1982, SC 65, David O. Moberg, WCSC.
45. Cable from American Consulate Cape Town to Secretary of State, Subject: Message from Secretary to Foreign Minister Botha, August 28, 1982, vol. I 1/20/81–12/31/82 [3 of 7], Box 4, South Africa, NSC: Country File: Records, National Security Council (NSC) Staff and Office Files, Executive Secretariat, RRPL.
46. Cable from American Consulate Cape Town to Secretary of State, Subject: Pik Botha's Views on Angolan Talks, Soviet Intentions, and US Analysis, March 4, 1983, vol. II 1/1/83–11/21/85, [1 of 3], Box 4, South Africa, NSC: Country File: Records, National Security Council (NSC) Staff and Office Files, Executive Secretariat, RRPL.
47. Cable from American Consulate Cape Town to Secretary of State, Subject: Senator Kassebaum's Meeting with Pik Botha, January 4, 1983, Box 4, South Africa, vol. II 1/1/83–11/21/85, [3 of 3], NSC: Country File: Records, National Security Council (NSC) Staff and Office Files, Executive Secretariat, RRPL.
48. Cable from American Consulate Cape Town to Secretary of State, Subject: South Africa Downgrades Talks with Angolans and Terminates Dialogue with Mozambique, March 6, 1983, vol. II 1/1/83–11/21/85, [1 of 3], Box 4, South Africa, NSC: Country File: Records, National Security Council (NSC) Staff and Office Files, Executive Secretariat, RRPL.
49. Cable from American Consulate Cape Town to Secretary of State, Subject: AS Abrams Meeting with Foreign Minister R. F. Botha, November 22, 1982, vol. I 1/20/81–12/31/82 [1 of 7], Box 4, South Africa, NSC: Country File: Records, National Security Council (NSC) Staff and Office Files, Executive Secretariat, RRPL.
50. Memorandum for the President from George P. Shultz, Subject: Southern Africa: Status of Our Negotiation Effort, June 6, 1983, vol. II 1/1/83–11/21/85, [3 of 3], Box 4, South Africa, NSC: Country File: Records, NSC Staff and Office Files, Executive Secretariat, RRPL.
51. Memorandum of Conversation, Subject: Presidential Meeting with Zambian President Kenneth Kaunda, March 30, 1983, Memorandums of Conversation—President Reagan (2/15/83–03/31/83), Box 51, NSC: Subject File, Executive Secretariat, RRPL.
52. Memorandum of Conversation, Subject: Presidential Meeting with Zaire President Mobutu, August 4, 1983, Memorandums of Conversation—President Reagan (07/27/83–08/14/83), Box 51, NSC: Subject File, Executive Secretariat, RRPL.
53. Memorandum of Conversation, Subject: Presidential Meeting with Zimbabwe Prime Minister Robert Mugabe, September 13, 1983, Memorandums of Conversation—President Reagan (08/15/83–09/25/83), Box 51, NSC: Subject File, Executive Secretariat, RRPL.
54. Memorandum of Conversation, Subject: Presidential Meeting with Cape Verde President Aristides Pereira, October 3, 1983, Memorandums of Conversation—President Reagan (October 1983), Box 52, NSC: Subject File, Executive Secretariat, RRPL.

55. *South African Digest* for the week ended February 25, 1983, Box VI A1.5, *South Africa Digest*, 1983, SC 65, David O. Moberg, WCSC.
56. *South African Digest* for the week ended October 14, 1983, Box VI A1.5 (19), *South Africa Digest*, SC 65, David O. Moberg, 1983, WCSC.
57. *South African Digest* for the week ended December 14, 1984, Box VI A1.5 (19), *South Africa Digest*, 1984, SC 65, David O. Moberg, WCSC.
58. Michael Hurry, *Who Holds the Balance? An Examination of Patterns of Subversion, Worldwide Conspiracy and Culture-Alienation, as Promoted in the Media of Mass Communication* (Veritas, 1984), 28, HV6275.H877 1984, Collection on Radicalism, Michigan State University Special Collections.
59. "High Stakes in the Divestment Campaign Against SA," *Aida Parker Newsletter*, no. 43, October 1984, Folder 8: General Correspondence, South African Embassy, 1982–88, Box 84, Collection, William A. Rusher Papers, 1940–2010, LOC.
60. "St. Louis Group Finds Media Distorts South Africa's Image," *Citizens Informer* 16, no. 3, Council of Conservative Americans, Summer 1984, Folder HH328A:124—Tri-State Informer, Box T-23, Part II, HHC.
61. Letter to William Rusher from Carl Nöffke, May 24, 1984, Folder 8: General Correspondence, South African Embassy, 1982–1988, Box 84, William A. Rusher Papers, 1940–2010, LOC.
62. Cable from American Consulate Cape Town to Secretary of State, Subject: Text of Letter from Botha to Reagan delivered by Fourie, February 22, 1984, South Africa: Presidential Correspondence (12/01/1983–05/18/1984), RAC Box 16, Collection: African Affairs Directorate, NSC, Box 8, African Affairs Directorate, NSC: Records, RRPL.
63. Letter from Ronald Reagan to P. W. Botha, May 11, 1984, South Africa: Presidential Correspondence (12/01/1983–05/18/1984), RAC Box 16, Collection: African Affairs Directorate, NSC, Box 8, African Affairs Directorate, NSC: Records, RRPL.
64. Letter from Jack Kemp to Howard Phillips, February 14, 1985, Folder 4A; CC 1:2, Box 111, CC 1-2-6, JFL, https://cdm17184.contentdm.oclc.org/digital/collection/p17184coll12/id/113589/rec/14.
65. Michael Weisskopf, "Kemp's Racial Awakening: Candidate's Experiences in Pro Football Led Him Away from Republican Mainstream," *Washington Post*, October 8, 1996, https://www.washingtonpost.com/archive/politics/1996/10/09/kemps-racial-awakening/6f0e831d-78c9-4d69-b2b0-7545842aee68/.
66. Memorandum for Robert C. McFarlane from Charles Hill, Subject: Recent South Africa Violence and US Reaction, September 11, 1984, Box 4, South Africa Vol II 1/1/83–11/21/85 [1 of 3], NSC: Country File: Records, National Security Council (NSC) Staff and Office Files, Executive Secretariat, RRPL; and Alex Thomson, *U.S. Foreign Policy Towards Apartheid South Africa, 1948–1994* (Palgrave Macmillan, 2008), 131.
67. Memorandum for Robert C. McFarlane from Charles Hill, Subject: Briefing for the President on Developments in Southern Africa, November 29, 1984, Box 4, South Africa, vol. II 1/1/83–11/21/85 [1 of 3], NSC: Country File: Records, NSC Staff and Office Files, Executive Secretariat, RRPL.

68. "The Struggle Against Apartheid," *South African Labour Bulletin* 28, no. 6 (December 2004): 33, https://www.southafricanlabourbulletin.org.za/wp-content/uploads/2021/11/The-struggle-against-apartheid-1984–1990.pdf; and Michael Parks, "200,000 Blacks Strike at Mines in South Africa," *Los Angeles Times*, August 10, 1987.
69. Allister Sparks, "S. Africa Expands Arrests in Crackdown on Unions," *Washington Post*, November 15, 1984, https://www.washingtonpost.com/archive/politics/1984/11/15/s-africa-expands-arrests-in-crackdown-on-unions/437782ab-aaaa-41a3-8240-b2ec3dbbdc59/; and Francis Njubi Nesbitt, *Race for Sanctions: African Americans Against Apartheid, 1946–1994* (Indiana University Press, 2004), 124.
70. Nesbitt, *Race for Sanctions*, 124.
71. Letter to Ronald Reagan from the Congressional Black Caucus, September 10, 1984, WHORM Subject File, (219000–246999), Box 165, CO 141, South Africa, RRPL.
72. Letter from Nancy Kassebaum and Richard Lugar to Ronald Reagan, November 30, 1984, WHORM Subject File, (259000–259399), Box 165, CO 141, South Africa, RRPL.
73. Memorandum for Robert McFarlane from Phillip Ringdahl, Subject: Crocker's Request for Assistance on South Africa, December 17, 1984, South Africa—Working Files 3 (10), October 1984 to June 1986, RAC Box 9, Collection: African Affairs Directorate, NSC, Box 2, African Affairs Directorate, NSC, Records, RRPL.
74. "Black People in South Africa Are Getting a Better Deal," *The Standard*, Student Moderate Alliance, 3rd Quarter, 1984, C3/9/136, 1984, Okt, Box 249, PV 203, Archive of Contemporary Affairs (ARCA) at the University of the Free State, Bloemfontein, South Africa.
75. "The Struggle Continues: Namibia Week," Student Moderate Alliance, 1984, 1984, Okt, C3/9/136, Box 249, PV 203, ARCA.
76. "Walking Down the Aisle to Constructive Change," Student Moderate Alliance, 1984, 1984, Okt, C3/9/136, Box 249, PV 203, ARCA.
77. "Apartheid—How Much Longer?," International Society for Human Rights, 1986, Folder M7/6/6, vol. 7, 1986, Box 183, PV 734, ARCA.
78. "A Misguided Weapon—Divestment," Student Moderate Alliance, 1984, 1984, Okt, C3/9/136, Box 249, PV 203, ARCA.
79. Ron Nixon, *Selling Apartheid: South Africa's Global Propaganda War* (Pluto, 2016), 179, 181.
80. The Inkathagate revelations exposed South African state funding for this Buthelezi launched project, which was designed to oppose the Congress of South African Trade Unions and their support for sanctions. Jeremy Baskin, *Striking Back: A History of COSATU* (Routledge, 1991), 134. The union and its Inkatha allies frequently clashed with ANC-aligned unions, including at one Inkatha rally in 1986 that led to the abduction and killing of three prominent Metal and Allied Workers' Union leaders, fueling union violence in Natal. Sarmcol Strike, "The Truth Commission," https://sabctrc.saha.org.za/glossary/sarmcol_strike.htm?tab=victims.
81. "Understanding Sanctions," International Freedom Foundation, 1988, 9, 17–25, 47–48, B8/26, 1988, Box 216, PV 203, ARCA.
82. A survey of over 500 industrial workers in South Africa conducted by Professor Lawrence Schlemmer, vice president of the South African Institute of Race Relations, shows

that divestment "cannot claim to be a campaign for the black rank-and-file people of South Africa." According to Schlemmer, over 75 percent of workers rejected US disinvestment. The study—paid for in part by the Reagan administration—proved a hit among pro-apartheid activists, despite widespread criticism of Schlemmer's methodology and assumptions by scholars and activists. The report's author, Dr. Lawrence Schlemmer, had close ties to Buthelezi, serving as director of the Inkatha Institute of South Africa for six years. For critiques of the Schlemmer study, see Michael Sutcliffe and Paul Wellings, "Disinvestment and Black Workers Attitudes in South Africa: A Critical Comment," *Review of African Political Economy* 34 (December 1985): 66–82; and Mark Orkin, "The Politics and Problematics of Survey Research," *American Behavioral Scientist* 42, no. 2 (October 1998), https://doi.org/10.1177/0002764298042002006.

83. "Understanding Sanctions," International Freedom Foundation.
84. Memo to Howard Phillips from David Sanders, July 1985, CC 1-2-6 CC 1:2 Box 117, JFL, https://cdm17184.contentdm.oclc.org/digital/collection/p17184coll12/id/103254/rec/15; "Member's Report," The Conservative Caucus, May 1986, CC 1-2-7 Folder 12C; CC 1:2 Box 128, JFL, https://cdm17184.contentdm.oclc.org/digital/collection/p17184coll12/id/130644/rec/8.
85. A memo for Helen Gombert from Howard Phillips from June 9, 1985, CC 1-2-6 Folder 15A; CC 1:2 Box 117, JFL, https://cdm17184.contentdm.oclc.org/digital/collection/p17184coll12/id/97866/rec/28.
86. Urgent Meeting, Conservative Caucus, August 2, 1985, CC 1-2-6 Folder 19B; CC 1:2 Box 120, JFL, https://cdm17184.contentdm.oclc.org/digital/collection/p17184coll12/id/99219/rec/32.
87. Sen. Wallop Denounces Hypocrisy of Lugar-Dole-Kennedy-Cranston Attack on South Africa, August 1985, CC 1-2-6 Folder 18B; CC 1:2 Box 118, JFL, https://cdm17184.contentdm.oclc.org/digital/collection/p17184coll12/id/105351/rec/38.
88. Jessica Ann Levy, "Black Power, Inc.: Global American Business and the Post-Apartheid City," *Enterprise and Society* 21, no. 4 (2020): 871.
89. Secretary George Shultz, "The U.S. Approach to South Africa," Current Policy No. 854, US Department of State Bureau of Public Affairs, 1986, 2, 4, Entry A1 1589, Records Relating to Major Publications, 1949–1990, Box 119, RG 59, NARA.
90. Jessica Levy, "Black Power in the Board Room: Leon Sullivan and the Corporate Anti-Apartheid Response," *Enterprise and Society* 21, no. 1 (March 2020): 185.
91. Mattie C. Webb, "'An Exercise in the Art of the Possible': Waging a Battle Against Apartheid in the South African Workplace," *Enterprise and Society* 25, no. 2 (2024): 334.
92. Leon Sullivan eventually called for a complete "withdrawal of all American companies doing business in South Africa" in an acknowledgement of the principles' ineffectiveness in 1987.
93. Howard Phillips, *Washington Dateline*, March 1985, V. 3 I, Box 2, History of South African Movement, 2/13/85–2/22/85, Personal Papers of Chris Bunker, Series No. PP/329, UKL.
94. Daniel O. Graham, "Intelligence Expert Defends South Africa Strategy for U.S.," *Spotlight*, March 4, 1985, V. 3 I, Box 2, History of South African Movement, 2/13/85–2/22/85, Personal Papers of Chris Bunker, Series No. PP/329, UKL.

95. John Chamberlain, "Otto J. Scott's *The Other End of the Lifeboat*," book review, The Chalcedon Foundation, June 1985, Folder 12, Chalcedon Foundation, Assorted Papers, 1988–1994, Carton 1, BANC MSS 98/70, Collection on the US Right [ca. 1950s–1997], Sara Diamond Papers, BLMC.
96. A draft of the Howard Phillips Issues and Strategies Bulletin, March 4, 1985, CC 1-2-6 Folder 4B; CC 1:2 Box 111, JFL, https://cdm17184.contentdm.oclc.org/digital/collection/p17184coll12/id/92754/rec/20.
97. A Letter to Conservative Caucus Supporter, CC 1-2-6 Folder 4B; CC 1:2 Box 111, JFL, https://cdm17184.contentdm.oclc.org/digital/collection/p17184coll12/id/90533/rec/21.
98. "Why Did Conservatives Join Anti-South Africa Briagde," *Human Events: The National Conservative Weekly*, vol. XLIV, no. 52, December 29, 1984, Box 5, 1982–1984, Collection: Human Events, RRPL.
99. Memorandum for Robert C. McFarlane, Subject: South African State President Botha's Letter to President Reagan, February 5, 1985, South Africa [1985] (3 of 3), RAC Box 9, Collection: African Affairs Directorate, NSC, Box 2, African Affairs Directorate, NSC: Records, RRPL.
100. Cable from American Consulate Pretoria to Secretary of State, Subject: Crocker Meeting with South African Minister of Cooperation Gerrit Viljoen, February 13, 1985, South Africa [1985] (3 of 3), RAC Box 9, Collection: African Affairs Directorate, NSC, Box 2, African Affairs Directorate, NSC: Records, RRPL.
101. South Africa: Two-Track Policy for Blacks, Bureau of Intelligence and Research—Analysis, February 24, 1985, South Africa [1985] (3 of 3), RAC Box 9, Collection: African Affairs Directorate, NSC, Box 2, African Affairs Directorate, NSC: Records, RRPL.
102. Memorandum for the President from Michael H. Armacost, Acting Secretary, March 2, 1985, Box 34, President Chron, 3/3/1985–3/4/1985, Situation Room, White House: Records, RRPL.
103. South Africa: A Dash of Reform in the Apartheid Stew, South Africa—Working Files 3 (9), October 1984 to June 1986, RAC Box 9, Collection: African Affairs Directorate, NSC, Box 2, African Affairs Directorate, NSC, Records, RRPL.
104. Statement on South African Arrests/Trials, March 1, 1985, South Africa [1985] (2 of 3), RAC Box 9, Collection: African Affairs Directorate, NSC, Box 2, African Affairs Directorate, NSC: Records, RRPL.
105. Memorandum for Robert C. McFarlane, Subject: Congressional Briefings on Southern Africa, March 9, 1985, South Africa—Congressional Briefings, RAC Box 16, Collection: African Affairs Directorate, NSC, Box 7, African Affairs Directorate, NSC: Records, RRPL.
106. Memorandum for Robert McFarlane from Phillip Ringdahl, Subject: Africa: Your Congressional Briefings on Southern Africa, March 20, 1985, South Africa—Congressional Briefings, RAC Box 16, Collection: African Affairs Directorate, NSC, Box 7, African Affairs Directorate, NSC: Records, RRPL.
107. Memorandum for Robert C. McFarlane from Ronald K. Sable, Subject: Congressional Briefing on Southern Africa, March 13, 1985, WHORM Subject File (220000-239999), Box 15, CO 001-01 (Africa), RRPL.

108. Alan Cowell, "South African Rightists Gain in Vote," *New York Times*, October 31, 1985, https://www.nytimes.com/1985/10/31/world/south-african-rightists-gain-in-vote.html.
109. Memorandum for the President from George P. Shultz, June 14, 1985, Box 35, President/NSC Chron, 6/15/1985–6/16/1985, Situation Room, White House: Records, RRPL.
110. Letter from John Sears to Pat Buchanan, June 17, 1985, WHORM Subject File (344500-347199), Box 167, CO 141, South Africa, RRPL.
111. Memorandum for Robert McFarlane from Phillip H. Ringdahl, Subject: South Africa—Meeting with Ambassador Nickel, Wednesday, 0900, June 19, 1985, June 20, 1985, South Africa—General—1985–1987 (1 of 4), RAC Box 10, Collection: African Affairs Directorate, NSC, Box 3, African Affairs Directorate, NSC: Records, RRPL.
112. "The Reagan Doctrine: Getting Out Before Really Getting Hurt," *American Review*, Institute for American Studies, Rand Afrikaans University, Summer 1985, Folder 8: General Correspondence, South African Embassy, 1982–88, Box 84, William A. Rusher Papers, 1940–2010, LOC.
113. "Naïve Congressmen Threaten South Africa," *Citizen's Informer* 17 (Winter 1985), CofCC, Folder HH328A:124—Tri-State Informer, Box T-23, Part II, HHC.
114. John Chamberlin, "Foreign Policy Dominated CPAC '85," *Human Events: The National Conservative Weekly* XLV, no. 12 (March 23, 1985), Box 6, 1985–1987, Collection: *Human Events*, RRPL.
115. The coalition was a who's who of South Africa's most ardent supporters, including Phillips, Paul Weyrich of the Coalitions for America, Jack Abramoff founder of the International Freedom Foundation (financed by apartheid South Africa), and Donald McAlvany. "Mr. President, Why Is Chester Crocker Trying to Sell 20 Million Black Africans Into Communist Slavery?," *Human Events: The National Conservative Weekly* XLV, no. 12 (March 23, 1985), Box 6, 1985–1987, Collection: *Human Events*, RRPL.
116. Ivor Benson's *Behind the News*, Ivor Benson, July 1985, Folder 3, Ivor Benson, Carton 31, Collection on the US Right [ca. 1950s–1997], Sara Diamond Papers, BANC MSS 98/70, UC Berkeley Bancroft Library Manuscripts Collection.
117. National Security Council Meeting on South Africa, July 26, 1985, NSC 119, July 26, 1985 (3/3), Box 6, Executive Secretariat NSC, NSC Meeting File, Collection: Executive Secretariat, NSC Meeting File, Box 12, RRPL.
118. Incoming Telegram from Pretoria, Subject: South Africa: Promise of Important Decisions, August 2, 1985, South Africa—Working Files 3 (3), October 1984 to June 1986, RAC Box 9, African Affairs Directorate, NSC, Records, Collection: African Affairs Directorate, NSC, Box 2, RRPL.
119. Note from Robert McFarlane to the NSDRF, Subject: Meeting with Pik Botha, August 8, 1985, South Africa: Public Diplomacy (10 of 11), RAC Box 16, Collection: African Affairs Directorate, NSC: Box 9, African Affairs Directorate, NSC: Records, RRPL.
120. "Address by State President P. W. Botha, August 15, 1985," O'Malley, https://omalley.nelsonmandela.org/index.php/site/q/03lv01538/04lv01600/05lv01638/06lv01639.htm.
121. Executive Secretariat Bureau of Intelligence and Research, Current Reports, August 16, 1985, South Africa—Working Files 3 (3), October 1984 to June 1986, RAC Box 9, Collection: African Affairs Directorate, NSC, Box 2, African Affairs Directorate, NSC, Records, RRPL.

122. Cable from Secretary of State to All African Diplomatic Posts, August 22, 1985, Subject: U.S. Assessment of South African Situation: After the P. W. Botha Speech, South Africa—Working Files 3 (2), October 1984 to June 1986, RAC Box 9, Collection: African Affairs Directorate, NSC, Box 2, African Affairs Directorate, NSC, Records, RRPL.
123. Memorandum for Phillip Ringdahl from William P. Martin, Subject: Secretary Shultz's Evening Report of, August 20, 1985, South Africa—Working Files 3 (2), October 1984 to June 1986, RAC Box 9, Collection: African Affairs Directorate, African Affairs Directorate, NSC, Records, NSC, Box 2, RRPL.
124. Robert McFarlane, "U.S. Says Talks Must Begin Quickly in South Africa," August 15, 1985, WHORM Subject File (344500-347199), Box 167, CO 141, South Africa, RRPL.
125. Memorandum to Chester Crocker from Herman Nickel, Subject: Our Public Diplomacy Initiative: The Theoretical Framework, South African: Public Diplomacy, (09/09/1985–09/05/1985), RAC Box 16, Collection: African Affairs Directorate, NSC: Box 9, African Affairs Directorate, NSC: Records, RRPL.
126. Meeting with the National Security Council, from Robert C. McFarlane, July 16, 1985, South Africa—Working Files 3 (5), October 1984 to June 1986, RAC Box 9, Collection: African Affairs Directorate, NSC, Box 2, African Affairs Directorate, NSC, Records, RRPL.

4. WHITE WOMEN FOR APARTHEID

1. *Winnie Mandela's Secret*, Accuracy in Media; Undated. Tape E168: South Africa Now Collection (MS 1818), 1990. Manuscripts and Archives, Yale University Library. For more on white women positioning as "mother figures," see Elizabeth Gillespie McRae, *Mothers of Massive Resistance: White Women and the Politics of White Supremacy* (Oxford University Press, 2018).
2. Although egregious claims about the mass killings of children are false, violence did target noncombatants as part of increasing unrest led by the ANC in the townships. Furthermore, the ANC did use necklacing as a tactic targeting "political sellouts" and those who opposed the ANC's vision for South Africa. Nevertheless, most violence in the township was at the hands of state forces and their Inkatha partners. Gary Kynoch, "Reassessing Transition Violence: Voices from South Africa's Township Wars, 1990–4," *African Affairs* 112, no. 447 (2013): 296, 283.
3. "1991: Mandela's Wife Jailed for Kidnaps," *BBC Home*, May 14, 1991, http://news.bbc.co.uk/onthisday/hi/dates/stories/may/14/newsid_2863000/2863807.stm, and Suzanne Daley, "Winnie Mandela's Ex-Bodyguard Tells of Killings She Ordered," *New York Times*, December 4, 1997, https://www.nytimes.com/1997/12/04/world/winnie-mandela-s-ex-bodyguard-tells-of-killings-she-ordered.html.
4. Emily Bridger, "From 'Mother of the Nation' to 'Lady Macbeth': Winnie Mandela and Perceptions of Female Violence in South Africa, 1985–91," *Gender and History* 27, no. 2 (August 2015): 446.
5. "Richardson Was a Police Informer: TRC Hears," *SAPA*, November 28 1997, https://www.justice.gov.za/trc/media%5C1997%5C9711/s971128r.htm. Although the Truth and

Reconciliation Commission implicated Madikizela-Mandela in a number of assaults and arrests, Richardson was allegedly a police informant who killed Stompie to hide his identity. For more on Stratcom, see Paul Erasmus, *Confessions of a Stratcom Hitman* (Jacana Media, 2021).

6. Bridger, "From 'Mother of the Nation' to 'Lady Macbeth,' " 452.
7. Kim Miller, "Moms with Guns: Women's Political Agency in Anti-Apartheid Visual Culture," *African Arts* 42, no. 2 (Summer 2009): 68–75.
8. These conservative feminists argued that "the problems which confront women can best be addressed by building on—rather than repudiating—the ideals and institutions of Western culture." Angela D. Dillard, "Adventures in Conservative Feminism," *Society* 42, no. 3 (March 2005): 26.
9. Karen Brodkin Sacks, "What's a Life Story Got to Do With It?," in *Interpreting Women's Lives: Feminist Theory and Personal Narratives*, ed. Personal Narratives Group (Indiana University Press, 1989), 91; and Karen Buenavista Hanna, " 'Centerwomen' and the 'Forth Shift:' Hidden Figures of Transnational Filipino Activism in Los Angeles, 1972–1992," in *Filipino American Activism: Diasporic Politics Among the Second Generation*, ed. Robyn Magalit Rodriguez (Brill, 2020), 156.
10. Kathleen Blee, *Inside Organized Racism Women in the Hate Movement* (University of California Press, 2002), 112–22, 128.
11. Blee, *Inside Organized Racism Women in the Hate Movement*, 134. It is crucial to note that pro-apartheid women often had more freedom than their cousins in the white power movement and racist hate groups like the Aryan Women's League, Ku Klux Klan Women, and Christian Identity Women. The virulent, regimented nature of these top-down, authoritarian hate groups provided little space for women to take on leadership roles, like those in the pro-apartheid movement. Nevertheless, the categorizations of white supremacist thinking about women's roles can be applied to the pro-apartheid movement.
12. The concept of "translating" political support into broader debates stems from the historian Elizabeth Gillespie McRae's discussion of Jim Crow organizing by white women. McRae, *Mothers of Massive Resistance*, 7.
13. Ronnee Schreiber, *Righting Feminism: Conservative Women and American Politics* (Oxford University Press, 2008), 3–17.
14. Kathleen M. Blee and Sandra Deutsch, *Women of the Right: Comparisons and Interplay Across Borders* (Pennsylvania State University Press, 2012); Seyward Darby, *Sisters in Hate: American Women on the Front Lines of White Nationalism* (Little, Brown, 2020); Abby Ferber, *Home-Grown Hate Gender and Organized Racism* (Taylor and Francis, 2012); Kathleen Blee, "Ethnographies of the Far Right," *Journal of Contemporary Ethnography* 36, no. 2 (2007): 119–28; Blee, *Inside Organized Racism*; Kathleen Blee, "Does Gender Matter in the United States Far-Right," *Politics, Religion and Ideology* 13, no. 2 (2012): 253–65; Anne Bonds, "Race and Ethnicity II: White Women and the Possessive geographies of White Supremacy," *Progress in Human Geography* 44, no. 4 (2020): 778–88; and Kathleen Belew, *Bring the War Home: The White Power Movement and Paramilitary America* (Harvard University Press, 2019).

15. For more on the unique roles of white women in international white power spaces, see Eviane Leidig, *The Women of the Far Right: Social Media Influencers and Online Radicalization* (Columbia University Press, 2023), especially Chapter 6, "From Protests to Parliaments."
16. Charl Blignaut, "Untold History with a Historiography: A Review of Scholarship on Afrikaner Women in South African History," *South African Historical Journal* 65, no. 4 (2013): 599–600; Jonathan Hyslop, "White Working-Class Women and the Invention of Apartheid: 'Purified' Afrikaner Nationalist Agitation for Legislation Against 'Mixed' Marriages, 1934–9," *Journal of African History* 36, no. 1 (1995): 57–81; Marijke Du Toit, "The Domesticity of Afrikaner Nationalism: Volksmoeders and the ACVV, 1904–1929," *Journal of Southern African Studies* 29, no. 1 (2003): 155–76; Marijke du Toi, "Framing Volksmoeders: The Politics of Female Afrikaner Nationalists, 1904–1930," in *Right-Wing Women: From Conservatives to Extremists Around the World*, ed. Paola Bacchetta and Margaret Power (Routledge, 2002); Christi van der Westhuizen, "(Un)sung Heroines: The Rise and Fall and Rise of the Afrikaner Nationalist Volksmoeder in South Africa," *Matatu* 50, no. 2 (2020): 258–79; Christi van der Westhuizen, "Reconstructed? White Afrikaans Women in Post-apartheid South Africa," in *The Palgrave Handbook of Critical Race and Gender*, ed. Shirley Anne Tate and Encarnación Rodríguez (Palgrave Macmillan, 2022), 429–48; Deborah Gaitskell and Elaine Unterhalter, "Mothers of the Nation: A Comparative Analysis of Nation, Race and Motherhood in Afrikaner Nationalism and the African National Congress," in *Women-Nation-State*, ed. Nira Yuval-Davis and Floya Anthias (Macmillan, 1989); and Christi van der Westhuizen, *Sitting Pretty: White Afrikaans Women in Postapartheid South Africa* (University of KwaZulu-Natal Press, 2017).
17. Keisha N. Blain, *Set the World on Fire: Black Nationalist Women and the Global Struggle for Freedom* (University of Pennsylvania Press, 2018).
18. Elisabeth Armstrong, "Before Bandung: The Anti-Imperialist Women's Movement in Asia and the Women's International Democratic Federation," *Signs: Journal of Women in Culture and Society* 41, no. 2 (2016): 305, 307.
19. Rachel Sandwell, "The Travels of Florence Mophosho: The African National Congress and Left Internationalism, 1948–1985," *Journal of Women's History* 30, no. 4 (Winter 2018): 101.
20. Rachel Sandwell, "South African Women and the Politics of Peace in the 1950s," *South African Historical Journal* 75, no. 1–2 (2023): 73.
21. Meghan Healy Clancy, "Women and Apartheid," *Oxford Research Encyclopedias, African History*, June 2017.
22. Philip I. Levy, "Sanctions on South Africa: What Did They Do?," *American Economic Review* 89, no. 2 (May 1999): 416.
23. Levy, "Sanctions on South Africa"; Martine Mariotti and Johan Fourie, "The Economics of Apartheid: An Introduction," *Economic History of Developing Regions* 29, no. 2 (2014): 116; William H. Kaempfer and Anton D. Lowenberg, "The Theory of International Economic Sanctions: A Public Choice Approach," *American Economic Review* 78 (1988): 786–93; and Terence Moll, "Did the Apartheid Economy 'Fail'?," *Journal of Southern African Studies* 17, no. 2 (June 1991): 271–91.

24. Mariotti and Fouri, "The Economics of Apartheid," 121; Servaas van der Berg, "The Transition from Apartheid: Social Spending Shifts Preceded Political Reform," *Economic History of Developing Regions* 29, no. 2 (2014): 234–44.
25. Martine Mariotti, "Labor Markets During Apartheid in South Africa," *Economic History Review* 65, no. 3 (2012): 1100.
26. Letter from Carl Nöffke to William A. Rusher, November 2, 1984, Folder 8: General Correspondence, South African Embassy, 1982–88, Box 84, William A. Rusher Papers, 1940–2010, LOC.
27. "The Media Target South Africa," AIM Report, October 1986, Box 1, AIM Report (Accuracy in Media Reporting), SC 79, Intercessors for the Suffering Church Collection, Mary Ann Gilbert, Serials Correspondence, WCSC.
28. I use the definition of "tastemaker" from Niamh Thornton in *Tastemakers and Tastemaking: Mexico and Curated Screen Violence* (State University of New York Press, 2020)—"influential or indicative individuals who are both determining and reflective of wider patterns and trends," with Pierre Bourdieu specifically identifying magazines as "assisting" tastemaking. Pierre Bourdieu, *Distinction: A Social Critique of the Judgement of Taste* (Harvard University Press, 1984), 232.
29. "Our 200th Issue," *Aida Parker Newsletter*, no. 200 (October 1996), *Aida Parker Newsletter*, January 1994–December 1996, APC Periodicals, APC.
30. McRae, *Mothers of Massive Resistance*, 88, 104. See also Lisa McGirr, *Suburban Warriors: The Origins of the New American Right* (Princeton University Press, 2015).
31. Michelle M. Nickerson, *Mothers of Conservatism: Women and the Postwar Right* (Princeton University Press, 2012), xvii.
32. Jacklyn Cock, "Keeping the Fires Burning: Militarization and the Politics of Gender in South Africa," *Review of African Political Economy* 45/46 (1989): 50.
33. Cock, "Keeping the Fires Burning," 53; Jacklyn Cock, "Women and the Military: Implications for Demilitarization in the 1990s in South Africa," *Gender and Society* 8, no. 2 (June 1994): 152.
34. "Veteran Journalist Dies," *News 24*, February 24, 2003, https://www.news24.com/News24/Veteran-journalist-dies-20030224. For more on the Argus Group, see Herman Wasserman, "The Ramifications of Media Globalization in the Global South for the Study of Media Industries," *Media Industries* 1, no. 2 (2014).
35. Aida Parker, "The Secret U.S. War Against South Africa," Americans Concerned About South Africa, 1977, Political Extremism and Radicalism: Far-Right Groups in America, GALE.
36. J. Brooks Spector, "Apartheid's InfoGate, Fresh and Relevant After All These Years," *Daily Maverick*, January 29, 2013, https://www.dailymaverick.co.za/article/2013-01-29-apartheids-infogate-fresh-and-relevant-after-all-these-years/.
37. According to the scholar Nicky Falkof, Parker was "secretly sponsored by intelligence divisions within the South African Police," but Falkof does not provide documentation of this claim. Nicky Falkof, *Satanism and Family Murder in Late Apartheid South Africa: Imagining the End of Whiteness* (Palgrave Macmillan, 2015), 129. "Warrant of Arrest Authorized for Nazi Sympathizer Jan Lamprecht," South African Jewish Board of

Deputies, March 12, 2021; and Jan Lamprecht, "South Africa's Mysterious AIDA Parker—The AIDA Parker Newsletter—I Met Her—Who Was She Really?," History Reviewed: The Truth They've Been Hiding From You!, December 15, 2017.

38. "Special Investigation Into Secret State Funding," subsection 1, part 4, chap. 6, vol. 2, *TRC Final Report*, 1998, 526, https://sabctrc.saha.org.za/reports/volume2/chapter6/part4/subsection1.htm.
39. "Aida Parker Newsletter Subscription Form," *Aida Parker Newsletter*, 1987, Folder 16, Aida Parker, carton 42, BANC MSS 98/70, Collection on the US Right [ca. 1950s–1997], Sara Diamond Papers, BLMC.
40. Memorandum from the South Africa File from Howard Phillips, April 13, 1990, CC 1-3-1 Folder 12A; CC 1:3 Box 6, JFL, https://cdm17184.contentdm.oclc.org/digital/collection/p17184coll12/id/116240/rec/5.
41. "The Enemies Within—Part I, the Priests Take on Pretoria, 'Comrade Jesus,' and the SA Revolution," *Aida Parker Newsletter Special Issue*, 1987, Folder: Jr, "Right-Wing Religion," Jr, Right-Wing Religion AG2843—Institute for Contextual Theology, UWHP.
42. "Aida's Asides," *Aida Parker Newsletter*, March 1983, no. 1 March 1983—no. 32 May 1984, APC Periodicals, + no. 71 (incomplete), APC.
43. "What About SA's Whites?," "American Ignorance: Criminal Neglect?," "Ideological Soul-Brothers: The ANC and the Marxists," and "The Anti-SA Campaign: A Classic of Soviet-Supported 'Active Measures,'" Special ANC Issue, *Aida Parker Newsletter*, November 26, 1986, Folder 19, NRB 87 South Africa, carton 42, Sara Diamond Papers, BANC MSS 98/70, Collection on the US Right [ca. 1950s–1997], BLMC.
44. Aida Parker, "The Misguided Policies of Western Leaders in South Africa," *Conservative Review* 3 (October 1992), Folder 3, Paleoconservatives, Conservative Review, vol. 3, 1992, carton 46, BANC MSS 98/70, Collection on the US Right [ca. 1950s–1997], Sara Diamond Papers, BLMC. *Conservative Review* was a magazine run by Roger Pearson, former leader of the World Anti-Communist League, proponent of racial science, and associate of neo-Nazis. Russ Bellant, *Old Nazis, the New Right, and the Republican Party: Domestic Fascist Networks and the U.S. Cold War* (South End Press, 1991), 60–62.
45. Larry Abraham, "The Crisis in South Africa," *Insider Report*, March 1986, CC 1-2-7 Folder 8A; CC 1:2 Box 125, JFL, https://cdm17184.contentdm.oclc.org/digital/collection/p17184coll12/id/124141/rec/27. Abraham is perhaps most infamous for his book *None Dare Call It Conspiracy* about the New World Order conspiracy that undermined the US economy.
46. "February 15," *Conservative Manifesto* no. 28, Conservative Caucus, April 1983, p. 26, CC 1-2-4 Folder 12B; CC 1:2 Box 65, JFL, https://cdm17184.contentdm.oclc.org/digital/collection/p17184coll12/id/57898/rec/22.
47. "South Africa Should Spotlight Human Rights Abuses in Zimbabwe" and "Farewell to Cape Town, Joberg, and RSA," *Conservative Manifesto*, no. 55, Conservative Caucus, July 1985, p. 10, 60, CC 1-2-6, Folder 17B; CC 1:2 Box 119, JFL, https://cdm17184.contentdm.oclc.org/digital/collection/p17184coll12/id/109317/rec/21.
48. Aida Parker Schedule, Conservative Caucus, April 1990, CC 1-3-1 Folder 12B; CC 1:3 Box 6, JFL, https://cdm17184.contentdm.oclc.org/digital/collection/p17184coll12/id/118125/rec/3.

49. "High Stakes in the Divestment Campaign Against SA," *Aida Parker Newsletter*; "Enclosures, RE South Africa and the Iran-Contra Temps," to Pat Buchanan from Phil Nicolaides, December 29, 1986, WHORM Subject File (448400-449499), Box 172, CO 141, South Africa, RRPL.
50. "This Is the Price SA Pays for Not Presenting Her Case," *Aida Parker Newsletter*, Special ANC Issue.
51. In his 1992 memoir, Crocker explicitly deemed the *APN* as part of the "attack journalism" of the transatlantic right wing. Chester Crocker, *High Noon in Southern Africa: Making Peace in a Rough Neighborhood* (Norton, 1992), 283.
52. "From ANC Files: The People Who Back Terror," *Aida Parker Newsletter*, Special ANC Issue.
53. "Randall Robinson: The ANC's 'Foreign Agent' in the US," *Aida Parker Newsletter Special Supplement*, 1985, Folder: Jr, Right-Wing Religion, "Right-Wing Religion," Jr, AG2843—Institute for Contextual Theology, UWHP.
54. Francis Njubi Nesbitt, *Race for Sanctions: African Americans Against Apartheid, 1946–1994* (Indiana University Press 2004), 99, 101, 135, 145.
55. "Who CAN You Trust?," *Aida Parker Newsletter*, Special Sanctions Issue, no. 115, February 1988, Folder 16, Aida Parker, carton 42, Sara Diamond Papers, BANC MSS 98/70, Collection on the US Right [ca. 1950s–1997], BLMC.
56. "The Anti-SA Campaign: A Classic of Soviet-Supported 'Active Measures,'" *Aida Parker Newsletter*, Special ANC Issue.
57. "Militant Black Lobbying Group Fuels Anti-SA Flames," *Aida Parker Newsletter*, Special ANC Issue.
58. "Facts About Southern Africa the International Media Will Not Give You," *Aida Parker Newsletter*, no. 119, August 1987, Folder 16, Aida Parker, carton 42, Sara Diamond Papers, BANC MSS 98/70, Collection on the US Right [ca. 1950s–1997], BLMC.
59. "ANC: 'Freedom Fighters' or Soviet Puppets?," *Aida Parker Newsletter*, no. 95, November 26, 1986, Folder 19, NRB 87 South Africa, carton 42, Sara Diamond Papers, BANC MSS 98/70, Collection on the US Right [ca. 1950s–1997], BLMC.
60. "Manipulating the World's Youth" and "Ideological Soul-Brothers: The ANC and the Marxists," *Aida Parker Newsletter*, Special ANC Issue.
61. "Facts About Southern Africa," *Aida Parker Newsletter*, August 1987, 20.
62. "American Ignorance: Criminal Neglect?," *Aida Parker Newsletter*, Special ANC Issue.
63. Nicole Hemmer, *Partisans: The Conservative Revolutionaries Who Remade American Politics in the 1990s* (Basic, 2022), 13.
64. Sean Wilentz, "Cofounding Fathers: The Tea Party's Cold War Roots," *New Yorker*, October 11, 2010, https://www.newyorker.com/magazine/2010/10/18/confounding-fathers.
65. Stephanie E. Jones-Rogers, *They Were Her Property: White Women as Slave Owners in the American South* (Yale University Press, 2019), 27.
66. Kimberly Killen, "Can You Hear Me Now? Race, Motherhood, and the Politics of Being Heard," *Politics and Gender* 15, no. 4 (December 2019): 627–29.
67. "Ted Koppel: Ideologue First, Journalist Second," December 1, 2005, http://howardphillips.com/archive1205.htm. Although the date of Phillips's blog entry is December 1, 2005, the entry references a 1985 appearance on *Nightline* by Victims Against Terrorism.

68. One of Cindy's companions—Ibhayi Mayor Tamsanqa Linda—who testified to the ANC murdering his friends and firebombing his mother's home, would travel on the sponsorship of the John Birch Society in 1990. "Black South African Leader to Speak at LCSC," *Lewiston Tribune*, November 19, 1990, and "Group to Host South African," *Oklahoman*, October 26, 1990, https://www.oklahoman.com/story/news/1990/10/26/group-to-host-south-african/62547986007/.
69. Mark Phillips, "From Partisanship to Neutrality? Changing Perspectives on the Role of SA Security Forces During Transition," Paper presented at the Centre for the Study of Violence and Reconciliation, seminar no. 4 (June 1990): 2.
70. Terry Bell, "Olaf Palme Assassination: The SA Connection," *Daily Maverick*, June 10, 2020, https://www.dailymaverick.co.za/article/2020-06-10-olaf-palme-assassination-the-sa-connection/.
71. "Mandela Mania," *AIM Report*, XIX-13, July A, 1990.
72. Conference on Namibia and Human Rights, International Society for Human Rights, March 27, 1986, Iwan Agrusow and Ndabezinhle Musa, "South Africa and Human Rights: A Way Between Apartheid and Revolution," September 1985.
73. "Introducing Victims Against Terrorism," Victims Against Terrorism, Folder: Jr, Right-Wing Religion, AG2843—Institute for Contextual Theology, UWHP.
74. "Victims Against Terrorism," South Africa, UK Parliamentary Records, June 11, 1985, https://api.parliament.uk/historic-hansard/written-answers/1985/jun/11/victims-against-terrorism-south-africa; Peter Goodspeed, "South Africans Plan to Picket Our Embassy," *Toronto Star*, October 13, 1987; and "Protest Targets Anti-Apartheid Office," *Washington Post*, May 21, 1987.
75. Memorandum for the Namibia File from Howard Phillips, January 2, 1990, CC 1-3-1 Folder 1A; CC 1:3 Box 1, JFL, https://cdm17184.contentdm.oclc.org/digital/collection/p17184coll12/id/87602/rec/7. This funding occurred until F. W. de Klerk unbanned the ANC in 1990. Phillips, "From Partisanship to Neutrality?"
76. Jill E. Kelly, "Political Violence as Routine," Africa Is a Country, December 7, 2012, https://africasacountry.com/2012/12/the-new-york-times-reports-on-political-violence-in-south-africa.
77. Letter to Howard Phillips from Jonathan Leontsinis, May 8, 1985, CC 1-2-6 Folder 14A; CC 1:2 Box 117, JFL, https://cdm17184.contentdm.oclc.org/digital/collection/p17184coll12/id/97442/rec/8. Because Cindy led Victims Against Terrorism, with little presence of John in the meetings or publications, John's introductory letter likely reflected gendered proprieties around introductions. Occasionally, descriptions of John Leontsinis only referred to him as a "horticulturalist." As the Conservative Caucus put it in their profile of the Victims Against Terrorism group, Leontsinis spent "most of her time" working for the organization, citing her "tremendous personality." Although undoubtedly the head of Victims Against Terrorism, limitations to Cindy's activism existed. Cindy's husband—not her—made the initial overture to Phillips and the Conservative Caucus. Victims Against South Africa Delegation, Conservative Caucus, May 28, 1985, CC 1-2-6 Folder 12B; CC 1:2 Box 116, JFL, https://cdm17184.contentdm.oclc.org/digital/collection/p17184coll12/id/98452/rec/1.

78. "TCC Launches Campaign to Defeat Sanctions," *Conservative Caucus Member's Report* 9, no. 2 (July 1985), CC 1-2-6 Folder 19B; CC 1:2 Box 120, JFL, https://cdm17184.contentdm.oclc.org/digital/collection/p17184coll12/id/113291/rec/6; "Falwell and Phillips Urge Media Focus on Marxist Terrorism and Violence in South Africa," Conservative Caucus, May 28, 1985, CC 1-2-6 Folder 12B; CC 1:2 Box 116, JFL, https://cdm17184.contentdm.oclc.org/digital/collection/p17184coll12/id/98454/rec/1.
79. "Victims Against Terrorism Hosted by TCC," *Conservative Manifesto*, no. 56, Conservative Caucus, August 1985, CC 1-2-6 Folder 16B; CC 1:2 Box 117 JFL, https://cdm17184.contentdm.oclc.org/digital/collection/p17184coll12/id/98925/rec/6.
80. "Draft of Soviet Strategy for Conquest of Southern Africa Must Be Blocked by American Conservatives," Howard Phillips, June 11, 1985, CC 1-2-6 Folder 15A; CC 1:2 Box 117, JFL, https://cdm17184.contentdm.oclc.org/digital/collection/p17184coll12/id/97898/rec/44.
81. *The Conservative Manifesto*, no. 56, Conservative Caucus.
82. Letter to Howard Phillips from Cindy Leontsinis, July 29, 1985, CC 1-2-6 Folder 20A; CC 1:2 Box 156, JFL, https://cdm17184.contentdm.oclc.org/digital/collection/p17184coll12/id/100413/rec/3.
83. "Immediate Objective," Howard Phillips, July 11, 1985, CC 1-2-6 Folder 16B; CC 1:2 Box 118, JFL, https://cdm17184.contentdm.oclc.org/digital/collection/p17184coll12/id/98458/rec/9.
84. Letter from Elsa Sandstrom to Ronald Reagan, July 29, 1985, WHORM Subject File, (275000–275949), Box 165, CO 141, South Africa, RRPL. On the Federation of Republican Women, "Lucile Hosmer: A Conservative Republican in the Mainstream of Party Politics," Women in Politics Oral History Project, University of California Berkely, 1983.
85. Letter from Vera Von Wiren-Garczynski to Ronald Reagan, August 11, 1985, WHORM Subject File (327750–327899), Box 166, CO 141, South Africa, RRPL. Vera von Wiren-Garczynski, born in Yugoslavia, was an avowed anticommunist and friend to the Reagan and Bush administrations. According to her obituary, she carried messages between the White House and Polish dissident Lech Walesa during the Solidary Movement in the 1980s. "Vera R. Von Wiren Garczynski," Find a Grave, 2013, https://www.findagrave.com/memorial/115648523/vera_r-garczynski.
86. Letter from Leslie C. Dutton to Ronald Reagan, August 29, 1986, WHORM Subject File (424000-424631), Box 170, CO 141, South Africa, RRPL.
87. Mary Lee Cake, "Cry the Beloved Country," *Bedford Bulletin*, July 25, 1986, WHORM Subject File (433800-434699), Box 170, CO 141, South Africa, RRPL.
88. Letter from John A. and Margaret G. Harper to Ronald Reagan, May 20, 1986, South Africa—General—1985–1987 (2 of 14), RAC Box 10, NSC: Records, Collection: African Affairs Directorate, NSC, Box 3, RRPL.
89. Letter from Diane Jacobs to Ronald Reagan, July 29, 1986, WHORM Subject File (420350-420599), Box 169, CO 141, South Africa, RRPL.
90. Gaitskell and Unterhalter, "Mothers of the Nation," 66.
91. Gospel Defense League, "A Tribute to Mrs. Dorothea Scarborough," May 27, 2022, http://gospeldefenceleague.org/index.php/test-3/164-a-tribute-to-mrs-dorothea-scarborough.

92. Letter from C. Van der Merwe to Desmond Tutu, January 18, 1985, Folder B34, Archbishops of Cape Town, Broadcasting, 1983–1985, B33–B37, AB2546—Archbishops of Cape Town, UWHP.
93. "The Gospel Defense League," Gospel Defense League, January 1987, Folder: 35 gel, Gospel Defense League (right-wing), Gospel Defense League, World Conference and Religion + Peace, 35.42–43, AC623—SACC, UWHP.
94. The Gospel Defense League's attacks on Tutu, specifically after he won the Nobel Peace Prize in 1985, drew coverage from the South African Broadcasting Corporation to the ire of the archbishop. *Gospel Defense League Newsletter*, Gospel Defense League, August 1985, Folder: 35 gel, Gospel Defense League (right-wing), Gospel Defense League, World Conference and Religion + Peace, 35.42–43, AC623—SACC, UWHP.
95. Gospel Defense League Newsletter, Gospel Defense League, June 1986, Folder: 35 gel, Gospel Defense League (right-wing), Gospel Defense League, World Conference and Religion + Peace, 35.42–43, AC623—SACC, UWHP.
96. For example, in 1989, Minister of Law and Order Adriaan Vlok and four police officers attempted to assassinate Frank Chikane by lacing his underwear with poison and SADF agents hung a baboon fetus in Tutu's garden. "Apartheid-Era Police Guilty of Attempted Murder of Activists," CNN, 2007, https://www.cnn.com/2007/WORLD/africa/08/17/southafrica.apartheid.reut/; and "Basoon: Baboon Foetus Not Mine," News 24, September 5, 2001, https://www.news24.com/News24/Basson-Baboon-foetus-not-mine-20010905.
97. Gospel Defense League Newsletter, Gospel Defense League, February 1986, JF-Ji, Folder: JG, Gospel Defense League, 1986–1989, AG2843—Institute for Contextual Theology, Special Topics, UWHP.
98. Gospel Defense League Newsletter, Gospel Defense League, October 1985, Box 3, Gospel Defense League Newsletters, 1985–1995, SC 79, Intercessors for the Suffering Church Collection, Mary Ann Gilbert, Serials Correspondence, WCSC.
99. Gospel Defense League Newsletter, Gospel Defense League, September 1985, Box 3, Gospel Defense League Newsletters, 1985–1995, SC 79, Intercessors for the Suffering Church Collection, Mary Ann Gilbert, Serials Correspondence, WCSC.
100. Gospel Defense League Newsletter, Gospel Defense League, September 1986, Box 3, Gospel Defense League Newsletters, 1985–1995, SC 79, Intercessors for the Suffering Church Collection, Mary Ann Gilbert, Serials Correspondence, WCSC.
101. Gospel Defense League Newsletter, Gospel Defense League, August 1986, Box 3, Gospel Defense League Newsletters, 1985–1995, SC 79, Intercessors for the Suffering Church Collection, Mary Ann Gilbert, Serials Correspondence, WCSC.
102. Director's Report, Annual Report 1986, Peter Hammond, Frontline Fellowship, Box 3, Frontline Fellowship, News/Prayer Letters, 1984–1995, SC 79, Intercessors for the Suffering Church Collection, Mary Ann Gilbert, Serials Correspondence, WCSC and Letter to Denis Walker from Peter Hammond, Conservative Caucus, December 11, 1984, CC 1-2-6 Folder 6A; CC 1:2 Box 113, JFL, https://cdm17184.contentdm.oclc.org/digital/collection/p17184coll12/id/91719/rec/1.

103. Letter from Anne Shipps to Mary Ann Gilbert, May 10, 1986, Box 9, Unto the Least of These Correspondence with Anne Ships + Harry Jones, SC 79, Intercessors for the Suffering Church Collection, Mary Ann Gilbert, Serials Correspondence, WCSC.
104. Father Lewis to Speak at Interchurch Meeting, sponsored by Anne E. Shipps and Harry Jones, May 29, 1984, Box 8, Rhodesia Christian Group Newsletter, 1982–1990, SC 79, Intercessors for the Suffering Church Collection, Mary Ann Gilbert, Serials Correspondence, WCSC.
105. Letter from Anne Shipps to Mary Ann Gilbert, January 18, 1989, Box 9, Unto the Least of These Correspondence with Anne Ships + Harry Jones, SC 79, Intercessors for the Suffering Church Collection, WCSC.
106. Confidential USA-Europe Preaching Tour, Peter Hammond, March 1988, Box 3, Frontline Fellowship, News/Prayer Letters, 1984–1995, SC 79, Intercessors for the Suffering Church Collection, Mary Ann Gilbert, Serials Correspondence, WCSC and Memorandum to Howard Phillips from Jay Hopkins, Re: Scheduling for Peter Hammond, March 3, 1988, CC 1-2-9 Folder 7B; CC 1:2 Box 148, JFL, https://cdm17184.contentdm.oclc.org/digital/collection/p17184coll12/id/106643/rec/1.
107. Report Back on USA Speaking Tour, Peter Hammond, April 1988, Box 3, Frontline Fellowship, News/Prayer Letters, 1984–1995, SC 79, Intercessors for the Suffering Church Collection, Mary Ann Gilbert, Serials Correspondence, WCSC.

5. BREAKING WITH THE REPUBLICAN PARTY

1. Richard Norton Smith, "Pat Buchanan Interview for the Gerald R. Ford Oral History Project," Gerald Ford Foundation, October 4, 2010, https://geraldrfordfoundation.org/centennial/oralhistory/pat-buchanan/.
2. For more on the difficulties of Reagan's second term, see Jane Mayer and Doyle McManus, *Landslide: The Unmaking of the President, 1984-1988* (Houghton Mifflin, 1989).
3. J. E. Davies, *Constructive Engagement? Chester Crocker and American Policy in South Africa, Namibia and Angola, 1981–8* (Ohio University Press, 2007); Alex Thomson, *U.S. Foreign Policy Towards Apartheid South Africa, 1948–1994* (Palgrave Macmillan, 2008); Thomas Borstelmann, *Apartheid's Reluctant Uncle: The United States and Southern Africa in the Early Cold War* (Oxford University Press, 1993); Alex Thomson, "Incomplete Engagement: Reagan's South Africa Policy Revisited," *Journal of Modern African Studies* 33, no. 1 (1995): 83–101; Alex Thomson, "A More Effective Constructive Engagement: US Policy Towards South Africa after the Comprehensive Anti-Apartheid Act of 1986," *Politikon* 39 (2012): 371–89; Mayer and McManus, *Landslide*; Kevin M. Kruse and Julian E. Zelizer, *Fault Lines: A History of the United States Since 1974* (Norton, 2019); Joel D. Aberbach and Gillian Peele, *Crisis of Conservatism? The Republican Party, the Conservative Movement, and American Politics After Bush* (Oxford University Press, 2010); Kevin Kruse, *White Flight: Atlanta and the Making of Modern Conservatism* (Princeton University Press, 2005); Kim Phillips-Fein, *Invisible Hands: The Businessmen's Crusade Against*

the New Deal (Norton, 2009); Joseph Crespino, *In Search of Another Country: Mississippi and the Conservative Counterrevolution* (Princeton University Press, 2007); and Matthew D. Lassiter, *The Silent Majority: Suburban Politics in the Sunbelt South* (Princeton University Press, 2006).

4. Kathleen Belew, *Bring the War Home: The White Power Movement and Paramilitary America* (Harvard University Press, 2019); Sara Diamond, *Roads to Dominion: Right-Wing Movements and Political Power in the United States* (Guilford, 1995); and Daniel Geary, Camilla Schofield, and Jennifer Sutton, eds., *Global White Nationalism: From Apartheid to Trump* (Manchester University Press, 2020).
5. US Congress, House, Anti-Apartheid Action Act of 1985, HR 1460, 99th Congress, 1st. sess., introduced in House on March 7, 1985, https://www.congress.gov/bill/99th-congress/house-bill/1460?r=9&s=5; and US Congress, Senate, Anti-Apartheid Act of 1985, 99th Congress, 1st sess., introduced in Senate on March 7, 1985, https://www.congress.gov/bill/99th-congress/senate-bill/635.
6. Representative Wolpe speaking on H.R. 1460, 99th Congress, 1st sess., *Congressional Record*, Hearings and Markup Before the Subcommittees on International Economic Policy and Trade and on Africa of the Committee on Foreign Affairs, April 17, 1985, NARA.
7. "NAACP Urges Senate Passage of Anti-Apartheid Act of 1985," *Atlanta Daily World*, August 25, 1985. On the NAACP's antiapartheid activism, see Carol Anderson, "International Conscience, the Cold War, and Apartheid: The NAACP's Alliance with the Reverend Michael Schott for South West Africa's Liberation, 1946–1951," *Journal of World History* 19 (2008): 297–325; Carol Anderson, *Bourgeois Radicals: The NAACP and the Struggle for Colonial Liberation, 1941–1960* (Cambridge University Press, 2015); and Robert Zebulun Larson, "The Transnational and Local Dimensions of the U.S. Anti-Apartheid Movement" (PhD diss., Ohio State University, 2019).
8. "Churches Continue Anti-apartheid Effort," *Afro American*, March 2, 1985; "JCRC Backs Anti-apartheid," *Philadelphia Tribune*, June 18, 1985; and Anna J. W. James, "3,000 at WMS Take Anti-apartheid State," *Philadelphia Tribune*, September 20, 1985. The robust antiapartheid activism of the National Council of Churches infuriated pro-apartheid religious actors, who singled out the organization as part of a grand communist conspiracy against the South African government.
9. Simon Anekwe, "60,000 March Against Hated, Evil Apartheid: Protestors Urge Ron to Act on Side of Justice," *New York Amsterdam News*, August 17, 1985.
10. M. A. Goodin, "Divestiture: Hitting South Africa Where It Hurts: Michigan to Join Anti-apartheid Ranks," *Michigan Chronicle*, September 28, 1985.
11. Margalit Fox, "Malcolm Wallop, Senator from Wyoming, Dies at 78," *New York Times*, September 15, 2011, https://www.nytimes.com/2011/09/16/us/malcolm-wallop-ex-senator-of-wyoming-dies-at-78.html; Brian Murphy, "Steve Symms, Senator Who Was the Voice of Conservative Ire, Dies at 86," *Washington Post*, August 10, 2024, https://www.washingtonpost.com/obituaries/2024/08/10/steve-symms-senate-dukakis-dies/.
12. Mark Memmott, "How Did Strom Thurmond Last Through His 24-Hour Filibuster?," NPR, March 7, 2013, https://www.npr.org/sections/thetwo-way/2013/03/07/173736882

/how-did-strom-thurmond-last-through-his-24-hour-filibuster. Senator Cory Booker (D-NJ) broke this record in 2025.

13. William A. Link, *Righteous Warrior: Jesse Helms and the Rise of Modern Conservatism* (St. Martin's, 2008), 2.
14. Steve Symms, "Anti-Apartheid Action Act of 1985," *Senate Congressional Record*, August 1, 1985, NARA
15. Malcom Wallop, "Consideration of Bill S.995, the Anti-Apartheid Action Act," *Senate Congressional Record*, July 11, 1985, US Congressional Record.
16. Neil A. Lewis, "Richard Lugar, G.O.P. Senator and Foreign Policy Force, Dies at 87," *New York Times*, April 28, 2019, https://www.nytimes.com/2019/04/28/obituaries/senator-richard-lugar-dead.html.
17. "Nancy L. Kassebaum: A Featured Biography," US Senate, https://www.senate.gov/senators/FeaturedBios/Featured_Bio_Kassebaum.htm; Tim Carpenter, "U.S. Sen. Kassebaum Looks in Mirror, Sees GOP Moderates Like Herself No Longer Viable in Kansas," *Kansas Reflector*, April 21, 2022, accessed August 22, 2024, https://kansasreflector.com/2022/04/21/u-s-sen-kassebaum-looks-in-mirror-sees-gop-moderates-like-herself-no-longer-viable-in-kansas/.
18. Adam Clymer, "Charles Mathias, Former U.S. Senator, Dies at 87," *New York Times*, January 25, 2010, https://www.nytimes.com/2010/01/26/us/politics/26mathias.html.
19. Senate Foreign Relations Committee, "Lugar-Dole-Mathias-Kassebaum Anti-Apartheid Action," Richard G. Lugar Senatorial Papers, http://collections.libraries.indiana.edu/lugar/items/show/154.
20. Fein, *Invisible Hands*; Jonathan Davis, "Thatcher, Reagan, and Free Markets: Ghost Towns, Rust Belts and a New Individualism," in *The Global 1980s: People, Power, and Profit*, ed. Jonathan Davis (Routledge, 2019); and Angus Burgin, *The Great Persuasion: Reinventing Free Markets Since the Depression* (Harvard University Press, 2012).
21. Current Policy 686, "South Africa: The Case Against Sanctions," State Department, April 15, 1985, Entry A1 1589, Records Relating to Major Publications, 1949–1990, Box 110, RG 59, NARA.
22. Address by George P. Shultz at the National Press Club, April 16, 1985, Hearings before the Committee on Banking, Housing, and Urban Affairs, US Senate and the Subcommittee on International Finance and Monetary Policy on S. 635, *U.S. Congressional Record*, NARA.
23. Chester Crocker, Current Policy 688, "The U.S. Response to Apartheid in South Africa," before the House Foreign Relations Committee, April 17, 1985, Entry A1 1589, Records Relating to Major Publications, 1949–1990, Box 110, RG 59, NARA.
24. Incoming telegram from AM Consul Johannesburg to Sec State Wash DC, "Black Activists on Likely Reaction to Botha Speech, U.S. Policy Moves," August 15, 1985, South Africa—Working Files 3 (2), October 1984 to June 1986, RAC Box 9, African Affairs Directorate, NSC, Records, Collection: African Affairs Directorate, NSC, Box 2, RRPL.
25. Memorandum for Robert C. McFarlane from Phillip Ringdahl, "South Africa—State Options Paper on the Sanctions Bill," August 27, 1985, South Africa—Working Files 3 (2), October 1984 to June 1986, RAC Box 9, African Affairs Directorate, NSC, Records, Collection: African Affairs Directorate, NSC, Box 2, RRPL.

26. Letter from Gordon Jones to Patrick Buchanan, September 9, 1985, WHORM Subject File (344500-347199), Box 167, CO 141—South Africa, RRPL.
27. Paul Lewis, "European Nations Order Sanctions on South Africa," *New York Times*, September 11, 1985, https://www.nytimes.com/1985/09/11/world/european-nations-order-sanctions-on-south-africa.html.
28. Telegram for George Shultz, from Hans-Dietrich Genscher, Subject: Genscher Letter on South Africa, September 20, 1985, South Africa—Working Files 3 (1), October 1984 to June 1986, RAC Box 9, African Affairs Directorate, NSC, Records, Collection: African Affairs Directorate, NSC, Box 2, RRPL.
29. Jeff Sallot, "Unified Action Sought on Apartheid, Commonwealth at Risk, Thatcher Told," *Globe and Mail*, October 17, 1985, and Joseph Lelyveld, "Thatcher Accepts Limited Sanctions on South Africa," *New York Times*, August 5, 1986.
30. Malcolm Fraser, "Sanctions May Be Our Last Chance: Without Them, West May Be Shut Out in Southern Africa," *Los Angeles Times*, August 3, 1986.
31. Letter from Malcom Fraser and Olusegun Obasanjo to Ronald Reagan, July 21, 1986, WHORM Subject File (445000-448399), Box 172, CO 141, South Africa.
32. "Botha Imposes Nationwide Emergency; U.S. Protests: Hundreds Seized in Roundup," *Los Angeles Times*, June 12, 1986, https://www.latimes.com/archives/la-xpm-1986-06-12-mn-10542-story.html.
33. "Britain Makes Formal Protest of South African State of Emergency with South Africa," *AP News*, June 25, 1986.
34. Jim Leach, providing for consideration on H. R. 4868, Anti-Apartheid Act of 1986, on June 18, 1986, 99th Congress, 2nd Session, *Congressional Record*, NARA.
35. Arlen Specter speaking on S. 2701—Relating to Sanctions Against South Africa, August 13, 1986, 99th Congress, 2nd Session, *Congressional Record*, NARA.
36. After the Mozambique–South Africa signing of the Nkomati Accord in 1984, which ostensibly ended support for the ANC and Renamo, the Reagan administration sent hundreds of millions of dollars in aid to Mozambique and Zimbabwe to try and bring them in line with the capitalist West. Ercilio Neves Brandão Langa, "Diplomacy and Foreign Policy in Mozambique: The First Post-Independence Government—Samora Machel," *Brazilian Journal of African Studies* 6, no. 11 (2021): 28. In practice, South Africa never stopped backing Renamo. Susana Cárdenas, "A Desk Study of U.S. Assistance to Mozambique's Complex Humanitarian Emergency," USAID, September 1998, 21, https://pdf.usaid.gov/pdf_docs/PNADL046.pdf; and Edward A. Dougherty, "Zimcord Conference Documentation," *African Issues* 11, no. 3–4 (August 2021).
37. Memorandum to Pat Buchanan from Phil Nicolaides, Subject: The *Real* Goal of the Sanctions Promoters, September 22, 1986, WHORM Subject File (440874)(1), Box 171, CO 141—South Africa, RRPL.
38. Ariel Remos, "The Objective in South Africa is to Place the Communists in Power," shared by Phil Nicolaides to Pat Buchanan, August 31, 1986, WHORM Subject File (436200-437499), Box 171, CO 141, South Africa, RRPL.
39. Letter from John Chettle to Patrick J. Buchanan, July 16, 1986, WHORM Subject File (430000-431999), Box 170, CO 141—South Africa, RRPL.

40. Letter from Pat Buchanan to John H. Chettle, July 17, 1986, WHORM Subject File (430000-431999), Box 170, CO 141—South Africa, RRPL.
41. Memorandum from Pat Buchanan to Ronald Reagan, July 17, 1986, WHORM Subject File (430000-431999), Box 170, CO 141—South Africa, RRPL.
42. Letter to Pat Buchanan from David L. Chew, July 21, 1986, WHORM Subject File (400950-401029), Box 168, CO 141—South Africa, RRPL.
43. Letter from Arthur K. Melin to Pat Buchanan, July 24, 1986, and Letter from Pat Buchanan to Arthur K. Melin, August 11, 1986, WHORM Subject File (433800-434699), Box 170, CO 141, South Africa, RRPL.
44. Note from David Chew to Donald T. Regan, November 5, 1986, Series I: Diskette File [Correspondence, Memos] (2), Dawson, Thomas C. II Files: Office of the Chief of Staff, RRPL.
45. Letter from a Knowledgeable US Government Official in the Region, June 30, 1986, [South Africa, Background Information, re Sanctions] (7 of 12), Series I: Subject File, Communications, Office of Buchanan, Patrick: Files, RRPL.
46. Letter from Charles Stockell to Patrick Buchanan, March 17, 1986, Letter from Richard Sanders to Patrick Buchanan, March 1, 1986, WHORM Subject File (397000-399999), Box 168, CO 141—South Africa, RRPL.
47. Memorandum for the Chief of Staff from Pat Buchanan, August 1, 1986, WHORM Subject File (435500-435999), Box 171, CO 141—South Africa, RRPL.
48. Letter from Mrs. Dexter Fee (Elizabeth), to Pat Buchanan, March 22, 1985, WHORM Subject File (308000-314999), Box 166, CO 141—South Africa, RRPL; Letter from W. J. Durrenberger to Ronald Reagan, July 23, 1986, WHORM Subject File (409900-410059), Box 169, CO 141—South Africa, RRPL; Letter from Earl E. T. Smith to Ronald Reagan, February 25, 1986, WHORM Subject File (383000-390999), Box 168, CO 141—South Africa, RRPL; Mary Lee Cake, "Cry the Beloved Country," *Bedford Bulletin*, August 5, 1986, WHORM Subject File (433800-434699), Box 170, CO 141—South Africa.
49. Letter from Richard Kelly to Ronald Reagan, February 13, 1981, WHORM Subject File (016900-023819), CO 141—South Africa, RRPL; Letter from Jack M. Strate to Ronald Reagan, December 27, 1984, WHORM Subject File (275950-286999), Box 165, CO 141—South Africa, RRPL; Letter from Joan Joyce Sellers to Ronald Reagan, January 28, 1985, WHORM Subject File, (287000–293089), Box 165, CO 141—South Africa, RRPL; Letter from J. Evetts Haley to Senator Boren, June 17, 1985, WHORM Subject File (326000-327749), Box 166, CO 141—South Africa, RRPL.
50. Letter from William Cain to Ronald Reagan, July 30, 1986, WHORM Subject File (420350-420599), Box 169, CO 141—South Africa; Letter to Edwin Meese from William P. Hanson, March 23, 1981, WHORM Subject File (016900-023819), Box 163, CO 141—South Africa, RRPL; Letter to Ronald Reagan from Alden J. Erskine, September 11, 1985, WHORM Subject File (339353-340999), Box 167, CO 141—South Africa, RRPL; Enclosure to a Letter from Duncan Mackenzie to Ronald Reagan, July 22, 1986, WHORM Subject File (420350-420599), Box 169, CO 141—South Africa, RRPL.
51. Letter from Joe Lane Travis to Mitch McConnell, September 16, 1986, WHORM Subject File (425900-426179), Box 170, CO 141—South Africa, RRPL.

52. Letter from Penny Pullen to Ronald Reagan, January 6, 1982, WHORM Subject File (299000-301999), Box 165, CO 141—South Africa, RRPL; Letter from Robert L. Sandvig to Robert McFarlane, May 28, 1985, WHORM Subject File (322900-325999), Box 166, CO 141—South Africa, RRPL; Letter from Robert J. Archer to Ronald Reagan, April 8, 1985, WHORM Subject File (299000-301999), Box 165, CO 141—South Africa, RRPL.
53. Letter from Patrick Buchanan to Bruce Hunter, August 21, 1986, WHORM Subject File (437500-438349), Box 171, CO 141—South Africa, RRPL.
54. Letter from Pat Buchanan to Mrs. Dexter Fee and Letter from Pat Buchanan to R. E. Forbes, April 4, 1985, WHORM Subject File, (308000–314999), Box 166, CO 141, South Africa, RRPL; and Letter from Pat Buchanan to Richard B. Sanders, May 21, 1986, WHORM Subject File (397000-399999), Box 168, CO 141, South Africa, RRPL.
55. Letter from Wirt Yerger, Jr. to Ronald Reagan, Subject: A Time for Statesmanship—South Africa, August 12, 1985, WHORM Subject File (356500-357999), Box 168, CO 141—South Africa, RRPL. Founding chairman of the Mississippi Republican Party, Yerger was a hardline "Lily White" Republican, rejecting the civil rights movement as communist influenced. Joseph Crespino, *In Search of Another Country: Mississippi and the Conservative Counterrevolution* (Princeton University Press, 2007), 84–85, 100.
56. Proposed Reply to Mr. Sanders, National Security Council, May 9, 1986, WHORM Subject File (397000-399999), Box 168, CO 141, South Africa, RRPL; From KF to Agnes Waldron, May 9, 1986, WHORM Subject File (397000-399999), Box 168, CO 141, South Africa, RRPL.
57. Memorandum for Jim Warner from Pat Buchanan, September 11, 1986, WHORM Subject File (426180-426299), Box 170, CO 141—South Africa, RRPL.
58. Note from Walter Raymond to Robert McFarlane, Subject: Dave Miller, August 29, 1985, South Africa [08/17/1985–09/09/1985], Box 8, NSC Staff and Office Files, Raymond, Walter: Files, Series I: Subject, RRPL.
59. For more on John Sears's tumultuous relationship with the Reagan administration—notably his disastrous stint as campaign manager and his eventual firing in a New Hampshire hotel room—see Craig Shirley, *Rendezvous with Destiny: Reagan and the Campaign That Changed America* (Intercollegiate Studies Institute, 2011).
60. Ron Nixon, *Selling Apartheid: South Africa's Global Propaganda War* (Pluto, 2016), 92.
61. Memorandum for the Chief of Staff from Pat Buchanan, January 29, 1986, White House Office of Records Management (WHORM) Subject File (366400-367999), Box 168, CO 141, RRPL.
62. Memorandum for John Poindexter from Pat Buchanan, June 9, 1986, WHORM Subject File (419000-420013), Box 169, CO 141, RRPL.
63. Letter from Herbert Beukes to Patrick J. Buchanan, June 13, 1986, WHORM Subject File (418050-418999), Box 169, CO 141—South Africa, RRPL.
64. Memorandum for John Poindexter from Pat Buchanan, June 13, 1986, WHORM Subject File (418050-418999), Box 169, CO 141—South Africa, RRPL.
65. Memorandum for John M. Poindexter from Nicholas Platt, June 18, 1986, WHORM Subject File (418050-418999), Box 169, CO 141—South Africa, RRPL.

66. Letter from Ronald Reagan to Pieter Willem Botha, June 23, 1986, WHORM Subject File (418050-418999), Box 169, CO 141—South Africa, RRPL.
67. Memorandum for Chief of Staff from Pat Buchanan, July 14, 1986, WHORM Subject File (400583-400949), Box 168, CO 141—South Africa, RRPL.
68. Pat Buchanan, "A Republican Sanctions Strategy," August 5, 1986, WHORM Subject File (401400-402999), Box 168, CO 141—South Africa, RRPL.
69. Baldwin was a well-known consultant with the United International Consultants, which raked in almost $400,000 in two years from the South African government. United International Consultants paid Baldwin $100,000 a year for her expertise as a former staffer with the Senate Republican Policy Committee and former Nixon administration aide. "Fees Paid to U.S. Agents by South African Government, Homelands, and Corporations," December 16, 1985, the US Department of Justice, Foreign Agents Act Registration Records, Center for Digital Humanities and Social Sciences, Michigan State University, http://kora.matrix.msu.edu/files/50/304/32-130-F42-84-al.sff.document.af000216.pdf.
70. Memorandum for Ambassador Beukes/Malcolm Ferguson from Jody Baldwin, Re: Elements needed to sustain the presidential veto of H.R. 4868, particularly in the Senate, September 16, 1986, WHORM Subject File (500900-500939), Box 173, CO 141—South Africa, RRPL.
71. Hoar was also famous for his work *Architects of Conspiracy: An Intriguing History* (Western Islands, 1984), a collection of articles written by Hoar in *American Opinion*, now *New American*, a periodical published by the John Birch Society. In *Architects of Conspiracy*, Hoar promotes the one-world government far-right conspiracy theory popular among the pro-apartheid movement.
72. Proposed Amendment List for Anti-Apartheid Bill, Box No. 15: South Africa, House Foreign Affairs Committee—Minority—General Files: South Africa—Soviet Union, RG 233 NARA.
73. Explanation of the Crane Amendment, Box No. 214, H.R. 4868, Mr. Gray of Pennsylvania, Committee on Ways and Means Legislative Files, H.R. 4807–4868, RG 233—United States House of Representatives, 99th Congress, NARA.
74. "Jesse Helms, Speaking on H.R. 4868 Comprehensive Anti-Apartheid Act of 1986—Veto Message," October 1, 1986, 99th Congress, 2nd session, *Congressional Record Permanent Digital Collection*, 27645; "Strom Thurmond, Speaking on H.R. 4868 Comprehensive Anti-Apartheid Act of 1986—Veto Message," October 1, 1986, 99th Congress, 2nd Session, *Congressional Record Permanent Digital Collection*, 27645; "Malcolm Wallop, Speaking on S.635 Anti-Apartheid Action Act of 1985," July 11, 1985, 99th Congress, 1st Session, *Congressional Record Permanent Digital Collection*, 18804; "Dan Burton, Speaking on H.R. 4868 Anti-Apartheid Act of 1986," June 18, 1986, 99th Congress, 2nd Session, *Congressional Record Permanent Digital Collection*, 14229.
75. Judith Miller, "Behind Senator Helms, a Cherubic Assistant Reigns," *New York Times*, April 22, 1981, https://www.nytimes.com/1981/04/22/world/behind-senator-helms-a-cherubic-assistant-reigns.html.
76. Themes from John Carbaugh to Pat Buchanan, July 15, 1986 [South Africa, Background Information, re Sanctions] (8 of 12), Box 2, Series I: Subject File, Communications, Office of, Buchanan, Patrick: Files, RRPL.

77. Reply to note of 07/04/86, note from Walter Raymond, Subject: South Africa, July 7, 1986, Communications, Office of, Buchanan, Patrick: Files, Series I: Subject File, Box 2 [South Africa, Background Information, re Sanctions] (7 of 12), RRPL.
78. Draft Presidential Speech on South Africa from Rodney B. McDaniel to Tony Dolan, July 10, 1986, Communications, Office of, Buchanan, Patrick: Files, Series I: Subject File, Box 2 [South Africa, Background Information, re Sanctions] (4 of 12), RRPL.
79. Memorandum for the President from John M. Poindexter, Subject: US Initiative Concerning South Africa, July 11, 1986, CO 141, South Africa, Box 172, WHORM Subject File (445000-448399), RRPL.
80. "A Secret Communist Document Reveals the Real Game Plan for South Africa," Heritage Foundation, Executive Memorandum, July 10, 1986, National Security Council (NSC) Staff and Office Files, Raymond, Walter: Files, Series I: Subject, Box 8, South Africa 2 [07/01/1986–07/10/1986], RRPL.
81. Memorandum to Pat Buchanan from Phil Nicolaides, Subject: George Shultz and the ANC Terrorists, July 11, 1986, Communications, Office of, Buchanan, Patrick: Files, Series I: Subject File, Box 2 [South Africa, Background Information, re Sanctions] (3 of 12), RRPL.
82. Memorandum for John M. Poindexter from Phillip Ringdahl, Subject: South Africa—Presidential Response to Chief Buthelezi, August 9, 1986, CO 141, South Africa, Box 169, WHORM Subject File (405690-406296), RRPL.
83. Letter from Gatsha Buthelezi to Ronald Reagan, July 11, 1986, CO 141, South Africa, Box 169, WHORM Subject File (405690-406296), RRPL.
84. Memorandum for Patrick J. Buchanan from Anthony R. Dolan, July 11, 1986 [South Africa, Background Information, re Sanctions] (6 of 12), Box 2, Series I: Subject File, Communications, Office of, Buchanan, Patrick, RRPL.
85. Draft Presidential Speech on South Africa, reviewed by Buchanan July 15, 1986, Box 2 [South Africa, Background Information, re Sanctions] (6 of 12), Series I: Subject File, Communications, Office of, Buchanan, Patrick: Files, RRPL.
86. Draft for RR Speech, Pat Buchanan, July 14, 1986 [South Africa, Background Information, re Sanctions] (6 of 12), Box 2, Series I: Subject File, Communications, Office of, Buchanan, Patrick, RRPL.
87. Memorandum for the Chief of Staff from Pat Buchanan, July 14, 1986, CO 141, South Africa, Box 168, WHORM Subject File (400583-400949), RRPL.
88. "Notes on South Africa," July 17, 1986, Box 14, South Africa, Series I, Subject File, Office of the Chief of Staff, Thomas, W. Dennis: Files, RRPL.
89. From Richard B. Wirthlin to Donald T. Regan, "Proposed President's Speech on South Africa," July 15, 1986, Box 14, South Africa, Series I, Subject File, Office of the Chief of Staff, Thomas, W. Dennis: Files, RRPL.
90. Nicholas Platt Memorandum to John M. Poindexter, Subject: South Africa Public Diplomacy Action Plan, 1986, Box 8, South Africa 2 [07/18/1986–07/22/1986], Raymond, Walter: Files, Series I: Subject, National Security Council (NSC) Staff and Office Files, RRPL.
91. Black American Invitees, 1986, Box 8, South Africa 2 [07/18/1986–07/22/1986], Raymond, Walter: Files, Series I: Subject, National Security Council (NSC) Staff and Office Files, RRPL.

92. Memorandum for John M. Poindexter from Pat Buchanan, July 18, 1986, CO 141, South Africa, Box 168, WHORM Subject File (400583-400949), RRPL.
93. Text of Remarks by the President and Members of the World Affairs Council and the Foreign Policy Association, July 22, 1986, House Foreign Affairs Committee—Minority—General Files: Shiite—South Africa, RG 233, NARA, 3, 5, 6.
94. "West European Press Supports Economic Sanctions Against South Africa," FMA-8/18/86, Entry P59, Foreign Media Trends and Analyses, 1984–94, Box 1, RG 306, U.S. National Archives, Letter to Anton Rupert from Walt Raymond, July 31, 1986, South Africa 2 [07/31/1986–08/10/1986], Box 8, Raymond, Walter: Files, Series I: Subject, National Security Council (NSC) Staff and Office Files, RRPL.
95. Gerald M. Boyd, "President Opposes Additional Steps on South Africa," *New York Times*, July 23, 1986.
96. "Reagan Resists Sanctions, but . . .," *New York Times*, July 27, 1986.
97. "Excerpts from Speech in Response to Reagan," *New York Times*, July 23, 1986.
98. Testimony by Secretary Shultz, Senate Foreign Relations Committee, July 23, 1986, WHORM Subject File (436000-436199), Box 171, CO 141—South Africa, RRPL.
99. Mr. President: DO THESE MEN SPEAK FOR YOU?, Coalition Against ANC Terrorism, WHORM Subject File (458000-459999), Box 172, CO 141—South Africa, RRPL.
100. Policy Forum on Strategic Minerals and US Policy Toward South Africa, vol. II, no. 3, Policy Forum, House Foreign Affairs Committee—Minority—General Files: South Africa—Soviet Union, Box No. 15: South Africa, RG 233, NARA.
101. From Phil Nicolaides to Pat Buchanan, July 15, 1986, Communications, Office of, Buchanan, Patrick: Files, Series I: Subject File, Box 2 [South Africa, Background Information, re Sanctions] (1 of 12), RRPL.
102. Patrick J. Buchanan, "Do We Have to Destroy South Africa in Order to Save Her," August 27, 1986, WHORM Subject File (424632)(1), Box 170, CO 141—South Africa, RRPL.
103. Patrick Buchanan, "The Unpardonable Heresy of the Boer Republic," 1986, South Africa (6), Box 18020, Public Affairs, Office of, Public Affairs Office of, Records, RRPL. It is unclear if Buchanan ever published it.
104. Note for Donald T. Regan from David Chew [Correspondence, Memos] (2), Series I: Diskette File, Office of the Chief of Staff, Dawson, Thomas C. II, RRPL.
105. "Destroy South Africa to Save It?," Pat Buchanan, September 18, 1986 [09/09/1986–09/21/1986], South Africa 2, Box 8, Series I: Subject, NSC Staff and Office Files, Raymond, Walter: Files, RRPL.
106. Memorandum for Donald T. Regan and John M. Poindexter from Pat Buchanan, August 22, 1986, South Africa 2 [08/23/1986–08/25/1986], Box 8, NSC Staff and Office Files, Raymond Walter: Files, Series I, RRPL.
107. Memorandum for Mari Maseng from Carl A. Anderson, Subject: Religious Group Activities on South Africa, September 24, 1986, WHORM Subject File (43900-439799), Box 171, CO 141—South Africa, RRPL.
108. During her tenure in the Reagan White House, Arey directly administered the women's portfolio, serving as the go-between for the administration and women's organizations. Arey Linda L.: Files, 1985–1987, "Ronald Reagan Presidential Library and Museum,"

https://www.reaganlibrary.gov/archives/white-house-inventory/arey-linda-l-files-1985-1987, accessed January 11, 2022.

109. Memorandum for Mari Maseng from Linda Arey, Subject: Constituent Activities in Support of Reagan's Position on South Africa, September 24, 1986, WHORM Subject File (439000-439799), Box 171, CO 141—South Africa, RRPL.
110. South Africa Update, September 24, 1986, WHORM Subject File (439000-439799), Box 171, CO 141—South Africa, RRPL.
111. The Eminent Black Persons Group, spearheaded by Director of African Affairs Phillip Ringdahl, was a proposed counter to the European Eminent Persons Group. Letter from Robert N. Cleaves to Phil Ringdahl, July 29, 1986 [South Africa], Sanctions (Including Legislation), (7), RAC Box 16, African Affairs Directorate, NSC: Records, Collection: African Affairs Directorate, NSC, Box 10, RRPL.
112. Urgent Action Memo to Pat Buchanan from Phil Nicolaides, September 25, 1986, CO 141, South Africa, Box 171, WHORM Subject File (440874)(1), RRPL.
113. Memorandum for Donald T. Regan and John M. Poindexter from Pat Buchanan, Subject: Sustaining the Sanctions Veto, September 21, 1986, WHORM Subject File (500900-500939), Box 173, CO 141—South Africa, RRPL.
114. Draft Letter to Republican Fundraisers by Pat Buchanan, September 21, 1986, WHORM Subject File (500900-500939), Box 173, CO 141—South Africa, RRPL.
115. Don Regan response to draft letter to Republican Fundraisers, September 21, 1986, CO 141, South Africa, Box 173, WHORM Subject File (500900-500939), RRPL.
116. Memorandum for Ambassador Beukes/Malcolm Ferguson from Jody Baldwin.
117. Memorandum for Donald T. Regan from Dennis Thomas, Subject: South Africa, September 23, 1986, WHORM Subject File (401400-402999), Box 168, CO 141, RRPL; memorandum for Donald T. Regan from Dennis Thomas, Subject: South Africa, September 25, 1986, WHORM Subject File (500900-500939), Box 173, CO 141—South Africa, RRPL.
118. "Categorized List of Senators," Jody Baldwin, Undated, WHORM Subject File (401400-402999), Box 168, CO 141—South Africa, RRPL.
119. Memorandum for the Chief of Staff from Pat Buchanan, August 18, 1986, WHORM Subject File (401030-401399), Box 168, CO 141—South Africa, RRPL.
120. Note for DTR from Will Ball, Re: South Africa, August 28, 1986, WHORM Subject File (401030-401399), Box 168, CO 141—South Africa, RRPL.
121. Memorandum for Donald T. Regan from Dennis Thomas, Subject: South Africa, September 22, 1986, WHORM Subject File (445000-448399), Box 172, CO 141, South Africa, RRPL.
122. Memorandum from Walter Raymond, Subject: South Africa and the E.O., August 22, 1986, South Africa 2 [08/26/1986–09/26/1986], Box 8, Raymond, Walter: Files, Series I: Subject, National Security Council (NSC) Staff and Office Files, RRPL.
123. Memorandum for the President from John M. Poindexter, Subject: Future U.S. Actions Concerning South Africa, September 2, 1986, WHORM Subject File (406297), Box 169, CO 141—South Africa, RRPL.
124. Memorandum for VADM John M. Poindexter, from Nicolas Platt, August 26, 1986, Subject: South Africa Executive Order and the Congress, WHORM Subject File (406297), Box 169, CO 141—South Africa, RRPL.

125. Comparison of South African Bill, Current Executive Order, E.C., Measures and Expanded Executive Order [South Africa], Sanctions (Including Legislation), (5), RAC Box 16, Collection: African Affairs Directorate, NSC, Box 10, RRPL, 1–2.
126. Comparison of South African Bill, Current Executive Order, E.C., Measures and Expanded Executive Order [South Africa], Sanctions (Including Legislation), (5), RAC Box 16, Collection: African Affairs Directorate, NSC, Box 10, RRPL, 2–6.
127. Subject: South Africa Executive Order and the Congress.
128. Jan Ad-Stemmet, "The Storms of Reforms: South Africa's Reform-Strategy, c. 1980–1989," *University of Free State Journal* 38, no. 2 (December 2013): 123.
129. Michael Parks, "Botha Outlines Apartheid Reforms; Blacks Unmoved," *Los Angeles Times*, February 1, 1986.
130. Incoming telegram from AM Embassy Pretoria to Sec State Wash DC, "My Presentation of Reagan's Letter to State President Botha," September 11, 1985, South Africa—Working Files 3 (6), October 1984 to June 1986, RAC Box 9, African Affairs Directorate, NSC, Records, Collection: African Affairs Directorate, NSC, Box 2, RRPL.
131. Memorandum to Pat Buchanan from Phil Nicolaides, Subject: Implementing the President's S.A. Policy, July 23, 1986 [South Africa, Background Information, re Sanctions] (7 of 12), Box 2, Series I, Subject File, Communications, Office of, Buchanan, Patrick: Files, RRPL.
132. Buchanan, "A Republican Sanctions Strategy."
133. Q&A in Response to 1985 Executive Order, South Africa [Press-1985], (2 of 4), RAC Box 9, African Affairs Directorate, NSC, Records, Collection: African Affairs Directorate, NSC, Box 3, RRPL.
134. Charter of the Advisory Committee on South Africa, December 18, 1985, South Africa Advisory Committee: [01/03/1986—01/23/1986], Box 16, African Affairs Directorate, NSC: Records, Collection: African Affairs Directorate, NSC, Box 6, RRPL.
135. Memorandum for Nicholas Platt from William Martin, "South Africa: Request for Plan of Action," November 11, 1985, South Africa—General—1985–1987 (1 of 4), RAC Box 10, African Affairs Directorate, NSC: Records, Collection: African Affairs Directorate, NSC, Box 3, RRPL; memorandum for Pat Buchanan from John M. Poindexter, "South Africa Advisory Committee," January 18, 1986, South Africa Advisory Committee: [01/03/1986—01/23/1986], Box 16, African Affairs Directorate, NSC: Records, Collection: African Affairs Directorate, NSC, Box 6, RRPL; Draft Presidential Speech on South Africa, July 15, 1986, Box 2 [South Africa, Background Information, re Sanctions] (6 of 12), Series I: Subject File, Communications, Office of, Buchanan, Patrick: Files, RRPL. Chairmen Cary and Colemen were seemingly not invited to Reagan's speech. Conservative /presidential supporters, Linas Kojelis, July 1986, Public Liaison, Office of, Kojelis, Linas: Files, OA 18283 [South Africa Speech 07/22/1986 Invitations] (2 of 6), RRPL.
136. Telegram to Secretary of State from US Mission, Subject: Meeting in New York with ANC Representative Neo Mnumzana, February 1986, South Africa: ANC (3 of 4), RAC Box 16, African Affairs Directorate, NSC, Records, Collection: African Affairs Directorate, NSC, Box 6, RRPL.
137. "Sanctions Scenarios," August 11, 1986, WHORM Subject File (400583-400949), Box 168, CO 141, RRPL.

138. "Sanctions Scenarios," August 11, 1986.
139. "Undiplomatic Diplomat: Outspoken Black Ambassador May Get Top State Department Post," *Post Standard*, June 18, 1985.
140. Note from Phil Nicolaides to Pat Buchanan, August 28, 1986, WHORM Subject File (440874)(1), Box 171, CO 141—South Africa, RRPL.
141. Memorandum from Phil Nicolaides to Pat Buchanan, September 29, 1986, WHORM Subject File (440874)(1), Box 171, CO 141—South Africa, RRPL.
142. "Standard Language on Contact with the ANC," WHORM Subject File (440874)(1), Box 171, CO 141, RRPL.
143. "The View from the State Department, Ambassador Ordered to Suppress News of African Support for the President," Shirley Abbot, July 30, 1986, WHORM Subject File (437500-438349), Box 171, Co 141—South Africa, RRPL.
144. Memorandum from Phil Nicolaides to Pat Buchanan, Subject: S.A. Update, September 10, 1986, WHORM Subject File (440874)(1), Box 171, CO 141—South Africa, RRPL.
145. Memorandum from Pat Buchanan to Donald T. Regan and John M. Poindexter, August 22, 1986, WHORM Subject File (419000-420013), Box 169, CO 141—South Africa, RRPL.
146. Memorandum for Donald T. Regan and John M. Poindexter from Pat Buchanan, Subject: The Reagan Plan, September 10, 1986, WHORM Subject File (426180-426299), Box 170, CO 141—South Africa, RRPL.
147. Presidential Veto Message: HR 4868, Comprehensive Anti-Apartheid Act of 1986 for Buchanan, September 25, 1986, OA 15539, South Africa: H.R. 4868 (3), McGrath, C. Dean: Files: RRPL.
148. David Hoffman, "Reagan Vetoes Sanctions Against South Africa," *Washington Post*, September 26, 1986, https://www.washingtonpost.com/archive/politics/1986/09/27/reagan-vetoes-sanctions-against-south-africa/af009ab1-2ed2-4e72-ab46-52fc2ec2d7e6/.
149. Steven V. Roberts, "Senate, 78 to 21, Overrides Reagan's Veto and Imposes Sanctions on South Africa," *New York Times*, October 3, 1986, https://www.nytimes.com/1986/10/03/politics/senate-78-to-21-overrides-reagans-veto-and-imposes-sanctions-on.html.
150. Tim Alberta, "'The Ideas Made It, But I Didn't': Pat Buchanan Won After All. But Now He Thinks It Might Be Too Late for the Nation He Was Trying to Save," *Politico Mag Profile*, May/June 2017, https://www.politico.com/magazine/story/2017/04/22/pat-buchanan-trump-president-history-profile-215042/.

INTERLUDE: APARTHEID THEOLOGY

1. Harold E. Winkler, "Bishop Masamba Comes to Town," Institute for Contextual Theology, 1990, Folder: Jr, Right-Wing Religion, AG2843—Institute for Contextual Theology, "Right-Wing Religion," Jr, UWHP. Portions of this chapter originally appeared in Augusta Dell'Omo "Infernal Handiwork: Trinity Broadcasting Network Aids Apartheid South Africa," *Diplomatic History* 45, no. 4, (September 2021): 767–793.
2. *Lekker* is an Afrikaans adjective meaning, in this context, nice or pleasant.
3. Winkler, "Bishop Masamba Comes to Town."

4. Frank Chikane, General Secretary's Report (1985–1986), Institute for Contextual Theology, April 29, 1987, Folder: B2, Institute for Contextual Theology Reports, Quarterly/Half Yearly Reports, Gen. Sec. Reports, Director Reports, Progress Reports, 1981–1991, B2–B6, AG2843—ICT, Reports: General/Divisional/Reports of Visits, UWHP.
5. Winkler, "Bishop Masamba Comes to Town."
6. T. Dunbar Moodie, "Confessing Responsibility for the Evils of Apartheid: The Dutch Reformed Church in the 1980s," *South African Historical Journal* 72, no. 4 (2020): 643; P. G. J. Meiring, "Reforum: A Brief but Not Unimportant Chapter in the Dutch Reformed Church's Apartheid Saga," *Verbum et Ecclesia* 42, no. 1 (2021): 1–8.
7. Kevin Jacobs, "Dissident Afrikaners Threaten to Split from Dutch Reformed Church," *UPI*, June 27, 1987; "A New Right-Wing Group Aksie Eie Toekoms (Action for our Own Future) (AET) Is Founded in Pretoria," *South African History Online*, February 14, 1981, https://www.sahistory.org.za/dated-event/new-right-wing-group-aksie-eie-toekoms-action-our-own-future-aet-founded-pretoria; Gary Thatcher, "An Afrikaner Who Wants to Be South Africa's Ronald Reagan," *Christian Science Monitor*, February 25, 1981, https://www.csmonitor.com/1981/0225/022548.html.
8. Brian Pottinger, *The Imperial Presidency: P.W. Botha: The First Ten Years* (Southern Book, 1988).
9. Simon Evenett, "The Impact of Economic Sanctions on South African Exports," *Scottish Journal of Political Economy* 49, no. 5 (2002): 557–73; John D. Battersby, "Sanctions Squeeze South Africa," *New York Times*, November 13, 1988, https://www.nytimes.com/1988/11/13/business/sanctions-squeeze-south-africa.html.
10. Franziska Rueedi, "'Our Bushes Are the Houses Our Bushes Are the Houses': People's War and the Underground during the Insurrectionary Period in the Vaal Triangle, South Africa," *Journal of Southern African Studies* 46, no. 4 (2020): 632.
11. Rueedi, "'Our Bushes Are the Houses Our Bushes Are the Houses,'" 239. On future South African president Ramaphosa's historic strike with the National Union of Mineworkers, see Kate Philip, *Markets on the Margins: Mineworkers, Job Creation, and Enterprise Development* (Boydell & Brewer, 2018); Andries Bezuidenhout and Sakhela Buhlungu, "From Compounded to Fragmented Labor: Mineworkers and the Demise of Compounds in South Africa," *Antipode* 43, no. 2 (March 2011): 237–63; and Sakhela Buhlungu and Andries Bezuidenhout, "Union Solidarity Under Stress: The Case of the National Union of Mineworkers in South Africa," *Labor Studies Journal* 33, no. 3 (September 2008): 262–67.
12. Gregory Houston, *The National Liberation Struggle in South Africa: A Case Study of the United Democratic Front, 1983–1987* (Ashgate, 1999).
13. Frank Chikane, *The Church's Prophetic Witness Against the Apartheid System in South Africa* (Johannesburg, 1988); John de Gruchy, Steve de Gruchy, and Desmond Tutu, *The Church Struggle in South Africa* (Fortress, 2005); Charles Villa-Vicencio, *Theology and Violence: The South African Debate* (Eerdmans, 1988).
14. Houston, *The National Liberation Struggle for South Africa*, 59–88.
15. J. E. Spence, "South Africa's General Election—the Point of No Return?," *The World Today* 43, no. 7 (July 1987): 117.

16. F. A. Mouton, "'Dr No': A.P. Treurnicht and the Ultra-Conservative Quest to Maintain Afrikaner Supremacy, 1982–1993," *South African Historical Journal* 65, no. 4 (2013): 585.
17. Stanley Uys, "White Elections—Black Times," *Front File—Southern African Brief*, no. 2, May 1987. Of the 2,062,000 white votes cast, over 1,200,000 were Afrikaners. The Conservative Party and the National Party pulled 604,595 Afrikaners.
18. In retrospect, many of those Progressive voters moved to the National Party, fearful of the rising power of the Conservative Party and unconvinced by the Progressive Federal Party's plans for apartheid reform. This shift in the vote became clearer with the assumption of power by F. W. de Klerk, but in 1987, national and international observers feared a shift to the right.
19. Dan O'Meara, *Forty Lost Years: The Apartheid State and the Politics of the National Party, 1948-1994* (Raven, 1997), 312.
20. Hermann Giliomee, "'Broedertwis': Intra-Afrikaner Conflicts in the Transition from Apartheid," *African Affairs* 91, no. 364 (July 1992): 339–64.
21. "The Kairos Theology and the Destabilization of the Region," EDICESA Conference, September 20, 1989, Folder: ICT, Kairos Doc. G9, Kairos Document—Responses, Responses, AG2843—Institute for Contextual Theology, UWHP.
22. "Commission of Inquiry Into the South African Council of Churches Held at Pretoria on 9 May 1983, Volume 61," Collection: Commissions of Inquiry, Struggles for Freedom: Southern Africa, *JSTOR*.
23. Izak J. J. Spangenberg, "The Bible, Theology, and the Dutch Reformed Church in South Africa, 1920–2020," *Hervormde Teologiese Studies* 76, no. 4 (2020): 5, 7
24. Subscriber Letter, Gospel Defense League, October 1987, Box 3, Gospel Defense League Newsletters, 1985–1995, Mary Ann Gilbert, Serials Correspondence, SC #9, Intercessors for the Suffering Church Collection, WCSC.
25. Subscriber Letter, Gospel Defense League, September 1987, Box 3, Gospel Defense League Newsletters, 1985–1995, Mary Ann Gilbert, Serials Correspondence, SC 79, Intercessors for the Suffering Church Collection, WCSC.
26. Subscriber Letter, Gospel Defense League, November 1987, Box 3, Gospel Defense League Newsletters, 1985–1995, Mary Ann Gilbert, Serials Correspondence, SC 79, Intercessors for the Suffering Church Collection, WCSC.
27. "Freedom of Religion: How Vital Is Religion in the New South Africa," Gospel Defense League, November 1991, Box 3, Gospel Defense League Newsletters, 1985–1995, Mary Ann Gilbert, Serials Correspondence, SC 79, Intercessors for the Suffering Church Collection, WCSC.
28. "Freedom of the Nation: The Challenge of Pluralism," Gospel Defense League, 1994, Box 3, Gospel Defense League Newsletters, 1985–1995, Mary Ann Gilbert, Serials Correspondence, SC 79, Intercessors for the Suffering Church Collection, WCSC.
29. "What Does the Bible Say About Democracy?," Gospel Defense League, August 1988, Folder: Jr, Right-Wing Religion, "Right-Wing Religion," Jr, AG2843—Institute for Contextual Theology, UWHIP.

30. "What Does the Bible Say About Ethnicity?," Gospel Defense League, February 1989, Box 3, Gospel Defense League Newsletters, 1985–1995, Mary Ann Gilbert, Serials Correspondence, SC 79, Intercessors for the Suffering Church Collection, WCSC.
31. The Gospel Defense League of South Africa, November 1987, Box 3, Gospel Defense League Newsletters, 1985–1995, Mary Ann Gilbert, Serials Correspondence, SC 79, Intercessors for the Suffering Church Collection, WCSC.
32. "Information Resources Available from the Gospel Defense League," 1991, Folder: Jr, Right-Wing Religion, "Right-Wing Religion," Jr, AG2843—Institute for Contextual Theology, UWHP.
33. Francis Nigel Lee, "The Christian Afrikaners: A Brief History of Calvinistic Afrikanerdom," Ensign Message, https://ensignmessage.com/articles/the-christian-afrikaners-6/; Peter Hammond, "A Tribute to Professor Dr. Peter Beyerhaus," Frontline Fellowship, January 29, 2020, https://www.frontlinemissionsa.org/in-memorium/a-tribute-to-prof-dr-peter-beyerhaus; "Leadership and Staff," Heritage Presbyterian Church, https://heritagepresbyterianchurch.com/leadership-staff/; "Dr Francis Nigel Lee," Frontline Fellowship, December 23, 2011, https://www.frontlinemissionsa.org/in-memorium/dr-francis-nigel-lee; "Who We Are," Pactum Institute, https://www.pactuminstitute.com/who-we-are.
34. "Information Resources Available from the Gospel Defense League."
35. "The Battle for a Biblical South Africa: A Report on the Conference for Christian Action held on Thursday 10th October, 1991, at the Evangelical Reformed Church, Bellville," Gospel Defense League, October 10, 1991, Box 3, Gospel Defense League Newsletters, 1985–1995, Mary Ann Gilbert, Serials Correspondence, SC 79, Intercessors for the Suffering Church Collection, WCSC.
36. 1988 Annual General Meeting Conference, Theme: The Misuse of Religion in South Africa, August 1–4, 1988, Institute for Contextual Theology, August 1–4, 1988, Folder: C6, ICT, AGM Conference, 1988, C1–C9, 1982–1991, AG2843—Institute for Contextual Theology, Institute for Contextual Theology Annual Conferences, UWHP.
37. Institute for Contextual Theology, Women's Sector Report, Institute for Contextual Theology, 1993, Folder: B5, Women's Sector, 1989–1993, B2–B6, AG2843—Institute for Contextual Theology, ICT, Reports: General/Divisional/Reports of Visits, UWHP.
38. Notes from ICT AGM on Misuse of Religion in South Africa, Institute for Contextual Theology, August 2, 1988, Folder: C6, ICT, AGM Conference, 1988, C1–C9, 1982–1991, AG2843—Institute for Contextual Theology, Institute for Contextual Theology Annual Conferences, UWHP.
39. South Africa Right Wing Religion, Institute for Contextual Theology, 1988, Folder: Jr, Right-Wing Religion, AG2843—Institute for Contextual Theology, "Right-Wing Religion," Jr, UWHP. Report on the Seminar of "Concerned Evangelicals" held on the 12th April 1986 at Funda Center Soweto, Concerned Evangelicals, April 12, 1986, Folder: JC, Institute for Contextual Theology, Concerned Evangelical, Meetings of CE mtg, CE Minutes, AG2843—Institute for Contextual Theology, Centre-Crisis, JC: UWHP.

40. Misuse of Religion: Interim Report, Concerned Evangelicals, July 20, 1988, Folder: JC, Institute for Contextual Theology, Concerned Evangelical, Meetings of CE mtg, CE Minutes, AG2843—Institute for Contextual Theology, Centre-Crisis, JC: UWHP.
41. "What Is the International Freedom Foundation?," Jeffrey Marishane, Institute for Contextual Theology, January 1993, Folder: I1, ICT, Memoranda, AG2843—Institute for Contextual Theology, I, Memoranda, Papers, Articles, UWHP.
42. The Rhema Christian Church presented itself as a "moderate" church that challenged ANC activists like Mandela to "declare" his Christian commitments, part of a scheme to undermine confidence in the ANC in favor of the "eminently Christian" National Party and the "Black moderates." These concerns from the ICT remain fascinating because of McCauley's contemporary ties to the ANC, particularly former president Jacob Zuma. "Inside the Most Powerful Church in South Africa," *Independent*, June 21, 2010, https://www.independent.co.uk/news/world/africa/inside-the-most-powerful-church-in-south-africa-2006129.html; Ebrahim Fakir, "Why Was Ray McCauley Trying to Play Peacemaker Between the ANC and EFF," *Sowetan Live*, February 12, 2015, https://www.sowetanlive.co.za/news/2015-02-12-why-was-ray-mccauley-trying-to-play-peacemaker-between-the-anc-and-eff2/; Mmanaledi Mataboge, "Why ANC Dumped Council of Churches," *Mail and Guardian*, September 18, 2009, https://www.sowetanlive.co.za/news/2015-02-12-why-was-ray-mccauley-trying-to-play-peacemaker-between-the-anc-and-eff2; Notes on Steering Committee Meeting at Aubrey House, Concerned Evangelicals, April 6, 1987, Folder: JC, Institute for Contextual Theology, Concerned Evangelical, Meetings of CE mtg, CE Minutes, AG2843—Institute for Contextual Theology, Centre-Crisis, JC: UWHP.
43. Evangelical Witness in South Africa (Evangelicals Critique Their Own Theology and Practice), Concerned Evangelicals, July 1986, Folder: JC, Institute for Contextual Theology, Concerned Evangelical, Meetings of CE mtg, CE Minutes, AG2843—Institute for Contextual Theology, Centre-Crisis, JC: UWHP.
44. "To Give the Winds a Mighty Voice," TBN Online, https://tbnfounders.org/founders-biographies/#paul.
45. "A Global Messenger of God's Love!," TBN Online, https://www.tbn.org/about.
46. Elaine Woo, "Paul Crouch Dies at 79; Founded Trinity Broadcasting Network," *Los Angeles Times*, November 30, 2013.
47. Darren Dochuk, *From Bible Belt to Sunbelt: Plain-Folk Religion, Grassroots Politics, and Evangelical Conservatism* (Norton, 2011), xviii, 2
48. Allen Anderson, *An Introduction to Pentecostalism: Global Charismatic Christianity* (Cambridge University Press, 2014), 1, 4.
49. Kathleen Hladky, "'The Prince of the Power of the Air': Media, the Word of Faith Movement, and the End of the World on Trinity Broadcasting Network," *Spectator* 28, no. 1 (2008): 40–52.
50. See Quentin J. Schultze, *Televangelism and American Culture: The Business of Popular Religion* (University of Oregon Press, 1991); Jeffrey K. Hadden, "The Rise and Fall of American Televangelism," *Annals of the American Academy of Political and Social Science* 527, no. 1 (1993): 113–30; Janice Peck, "Selling Goods and Selling God: Advertising,

Televangelism, and the Commodity Form," *Journal of Communication Inquiry* 17, no. 1 (1993): 5–24; and Hladky, " 'Prince of the Power,' " 5.

51. "Africa—A Call to Arms!," *Praise the Lord Newsletter* XIII, no. III (March 1985), *Trinity Broadcasting Network Thirtieth Anniversary Publications 1973–2003* (hereafter *TBN Thirtieth Anniversary*), vol. 2.
52. Sekibakiba Peter Lekgoathi, " 'You Are Listening to Radio Lebowa of the South African Broadcasting Corporation': Vernacular Radio, Bantustan Identity and Listenership, 1960–1994," *Journal of Southern African Studies* 35, no. 3 (2009): 1.
53. Adrian Hadland, Joshua Ogada, and Mike Aldridge, *Re-visioning Television: Policy, Strategy and Models for the Sustainable Development of Community Television in South Africa* (Human Science Research Council Press, 2006); Kristin Skare Ogeret, "From 'The Devil in the Black Box' to a Nation-Building Tool: Early TV in South Africa—A New Medium for a New Nation," in *Modernization, Nation-Building, and Television History*, ed. Stewart Anderson and Melissa Chakars (Routledge, 2015), 191; Ron Krabill, *Starring Mandela and Cosby: Media and the End(s) of Apartheid* (University of Chicago Press, 2010), 3.
54. Sean Jacobs, *Media in Post Apartheid South Africa: Postcolonial Politics in the Age of Globalization* (Indiana University Press, 2019), 18.
55. "Republic of South Africa, Government Gazette," National Key Points Act, July 25, 1980, https://www.gov.za/sites/default/files/gcis_document/201503/act-102-1980.pdf; and Gavin Cawthra, *Policing South Africa: The South African Police and the Transition from Apartheid* (Zed Books, 1993).
56. Krabill, *Starring Mandela and Cosby*, 6.
57. Jacobs, *Media in Post Apartheid South Africa*, 19.
58. Jacobs, *Media in Post Apartheid South Africa*, 21; and Krabill, *Starring Mandela and Cosby*, 1.
59. Tinyiko Maluleke, "South Africa," in *Christianity in Sub-Saharan Africa*, ed. Kenneth R. Ross, J. Kwabena Asamoah-Gyadu, and Todd M. Johnson (Edinburgh University Press, 2017), 44.
60. Matthew Schoffeleers, "The Zion Christian Church and the Apartheid Regime," *Leidschrift: Black Culture in South Africa* 4 (June 1988): 42, 47.
61. "Spirit and Power—A 10-Country Survey of Pentecostals: Historical Overview of Pentecostalism in South Africa," PEW Research Center, October 5, 2006, https://www.pewresearch.org/religion/2006/10/05/historical-overview-of-pentecostalism-in-south-africa/. The ZCC later joined up with the African Christian Democratic Party and Mangope's United Christian Democratic Party, campaigning against abortion and homosexuality.
62. Maria Frahm-Arp, "Pentecostal Charismatic Christianity and Social Media in South Africa: Mitigating Marginality, Prosperity Teachings, and the Emergence of a Black Middle Class," in *Religion, Media, and Marginality in Modern Africa*, ed. Felicitas Becker, Joel Cabrita, and Marie Rodet (Ohio University Press, 2018), 76.
63. The "black middle class" of sympathetic conservative South Africans also included Colored and Indian South Africans. The majority of Colored South Africans live in the Western Cape, specifically Cape Town, where they make up nearly half the total population, the result of "intermingling" between "European men and the Indigenous and slave populations of the Cape" in the seventeenth century. The United Democratic Front and

the internal wing of the ANC based their operations in Western Cape in the 1980s, and high-profile Colored activists included Cheryl Carolus, Trevor Manuel, and Allan Boesak. Several of the pro-apartheid movement's most critical actors called Cape Town home—Dorothea Scarborough and Ed Cain. In the initial years after apartheid's formation in 1948, the Colored People's National Union was the largest political organization for Colored South Africans but was "dominated by moderate and conservative rural Coloureds" who "favored a policy of negotiation and compromise." Explicit attempts to bring Colored South Africans into the National Party vision of South Africa occurred politically in the 1980s with the 1983 Tricameral Parliament, but it was also religious and cultural, a result of shared Christian religiosity and Afrikaans language. In 1994, over half of Colored voters in the Western Cape voted for the National Party in the first open elections, and only a third of their vote went to the ANC. Divisions also existed within the Muslim community in South Africa—which included Colored and Indian South Africans in the Western Cape, Transvaal, and Natal regions—over participation in the Tricameral Parliament, where "many of the conservative Muslim leaders urged against challenging the apartheid regime." Peter Hammond based his operations in the Transvaal and Natal regions. Although not explicitly seeking to reach Muslim South Africans, the pro-apartheid movement's most ardent defenders actually represented a far wider category of "conservative black South Africans" who did not map neatly onto the ANC's vision of a post–white rule South Africa. These divisions also included South Africa's Jewish population, which "counted" as "white" within the apartheid system and largely benefited from its policies, even as progressive and leftist Jewish South Africans joined the antiapartheid movement. Sean Jacobs, "Making Sense of the 'Coloured' Vote in Post-Apartheid South Africa: Comparing the 1994 and 1999 Provincial Results in the Western Cape," *Journal of African Elections* 1, no. 1 (May 2001): 24–25; Eugene Baron, "'Coloured', You're On Your Own? A Dialectic Between Biko's Black Consciousness Thought and the Post-Apartheid Conditions of the 'Coloured' People in South Africa," *Black Theology: An International Journal* 20, no. 2 (2022): 128; "South African Coloured People's Organization (SACPO)," South African History Online, https://www.sahistory.org.za/article/south-african-coloured-people-organisation-sacpo; Jill E. Kelly, "'It Is *Because* of Our Islam That We Are There:' The Call of Islam in the United Democratic Front Era," *African Historical Review* 41, no. 1 (2009): 120; and Shirli Gilbert and Deborah Posel, "The Holocaust, Apartheid, and Contemporary South African Jewish Perspectives on Victimhood," *Journal of Jewish Identities* 14, no. 2 (2021): 155–70.

64. Paul Crouch, "Rio Grande Valley on the Air!," *Praise the Lord Newsletter* XII, no. VIII, August 1984, *TBN Thirtieth Anniversary*, vol. 2.
65. "South Africa—On the Air!," *Praise the Lord Newsletter* XIV, no. I, January 1987, *TBN Thirtieth Anniversary*, vol. 2.
66. Augusta Dell'Omo, "Infernal Handiwork: Trinity Broadcasting Network Aids Apartheid South Africa, 1980–1995," *Diplomatic History* 45, no. 4 (September 2021): 785.
67. Mark I. Pinsky, "Ruler of S. African Sector Visits Here, Talks with Crouch," *Los Angeles Times*, April 1, 1989.
68. "I Had a Dream," *Praise the Lord Newsletter* XIV, no. VIII, August 1987, Folder HH84/1/3—Trinity Broadcasting Network, Box 15–32, Ms. 76.15, HHC.

69. "I Had a Dream."
70. "'Shall Come in Like Manner,'" *Praise the Lord Newsletter* XV, no. X, October 1988, *Trinity Broadcasting Network Thirtieth Anniversary*, vol. 2.
71. Louis Prisock, *African Americans in Conservative Movements* (Springer, 2018), 297–334.
72. "Angel III—Heaven Bound!," *Praise the Lord Newsletter* XIX, no. V, May 1992, Folder 27C:81—Trinity Broadcasting Inc., Box T-22, Ms. 76, Part II, HHC.
73. "Angel III—Heaven Bound!"; and "TBN Satellite Schedule," Trinity Broadcasting Network, Folder 75C—Trinity Broadcasting Inc., Box T-22, Ms. 76, Part II, HHC.
74. "African Station Number Two—Granted," *Praise the Lord Newsletter* XV, no. XI, November 1988, *TBN Thirtieth Anniversary*, vol. 2.
75. "1991—What a Year!," *Praise the Lord Newsletter* XIX, no. I, January 1992, *TBN Thirtieth Anniversary*, vol. 2
76. "African Station Number Two—Granted."
77. "What a Year!," *Praise the Lord Newsletter* XVII, no. I, January 1990, *TBN Thirtieth Anniversary*, vol. 2.
78. "South Africa—On the Air!"
79. *Praise the Lord*, "April 30, 1992," directed and written by Paul Crouch, Trinity Broadcasting Network, aired on April 30, 1992, https://www.youtube.com/watch?v=oB1VYnzB7PQ.
80. National Religious Broadcasters, Convention/Exhibition, February 2–6, 1986, B9/1/4, 1986, Mrt.-Mei, Box 220, PV 203, ARCA.
81. Mark I. Pinsky, "Ruler of S. African Sector Visits Here, Talks with Crouch," *Los Angeles Times*, April 1, 1989.
82. "I Had a Dream."
83. "Developing the Ciskei: In Search of a Strategy," *Rural and Regional Monitor, Indicator South Africa* 3, no. 4 (1986): 6.
84. "African Station Number Two—Granted."
85. Mark I Pinsky, "Asia to Africa: Crouch Takes His TV Gospel Worldwide Series, 'Trinity Broadcasting,' 'Into All the World,'" *Los Angeles Times*, January 27, 1989.
86. On US evangelicals' use of human rights, see Lauren Turek, *To Bring the Good News to All Nations: Evangelical Influence on Human Rights and U.S. Foreign Relations* (Cornell University Press, 2020).
87. Wesley M. Mabuza and McGlory Speckman, "Institute for Contextual Theology (ICT) Further Submission Truth and Reconciliation Commission (TRC)," November 17–19, 1997, https://humanities.uct.ac.za/sites/default/files/content_migration/humanities_uct_ac_za/309/files/Institute_for_Contextual_Theology.pdf.
88. The Institute for Contextual Theology: The Research and Education Department, Institute for Contextual Theology, 1993, Folder: B4, Research + Formation Department, Reports, Papers, B2–B6, AG2843—Institute for Contextual Theology, ICT, Reports: General/Divisional/Reports of Visits, UWHP.
89. Report: Department of Research Education and Formation, Institute for Contextual Theology, April 29, 1993, Folder: B4, Research + Formation Department, Reports, Papers, B2–B6, AG2843—Institute for Contextual Theology, ICT, Reports: General/Divisional /Reports of Visits, UWHP.

90. Report of the Department for Research Education and Formation on Implementation of Restructuring and Planning, Institute for Contextual Theology, February 5, 1992, Folder: B4, Research + Formation Department, Reports, Papers, B2–B6, AG2843—Institute for Contextual Theology, ICT, Reports: General/Divisional/Reports of Visits, UWHP.
91. "Misuse of Religion: Interim Report."
92. James R. Cochrane, "A Balance of Forces: The South African Church in the Present Context," University of Natal, Pietermaritzburg, 1990, Folder: I2, ICT, Articles Misc, AG2843—ICT, I, Memoranda, Papers, Articles, UWHP.
93. Harold Winkler Final Report on the Pilot Study on Right Wing Church Groups, University of Cape Town, January 1988, Folder: J1, Right-Wing Religion, AG2843—Institute for Contextual Theology, "Right-Wing Religion," J1, UWHP.
94. 1989 Annual General Meeting Conference, May 23–26, 1989, Institute for Contextual Theology, May 23–26, 1989, Folder: C7, Institute for C. Theology, AGM 1988 (+ Conference), C1–C9, 1982–1991, AG2843—Institute for Contextual Theology, Institute for Contextual Theology Annual Conferences, UWHP.
95. Notes from ICT AGM on Misuse of Religion in South Africa.
96. "1989 Annual General Meeting," Institute for Contextual Theology, May 23, 1989, Folder: C7, Institute for C. Theology, AGM 1988 (+ Conference), C1–C9, 1982–1991, AG2843—ICT, Annual Conferences, UWHP.
97. Cedric Mayson, "Memorandum for Brainstorming Session on a Pilot Project for an ANC Religious Desk," Institute for Contextual Theology, March 1992, Folder: B4, Research + Formation Department, Reports, Papers, B2–B6, AG2843—Institute for Contextual Theology, ICT, Reports: General/Divisional/Reports of Visits, UWHP.
98. EDICESA Project on Right-Wing Christian Groups, EDICESA, December 1989–August 1990, Folder: J1, Right-Wing Religion, AG2843—Institute for Contextual Theology, "Right-Wing Religion," J1, UWHP.
99. Siphiwe Dube, "Muscular Christianity in Contemporary South Africa: The Case of the Mighty Men Conference," *Hervormde Teologiese Studies* 71, no. 3 (2015): 1–9; Siphiwe Ignatius Dube, "The New Religious Political Right in Neo-Apartheid South Africa," *Religion and Theology* 28 (2021); Douglas Bafford, "The Sins of Our Ancestors: Conservative Evangelical Christianity and Cosmological Responses to Racial Division in Post-Apartheid South Africa" (PhD diss., Brandeis University, 2022); and André Czeglédy, "A New Christianity for a New South Africa: Charismatic Christians and the Post-Apartheid Order," *Journal of Religion in Africa* 38, no. 3 (2008): 284–311.
100. EDICESA Project on Right-Wing Christian Groups.
101. Half Yearly Report on the Department of Ministries, Outline Report on Activities, Priorities, and Future plans, ICT, January-June 1990, Folder: B8, ICT, Department of Ministries, Reports 1990–1994, B7–B10, AG2843—ICT, UWHP.
102. Ministry Department—Annual Report—1991, Institute for Contextual Theology, 1991, Folder: B8, ICT, Department of Ministries, Reports 1990–1994, B7–B10, Reports (Divisions and Misc), AG2843—ICT, Institute for Contextual Theology Resolutions Adopted at the 1990 Annual General Meeting, July 19, 1991, Institute for Contextual Theology, July 19, 1991, Folder: C8, ICT, AGM Conference 1990, C1–C9, AG2843—Institute for Contextual Theology, Institute for Contextual Theology Annual Conferences, 1982–1991, UWHP.

6. HUMAN RIGHTS FOR WHITE POWER

1. Arnaud de Borchgrave, "Botha: World Should Let Pretoria Change at Its Own Pace," *Washington Times*, March 14, 1988, PS 12/106/1, 1988, Box 334, PV 203, ARCA.
2. Christopher S. Wren, "Botha, Rebuffed by His Party, Quits South Africa Presidency," *New York Times*, August 15, 1989, https://www.nytimes.com/1989/08/15/world/botha-rebuffed-by-his-party-quits-south-africa-presidency.html.
3. David Welsh, *The Rise and Fall of Apartheid* (University of Virginia Press, 2009), 347.
4. "The South African Right: Searching for Allies Abroad," *Freedom Bulletin*, International Freedom Foundation (1990), Folder: Ji, International Freedom Foundation, 1990–93, AG2843—Institute for Contextual Theology, Special Topics, JF-Ji, UWHP.
5. See Jamie Miller, *An African Volk: The Apartheid Regime and Its Search for Survival* (Oxford University Press, 2016).
6. Alex Thomson, "A More Effective Constructive Engagement: US Policy Towards South Africa after the Comprehensive Anti-Apartheid Act of 1986," *Politikon* 39 (2012): 374.
7. Edward Perkins, *Mr. Ambassador: Warrior for Peace* (University of Oklahoma Press, 2006), 310–16.
8. Thomson, "A More Effective Constructive Engagement," 375.
9. Kathryn O'Neill and Barry Munslow, "Ending the Cold War in Southern Africa," *Third World Quarterly* 12, no. 3 (1990): 83; Piero Gleijeses, "From Cassinga to New York: The Struggle for the Independence of Namibia," in *Cold War in Southern Africa: White Power, Black Liberation*, ed. Sue Onslow (Routledge, 2009).
10. Theresa Edlmann, "The Lingering, Unspoken Pain of White Youth Who Fought for Apartheid," *Conversation*, September 2, 2015, https://theconversation.com/the-lingering-unspoken-pain-of-white-youth-who-fought-for-apartheid-46218.
11. Daniel Conway, *Masculinities, Militarization, and the End Conscription Campaign* (Manchester University Press, 2012), 107, 117.
12. Conway, *Masculinities, Militarization, and the End Conscription Campaign*, 149–50. For novels on the impact of mandatory military service on white South African society, see Tony Eprile, *The Persistence of Memory* (Norton, 2004) and Rehana Rossouw, *New Times* (Jacana Media, 2017).
13. Raymond Duncan, *Moscow and the Third World* (Taylor & Francis, 2020); Francis Fukuyama, *Gorbachev and the New Soviet Agenda in the Third World* (RAND, 1989); Melvin Goodman, *Gorbachev's Retreat: The Third World* (Praeger, 1991).
14. Chris Saunders, "The Angola/Namibia Crisis of 1988 and Its Resolution," in Onslow, *Cold War in Southern Africa*, 231.
15. Saunders, "The Angola/Namibia Crisis of 1988 and Its Resolution," 234. On the Soviet rapprochement with the United States, see James Wilson, *The Triumph of Improvisation* (Cornell University Press, 2015); and Simon Miles, *Engaging the Evil Empire: Washington, Moscow, and the Beginning of the End of the Cold War* (Cornell University Press, 2020).
16. Chester Crocker, *High Noon in Southern Africa: Making Peace in a Rough Neighborhood* (Norton, 1993), 395; and Lionel Cliffe et al., *The Transition to Independence in Namibia* (Rienner, 1994).

17. Chris Miller, *The Struggle to Save the Soviet Economy: Mikhail Gorbachev and the Collapse of the USSR* (University of North Carolina Press, 2016), 4.
18. Welsh, *The Rise and Fall of Apartheid*, 356.
19. Adrian Guelke, *Rethinking the Rise and Fall of Apartheid* (Palgrave Macmillan, 2004), 156.
20. Rupert Taylor, "Between Apartheid and Democracy," *Round Table* 79, no. 314 (1990): 157–66; "Mass Democratic Movement," O'Malley Archive, https://omalley.nelsonmandela.org/index.php/site/q/03lv03445/04lv03446/05lv03480.htm.
21. Barbara Keys, *Reclaiming American Virtue* (Harvard University Press, 2014), 13.
22. James Peck, *Ideal Illusions: How the U.S. Government Co-Opted Human Rights* (Henry Holt, 2010).
23. Sarah Snyder, *Human Rights Activism and the End of the Cold War* (Cambridge University Press, 2011), 4.
24. Keys, *Reclaiming American Virtue*, 277.
25. Nicole Hemmer, *Partisans: The Conservative Revolutionaries Who Remade American Politics in the 1990s* (Basic, 2022); Steven A. Holmes, "The 1992 Campaign: Republicans; Buchan's Run Exposes Fissures in the Right," *New York Times*, February 4, 1992. Perhaps the best encapsulation of the power of the new right wing in the Republican Party was former Reagan official Pat Buchanan's 1992 run for the Republican presidential nominee, running on his new "paleoconservative agenda": anti-immigration, anti-multinationalism, and anti–societal liberalism, ultimately netting three million total votes and coining the "culture wars" phrase in his eventual concession speech. Patrick J. Buchanan, "Address to the Republican National Convention," August 17, 1992, https://www.americanrhetoric.com/speeches/patrickbuchanan1992rnc.htm.
26. National Security Review 15—South Africa, April 9, 1989, George H. W. Bush Presidential Library, April 9, 1989, https://bush41library.tamu.edu/files/nsr/nsr15.pdf.
27. "Statement on Meeting with South African Anti-Apartheid Activist Albertina Sisulu," June 30, 1986, https://bush41library.tamu.edu/archives/public-papers/624; Meetings with Foreigners, 1989–1990, George H. W. Bush Presidential Library https://bush41library.tamu.edu/files/Press--Meetings%20with%20Foreigners%201989.pdf.
28. Memorandum of Telephone Conversation, Subject: Telecon with President F.W. de Klerk of South Africa, August 13, 1990, Memorandum of Telephone Conversation, Subject: Telephone Conversation with F.W. de Klerk of South Africa, June 27, 1990, Memorandum of Telephone Conversation, Subject: Telephone Conversation with State President F. W. de Klerk of South Africa, February 10, 1990, accessed September 11, 2024, https://bush41library.tamu.edu/files/memcons-telcons/1990-08-13--de%20Klerk.pdf; https://bush41library.tamu.edu/files/memcons-telcons/1990-02-10--de%20Klerk.pdf; https://bush41library.tamu.edu/files/memcons-telcons/1990-06-27--de%20Klerk.pdf.
29. Memorandum of Conversation, Subject: Plenary Meeting with President F. W. de Klerk of South Africa, September 24, 1990, https://bush41library.tamu.edu/files/memcons-telcons/1990-09-24--de%20Klerk.pdf.
30. Memorandum of Telephone Conversation, Subject: Telecon with Nelson Mandela, Deputy President of the ANC, South Africa, on October 5, 1990, October 5, 1990, https://bush41library.tamu.edu/files/memcons-telcons/1990-10-05--Mandela.pdf.

31. Memorandum of Conversation, Subject: Plenary Meeting with President F. W. de Klerk of South Africa, September 24, 1990, https://bush41library.tamu.edu/files/memcons-telcons/1990-09-24--de%20Klerk.pdf.
32. George H. W. Bush, "Address Before a Joint Session of the Congress on the End of the Cold War," March 6, 1991, Miller Center of Public Affairs, University of Virginia, https://millercenter.org/the-presidency/presidential-speeches/march-6-1991-address-joint-session-congress-end-gulf-war.
33. Neus Torbisco Casals, *Group Rights as Human Rights: A Liberal Approach to Multiculturalism* (Springer, 2006), 5.
34. "Document of the Copenhagen Meeting of the Conference on the Human Dimension of the CSCE," Organization for Security and Cooperation in Europe, June 29, 1990, https://www.osce.org/odihr/elections/14304.
35. E. J. Hobsbawm, "Ethnicity and Nationalism in Europe Today," *Anthropology Today* 8, no. 1 (February 1992): 2–8; and *The Protection of Minorities: Collected Texts of the European Commission for Democracy Through Law* (Council of Europe Press, 1994).
36. Saul Dubow, *South Africa's Struggle for Human Rights* (Ohio University Press, 2012), 14, 17, 88, 107.
37. "Election Special: Intervention Must Work Both Ways," *Aida Parker Newsletter*, April 22, 1987, *Aida Parker Newsletter*, April 1986–December 1990 (incomplete), APC Periodicals, APC.
38. "The Enemies Within—Part 2—SA's Newly Organized Labour?," *Aida Parker Newsletter Special Issue*, 1987, *Aida Parker Newsletter*, April 1986–December 1990 (incomplete), APC Periodicals, APC.
39. "Uncle Sam's Moral Balancing Act Over South Africa: It's Time to Hit Back," *Aida Parker Newsletter*, September 1988, *Aida Parker Newsletter*, April 1986–December 1990 (incomplete), APC Periodicals, APC.
40. "Racism Around the World, Accusing Our Accusers," *Aida Parker Newsletter*, Summer 1989/90, APC Periodicals, *Aida Parker Newsletter*, April 1986–December 1990 (incomplete), APCSA, UKZNP.
41. "The Realities and Dangers of Glasnost/Perestroika," *McAlvany Intelligence Advisor*, November 1988, *Aida Parker Newsletter*, April 1986–December 1990 (incomplete), APC Periodicals, APC.
42. "Why We Must Support South Africa," National Association for the Advancement of White People News, Folder M7/2/13, vol. 13, 1987, PV 734, Box 133, ARCA.
43. Christi van der Westhuizen, *White Power and the Rise and Fall of the National Party* (Zebra, 2007), 174–76.
44. "I Am Not a Racist, but . . .," Independent Board of Inquiry, 1994, Folder: A9.3, "I Am Not a Racist," A9, AG2543—IBI, Right-Wing Organizations, UWHP.
45. J. A. Marais, "The Founders of the New South Africa," Christian Defense League, 1994, Radicalism, DT1757.M373 1994, Michigan State University Special Collections.
46. Martin Childs, "Eugene Terre'Blanche: Leader of the Far-Right AWB Party Who Led the Resistance to Majority Rule in South Africa," *Independent*, April 6, 2010, https://www.independent.co.uk/news/obituaries/eug-egrave-ne-terre-blanche-leader-of-the-farright-awb-party-who-led-the-resistance-to-majority-rule-in-south-africa-1936550.html.

47. Krista Johnson and Sean Jacobs, "Afrikaner Weerstandsbeweging," *Encyclopedia of South Africa* (Lynne Rienner, 2011), 11.
48. Krista Johnson and Sean Jacobs, (eds.), "Boer Republics," *Encyclopedia of South Africa*, (Lynne Reinner, 2011), 37.
49. Terre'Blanche also boasted of an underwater unit, a motorcycle gang, and an air force with private planes. "South African Police and South African Defense Force Involvement in Rightwing Extremists," Independent Board of Inquiry, November 13, 1989, Folder: A5.9, Police Brutality OFS, A5.9–13, AG2543—IBI, Police Conduct + Policing, UWHP.
50. One leader, Rooi Rus Swanepoel interrogated the fifteen Rivonia trialists, most prominently Nelson Mandela, Govan Mbeki, and Walter Sisulu, convicted and charged with 221 acts of sabotage designed to "ferment violent revolution" in 1964. Personal Profile on Political Right-Wingers, Independent Board of Inquiry, 1994, Folder: A9.1, Right-wing organizations, A9, AG2543—IBI, Right-wing organizations, UWHP.
51. The police's role in defending racial apartheid informed policing practices and training, and black South Africans unfavorably contrasted their zeal in policing the state of emergency with right-wing terror. The conviction of Barend Strydom, a dismissed former police officer, in November 1988 for a shooting spree in Strijdom Square, Pretoria, that killed eight people and injured sixteen others seemed to suggest that right-wing violence was the work of racist police officers. Report of the IBIIR for the Month of June 1991, Independent Board of Inquiry, June 1991, AG2543-2-2-15-01, UWHP; Nicholas Haysom, "Police Deviance in the Policing of South Africa," Article for *Human Rights and Labour Yearbook, University of Natal (Durban)*, vol. 1, 1990, Folder: A5.10, Police Conduct and Policing, A5.9–13, AG2543—IBI, Police Conduct + Policing, UWHP.
52. "South African Police and South African Defense Force Involvement in Rightwing Extremists."
53. The SADF was aware of this overlap—commanders admitted to high right-wing presence in its ranks in Western and Northern Transvaal, the Orange Free State, and parts of the Eastern Cape.
54. Force or Fallacy? The Right Wing and the SADF Commando System, Independent Board of Inquiry, 1993, Folder: A9.1, Right-Wing Organizations, A9, AG2543—IBI, Right-Wing Organizations, UWHP.
55. Memorandum on Extreme Rightwing Organizations in South Africa, Independent Board of Inquiry, August 24, 1990, Folder: 3.8–3.43, Independent Board of Inquiry, 3.1–3.42, Memoranda, AG2543—IBI, Memoranda, Photographs, UWHP.
56. John Battersby, "Afrikaners Propose White Homeland in South Africa," *Christian Science Monitor*, August 9, 1990, accessed September 10, 2024, https://www.csmonitor.com/1990/0809/otrek.html.
57. Liz Sly, "South Africa's Future—'All White' Town Finds It Can't Live Without Blacks," *Seattle Times*, March 16, 1992, https://archive.seattletimes.com/archive/?date=19920316&slug=1481260, and Scott Macleod, "South Africa Angst in Afrikanerdom," *Time*, December 10, 1990, https://time.com/archive/6716669/south-africa-angst-in-afrikanerdom/.
58. Battersby, "Afrikaners Propose White Homeland in South Africa."
59. Hercules Booysen, "Prabook," https://prabook.com/web/hercules.booysen/338247.

60. Leonard Thompson, *The Political Mythology of Apartheid* (Yale University Press, 1985), 26–27, 70.
61. Shula Marks, "South Africa: 'The Myth of the Empty Land,'" *History Today* 30, no. 1 (January 1980): 8. As Marks put it, "despite the abundant scientific evidence conclusively disproving these views," they persist.
62. "For Attention Miss Mickey Carter," Vereniging van Oranjewerkers, 1987, Folder I4, Tydperk, 1983–1985, Box 5, PV 611, ARCA.
63. Hermann Rex, "Geografiese Verspreiding van die Bantoe," *Sweesplag*, Afrikaner-Weerstandsbeweging, 1982, Folder: 1/A5/1, Date 1982–1986, Box 6, PV 357, ARCA.
64. "Programme of Principles and Policy," Conservative Party of South Africa, August 4, 1982, Folder 10/2/2/1, 1982–1987, Box 66, PV 873, ARCA.
65. H. F. Verwoerd Jr., "An Afrikanerviewpoint: A Look Into the Future, for Publication in 'the South Africans: Views for the Future,'" in *Leadership*," 1985, Folder A21: Tydperk, 1985, Box 1, PV 611, ARCA.
66. C. W. H. Boshoff, "'We Shall Never Surrender'—An Afrikaner Point of View," 1985, Folder A21: Tydperk, 1985, Box 1, PV 611, ARCA.
67. H. Booysen, "Political Thinking Among White Conservatives in South Africa," Folder A21: Tydperk, 1985, Box 1, PV 611, ARCA.
68. C. W. H. Boshoff, "Die Afrikaner Beslis oor sy Toekoms," PS 3/2/6, 1988, Box 283, PV 203, ARCA, UFS.
69. Carel Boshoff, "Orania and the Third Reinvention of the Afrikaner—Carel Boshoff," *Politics Web*, October 7, 2014.
70. C. W. H. Boshoff, "Erste Uitreking van die Stigting: Afrikanervryheid," March 22, 1988, PS 3/2/6, 1988, Box 283, PV 203, ARCA.
71. "Points for Dr. Treurnicht from Overseas Intelligence Sources in the Run-Up to 6th September," August 19, 1989, Clive Derby-Lewis, "Financial and Economic Situation," *Die Patriot*, August 16, 1989, Folder 8/5/5/1, 1985–1989, Box 64, PV 873, ARCA.
72. Van der Westhuizen, *White Power*, 176–80, 184.
73. F. W. de Klerk, *The Last Trek—A New Beginning* (Pan, 2000), 160–61.
74. Robin Lee and Lawrence Schlemmer, *Transition to Democracy: Policy Perspectives, 1991* (Oxford University Press, 1991), 16.
75. Allister Sparks, *Tomorrow Is Another Country: The Inside Story of South Africa's Negotiated Revolution* (Struik, 1994), 98.
76. Van der Westhuizen, *White Power*, 184–85.
77. Glenn Frankel, "F.W. de Klerk, South Africa's Last Apartheid President and Nobel Peace Prize Laureate, Dies at 85," *Washington Post*, November 11, 2021, https://www.washingtonpost.com/local/obituaries/fw-deklerk-death-south-africa/2021/11/11/761faa64-8fd4-11e6-a6a3-d50061aa9fae_story.html?utm_source=rss&utm_medium=referral&utm_campaign=wp_world.
78. Courtney Jung and Ian Shapiro, "South Africa's Negotiated Transition: Democracy, Opposition, and the New Constitutional Order," *Politics and Society* 23, no. 3 (September 1995): 285.
79. Heidi Brooks, *The African National Congress and Participatory Democracy: From People's Power to Public Policy* (Palgrave Macmillan, 2019), 117–63.

80. ANC Press Conference, "BBC Summary of World Broadcasts," April 9, 1992. This statement reflected the ANC's refusal to accept anything less than majority rule, rejecting "fancy" power-sharing proposals by the South African government.
81. The first two freedom struggles were against British colonial rule, with the First Boer War (1880–1881) resulting in Boer independence in the South African Republic and the Second Boer War (1899–1902) resulting in British control over the Orange Free State and the Transvaal. The AWB's use of the terms "First" and "Second" Boer War have largely fallen out of fashion as a result of its mythologizing within Afrikaner nationalism, in favor of the "Anglo-Boer War," to recognize the Commonwealth's contributions, or, as is most common in South Africa, the "South African War" because of the entrenchment, involvement, and impact of Africans on the conflict. Bill Nasson, *The South African War, 1899–1902* (Oxford University Press, 1999) and *Abraham Esau's War: A Black South African War in the Cape, 1899–1902* (Cambridge University Press, 1991).
82. IBIIR Report May 1990, Independent Board of Inquiry, May 1990, AG2543-2-2-3-01, accessed via UWHP online portal.
83. Memorandum on Extreme Rightwing Organizations in South Africa, Independent Board of Inquiry, August 24, 1990, Folder: 3.8–3.43, Independent Board of Inquiry, Memoranda, 3.1–3.42, AG2543—IBI, Memoranda, Photographs, UWHP.
84. IBIIR-Report-April 1990. These vigilante groups were part of a long history of self-formed militias within South Africa to uphold imperial and racist projects, leading to, at times, genocidal outcomes. See Mohamed Adhikari, *The Anatomy of a South African Genocide: The Extermination of the Cape San Peoples* (Ohio University Press, 2011); Stephen Miller, *Soldiers and Settlers in Africa, 1850–1918* (Brill 2009); and Nigel Penn, *The Forgotten Frontier: Colonist and Khoisan on the Cape's Northern Frontier in the 18th Century* (Ohio University Press, 2005).
85. David B. Ottaway, "White Terrorism Increases in South Africa; Right-Wing Resistance Groups Proliferate, Claim Responsibility for Recent Bombings," *Washington Post*, July 21, 1990.
86. SABC, "Truth Commission, TRC Victims, Letter H," https://sabctrc.saha.org.za/victims/h.htm?start=300.
87. Maxwell Shamase, "The Pattern of Political Conflict in South Africa and the White Right-Wing Violation of Civil Liberties, 1990–1994," *Ubuntu* (March 2019): 92.
88. Christopher S. Wren, "South Africa Arrests 12 Whites for Racial Attack," *New York Times*, December 1, 1990.
89. David B. Ottaway, "White Terrorism Increases in South Africa; Right-Wing Resistance Groups Proliferate, Claim Responsibility for Recent Bombings," *Washington Post*, July 21, 1990.
90. Christopher S. Wren, "Rumbling on the Right: A Strident, Well-Armed Minority of South African Whites Is Preparing to Foil Further Dismantling of Apartheid," *New York Times*, October 7, 1990.
91. Personal Profile on Political Right-Wingers, Independent Board of Inquiry, 1994, Folder: A9.1, Right-Wing Organizations, A9, AG2543—IBI, Right-Wing Organizations, UWHP.

92. Jack Reed, "White Extremist Talks with South African Government," *UPI*, May 14, 1990, https://www.upi.com/Archives/1990/05/14/White-extremist-talks-with-South-African-government/4683642657600/.
93. "I Am Not a Racist, but. . . ."
94. Reports of the IBIIR for the Period June 1990, Independent Board of Inquiry, June 1990, AG2543-2-2-4-01, UWHP.
95. "Freedom Manifesto for Our People," Conservative Party, May 26, 1990, Folder 10/1/1, 1949–1992, Box 65, PV 873, ARCA.
96. Boervolk Identiteitsdokument, February 15, 1990, Folder 8/5/5/2, 1990–92, Box 64, PV 873, ARCA. These pass documents were a twisted inversion of the complaints raised by black South Africans, who were forced to carry identity documents.
97. "Special Issue: South Africa at the Crossroads, the Path to Power," *Aida Parker Newsletter*, First Quarter 1990, *Aida Parker Newsletter*, January 1991–December 1993, APC Periodicals, APC.
98. "Toward a Soviet South Africa: Plunging Down the Slippery Slope of Surrender," *McAlvany Intelligence Advisor*, Winter 1990, *Aida Parker Newsletter*, January 1991–December 1993, APC Periodicals, APC.
99. "P.W. Botha blasts F.W. de Klerk for Carrying National Party Policies to Their Logical Conclusion in South Africa," *Howard Phillips Issues and Strategy Bulleting*, May 28, 1990, *Aida Parker Newsletter*, January 1991–December 1993, APC Periodicals, APC.
100. "Dear Subscriber," *Aida Parker Newsletter*, 1990, *Aida Parker Newsletter*, January 1991–December 1993, APC Periodicals, APC.
101. "Time for Courage . . . Action," *Aida Parker Newsletter*, June 1990, APC Periodicals, *Aida Parker Newsletter*, January 1991–December 1993, APC Periodicals, APC.
102. "Minutes and Accords Between the ANC and the South African Government, May 1990-February 1991," African National Congress, November 19, 1997.
103. Christopher S. Wren, "South Africa Ends Emergency Decree in 3 of 4 Provinces" and "De Klerk Lifts Emergency Rule in Natal Province, *New York Times*, June 8 and October 19, 1990.
104. Phiroshaw Camay and Anne J. Gordon, *The National Peace Accord and its Structures: South Africa Civil Society and Governance Case Study No. 1* (Cooperative for Research and Education, 2010).
105. Peter Harris, *Birth: The Conspiracy to Stop the '94 Elections* (Umuzi, 2010), 12.
106. Memorandum of Telephone Conversation, Subject: Telephone Conversation with F. W. de Klerk of South Africa, February 4, 1991, https://bush41library.tamu.edu/files/memcons-telcons/1991-02-04--de%20Klerk.pdf.
107. Memorandum of Conversation, Subject: Meeting with Gatsha Mangosuthu Buthelezi, Chief Minister of KwaZulu, South Africa, June 20, 1991, George H. W. Bush Presidential Library, https://bush41library.tamu.edu/files/memcons-telcons/1991-06-20--Buthelezi.pdf.
108. I. W. B. de Villiers, "Human Rights and Group Rights," 1991, Folder 3/1/10, s.d, Box 27, PV 873, ARCA.

109. Verslag van Subkomittee twee van die Voorsettingskomitee vir staatkundige aangeleenthede, Conservative Party, 1991, Folder 7/5/1/2, s.d., Box 61, PV 873, ARCA.
110. F. A. Mouton, "'Dr No': A.P. Treurnicht and the Ultra-Conservative Quest to Maintain Afrikaner Supremacy, 1982–1993," *South African Historical Journal* 65, no. 4 (2013): 578–82.
111. Bulletin 8/91-E, *Bulletin: Information Service of the National Party*, April 1991, Folder 8/5/5/2, 1990–92, Box 64, PV 873, ARCA.
112. "2 Killed as Apartheid Supporters Battle Police at de Klerk Speech," *Associated Press*, August 10, 1991.
113. "Two Dead, 54 Hurt in S. African Clash; Police and Neo-Nazis Battle as de Klerk Gives Speech in Conservative Town," *Edmonton Journal*, August 10, 1991.
114. "I Am Not a Racist, but. . . ."
115. "South African Police, Rightists Battle; 4 Killed," *Los Angeles Times*, August 10, 1991.
116. Interdepartementele Veiligheidsoorsig: Die bedreigingspotensiaal van verregse groeperinge, National Intelligence, August 1991, Folder J/1-J1/3, 1990, Box 280, PV 357, ARCA.
117. "Turmoil and Tragedy: What Is Happening in South Africa?," Frontline Fellowship, September 1992, Box 3, Frontline Fellowship, 1988–1995 News, SC 79, Intercessors for the Suffering Church Collection, Mary Ann Gilbert, Serials Correspondence, WCSC.
118. Exchanges Between O. H. Bates and Strydom, October 28, 1991, Folder A5(2), Tydperk, 1982–1992, Box 1, PV 611, ARCA.
119. Robert L. Slimp, "South African Update: The Government Is Losing Its Grip," *Citizens Informer* 22, no. 3, CofCC, Summer 1991, Folder HH334C:5—Tri-State Informer, Box T-23, Part II, HHC.
120. "Whites Want a New Partition Plan," *Monitor*, Center for Democratic Renewal, August 1990, Folder 13, Articles and Book Photocopies Regarding Homosexuality and Nazism, 1990, Box 4, RH WL MS 48, John Scoville Papers, Wilcox Collection, UKL.
121. "Toward a Soviet South Africa: Plunging Down the Slippery Slope of Surrender," *McAlvany Intelligence Advisor*, Winter 1990, Box 5, *McAlvany Intelligence Adviso*r, n.d. 1990 + 1991, SC 79, Intercessors for the Suffering Church Collection, Mary Ann Gilbert, Serials Correspondence, WCSC.
122. Instauration is "an obscure term" that means the "restoration" after a "significant time lapse," here referring to the white American. Editor-in-chief Wilmot Robertson, the pen name of Humphrey Ireland, is most infamous for writing *The Dispossessed Majority* and *The Ethnostate: An Unblinkered Prospectus on the Art of Statecraft*, which railed against a future white genocide brought about by US liberal weakness. He published *Instauration* from 1975 to 2000. "The Besiegers and the Besieged: What Hath Bush Wrought?," *Instauration*, March 1991, Folder 8, carton 31, From the Mountain, BANC MSS 98/70, Collection on the US Right [1950s–1997], Diamond Papers, BLMC; Arnold Birenbaum, *A Nation Apart: The African-American Experience and White Nationalism* (Routledge, 2019), 154–55.
123. Robert L. Slimp, "What Is Really Happening in South Africa," *Citizens Informer* 21, no. 1, CofCC, Spring 1990, Folder HH167.47—Tri-State Informer, Box T-23, Part II, HHC.
124. Letter from Denis Walker to Mary Ann Gilbert, October 22, 1990, Box 8, Rhodesia Christian Group, Correspondence, SC 79, Intercessors for the Suffering Church Collection, Mary Ann Gilbert, Correspondence, WCSC.

125. "South Africa: The State of the Nation," *Conservative Party*, September 1991, Folder 8/5/5/2, 1990–92, Box 64, PV 873, ARCA.
126. "The Fight for Freedom: Nationalism and the Desire for Ethnic Independence," *Aida Parker Newsletter*, September/October 1991, Aida Parker Newsletter, January 1991–December 1993, APC Periodicals, APC.
127. "The Fight for Freedom." Parker likely allied herself with the far-right cabinet ministers within the de Klerk administration. Van der Westhuizen, *White Power*, 181, 222. For more on this, see chapter 7.
128. "The Fight for Freedom."
129. "SA's Last Chance," *Referendum Special: The Aida Parker Newsletter*, March 1992, *Aida Parker Newsletter*, January 1991–December 1993, APC Periodicals, APC.
130. A. P. Treurnicht, "A Yes Vote Is a Blank Cheque," *Conservative Party Herald*, March 5, 1992, Folder 8/5/5/2, 1990–92, Box 64, PV 873, ARCA.
131. "1992: South Africa Votes for Change," *BBC: On This Day*, http://news.bbc.co.uk/onthisday/hi/dates/stories/march/18/newsid_2524000/2524695.stm; Christopher S. Wren, "South African Whites Ratify de Klerk Move to Negotiate with Blacks on a New Order," *New York Times*, March 19, 1992.
132. The only exception to this was Pietersburg in Northern Transvaal, Treurnicht's seat.
133. Annette Strauss, "The 1992 Referendum in South Africa," *Journal of Modern African Studies* 31, no. 2 (June 1993): 343.
134. Strauss, "The 1992 Referendum in South Africa," 343–50. For more on the changes in Inkatha, see chapter 7.
135. "The New Face of Fascism," *Aida Parker Newsletter*, April 1992, *Aida Parker Newsletter*, January 1991–December 1993, APC Periodicals, APC.
136. "Time to Save Our Country," *Aida Parker Newsletter*, June 1992, *Aida Parker Newsletter*, January 1991–December 1993, APC Periodicals, APC.
137. "Crisis Survival Issue," *Aida Parker Newsletter*, June 1992, *Aida Parker Newsletter*, January 1991–December 1993, APC Periodicals, APC.
138. Hoofmagsbasisse in die Volkstryd, October 1992, Folder 8/5/5/2, 1990–92, Box 64, PV 873, ARCA.
139. "The Boer People's State Is Here!," Boer Freedom Foundation, 1990, Folder: A9.2, Right Wing Organizations, A9, AG2543—IBI, Right-Wing Organizations, UWHP.

7. THE COLORBLIND FAR RIGHT AT APARTHEID'S END

1. "A Conference for Concerned South Africans," October 6, 1992, 26/2 Organisasks, 301–600 1990, PV 897—Nov. 1995, ARCA.
2. "Address by His Excellency, the State President of Bophuthatswana Kgosi Lucas Manyane Mangope at the Meeting Between Bophuthatswana, KwaZulu, Ciskei, and Other Interested Parties," "Speech by Andries Beyers MP, Leader of the Volksunie, Delivered at the Conference for Concerned South Africans," "Conference for Concerned South Africans by Dr. A. Treunicht, Conservative Party," and "Presentation of Brigadier OJ Gqozo,

Chairman of the Ciskei Council of State to Leaders Attending a Meeting at the Indaba Hotel," October 6, 1992, 26/2 Organisasks, 301–600 1990, PV 897, ARCA.

3. "Issues of Consensus," Conference of Concerned South Africans, October 6, 1992, 26/2 Organisasks, 301–600 1990, PV 897, ARCA.
4. "New Hope from Conference," *Aida Parker Newsletter*, October 1992, APN, January 1991—December 1993, APC Periodicals, APC.
5. Michael Lawrence and Andrew Manson, "The 'Dog of the Boers': The Rise and Fall of Mangope in Bophuthatswana," *Journal of Southern African Studies* 20, no. 3 (September 1994): 447–461; Maxwell Z. Shamase, "The Pattern of Political Conflict in South Africa and the White Right-Wing Violation of Civil Liberties, 1990–1994," *Ubuntu: Journal of Conflict and Social Transformation* 8, no. 1 (2019): 89–116; and Y. G. Muthien and M. M. Khosa, "The Kingdom, the Volkstaat and the New South Africa, Drawing South Africa's New Regional Boundaries," *Journal of Southern African Studies* 21, no. 2 (1995): 303–22.
6. Jason Robinson, "Fragments of the Past: Bantustan Politics and the South African Transition, 1990–2014," *Journal of Southern African Studies* 41, no. 5 (2015): 953–67; William Beinart, "Beyond 'Bantustans:' Some Ideas About the History of African Rural Areas in South Africa," *South African Historical Journal* 64, no. 1 (2012): 5–21; and Maano Freddy Ramutsindela, "Afrikaner Nationalism, Electioneering and the Politics of a Volkstaat," *Politics* 18, no. 3 (1998): 179–88.
7. Gary Kynoch, *Township Violence and the End of Apartheid: War on the Reef* (Wits University Press, 2018), 2.
8. Bill Berkeley, "The Warlords of Natal," *Atlantic*, March 1994, Folder: A17(3), Affidavits by People Trained for Hit Squads Activities, Accounts by Nico Basson of Destabilization Activities, etc., A16–A17, AG2543—IBI, Private Security Industry, SADF/SANDF, UWHP, 3.
9. Franziska Rueedi, "The Hostel Wars in Apartheid South Africa: Rumor, Violence and the Discourse of Victimhood," *Social Identities* 26, no. 6 (2020): 767.
10. The extent of collaboration between the South African state, right-wing vigilante groups, and the IFP will never be fully known due to record destruction by all parties involved. However, it is well-established that the South African government intentionally fueled violence during the transition, actively backed the IFP, and sought to preserve their own power through the violent security forces. James Gump, Anthony Minnaar, Ian Libenberg, Charl Schutte, and Anette Seegers conclude that the South African government extensively used surrogates throughout the 1990s to wage war on the ANC to provide the cover of plausible deniability and reinforce a culture of impunity. James Sanders's *Apartheid's Friends* is perhaps the most extensive accounting of the evolution of the security forces beginning in the early Cold War and the extensive "dirty tricks" used to brutalize antiapartheid activists, crush dissent, and pull collaborators into their wake. Brian Morrow's account of IFP and National Party collaboration, a memoir starting from his early years as a conscript into the Security Branch of the South African Police to his time as a whistleblower, uncovered the South African government's funding of a range of groups including the National Students Federation, copies of checks sent to

Inkatha, and documentation from senior police officials outlining the exact reasons to support Inkatha and Buthelezi. Ultimately, Morrow fled South Africa, becoming a whistleblower who exposed Adriaan Vlok and Magnus Malan's involvement in "Inkathagate." As Stephen Ellis put it, although the Third Force was not responsible for all the political violence in the period, "there is reason to believe that they were by some way its most important sponsors." The origins of the Natal Civil War and the covert support for the IFP by the apartheid state originate in, as historian Jabulani Sithole argues, the "muzzling" of political dissent by Buthelezi and his supporters, who wielded the bantustan's bureaucratic structures to "mediate the settlement of conflicts between the Zulu monarch and Buthelezi in favor of the latter," as Buthelezi gained power from the "extra-parliamentary formations that operated in the rest of the province." However, some historians remain concerned about the overdetermination of the Third Force narrative that masks political violence committed by the ANC and other parties. Scholars like Gary Kynoch argue against the "enduring narrative" of an alliance between security forces and the IFP against the ANC, instead arguing that all political parties used violence to jostle for power in the lead-up to the election. Although concluding that the apartheid state created the conditions of political violence in the Vaal Triangle, Kynoch cautions against simplistic narratives that reify the ANC as the only victims of the IFP's violent collaboration with the South African government. James Sanders, *Apartheid's Friends: The Rise and Fall of South Africa's Secret Service* (Murray, 2006); James Gump, "Unveiling the Third Force: Toward Transitional Justice in the USA and South Africa, 1973–1994," *Safundi: The Journal of South African and American Studies* 15, no. 1 (2014): 75–100; Anthony Minnaar, Ian Liebenberg, and Charl Schutte, eds., *The Hidden Hand: Covert Operations in South Africa* (Human Sciences Research Council, 1994); Annette Seegers, *The Military in the Making of Modern South Africa* (Tauris Academic Studies, 1996); Brian Morrow as told to Laurence Piper, *"To Serve and Protect": The Inkathagate Scandal* (Unisa, 2010); Jabulani Sithole, "Neither Communists nor Saboteurs: KwaZulu Bantustan Politics," in *The Road to Democracy in South Africa*, vol. 2 [1970–1980] (Unisa, 2006): 808–9; Stephen Ellis, "The Historical Significance of South Africa's Third Force," *Journal of Southern African Studies* 34, no. 2 (1998): 261–99; and Kynoch, *Township Violence and the End of Apartheid.*

11. "11 Die When the South African Defense Force (SADF) Opens Fire on Negotiators in Sebokeng, 4 September, 1990," South African History Online, https://www.sahistory.org.za/dated-event/11-die-when-south-african-defence-force-sadf-opens-fire-negotiators-sebokeng.
12. Rueedi, "The Hostel Wars in Apartheid South Africa," 757.
13. Mxolisi R. Mchunu, *Violence and Solace: The Natal Civil War in Late-Apartheid South Africa* (University of Virginia Press, 2020), 2. What drove the Natal Civil War remains a subject of debate among scholars. The politics of the conflict, pitting the UDF-ANC alliance against the IFP for control of a new democratic South Africa, remains the dominant interpretation and indeed the "mega-narrative" that fueled the conflict. But as political violence continues to ravage KwaZulu-Natal, scholars are broadening their scope on the drivers and legacies of conflict in the region and reexamining the dominant

narrative of the ANC and allies versus the IDF and the Third Force. As Philippe Denis argues, "political rivalries . . . do not explain everything," and historians have excavated the role of socioeconomic factors, gender, and religion in fueling the violence. The historian Jill Kelly, for instance, highlights the "complicated relationship between chiefs, white minority rule, and land in South Africa" that drove competition among the ANC and UDF and IFP for support from traditional authorities, through the "politics of the people," known in isiZulu as *ukukhonza*. Jill Kelly, *To Swim with Crocodiles: Land Violence and Belonging in South Africa, 1980–1996* (Michigan State University Press, 2018), xxx, xxxiv; Philippe Denis, "Indians Versus Russians: An Oral History of the Political Violence in Nxamalala (1987–1992)," *Journal of Natal and Zulu History* 24–25 (2006): 66. For more on the Natal Civil War, see Mlungisi Phakathi, "Rethinking Political Violence in Post-Apartheid KwaZulu-Natal, South Africa," *African Journal of Peace and Conflict Studies* 8, no. 1 (2019): 99–119; John Aitchison, *Numbering the Dead: The Course and Pattern of Political Violence in the Natal Midlands, 1987–1989* (Natal Society Foundation, 2015); Debby Bonnin, "Claiming Spaces, Changing Places: Political Violence and Women's Protests in KwaZulu-Natal," *Journal of Southern African Studies* 26, no. 2 (June 2002): 301–16; Anthony de Villiers Minnaar, *Patterns of Violence: An Overview of Conflict During the 1980s and 1990s* (Human Sciences Research Council, 1992); Paulus Zulu, "Durban Hostels and Political Violence: Case Studies in KwaMashu and Umlazi," *Transformation* 21 (1993): 1–23; and Rupert Taylor, "Justice Denied: Political Violence in KwaZulu-Natal After 1994," *African Affairs* 101, no. 405 (2002): 473–508.

14. Rueedi, "The Hostel Wars in Apartheid South Africa," 759; "Truth and Reconciliation Committee Final Report," vol. 3, chap. 6, Regional Profile Transvaal, 676, https://sabctrc.saha.org.za/originals/finalreport/volume3/split/BMvolume3_s1ch6_pg149.pdf.
15. Rueedi, "The Hostel Wars in Apartheid South Africa," 759–61.
16. "Truth and Reconciliation Committee Final Report."
17. "Violence in the Transvaal," Human Rights Watch Report, January 1991, https://www.hrw.org/legacy/reports/1991/southafrica1/8.htm.
18. "Where a Massacre Is a Way of Life," *Mail and Guardian*, July 3, 1992, https://mg.co.za/article/1992-07-03-00-where-a-massacre-is-a-way-of-life/.
19. Memorandum on Violence in Sebokeng, IBI, September 4, 1990, May 1991, October 1990, Folder: 3.8–3.43, IBI, Memoranda, 3.1–3.42, AG2543—IBI, Memoranda, Unidentified Photographs, UWHP.
20. "S. Africa Rivals Mandela, Buthelezi Meet," *Los Angeles Times*, January 29, 1991, https://www.latimes.com/archives/la-xpm-1991-01-29-mn-420-story.html.
21. Liz Carmichael, *Peacemaking and Peacebuilding in South Africa: The National Peace Accord, 1991–1994* (Boydell & Brewer, 2022), 1, 124, 126.
22. Carmichael, *Peacemaking and Peacebuilding in South Africa*, 167.
23. Goldstone Commission of Inquiry Public Violence and Intimidation, Role of South African Defense Force, Lawyers for Human Rights, January 30, 1992, Folder: A15.2, Goldstone Commission, Memorandum submitted by the Weekly Mail and by LHR, A15.2, AG2543—IBI, Goldstone Commission, W.M. Allegations r.e. SADF, UWHP.

24. Affidavit—Johnny Zamani Xulu, Independent Board of Inquiry, 1991, Folder: A17(3), Affidavits by People Trained for Hit Squads Activities, Accounts by Nico Basson of Destabilization Activities, etc., A16–A17, AG2543—IBI, Private Security Industry, SADF/ SANDF, UWHP.
25. Inquiry Into Allegations by Weekly Mail, Commission on the Prevention of Public Violence and Intimidation, March 5, 1992, Folder: A15.2, Goldstone Commission, Records of Inquiry into Allegations by Weekly Mail, pp. 597–943, 1992, A15.2, AG2543—IBI, Goldstone Commission, W.M. Allegations r.e. SADF, UWHP.
26. "Truth and Reconciliation Commission Final Report," vol. 3, chap. 3, subsection 26, October 29, 1998, https://sabctrc.saha.org.za/reports/volume3/chapter3/subsection26.htm.
27. Jackie Dugard, "South Africa's Internal Low-Intensity Conflict," in *The Role of Political Violence in South Africa's Democratization*, ed. Ran Greenstein (CASE, 2003).
28. Overview of the South African Situation 1991, ICT, 1991, Folder: B2, Institute for Contextual Theology Reports, Quarterly/Half Yearly Reports, Gen. Sec. Reports, Director Reports, Progress Reports, 1981–1991, B2–B6, AG2843—Institute for Contextual Theology, ICT, Reports: General/Divisional/Reports of Visits, UWHP.
29. Report of the IBIIR for the Month of July 1991, Independent Board of Inquiry, July 1991, AG2543-2-2-16-01, UWHP.
30. Mangosuthu Buthelezi, Statement from Buthelezi at a Press Conference from China and Hong Kong, August 8, 1991, Box 9, Unto the Least of These Correspondence with Anne Ships + Harry Jones, SC 79, Intercessors for the Suffering Church Collection, Mary Ann Gilbert, Serials Correspondence, WCSC.
31. Christopher S. Wren, "De Klerk Begins Major Tour of West Europe," *New York Times*, May 9, 1990, https://www.nytimes.com/1990/05/09/world/de-klerk-begins-major-tour-of-west-europe.html.
32. "Inkathagate: FINAL Edition," *Baltimore Sun*, July 25, 1991.
33. David Beresford, "New Inkathagate Claims Put de Klerk on the Spot: Pretoria Has Continued Covert Funding," *Guardian*, December 13, 1991; "de Klerk Axes Malan and Vlok Over Inkathagate," *Guardian*, July 30, 1991; Anton Harber, "How de Klerk Sold the Pass," *Guardian*, August 1, 1991.
34. "De Klerk's Response on 'Inkathagate' Fails to Convince His Critics," *Christian Science Monitor*, August 1, 1991.
35. Scott Kraft, "Inkatha Members on Trial, and So Is the Organization," *Los Angeles Times*, December 7, 1991; and Zach de Beer, "De Klerk Is Nearing High Noon: The Alternatives Are Stark-Plunge Back Into Apartheid or Go Forward Toward Hope and Democracy," *Los Angeles Times*, March 9, 1992.
36. "South African Choices," *Asian Wall Street Journal*, August 7, 1991.
37. "SA Catholic Bishops' Bid to Influence Municipal Elections," United Christian Action, January 1990, An Urgent Call for Prayer and Action, UCA, March 29, 1990, Box 9, United Christian Action, UCA News 1986–1992, South Africa, SC 79, Intercessors for the Suffering Church Collection, Mary Ann Gilbert, Serials Correspondence, WCSC.

38. "How Firm Are Your Foundations?," Signposts, 1991, Box 8, Signposts, 1985–1991, SC 79, Intercessors for the Suffering Church Collection, Gilbert, Correspondence, WCSC, Report of the IBIIR for the Month of July 1991.
39. Aida Parker, "Misguided Policies of Western Leaders in South Africa," *Conservative Review*, October 1992, Folder 3, Paleoconservatives, Conservative Review, vol. 3, 1992, carton 46, BANC MSS 98/70, Collection on the US Right [ca. 1950s–1997], Sara Diamond Papers, BLMC.
40. Hermann Giliomee, *The Last Afrikaner Leaders: A Supreme Test of Power* (Tafelberg, 2012), 339.
41. Ben Temkin, *Buthelezi: A Biography* (Frank Cass, 2003), 277.
42. Kenneth W. Grundy, "South Africa's Torturous Transition," *Current History* 92, no. 574 (May 1993): 229, 335–336.
43. D. W. Schoeman, "CODESA Progress Reporting, Period 21/12/1991-17/01/1992," 08/76 Ekonomie & Handll, 22501–22602, PV 897—Nov. 1995, ARCA.
44. "Working Group 2, Bophuthatswana Government, Position Statement on Constitutional Proposals," 1991, 01/7 Arbeid, Boeke, 801–2100, PV 897—Nov. 1995, ARCA. After the discovery of diamonds in the Northern Cape, the British government decided to award control of the diamond digging sites to the Griqua, descendants of the first African inhabitants and first Dutch settlers. Eventually, the Griqua saw their regional hegemony swallowed up by Western missionaries, Boer Great Trekkers, and the Sotho-Tswana groups, which later became the basis of the "Tswana homeland" of Bophuthatswana, created by the apartheid state. "Who Owned the Diamond Fields?," *City Press*, August 9, 2020; and Krista Johnson and Sean Jacobs, *Encyclopedia of South Africa* (Lynne Rienner, 2011), 132; Martin Chatfield Legassick, *The Politics of a South African Frontier: The Griqua, the Sotho-Tswana and the Missionaries, 1780–1840* (Basler Afrika Bibliographien, 2010), 292. For more on the Sotho and regional mining, see Laura Helen Phillips, "From Lebowa to Limpopo: Differentiation, Stratification and Class Formation in South Africa, 1972–2009" (PhD diss., New York University, 2020).
45. Bertus de Villiers, "Memorandum: Constitutional Alternatives and Implications for Bophuthatswana," Centre for Constitutional Proposals, September 30, 1991, 08/76 Ekonomie & Handll, 22501–22602, PV 897—Nov. 1995, ARCA.
46. "Afrikaner-Volksunie: Proposal for Regional Demarcation," Commission on Regions, January 1991, Ref: 1/11/11/112, http://www.nationalarchives.gov.za/sites/default/files/ITEM_NEG-0070-0011-_-112.pdf.
47. "Research into Restructuring of State Departments: Executive Summary, August 1991," Deloitte Pim Goldby, 08/36 Ekonomie + Handel, 10501–10800, PV 897—Nov. 1995, ARCA.
48. "The Scope of the Study," Bophuthatswana Economics Working Group, April 4, 1991, 26/2 Organisasks, 301–600 PV 897—Nov. 1995, ARCA.
49. "The SATSWA Initiative: The Current Status, 1993," the SATSWA Council, 19/9 Landboy, 2401–2700, PV 897, No. 1995, ARCA. For more on SATSWA, see Lawrence and Manson, "The 'Dog of the Boers.'"
50. D. W. Schoeman, "Summary Report," September 19, 1991, 08/76 Ekonomie & Handll, 22501–22602, PV 897—Nov. 1995, ARCA.

51. Heidi Brooks, *The African National Congress and Participatory Democracy: From People's Power to Public Policy* (Palgrave Macmillan, 2019), 134.
52. "South African Hotelier Did It His Way; Built Controversial Sun City Casino in '70s to Cater to Well-Heeled Clientele," *National Post*, March 30, 2020. For more on the global financial efforts of the bantustans, see Quinn Slobodian, "Libertarian Bantustans," in *Crack-Up Capitalism: Market Radicals and the Dream of a World Without Democracy* (Metropolitan, 2023); Julio Rodríguez Matute, "Miss World History," https://rodriguezmatute.home.blog/2020/11/30/miss-world-1992/.
53. "Miss World," DetailedPedia, https://www.detailedpedia.com/wiki-Miss_World_1992.
54. "Russia's Julia Kurochinka Crowned Miss World," *UPI*, December 12, 1992, https://www.upi.com/Archives/1992/12/12/Russias-Julia-Kurochinka-crowned-Miss-World/7738724136400/.
55. "Miss World 1992 Crowning," YouTube, September 16, 2024, https://www.youtube.com/watch?v=CEBg5nMpuEo.
56. Alan Cowell, "Out There: Sun City; Adorning Apartheid's Stage," *New York Times*, December 20, 1992, https://www.nytimes.com/1992/12/20/style/out-there-sun-city-adorning-apartheid-s-stage.html.
57. "Boipatong Massacre—17 June 1992," South African History Online, https://www.sahistory.org.za/article/boipatong-massacre-17-june-1992; Report of the IBI for the Month of July and August 1992, Independent Board of Inquiry, July and August 1992, AG2543-2-2-26-01, UWHP; Franziska Rueedi, "The Boipatong Massacre of 1992: Traces, Silences, and Truth(s)," *Journal of South African History* 74, no. 4 (2023): 683.
58. Lehlohonolo Kennedy Mahlatsi, "We Must Never Forget the Boipatong Massacre on June 17, 1992," *IOL*, June 19, 2022, https://www.iol.co.za/sundayindependent/analysis/we-must-never-forget-the-boipatong-massacre-on-june-17-1992-eed185ca-6b62-445e-a7b8-53ed4f752147; Rueedi, "The Boipatong Massacre of 1992," 686.
59. Rueedi, "The Boipatong Massacre of 1992," 686; Richard Carver, "KwaZulu-Natal—Continued Violence and Displacement," WRITENET, July 1, 1996.
60. Mahlatsi, "We Must Never Forget the Boipatong Massacre on June 17, 1992."
61. Rueedi, "The Boipatong Massacre of 1992," 685–86.
62. Mahlatsi, "We Must Never Forget the Boipatong Massacre on June 17, 1992."
63. Hassen Ebrahim, *The Soul of a Nation: Constitution-making in South Africa* (Oxford University Press, 1999), 136–37. As Mathethe Jeffrey Sehume and Dan Motaung put it, mass mobilization represented a "third way, meaning neither passive acceptance of oppression nor violent opposition to it, but an active commitment to nonviolent means (e.g. direct action, civil disobedience, boycotts, strikes, protests, and education)." Mathethe Jeffrey Sehume and Dan Motaung, "The Evolution of Internal Mass Mobilization as an Instrument Against Colonialism: From Pre-1912 to 1994," in *The Future We Chose: Emerging Perspectives on the Centenary of the ANC*, ed. Busani Ngcaweni (Africa Institute of South Africa, 2013).
64. "Bisho Massacre of 1992," South African History Online, September 13, 2024, https://www.sahistory.org.za/article/bisho-massacre-1992.
65. "The Bisho Massacre," *The Sun*, September 9, 1992.

66. "Mass Funeral for the Victims of the Bisho Massacre," South African History Online, September 18, 1992, published September 17, 2020, https://www.sahistory.org.za/dated-event/mass-funeral-victims-bisho-massacre.
67. Report on the Bisho Incident, Commission on the Prevention of Public Violence and Intimidation, September 7, 1992, Folder: 15.9, Goldstone Commission (Report on Bisho Incident), also: Pickard Commission Report 1992, A15.3–15.9, AG2543—IBI, Goldstone Commission Reports, UWHP.
68. Report of the Pickard Commission on the Shooting Incident at Bisho, Pickard Commission, September 7, 1992, Folder: 15.9, Goldstone Commission (Report on Bisho Incident), also: Pickard Commission report 1992, A15.3–15.9, AG2543—IBI, Goldstone Commission Reports, UWHP.
69. Special Report on Bisho, Ciskei Shooting: September 7, 1992, IBI, September 7, 1992, AG2543-2-2-28-01, UWHP.
70. Mark Gevisser, "Bloody Bisho," *Nation*, October 5, 1992.
71. Stephanie Victor, "The Politics of Remembering and Commemorating Atrocity in South Africa: The Bisho Massacre and Its Aftermath, 1992–2012," *Journal of Southern Africa Studies* 41, no. 1 (2015): 83–102; Adrian Guelke, "Interpretations of Political Violence During South Africa's Transition," *Politikon* 27, no. 2 (2000): 239–54; "Record of Understanding Is Agreed to by the SA Government and the ANC," September 26, 1992, https://www.sahistory.org.za/dated-event/record-understanding-agreed-sa-government-and-anc.
72. "The Record of Understanding," *Track Two* 11, no. 4 (September 2002), https://journals.co.za/doi/pdf/10.10520/EJC111569.
73. Temkin, *Buthelezi*, 282.
74. Temkin, *Buthelezi*, 282.
75. "Working Group 4, Bophuthatswana Position Paper, Participation in Interim Government," 1992, "Maintaining the Status Quo and the Confederal Option," 08/76 Ekonomie & Handll, 22501–22602, PV 897—Nov. 1995, ARCA; "Ciskei Government: Submission to Working Group 2 Regarding a Constitution-Making Body and Process," March 24, 1992, Landboy, 2401–2700, PV 897, No. 1995—19/9, ARCA.
76. "Why the Inkatha Freedom Party Objects to the Idea of the New Constitution Being Written by a Popularly Elected Assembly (Whether Called 'Constituent Assembly' or Called by Any Other Name)," Inkatha Freedom Party, 1992, Landboy, 2401–2700, PV 897, No. 1995—19/9, ARCA.
77. "Working Group II: Proposals of the Inkatha Freedom Party on the Body and Procedures for Drafting a New Constitution," Landboy, 2401–2700, PV 897, No. 1995—19/9, ARCA.
78. "Issues of Consensus," Conference of Concerned South Africans, October 6, 1992, 26/2 Organisasks, 301–600 1990, PV 897, ARCA.
79. "COSAG: SA's Key to Freedom," *Aida Parker Newsletter*, No. 161, March 1993, January 1991—December 1993, *Aida Parker Newsletter*, APC Periodicals, APC.
80. "Urgent Attention Mr. Johan Ferreira, Please," February 1993, Organisaks, 1–300, 1990PV 897—Nov. 1995; "To ACTSA attention Mrs. A. Budd/Mrs. A Parker, Steering Committee Meeting," "Dear COSAG with Enclosures from United Christian Action, Concerned Christian Women for South Africa, UCA News, Christian Mission International, *Signposts*," from Aida Parker, 1992, April 21, 1993, 7/33 9601–9900, PV 897—Nov. 1995 ARCA.

81. "Please, NO Third Boer War," *Aida Parker Newsletter*, May 1993, *Aida Parker Newsletter*, January 1991—December 1993, APC Periodicals, APC.
82. The "New World Order" conspiracy, popularized in 1991 by Pat Robertson's *The New World Order*, alleged the development of a totalitarian world government via a series of cabals embedded within the world's financial and political institutions.
83. "Choosing Values in Changing Times, Signposts: A Digest of Researched Information for Concerned Christians," 1991, Box 8, Signposts, 1985–1991, SC 79, Intercessors for the Suffering Church Collection, Gilbert, Serials, WCSC.
84. "Media Update on Church and Revolution in South Africa," United Christian Action, May 1991, Box 9, United Christian Action, UCA News 1986–1992, South Africa, SC 79, Intercessors for the Suffering Church Collection, Mary Ann Gilbert, Serials Correspondence, WCSC.
85. "Communism and Christianity in South Africa," UCA News, June 1991, Box 9, United Christian Action, UCA News 1986–1992, South Africa, Mary Ann Gilbert, Serials Correspondence, SC 79, Intercessors for the Suffering Church Collection, WCSC.
86. "Deathtoll Mounts—As Murderers Go Free," UCA News, May 1991, Box 9, United Christian Action, UCA News 1986–1992, South Africa, Mary Ann Gilbert, Serials Correspondence, SC 79, Intercessors for the Suffering Church Collection, WCSC.
87. "Two New Year's Messages," UCA News, February 1991, Box 9, United Christian Action, UCA News 1986–1992, South Africa, Mary Ann Gilbert, Serials Correspondence, SC 79, Intercessors for the Suffering Church Collection, WCSC.
88. "Special Introductory Offer for Roca Report," Ed Cain, *The Roca Report*, February 10, 1992, Folder: Jr, Right-Wing Religion, Jr, AG2843—Institute for Contextual Theology, "Right-Wing Religion," UWHP.
89. "Letter from Ed Cain to Johan Ferreira," April 7, 1993; "Letter from Cain to Ferreira," April 27, 1993; "Letter from Cain to Ferreira, May 21, 1993," 25/10 Onderwys Stedlike Swartes, 2701–3000, PV 897—Nov. 1995, ARCA.
90. "Special Introductory Offer for Roca Report."
91. F. Mc.A. Clifford-Vaughn, "Terrorist Activities of the African National Congress," *Conservative Review*, February 1990, Folder 1, Paleoconservatives, *Conservative Review* 1, 1990, carton 46, BANC MSS 98/70, Collection on the US Right [ca. 1950s–1997], Sara Diamond Papers, BLMC.
92. "Mandela Mania," Accuracy in Media, July 1990, Folder 17, Accuracy in Media, carton 46, BANC MSS 98/70, Collection on the US Right [ca. 1950s–1997], Sara Diamond Papers, BLMC.
93. Pat Buchanan, "What Manner of Mission," *Washington Times*, June 20, 1990; Pat Buchanan, "Sometime Sanction," *Washington Times*, June 3, 1991, Folder 8, Buchanan, carton 45, Sara Diamond Papers, BANC MSS 98/70, Collection on the US Right [ca. 1950s–1997], BLMC.
94. William K. Shearer, "The California Stateman's Foreign Policy Review," November 1991, Folder 4, California Statesman's, carton 31, Sara Diamond Papers, BANC MSS 98/70, Collection on the US Right [ca. 1950s–1997], BLMC.
95. Report on Violence Between ANC and Inkatha in Natal, IBI, 1992, Folder: 3.8–3.43, Independent Board of Inquiry, Memoranda, 3.1–3.42, AG2543—IBI, Memoranda, Unidentified Photographs, UWHP.

96. Report on Border-Kei Region for IBI, IBI, May 24, 1993, Folder: 3.8–3.43, IBI, Memoranda, 3.1–3.42, AG2543—IBI, Memoranda, Unidentified Photographs, UWHP.
97. Re: Memorandum on the Activities of Mbhekiseni Khumalo, IBI, February 24, 1993, Folder: 3.8–3.43, Independent Board of Inquiry, Memoranda, 3.1–3.42, AG2543—IBI, Memoranda, Unidentified Photographs, UWHP.
98. Report for September 1993, Independent Board of Inquiry, September 1993, AG2543-2-2-38-01, UWHP.
99. "Items Most Needed," *Aida Parker Newsletter*, no. 170, January/February 1994, January 1994—December 1996, *Aida Parker Newsletter*, APC Periodicals, APC.
100. "Helping Us to Help IFP," *Aida Parker Newsletter*, no. 171, March 1994, January 1994—December 1996, *Aida Parker Newsletter*, APC Periodicals, APC.
101. Seshupo Mosala, "From a Liberation Movement to a Governing Party: An Interrogation of the African National Congress (ANC)," *Journal of Nation-Building and Policy Studies* 6, no. 3 (December 2022): 76; S. J. Mosala, J. C. M. Venter, and E. G. Bain, "The National Democratic Revolution (NDR) in South Africa: An Ideological Journey," *KOERS—Bulletin for Christian Scholarship* 84, no. 1 (2019): 12.
102. Brian Ganson, "Business in the Transition to Democracy in South Africa: Historical and Contemporary Perspectives," *Business and Peace Case Study*, March 2017.
103. Fritz Bartel, *The Triumph of Broken Promises: The End of the Cold War and the Rise of Neoliberalism* (Harvard University Press, 2022), 3.
104. Roger Southall, "The ANC for Sale? Money, Morality and Business in South Africa," *Review of African Political Economy* 35, no. 116 (June 2008): 283.
105. Southall, "The ANC for Sale?," 283, 289. For more on the black middle class, see Dunacn James Randall, "Prospects for the Development of a Black Business Class in South Africa," *Journal of Modern African Studies* 34 (1996): 661–86.
106. Southall, "The ANC for Sale?," 291, 292.
107. Neil Davidson, *What Was Neoliberalism: Studies in the Most Recent Phase of Capitalism 1973–2008* (Haymarket, 2023), 106
108. Robert van Niekerk and Vishnu Padayachee, "The Rise and Fall of a Social Democratic Economic and Social Policy Alternative in the ANC (1990–1996)," *Journal of Contemporary African Studies* 39, no. 2 (2021): 233.
109. Carolyn Holmes, *The Black and White Nation: Reconciliation, Opposition, and Nation-Building in Democratic South Africa* (University of Michigan Press, 2020), 7.
110. van Niekerk and Padayachee, "Rise and Fall of a Social Democratic Economic and Social Policy Alternative in the ANC," 239.
111. Memorandum of Conversation, Subject: Meeting Between the President and Nelson Mandela, President of African National Congress (ANC), December 5, 1991, George H. W. Bush Presidential Library, https://bush41library.tamu.edu/files/memcons-telcons/1991-12-05--Mandela.pdf.
112. F. T. Mdlalose, "COSAG—An Assessment a Few Thoughts on the Way Forward," December 7, 1992, 7/33 9601–9900 PV 897—Nov. 1995, ARCA.
113. "Working Documentation Presented by the IFP to the Brainstorming Session of COSAG 11–12 March, 1993," 26/1 Organisaks, 1–300, 1990, PV 897—Nov. 1995, ARCA.

114. "The Purposes and Functions of the Multi-Party Planning Conference: The Determination of the Form of State and Negotiation of the Process of Transformation of South Africa," Organisaks, 1–300, 1990, PV 897—Nov. 1995, ARCA.
115. Temkin, *Buthelezi*, 282, 285.
116. Stephen Ellman, "Federalism Awry: The Structure of Government in the KwaZulu/Natal Constitution," *South African Journal on Human Rights* 9, no 2 (1993): 165–66, 168.
117. "IFP Proposal to Erect Federalism in South Africa," Organisaks, 1–300, 1990, PV 897—Nov. 1995, ARCA.
118. Ellman, "Federalism Awry," 169, 171–73.
119. " 'Traditional' Dictatorship: One Party State in KwaZulu Homeland Threatens Transition to Democracy," *Human Rights Watch* 5, no. 12 (September 1993).
120. "Record of Discussion of Steering Committee Meeting, Transvaal Agricultural Union, Pretoria, Monday, 7 December 1992," 7/33 9601–9900 PV 897—Nov. 1995, ARCA.
121. Although COSAG members appointed Mdlalose as chairman, reflecting early IFP initiative in the organization's formation, at some point before COSAG met with the South African government in January 1993, the chairmanship passed to Cronjé, representing the IFP's desire to work within—but also outside of and beyond COSAG—and Bophuthatswana's efforts to make COSAG the legitimizing platform for its anti-integrationist aims.
122. Jason Robinson, "Fragments of the Past: Homeland Politics and the South African Transition, 1990–2014," *Journal of Southern African Studies* 41, no. 5 (2015): 953–67; "Rhodesia Plans to Recruit More Into Security Forces," *New York Times*, March 1, 1977.
123. John F. Burns, "Muzorewa Names a Cabinet, Reserving Key Roles for Himself and Smith," *New York Times*, May 31, 1979.
124. Bill Keller, "Homeland, Apartheid's Child, Is Defying Change," *New York Times*, November 28, 1993.
125. Keith B. Richburg, "Behold the Land of Bop—A Figment of Apartheid That Won't Go Away," *Washington Post*, September 16, 1993.
126. "Memorandum for Discussion with President Mangope, President of Bophuthatswana and Brigadier Gqozo, Chairman of the Military Council of Ciskei," Mangosuthu Buthelezi, Chief Minister of KwaZulu and President of the Inkatha Freedom Party, December 7, 1992, 26/2 Organisasks, 301–600, PV 897—Nov. 1995, ARCA.
127. "Embargo: Immediate: Joint Statement by President F.W. de Klerk, President L. Mangope, Chief Minister M. Buthelezi and Brigadier O. Gqozo: 10 December 1992," 7/33 9601-9900PV 897—Nov. 1995, ARCA.
128. Talks Between COSAG and the SA Government Held on 8 and 9 January 1993, 26/1 Organisaks, 1–300, PV 897—Nov. 1995, ARCA, 29.
129. "COSAG Steering Committee January 9, 1993," 7/33 9601–9900, PV 897—Nov. 1995, ARCA.
130. "Unity Is Not Strength!" *Aida Parker Newsletter*, January/February 1993, *Aida Parker Newsletter*, January 1991—December 1993, APC Periodicals, APC.
131. Notes for COSAG Meeting: 18 January 1993, 26/2 Organisasks, 301–600, PV 897—Nov. 1995, ARCA.

132. Meeting Between Delegations of the South African and the Bophuthatswana Governments Held at Katlego, Mmbatho, on 21 April 1993 and Remarks on the Bophuthatswana/South African Government meeting on 11 March 1993, 26/2 Organisasks, 301–600, PV 897—Nov. 1995, ARCA
133. Meeting with F. Schoeman, A. Ventas, D. de Villiers, P. Botha, R. Meyer, L. Wessels, March 11, 1993, Report of the Meeting Between the Governments of South Africa and Bophuthatswana, March 26–27, 1993, at the CDS Guest House, Pretoria, Organisasks, 301–600, PV 897—Nov. 1995, ARCA.
134. "Press Release, UN Chief Meets Mangope and Buthelezi for Talks," Information Service of Bophuthatswana, April 19, 1993, 26/2 Organisasks, 301–600, PV 897—Nov. 1995, ARCA.
135. "New State Gets Constitution: Tswanas and Afrikaners Unanimously Endorse 'Satswa' Regional Initiative," *Bop Bulletin*, Summer 1993, 46/7 TBVC, 1801–2100, 1992, No. 1995, PV 898, ARCA.
136. Letter from Joe Szlavik and Rick Sincere to Gary Dixon, August 24, 1993, Subject: COSAG Delegation, 20/8 Verdediging, 2101—2400, 1992, No. 1995, PV 898, ARCA. In May 2017, federal agents seized almost $500,000 from Joseph Szlavik, alleging that he and his firm engaged in "unlicensed international money transmitting" for ruling parties and elites in Gabon, Abu Dhabi, and Switzerland. James Kirchick, "Devils' Advocates," *New Republic*, August 12, 2008; Joe Palazzolo and Drew Hinshaw, "U.S. Seizes Assets from Lobbyist with Alleged Ties to Gabon's Leader: Move Part of Yearslong Probe Into Flows of Funds from the Central African Nation," *Wall Street Journal*, May 17, 2017.
137. Listing of Rightwing Groups Operating in South Africa, Independent Board of Inquiry, 1994, Folder: A9.1, Right-wing organizations, A9, AG2543—IBI, Right-wing organizations, UWHP.
138. "Confidential: Minutes of Meeting Held on 12 May 1993 at Val de Grace, Pretoria," 26/2 Organisasks, 301–600, PV 897—Nov. 1995, ARCA.
139. "I Am Not a Racist, but . . .," Independent Board of Inquiry, 1994, Folder: A9.3, "I Am Not a Racist," A9, AG2543—IBI, Right-Wing Organizations, UWHP.
140. Profiles of Right-Wing Organizations in South Africa, IBI, January 25, 1994, AG2543—IBI, Right-Wing Organizations, A9, Folder: A9.1, Right-Wing Organizations, UWHP.
141. Report for April 1993, Independent Board of Inquiry, April 1993, AG2543-2-2-34-01, UWHP.
142. "Christians Under Fire and Treachery and Tragedy in Angola," Frontline Fellowship, 1993, Box 3, Frontline Fellowship, 1988–1995 News, SC 79, Intercessors for the Suffering Church Collection, Mary Ann Gilbert, Correspondence, WCSC.
143. "South Africa Betrayed," Frontline Fellowship, September 1993, Box 3, Frontline Fellowship, 1988–1995 News, SC 79, Intercessors for the Suffering Church Collection, Mary Ann Gilbert, Serials Correspondence, WCSC.
144. "Rightists in S. Africa Pick Leader," *Chicago Tribune*, May 16, 1993.
145. Although they insisted that they represented the will of white South Africans, surveys conducted by the Human Science Research Council indicated that only about 6 percent of the white population—about 200,000 to 250,000 people—supported a *volkstaat*. The

AVF remained concentrated in Transvaal small towns and rural communities. Predominately made up of the middle class, the AVF, although undoubtedly insecure at the prospect of the loss of white majority rule, did stand to suffer material losses if they chose to engage in paramilitary action. "I Am Not a Racist, but. . . ."

146. Report for June and July 1993, IBI, June and July 1993, AG2543-2-2-36-01, Report for May 1993, IBI, May 1993, AG2543-2-2-35-01, UWHP.

147. Church of the Creator, Covert Action Information Bulletin, Summer 1993, Folder 25, Book photocopies on the topics of Nazism, 1993, Box 4, RH WL MS 48, John Scoville Papers, Wilcox Collection, UKL.

148. *Citizens Informer* 24, no. 1–2, Council of Conservative Americans, 1993, Folder HH 365C/22—Tri State Informer Inc., Box T-23, Part II, HHC.

149. Introduction to IBI, Independent Board of Inquiry, August 16, 1993, AG2543—IBI, Memoranda, Unidentified Photographs, 3.1–3.42, Folder: 3.3–3.7, IBI Memoranda, UWHP; Scott Kraft, "Rightists Lay Siege to S. Africa Talks Violence: Armed Whites Storm Negotiations Site. Mandela Charges That Police Were Slow to Act," *Los Angeles Times*, June 26, 1993.

150. Kraft, "Rightists Lay Siege to S. Africa Talks Violence."

151. David Beresford, "Police Finally Move Against Storm Troopers in South Africa," *Guardian*, June 29, 1993.

152. Kraft, "Rightists Lay Siege to S. Africa Talks Violence."

153. Report on the Inquiry Into the Events at the World Trade Center, Commission on the Prevention of Public Violence and Intimidation, June 25, 1993, AG2543—IBI, Goldstone Commission Reports, A15.20–15.25, Folder: A15.23, Interim Reports, re Hostels, Taxis (KWT and Queenstown area) and general reports, UWHP.

154. Report for June and July 1993, Independent Board of Inquiry, June and July 1993, AG2543-2-2-36-01, UWHP.

155. "A Fumbled Opportunity," *Resistance*, July 1993, Folder, 16, Mohimont, Lewis, 1988–97, Box 10, Papers of James N. Mason, RH WL MS 41, Kansas Collection, UKL.

156. "Neo-Nazis Storm Negotiations in South Africa," *Dignity Report*, Coalition of Human Dignity Research Development, July 1, 1993, Folder 4, Anti-Right Research, carton 50, Collection on the US Right [ca. 1950s–1997], BANC MSS 98/70, Sara Diamond Papers, BLMC.

157. "A Shot in the Foot: South Africa," *Economist (London)* 328, no. 7818 (1993): 41.

158. "Collision Course," *Aida Parker Newsletter*, December 1993, Aida Parker Newsletter, January 1991—December 1993, APC Periodicals, APC.

159. Freedom Alliance/Vryheidsalliansie, Minutes of Meeting Between Their Excellencies Pres. L. M. Mangope, Chief Minister M. G. Buthelezi, Brig O. J. Gqozo, Gen C. Viljoen, and Dr. F. Hartzenberg, held at Pretoria on October 7, 1993, Verdediging, 2101—2400, 1992, 20/8, No. 1995, PV 898, ARCA.

160. Meeting Minutes of FA, October 7, 1993, 20/8 Verdediging, 2101—2400, 1992, No. 1995, PV 898, ARCA.

161. Basic Approach to Possible Political Alliance, FA, October 12, 1993, Verdediging, 2101—2400, 1992, 20/8, No. 1995, PV 898, ARCA.

162. "Let's Take SA Back," *Aida Parker Newsletter*, January/February 1994, *Aida Parker Newsletter*, January 1994–December 1996, APC Periodicals, APC.
163. "I Am Not a Racist, but. . . ."
164. Situation in Tshing, IBI, April 21, 1994, Folder: A9.1, Right-Wing Organizations, A9, AG2543—IBI, UWHP.
165. Gavin Cawthra, "Arms for Apartheid: The Secret World of Sanctions Busting," *Index on Sanctioning* 20, no. 10 (1991), https://doi.org/10.1080/030642291085352.
166. Hennie van Vuuren, *Apartheid, Guns, and Money: A Tale of Profit* (Hurst, 2019), 4.
167. Tweegesprek: Regering/Vryheidsalliansie D'Nyala: 2–4 November 1993, FA Meeting November 3, 1993, 20/8 Verdediging, 2101—2400, 1992, No. 1995, PV 898, ARCA.
168. "Issue of the Form of State," Freedom Alliance, October 26, 1993, 20/8 Verdediging, 2101—2400, 1992, No. 1995, PV 898, ARCA.
169. Executive Meeting, October 15, 1993, Freedom Alliance, 20/8 Verdediging, 2101—2400, 1992, No. 1995, PV 898, ARCA. It was more than just the IFP who hated the idea of a white ethno-state. In 1992, the Cape Town liberal newspaper the *Argus* called the *volkstaat* "a bizarre attempt to live out the far-right's fantasy of a white homeland." "Living Out the Fantasy of the White Far-Right," *Argus*, November 30, 1993.
170. The Volkstaat Animal in SA, November 11, 1993, 20/8 Verdediging, 2101—2400, 1992, No. 1995, PV 898, ARCA.
171. "Prudence Will Pay," *Aida Parker Newsletter*, Spring 1993, *Aida Parker Newsletter*, January 1991—December 1993, APC Periodicals, APC.
172. Freedom Alliance Statement on Boundaries, November 15, 1993, 20/8 Verdediging, 2101—2400, 1992, No. 1995, PV 898, ARCA.
173. Jack Spence and David Welsh, *Ending Apartheid* (Taylor and Francis, 2010), 136–38.
174. Mosala, "From a Liberation Movement to a Governing Party," 78; N. F. Shivambu, "South Africa's Negotiated Transition from Apartheid to an Inclusive Political System: What Capitalist Interests Reigned Supreme" (master's diss., University of Witwatersrand, 2014); S. Terre'Blanche, *Lost in Transformation: South Africa's Search for a New Future Since 1986* (KMM Review, 2012).
175. Report on Bilateral Meeting with the ANC at the WTC, October 19, 1993, 20/8 Verdediging, 2101—2400, 1992, No. 1995, PV 898, ARCA.
176. Opening Statement at the Bilateral Discussion with the ANC/SACP Alliance on October 25, 1993, List of Irreconcilable Differences in Constitutional Positions Between the Freedom Alliance and the World Trade Center Process and the Way Forward to Constructive Negotiations, Freedom Alliance, October 24, 1993, 20/8 Verdediging, 2101—2400, 1992, No. 1995, PV 898, ARCA.
177. FA Report from Communications, October 11, 1993, 20/8 Verdediging, 2101—2400, 1992, No. 1995, PV 898, ARCA. Suzanne Vos was part of the IFP's press team. Bill Keller, "A 2nd Homeland Is Taken Over by South Africa," *New York Times*, March 23, 1994. Vos was interviewed for Denise Walsh's "The Liberal Moment: Women and Just Debate in South Africa, 1994–1996," *Journal of Southern African Studies* 32, no. 1 (2006): 85–105.
178. FA Meeting: Briefing of Executive Members, October 11, 1993, 20/8 Verdediging, 2101—2400, 1992, No. 1995, PV 898, ARCA.

179. Leaders' Meeting, Freedom Alliance, October 26, 1993, 20/8 Verdediging, 2101—2400, 1992, No. 1995, PV 898, ARCA.
180. Report from Sub-committee on Foreign Affairs, October 26, 1993, 20/8 Verdediging, 2101—2400, 1992, No. 1995, PV 898, ARCA.
181. Report of the Sub-Committee on Foreign Affairs to the Leaders' Summit to be held, January 14, 1994, 20/8 Verdediging, 2101—2400, 1992, No. 1995, PV 898, ARCA.
182. Minutes of a Meeting of the Subcommittee on Foreign Affairs of the Freedom Alliance, held on the November 10, 1993, Freedom Alliance, 20/8 Verdediging, 2101—2400, 1992, No. 1995, PV 898, ARCA.
183. Thomas M. Seitloane, "Bophuthatswana Stands Up for Human Rights in South Africa," *Precinct Reporter*, October 7, 1993; Thomas M. Seitloane, "Protecting the Liberties of All South Africans: FINAL Edition," *Washington Post*, October 10, 1993.
184. Freedom Alliance: Threat Assessment and Analysis of Short Term Options, November 26, 1993, 20/8 Verdediging, 2101—2400, 1992, No. 1995, PV 898, ARCA.
185. FA Leaders, Gqozo Statement, January 3, 1994, 20/8 Verdediging, 2101—2400, 1992, No. 1995, PV 898, ARCA.
186. "Fissures in the Granite," *Star*, January 12, 1994, 20/8 Verdediging, 2101—2400, 1992, No. 1995, PV 898, ARCA.
187. FA Executive Meeting, January 10, 1994, 20/8 Verdediging, 2101—2400, 1992, No. 1995, PV 898, ARCA, UFS.
188. FA Executive and Leaders Meeting, January 14, 1994, 20/8 Verdediging, 2101—2400, 1992, No. 1995, PV 898, ARCA.
189. Trilateral Negotiations from Felgate to Buthelezi, February 3, 1994, Statement by Freedom Alliance Executive, February 21, 1994, On Latest Amendments to the RSA Interim Constitution, 20/8 Verdediging, 2101—2400, 1992, No. 1995, PV 898, ARCA.
190. The FA as a Political Alliance, January 13, 1994, 20/8 Verdediging, 2101—2400, 1992, No. 1995, PV 898, ARCA.
191. FA Executive Meeting, February 21, 1994, 20/8 Verdediging, 2101—2400, 1992, No. 1995, PV 898, ARCA.
192. "Transvaal Regional Workshop Report, Theme: Education Towards Democracy; Breaking the Culture of Silence," Institute for Contextual Theology, March 11–13, 1994, Natal Regional Workshop, 1994, Institute for Contextual Theology, April 16, 1994, Transvaal Regional Workshop Report, March 11–13, 1994, Folder: H4.2, ICT, Regions: Transvaal 1994–95, H4–H5, Staffing & Admin, Personal Files, AG2843—Institute for Contextual Theology, UWHP.
193. "South Africa—Hostages to a Rightwing Agenda—Human Rights Violations Against Bophuthatswana Residents on the Eve of the South African Elections," Amnesty International, March 11, 1994, Folder: A27, Amnesty International Reports, A27–A32, AG2543—IBI, Amnesty International, List of Detainees, Exiles, NUMSA—Arson, Deportation, Natal, UWHP.
194. Peter Harris, *Birth: The Conspiracy to Stop the '94 Elections* (Umuzi, 2010), 107, 109.
195. Terre'Blanche's use of the "communist invasion" metaphor shows the resilience and potency of the *swaar gevaar* narrative, his somewhat "out of touch" nature from the rest

of the white right, and the continued persistence of demonizing any opponents to the right wing as "communist."

196. Bob Drogin, "Executions Underscore Bophuthatswana Chaos," *Los Angeles Times*, March 12, 1994.
197. Interestingly, in private FA meetings, Cronjé expressed his distrust of the AWB, with the AWB joining the FA seen as a nonstarter. FA Leaders, February 7, 1994, 20/8 Verdediging, 2101—2400, 1992, No. 1995, PV 898, ARCA. "South Africa: Securing the Peace—Issues of Justice and Accountability in the Wake of the Bophuthatswana Uprising," Amnesty International, March 29, 1994, Folder: A27, Amnesty International Reports, A27–A32, AG2543—IBI, Amnesty International, List of Detainees, Returned Exiles, NUMSA—Arson, Deportation, Natal, UWHP.
198. Drogin, "Executions Underscore Bophuthatswana Chaos."
199. "Zulu Christians Massacred," Frontline Fellowship, 1994, Box 3, Frontline Fellowship, 1988–1995 News, SC #9, Intercessors for the Suffering Church Collection, Mary Ann Gilbert, Serials Correspondence, WCSC.
200. "Bophuthatswana: A Pillar of Apartheid Falls, Violent Collapse of Homeland Has Turned the Tide Against Forces Trying to Sabotage South Africa's All-Race Elections," *Christian Science Monitor*, March 14, 1994.
201. "TEC Takes Over Ciskei as Gqozo Quits," *Business Day*, March 23, 1994.
202. "ANC Tries to Placate Rights to Avoid Right-Wing Undercutting of the Democratic Transition, South African Leaders Are Mulling a Proposed Plebiscite on an Afrikaner Homeland," *Christian Science Monitor* November 22, 1993.
203. Election Special, Independent Board of Inquiry, May 1994, AG2543-2-2-42-01, UWHP; "Foes of S. African Elections Register," *The Sun*, March 1994.
204. Hilary Lynd, "The Peace Deal: The Formation of the Ingonyama Trust and the IFP Decision to Join South Africa's 1994 Elections," *South African Historical Journal* 73, no. 2 (2021): 321.
205. Harris, *Birth*, 172.
206. "Buthelezi: The BOSS Connection," *Mail and Guardian*, November 27, 1998.
207. "Message from Middle America," *Citizens Informer* 25, Council of Conservative Citizens, Spring 1994, Folder HH634—Tri-State Informer, Box T-23, Part II, HHC.
208. Brian Abshire, "Christianity in Crises: The Church in South Africa," *Chalcedon Report*, May 1994, Folder 6, Chalcedon Foundation, *Chalcedon Report* 1994, carton 1, Collection on the US Right [ca. 1950s–1997], BANC MSS 98/70, Sara Diamond Papers, BLMC.
209. "SA Betrayed: Whom Will History Indict," *Aida Parker Newsletter*, April 1994, *Aida Parker Newsletter*, January 1994–December 1996, APC Periodicals, APC.
210. "I Am Not a Racist, but. . . ."
211. Harris, *Birth*, 167, 174.

CONCLUSION

1. "Life After Apartheid," *Aida Parker Newsletter*, no. 179, November/December 1994, *Aida Parker Newsletter*, January 1994–December 1996 APC, APC Periodicals, APC.

2. "Don't Write South Africa Off!," Frontline Fellowship, March 1995, Box 3, Frontline Fellowship, News/Prayer Letters, 1984-1995, SC 79, Intercessors for the Suffering Church Collection, Mary Ann Gilbert, Serials Correspondence, WCSC.9
3. Joseph Sobran, "After Apartheid," and Bob Slimp, "ANC Obsessed with Race," *Citizen Informer* 27, Fall 1996, CofCC, Folder HH23B—Tri-State Informer, Box T-23, Part II, Hall Hoag Collection, BUSC.
4. "Doelstelling—Welcome," *By Die Vlagpaal*, September 1994, Folder: A9.2, Right Wing Organizations, A9, AG2543—IBI, Right-Wing Organizations, UWHP.
5. Re: Objection to the Certification of the New Constitution by the Constitutional Court [1996], United Christian Action, Ed Cain and Peter Hammond, May 31, 1996, https://www.saflii.org/za/other/ZAConAsmRes/1996/62.html.
6. "White Rightwing Extremism in South Africa," Truth and Reconciliation Commission, 1995, 7-15, Folder: A14.4, TRC Submissions, TRC Reports, A14.3-5, AG2543—IBI, TRC—Papers, Reports, General Info on TRCs, UWHP.
7. "Quo Vadis, Afrikaners?," *Aida Parker Newsletter*, no. 191, January 1996, Aida Parker Newsletter, January 1994–December 1996, APC Periodicals, APC.
8. Hennie Serfontein, "Rightwing Afrikaners on Collision Course with ANC," *New Nation*, January 19, 1996, Folder: 5.9, Police Conduct, Reports of Police Misconduct, A5.9-13, AG2543—IBI, Police Conduct + Policing, UWHP.
9. Neil Southern, "The Government of National Unity and the Demise of the National Party in Post-Settlement South Africa," *Politikon* 42, no. 2 (2015): 235–54.
10. "South African Election Once Again Amplifies the Need for Boers to Look Beyond the Voting Booth," Pactum Institute, June 1, 2024, https://www.pactuminstitute.com/press-statements/south-african-election-once-again-amplifies-the-need-for-boers-to-look-beyond-the-voting-booth.
11. Rachel Jackson and Tumi Makgetla, "Redrawing the Map for Democracy: How South Africa's Post-Apartheid Government Tried to Do Away with the Territorial Legacy of Racial Segregation," *Foreign Policy*, October 11, 2013.
12. Candace Smith and Byron Pitts, "Inside the All-White 'Apartheid Town' of Orania, South Africa," *ABC News*, April 11, 2019, https://abcnews.go.com/International/inside-white-apartheid-town-orania-south-africa/story?id=62337338.
13. Stephen Piggott, "Paypal Co-founder Peter Thiel to Address White Nationalist-Friendly 'Property and Freedom Society' Conference in September," *SPLC Hatewatch*, June 9, 2016, https://www.splcenter.org/hatewatch/2016/06/09/paypal-co-founder-peter-thiel-address-white-nationalist-friendly-%E2%80%9Cproperty-and-freedom.
14. Carel Boshoff, "Orania and the Third Reinvention of the Afrikaner," *Politics Web*, October 7, 2014.
15. F. C. de Beer, "Exercise in Futility, or Dawn of Afrikaner Self-Determination: An Exploratory Ethno-Historical Investigation of Orania," *Ethnoculture* 1 (2007): 45–58, https://www.emich.edu/coer/Journal_2007/De_Beer.html.
16. "Mbeki Shoots Himself in Foot," *Aida Parker Newsletter*, no. 260, April 2002, *Aida Parker Newsletter*, January 2000–September 2002, APC Periodicals, APC; Wessel Visser, "The Establishment of Solidarity's Helping Hand as a Successful Community Based Welfare Organization," *Tydskrif vir Geeteswetenskappe* 51, no. 1 (March 2011): 21–53.

17. Siphokazi Mbolo and Ashley Nyiko Mabasa, "Nativism and Narrow Nationalism in South African Politics," *Africa Is a Country*, September 6, 2019, https://africasacountry.com/2019/09/nativism-and-narrow-nationalism-in-south-african-politics/; and Bright Nkrumah, "Think Tanks and Democratization in South Africa," *Cosmopolitan Civil Societies: An Interdisciplinary Journal* 14, no. 1 (2022): 26.
18. Stephen Khan, "South Africa's White Right, the Alt-Right and the Alternative," *Conversation*, October 4, 2018; The Afrikaner Foundation, "Orania," https://afrikaner.org/city/.
19. "The New Right-Wing: Right-Wing Election Bomb Suspects in Dramatic Jailbreak—Police Order a Nationwide Search for Four Alleged Afrikaner Weerstandsbeweging Bombers—and 'Inside Job' Is Not Ruled Out," Independent Board of Inquiry, March 1996, Folder: A9.2, Right Wing Organizations, A9, AG2543—IBI, Right-Wing Organizations, UWHP.
20. Hilary Lynd, "The Peace Deal: The Formation of the Ingonyama Trust and the IFP Decision to Join South Africa's 1994 Elections," *South African Historical Journal* 73, no. 2 (2021): 321; and Peter Harris, *Birth: The Conspiracy to Stop the '94 Elections* (Umuzi, 2010).
21. "Report of the Independent Electoral Commission: The South African Elections of April 1994," Independent Electoral Commission, 1994, 54.
22. Jill E. Kelly and Liz Timbs, "The Rise and Fall of Mangosuthu Buthelezi," *Africa Is a Country*, December 2017, https://africasacountry.com/2017/12/the-rise-fall-and-retirement-of-mangosuthu-buthelezi; Jaspreet Kindra, "Felgate Damns Buthelezi," *Mail and Guardian*, February 14, 2003, and "Buthelezi: The BOSS Connection," *Mail and Guardian*, November 27, 1998.
23. "NDJ," Independent Board of Inquiry, 1995, Folder: A12, Guns. Etc, A11-12, AG2543—IBI, Inkatha/Gun-Running, UWHP.
24. Jason Robinson, "Fragments of the Past: Homeland Politics and the South African Transition, 1990-2014," *Journal of Southern African Studies* 41, no. 5 (2015): 963, 964.
25. Sobran, "After Apartheid"; and Slimp, "ANC Obsessed with Race."
26. Bob Slimp, "South Africa Shows Its True Colors—Color It Red," *Citizens Informer* 28, Summer 1997, Folder HH614: Tri-State Informer, Box T-23, Part II, HHC.
27. Sue Huck, "Suppressing the 'White Tribe:' The War Against South Africa," *Conservative Review* 5, no. 2 (March/April 1994), Folder 5, Paleoconservatives, *Conservative Review*, Vol. 5, 1994, carton 46, Sara Diamond Papers, BANC MSS 98/70, Collection on the US Right [ca. 1950s–1997], BLMC.
28. Bob Slimp, "Black Rule in South Africa Is a Total Failure," *Citizens Informer* 28, CofCC, Winter 1997, Folder HH83C:51—Tri-State Informer, Box T-23, Part II, HHC.
29. Samuel Francis, "South Africa's Violent Future May Be Ours," *Citizens Informer* 29, 3rd Quarter, 1998, Folder HH136B:67—Tri-State Informer, Inc./Council of Conservative Americans, Box T-23, Part II, HHC.
30. Larry Harlow, "South African Refugee," *Citizens Informer* 29, Spring 1998, CofCC Folder HH136B:67—Tri-State Informer, Inc./Council of Conservative Americans, Box T-23, Part II, HHC.
31. Kathleen Belew, *Bring the War Home: The White Power Movement and Paramilitary America* (Harvard University Press, 2019), 2.

32. Brad Knickerbocker, "New Armed Militias Recruit Growing Membership in US," *Christian Science Monitor*, April 3, 1995.
33. "Victims of the Oklahoma City Bombing," *USA Today*, June 20, 2001.
34. Stuart A. Wright, *Patriots, Politics, and the Oklahoma City Bombing* (Cambridge University Press, 1997).
35. Alasdair Spark, "Conjuring Order: The New World Order and Conspiracy Theories of Globalization," *Sociological Review* 48 (October 2000): 46–62.
36. Susan Huck, "Letter from America," *Aida Parker Newsletter*, no. 250, May 2001, *Aida Parker Newsletter*, January 1994–December 1996, APC Periodicals, APC.
37. Huck, "Letter from America"; "Susan Huck Obituary," 2007, https://www.legacy.com/us/obituaries/dfw/name/susan-huck-obituary?id=25224596.
38. Benjamin C. Waterhouse, "Donald Trump: Campaigns and Elections," Miller Center, https://millercenter.org/president/trump/campaigns-and-elections.
39. Stephen Knott, "George H.W. Bush: Campaigns and Elections," Miller Center, University of Virginia, https://millercenter.org/president/bush/campaigns-and-elections.
40. "Quarterly Report," Patrick J. Buchanan, *From the Right* 2, no. 11 (September 1991), Folder 3, Buchanan, carton 45, BANC MSS 98/70, Collection on the US Right [ca. 1950s–1997], Sara Diamond Papers, BLMC.
41. Nicole Hemmer, *Partisans: The Conservative Revolutionaries Who Remade American Politics in the 1990s* (Basic, 2022), 140, 163.
42. Marty Cohen, *Moral Victories in the Battle for Congress: Cultural Conservatism and the House GOP* (University of Pennsylvania Press, 2019), 2.
43. Hemmer, *Partisans*, 219, 255.
44. Adam Nagourney, "Obama Elected President as Racial Barrier Falls," *New York Times*, November 4, 2008, https://www.nytimes.com/2008/11/05/us/politics/05elect.html; Vanessa Williamson, Theda Skocpol, and John Coggin, "The Tea Party and the Remaking of Republican Conservatism," *Perspectives on Politics* 9, no. 1 (March 2011): 25–43; Cornell Belcher, *A Black Man in the White House: Barack Obama and the Triggering of America's Racial-Aversion Crisis* (Water Street, 2016); and Matthew W. Hughey and Gregory S. Parks, *The Wrongs of the Right: Language, Race, and the Republican Party in the Age of Obama* (New York University Press, 2014).
45. "How South Africa Has Changed 30 Years After Apartheid," *Economist*, May 2, 2024.
46. "Farms and Freedom Under Fire in South Africa," Gospel Defense League, 2018, 3, 6, https://issuu.com/africachristianaction/docs/practical_solutions_for_south_afric.
47. "Fact Check: The Truth About Farm Murders in South Africa," *The Week*, November 10, 2017, https://theweek.com/89629/fact-check-the-truth-about-farm-murders-in-south-africa.
48. Global Initiative Against Transnational Organized Crime, "'The Underworld Runs the ANC'—Assassinations Analysis Shows the Stark Reality of Violence in KZN," *Daily Maverick*, June 27, 2022.
49. Rupert Taylor, "Justice Denied: Political Violence in KwaZulu-Natal after 1994," *African Affairs* 101, no. 405 (2002): 475.
50. Baldwin Ndaba, "Retired General and Son of Former Bophuthatswana Leader Mangope Is New Chairperson for ActionSA in North West," *IOL*, December 23, 2021, https://www

.iol.co.za/news/politics/retired-general-and-son-of-former-bophuthatswana-leader-mangope-is-new-chairperson-for-actionsa-in-north-west-655ffcd1-def9-46c1-9068-20c74d992290; and Cliff Shiko, "Kwena Mangope Announced as ActionSA's NW Premier Candidate," JacarandaFM, October 11, 2023, https://www.jacarandafm.com/news/news/kwena-mangope-announced-actionsas-nw-premier-candidate/.

51. ActionSA, "Kgosi Kwena Mangope," https://www.actionsa.org.za/kgosi-kwena-mangope/.
52. Laura Phillips, "The Peculiar Nostalgia for the Former Bantustans in South Africa," *Africa Is a Country*, March 27, 2018, https://africasacountry.com/2018/03/the-peculiar-nostalgia-for-the-former-bantustans-in-south-africa/; Jill E. Kelly, "The Strange Non-death of Bantustans," *Africa Is a Country*, September 15, 2023; Bongani Ngqulunga, "The Changing Face of Zulu Nationalism: The Transformation of Mangosuthu Buthelezi's Politics and Public Image," *Politikon: South African Journal of Political Studies* 47, no. 3 (2020): 287–304.
53. Ronelle Burger et al., "The Emergent Middle Class in Contemporary South Africa: Examining and Comparing Rival Approaches," *Development Southern Africa* 32, no. 1 (2015): 38.
54. Roger Southall, *The New Black Middle Class in South Africa* (Boydell & Brewer, 2016), xiv, xvi. For more from Southall, see "Political Change and the Black Middle Class in Democratic South Africa," *Canadian Journal of African Studies/La Revue Canadienne des Études Africaines* 38, no. 3 (2004): 521–42, and "The Black Middle Class and Democracy in South Africa," *Journal of Modern African Studies* 52, no. 4 (2014): 647–70
55. Southall, *The New Black Middle Class in South Africa*, 36.
56. Southall, *The New Black Middle Class in South Africa*, 191, South Africa has also seen the rise of African Independent Churches, particularly in the townships that are deeply embedded in the fabric of social and political community life. Barbara Bompani, "African Independent Churches in Post-Apartheid South Africa: New Political Interpretations," *Journal of Southern African Studies* 34, no. 3 (September 2008): 665–77.
57. Josiah Taru, "The Rise of African Prophets: The Unchecked Power of the Leaders of Pentecostal Churches," *Conversation*, February 8, 2024, https://theconversation.com/the-rise-of-african-prophets-the-unchecked-power-of-the-leaders-of-pentecostal-churches-221887.
58. Kepya Kaoma and Petronella Chlawe, "The Good Samaritan and Minorites in Africa: Christianity, the US Christian Right, and the Dialogical Ethics of *Ubuntu*," *Journal of Theology for Southern Africa* 155 (July 2016): 187.
59. Dale Wallace, "Resurgent Fundamentalism, Politics, and the Anti-Liberal Agenda: Challenges for South Africa's Constitutional Democracy," *Journal for the Study of Religion* 33, no. 1 (2020): 4, 21.
60. "Farms and Freedom Under Fire in South Africa," 11
61. Ismail Lagardien, "SA's Coloured People Crushed Between Ethnonationalism and African Nationalism," *Daily Maverick*, May 2, 2024, https://www.dailymaverick.co.za/opinionista/2024-05-02-sas-coloured-people-crushed-between-ethnonationalism-and-african-nationalism/.

62. Eric Naki, "DA and ANC Dismiss Western Cape Secession as 'Myth' and 'Self-Serving,'" *Citizen*, September 2, 2020, https://www.citizen.co.za/news/south-africa/politics/da-and-anc-dismiss-western-cape-secession-as-myth-and-self-serving/.
63. Oscar van Heerden, "Independent Republic of the Western Cape: Dream On, Suckers, It Ain't Gonna Happen," *Daily Maverick*, October 1, 2021.
64. Yonela Diko, "DA's Secession Bill—In Search of a Volkstaat?," *Eyewitness News*, January 22, 2024, https://www.ewn.co.za/2024/01/22/yonela-diko-das-secession-bill-in-search-of-a-volkstaat.
65. Tim Alberta, "'The Ideas Made It, but I Didn't': Pat Buchanan Won After All. But Now He Thinks It Might Be Too Late for the Nation He Was Trying to Save," *Politico Magazine*, May/June 2017, https://www.politico.com/magazine/story/2017/04/22/pat-buchanan-trump-president-history-profile-215042/.
66. Carolyn Holmes, "Tucker Carlson, Those South African White Rights Activists Aren't Telling You the Whole Truth," *Washington Post*, May 15, 2019.
67. Simon Kuper, "Musk, Thiel and the Shadow of Apartheid South Africa," *Financial Times*, September 19, 2024.
68. Zolan Kanno-Youngs and Hamed Aleaziz, "'Mission South Africa': How Trump Is Offering White Afrikaners Refugee Status," *New York Times*, March 30, 2025, https://www.nytimes.com/2025/03/30/us/politics/trump-south-africa-white-afrikaners-refugee.html; and Gerald Imray, "Why Is Trump Punishing South Africa and Who Are the Afrikaners He Wants to Give Refugee Status to?," *AP News*, February 8, 2025, https://apnews.com/article/south-africa-trump-musk-afrikaners-0f58dfe1651671d30fcbe16d00c3d99c.
69. Siphiwe Ignatius Dube, "The New Religious Political Right," *Religion and Theology* 28 (2021): 157, 161.
70. Patrick Ruffini, *Party of the People: Inside the Multiracial Populist Coalition Remaking the GOP* (Simon & Schuster, 2023), 22.
71. Ed Kilgore, "Why Non-white Voters and Young Men Drifted to Trump," *New York Magazine*, March 18, 2025, https://nymag.com/intelligencer/article/why-nonwhite-voters-and-young-men-drifted-to-trump.html.

INDEX

GPSR Authorized Representative: Easy Access System Europe, Mustamäe tee 50, 10621 Tallinn, Estonia, gpsr.requests@easproject.com

www.ingramcontent.com/pod-product-compliance
Lightning Source LLC
Chambersburg PA
CBHW022131020426
42334CB00015B/848

* 9 7 8 0 2 3 1 2 1 5 8 9 3 *